Animal
Revolution

To Emily, Henry, Leo and Guinevere

Animal Revolution

Changing Attitudes towards Speciesism

RICHARD D. RYDER

BERG

Oxford • New York

First published in 1989 by Basil Blackwell Ltd.
Revised and updated edition published in 2000 by
Berg
Editorial offices:
150 Cowley Road, Oxford, OX4 1JJ, UK
70 Washington Square South, New York, NY 10012, USA

Berg is an imprint of Oxford International Publishers Ltd.

Library of Congress Cataloging-in-Publication Data
A catalogue record for this book is available from the Library of Congress.

British Library Cataloguing-in-Publication Data
A catalogue record for this book is available from the British Library.

ISBN 1 85973 325 5 (Cloth)
      1 85973 330 1 (Paper)

Typeset by JS Typesetting, Wellingborough, Northants.
Printed in the United Kingdom by Biddles Ltd, Guildford and King's Lynn.

Contents

List of Abbreviations

AHA	American Humane Association
ALDF	Animal Legal Defense Fund
ALF	Animal Liberation Front
ASPCA	American Society for the Prevention of Cruelty to Animals
AWI	Animal Welfare Institute
BFSS	British Field Sports Society
BUAV	British Union for the Abolition of Vivisection
CALL	Central Animal Liberation League
CITES	Convention on International Trade in Endangered Species of Wild Fauna and Flora
CIWF	Compassion in World Farming
CRAE	Committee for the Reform of Animal Experimentation
FAWC	Farm Animal Welfare Council
FAWCE	Farm Animal Welfare Co-ordinating Executive
FOE	Friends of the Earth
FRAME	Fund for the Replacement of Animals in Medical Research
GECCAP	General Election Co-ordinating Committee for Animal Protection
JSA	Hunt Saboteurs Association
HSUS	Humane Society of the United States
IFAW	International Fund for Animal Welfare
IPPL	International Primate Protection League
ISPA	International Society for the Protection of Animals
IUCN	International Union for the Conservation of Nature
IWC	International Whaling Commission
LACS	League Against Cruel Sports
MFH	Master of Foxhounds
NAVS	National Anti-Vivisection Society
NSPCC	National Society for the Prevention of Cruelty to Children
PAL	Political Animal Lobby
PETA	People for the Ethical Treatment of Animals

PsyETA	Psychologists for the Ethical Treatment of Animals
RSPCA	Royal Society for the Prevention of Cruelty to Animals
SELFA	Stop the Export of Live Food Animals
SPCA	Society for the Prevention of Cruelty to Animals
SSPV	Scottish Society for the Prevention of Vivisection
UFAW	Universities Federation for Animal Welfare
WFPA	World Federation for the Protection of Animals
WSPA	World Society for the Protection of Animals

Foreword

Growing interest in the relationship between humankind and the other animals has prompted a new and updated edition of this book which was first published in 1989.

I have omitted entirely those chapters of the first edition that have become outdated, and I have added new illustrations and a new chapter (Chapter 11) which reflects recent developments in ethical theory, the science of animal welfare and the more sophisticated political campaigns of the 1990s. The book still tries to give fair emphases to both the American and European experiences while giving more attention to the implications of global free trade.

I would like to thank all those who, through their writings or otherwise, have helped me to maintain my commitment to the cause of animal protection over the years and to find the energy and material to produce this book.

These include, Richard Adams, Mike Baker, Don Broom, Anne Campbell-Dixon, Birgitta Carlsson, Stephen Clark, Jan Creamer, Brian Davies, Peter Davies, Hugh Denman, John Douglass, Joyce D'Silva, Kathryn Earle, Sara Everett, Ian Fergusson, Nicola Furrie, Robert Garner, Mark Glover, Mark Gold, Rebecca Hall, Clive Hollands, Hugh Hudson, Maggy Jennings, Gill Langley, Carmen Lee, Andrew Linzey, Ian Macphail, Olive Martyn, Colin McGinn, Mary Midgeley, Cindy Milburn, Frank Milner, Julia Neuberger, Anthony Podberscek, Mike Radford, Tom Regan, Jane and Vernon Reynolds, Peter Roberts, John Rolls, Steve Sapontzis, Derek Sayce, Peter Singer, Angela Smith, Kim Stallwood, Peter Stevenson, Ginny Stroud-Lewis, Caroline Vodden, Emma Wildsmith and Jon Wynne-Tyson.

My thanks go to them all and, particularly, to Penny Merrett who typed (and retyped) the manuscript.

It is fitting, surely, that this edition appears at this time. The millennium marks a moment when the human species can take stock of its condition and of its attitude to the rest of creation. It is also a time when other basic questions about the human journey can be addressed: Why am I here? Where do I want to go in the new millennium? What is the moral way I should be following?

It may at first glance seem strange that those of us interested in animal protection have contributed to the formulation of modern moral theory. But we have done so. The great interest in the subject of speciesism shown by philosophers in the last quarter of the twentieth century has sharpened the whole moral debate and concentrated it upon painience – the capacity to experience pain and distress.

The story of humankind's relationship to the other painients is an interesting one. The interaction between humans and nonhumans is not a trivial matter to be dismissed with a cynical smile; it has underlain the economic, artistic, religious and literary histories of our species. Our ancestors' fear, respect and even worship of the other animals gave way two millennia ago to an exaltation at their conquest. Gradually, as our species became dominant, so the other creatures were made our slaves. Today, secure in the knowledge of our effortlessly superior technological status, we are beginning to think again.

That is what this book is about.

Richard D. Ryder, Devon

Prologue

It is all too tempting to assume that the intellectuals and writers of any period represent the common opinions of their times. Similarly it is easily insinuated that these same writers are the leaders of society and that their doctrines substantially influenced the conduct of their less articulate contemporaries. How far are these two assertions true? Is it not possible that, in some instances at least, the writer who is remembered was not typical of his age and that the masses scarcely noticed or were affected by what he or she had to say?

Unfortunately for the historian, the records of the lives of the inarticulate are less well preserved, and so it is simpler to rely upon the written record. Besides, the historian, being a scholar and a writer, may naturally prefer to believe that it is the written word which fashions the deed and that the pen is always mightier that the sword! Yet there is a tide in the development of cultures which ebbs and flows as much through the tendency of human thinking to swing spontaneously between extremes, and by the natural response to events, as under any influence from intellectuals and theorizers. Sometimes, perhaps, the shift in doctrine *follows* rather than precedes the change in practice. Nevertheless, a survey of the written word on the subject of cruelty is a necessary element in any attempt to grasp the development of the past. There are many disturbing questions to be answered.

1 Introduction

This book is not another catalogue of cruelties. Lists of atrocities perpetrated by humans against other sentients have been widely and effectively published in recent years.[1] Rather, this is an attempt to look behind such phenomena to establish explanatory links, and to examine the changing relationships between human and nonhuman over the centuries, using history − chiefly British history − as a framework for new ideas.

The positive side of this human-to-nonhuman relationship − that is to say its manifestation in the writings and campaigns of those concerned to improve the protection of nonhuman animals − is given priority. Sometimes I have only scratched the surface of a large but relatively unexplored field − as when I cover the active period of the nineteenth century − and I hope such inadequacies will stimulate further research. I do not claim to be writing a comprehensive or definitive history, but to be providing a few findings and observations.

We are, I believe, discussing a matter of fundamental importance for the future of our planet. The struggle against speciesism is not a sideshow; it is one of the main arenas of moral and psychological change in the world today. It is part of a new and enlarged vision of peace and happiness.

The time has come for a revolution in our attitudes − attitudes which can and must change because there has been a huge and rapid shift in power. For hundreds of millennia our ancestors were one weak species in the struggle for survival, but now we rule the world. For almost our whole existence as a species we have been shaped by our environment, but now we are shaping it. We can destroy rain forests, alter the weather, cultivate deserts or make them. We can even change the other animals to suit our whims for meat, fur, laboratory utensils or playthings. We have wiped scores of species off the face of Earth and are now beginning to create new ones. Our power is already immense and, in the future, it will be greater still. Such power demands, at least, a reappraisal.

A NEW LANGUAGE

Some aspects of the language I use may surprise the reader. This is because I have tried, when appropriate in the context, to dismantle the speciesism inherent in the words we use. Phrases like 'men and animals', for example, insult not only women but nonhumans also, for humans are animals too.

Using the word 'animal' in opposition to the word 'human' is clearly an expression of prejudice. So how can this be avoided when describing those sentient creatures who are not of the human species? Does a phrase such as 'animals and human animals' help? It might, but it is rather clumsy. Slightly less cumbersome is the phrase 'nonhuman animal' and its inevitable abbreviation 'nonhuman'. To some this may itself sound speciesist, in that it could be asserting that human is the norm and that nonhuman is inferior. All I can say is that no such inferiority is intended or understood. In the absence of other appropriate words I use 'nonhuman' or 'nonhuman animal' in the hope that their use reminds the reader, as it does me, of the kinship between those of my own species and others.

Admittedly, in dealing with the past, it is difficult to use new terms and concepts consistently, so the early chapters do contain some speciesist phrasing. I defend the use of the word 'animal' in the title on the grounds that the revolution to which I refer applies to the human animal as well as to others; and because the revolution, to a large extent, is about the concept of 'animal' itself.

The hostility towards so-called antropomorphism during this century has been so extreme that the use of certain adjectives, pronouns such as 'he' or 'she' and verbs in a nonhuman context has been abhorred, particularly by those intellectuals who should have known better. Nevertheless, if I believe it appropriate I have, and without shame, deliberately attributed behavioural and emotional qualities to nonhumans which some may regard as far-fetched. So, if I believe a dog is angry then I say so, and if she is a dog who feels angry with speciesists, then I sympathize!

THE MODERN REVOLUTION

This book considers the history of humankind's changing attitudes towards the other animals; the story, by and large, of the gradual triumph of reason and compassion over habit, vested interest and convenience. I have tried to analyse causes and to provide arguments for further progress at a period when our relationships with other sentients and the environment generally are under scrutiny. Progress may not be a fashionable concept, yet I consider that some progress *has* been made towards a greater respect for nonhumans on our shared planet, and that the 1970s and 1980s have seen a quickening of this progress. The historian W. E. H. Lecky asserted over a century ago that 'the general tendency of nations is undoubtedly to become more gentle and humane in their actions; but this, like many other general tendencies in history, may be counteracted or modified by many special circumstances'.[2] There is much evidence to support this hypothesis.

The connections between animal liberation and the modern environmental movement are complex, yet the differing rationales of the two movements often lead to similar actions. When environmentalism arises from a generalized 'respect for nature' the step to animal liberation is a short one; but where the environmentalist's motive is an anthropocentric desire to preserve for the benefit of the human species, then therein lie seeds of conflict. Both movements have, in recent years, become more ideological and more effective. Environmentalists have illegally sailed ships into nuclear test zones and animal rightists have broken into factory-farms and animal research laboratories. They have lobbied with spectacular results.

The change in phraseology from a concern for 'animal welfare' to a concern for 'animal rights' indicates the movement's increasingly ideological complexion, its emphasis on the right to *life* as well as the avoidance of *suffering* and, perhaps, the youthfulness of many of its adherents. Whereas some of the great religions of the East have emphasized the desirability of protecting nonhuman *life* while tending to ignore nonhuman *suffering,* the animal welfare movement of the West has emphasized the reduction of suffering while condoning killing for food and other purposes. Now the modern animal rights ideology brings both threads together in its quest to conquer suffering and to protect nonhuman life universally.

Since the 1960s the pace of the change in outlook towards other species has accelerated and a powerful moral concern has emerged for the well-being of the other individual sentients of our planet. To an extent, this arose in the context of the still maligned 'hippy' culture of that decade which placed a new value on compassion and allowing others to 'do their own thing'. The return-to-nature element of this 'Flower Power' philosophy helped to blur the dividing line between human and nonhuman, implying that *all* sentients should be respected. Hippydom (a view of life rarely claimed to be, yet in some ways not far removed from, the teachings of Jesus) also questioned the priority of the commercial motive and consciously tried to demote the power of the 'macho' ideal after the disillusionment of the Vietnam war.

As Harlan Miller has suggested, there are also other reasons for the new interest in the relationship between nonhumans and humans.[3] First, anti-speciesism is a logical extension of the liberation movements against racism and sexism which flourished in the 1960s and 1970s. Secondly, we live in a scientific and science-fiction age which has given us a completely new perspective of the human animal as being possibly only one sentient species among many in the universe, some of whom may be far more intelligent than ourselves. Thirdly, various scientific disciplines – psychology, anthropology, zoology, ethology, neurophysiology and other biological sciences – have permeated popular thinking to an unprecedented degree and have helped to 'demystify' the human being, putting us on a level with the other animals. Finally, our greater scientific knowledge of nonhumans and of their capacity for intelligence, for rudimentary language and for suffering pain, has helped narrow the conceptual gap between us.

The dissemination of such information through higher education and television is now practically universal in the West and challenges the blind acceptance of the old speciesist status quo. The reawakening of interest in the 'rights of animals' in the 1960s and 1970s was not due, initially, to proselytizing, but to the spontaneous conclusion arrived at by many people that it was plainly *illogical* as well as unjust to discriminate so grossly on the basis of species. We recognized the huge extent of suffering in this Fourth World – the world of the nonhuman sentients.

Just as animal liberation of the 1970s had its roots in the swinging sixties, so the 1960s were, in part, born out of the concerns of the 1950s. The reaction against the semi-militaristic culture of the Cold War period eventually encouraged the liberation movements in America. Individualism was trying to assert itself against authority – an authority which appeared to deny pleasure, justice and freedom. It was not a class war but the mainly middle-class product of prosperity and education. Furthermore it was augmented by the attentions of an increasingly internationalized media, television particularly. The hedonistic hippy subculture survived well into the 1970s, with a strong emphasis upon sexual freedom and an insistence that each individual had a right to find his or her own pleasures. In America, genuine progess was made against racism and sexism and the liberation of thought of this period naturally and logically was extended to cover the oppression of nonhuman sentients. This development became clear from 1969.

Unlike the two previous periods in Britain of rapid progress in the movement against speciesism, which occurred around the end of the eighteenth century and the end of the nineteenth, on this occasion the revolution attracted support from men and women of *all* classes and now permeates the whole of the developed world. Initial developments in Britain have been followed in Australia and then in the USA and other Western nations. Whereas Europe followed the USA in its Women's Liberation and Civil Rights movements, it is America which followed Britain in the animal revolution.

A revolution, to be a revolution, does not merely entail a total change of attitude; it must affect aspects of the human condition which are fundamental. Too often a concern for nonhumans has been dismissed by politicians and intellectuals as being of only peripheral importance. Yet a moment's reflection will show that the whole development of human civilization has depended on the relationship between the human and nonhuman animals, and how that relationship was perceived and justified in the moral, cultural and religious contexts of the time. Humans have conquered the planet, taking control over the other species, some of whom have been both rivals for food and territory and often downright foes; we had to pit our brains against their brawn. Now that that war has been all but won, and the human ape has emerged triumphant over the other vertebrates, surely it behoves us to be magnanimous in victory? Only the battle against the microbe remains important.

Our cave-dwelling ancestors depended upon other sentients for food, and needed their skins for clothing and their bones for tools. But human exploitation and domination of nonhumans is no longer the urgent necessity that once it was; we now have alternative foods, clothing materials, methods of transport and sources of power. Yet we continue to trap, poison and shoot our evolutionary cousins, inflict agonies upon them in the name of science, imprison them in factory-farms and devour them, quite unnecessarily, by the million. Changing all this will have revolutionary consequences, affecting what we wear, what we eat, the price of food, the development of science, the appearance of our environment, the character of industries and the way we spend our leisure.

The twentieth century has been a remarkable period of anti-speciesist enlightenment, but, paradoxically, it also has been an era of worsening exploitation and encroachment. While the human population explosion has made ever-greater demands upon habitat, and expanding worldwide industry has destroyed wildlife with pollution, science and agricultural technology have devised new means of oppression and justified all by results.

SPECIESISM

The Battle of Ideas

The moral basis for animal liberation has been given much attention by modern philosophers since the publication of the well-known novelist Brigid Brophy's major article entitled 'The Rights of Animals' in the *Sunday Times* in 1965. Brophy wrote:

The relationship of homo sapiens to the other animals is one of unremitting exploitation. We employ their work; we eat and wear them. We exploit them to serve our superstitions: whereas we used to sacrifice them to our gods and tear out their entrails in order to foresee the future, we now sacrifice them to science, and experiment on their entrails in the hope – or on the mere offchance – that we might thereby see a little more clearly into the present.[4]

Six years later *Animals, Men and Morals* was published, a book edited by three young Oxford philosophers, Stanley and Roslind Godlovitch and John Harris; Roslind Godlovitch's essay 'Animals and Morals' came out in the same year.[5] Anti-vivisection letters in the *Daily Telegraph,* the first entitled 'Rights of Non Human Animals', were my own opening shots.[6] At that time I had no contacts with the then rather stagnant animal welfare movement, nor with the other people in Oxford who were beginning to think along similar lines; for me, it was spontaneous eruption of thought and indignation arising out of the conflict between my natural sympathy for nonhuman animals and what I had witnessed in university laboratories in Cambridge, Edinburgh, New York and California in the 1960s. Brophy, reading my letters in the *Daily Telegraph*, put me in touch with the Godlovitches and John Harris in 1969, and I was able to contribute to *Animals, Men and Morals*. This was reviewed in the *New York Review of Books* in 1973 by Peter Singer, who had known us in Oxford two years earlier.[7] Andrew Linzey then became part of our circle and so did Stephen Clark; we formed what, retrospectively, can be called an informal Oxford Group. With the support of John Harris, the Godlovitches and others, I organized campaigns against otter-hunting and animal experiments. Years later the Group was superseded by Oxford Animal Rights – a body run by Macdonald Daly of Balliol.

A spate of serious books on the subject followed, many or most written by members of this group, including my *Victims of Science* in 1975 and Peter Singer's *Animal Liberation* published in America in the same year and in Britain in 1976.[8] The Oxford Group's powerful contingent of academic philosophers started a discussion which has continued ever since among their colleagues around the English-speaking world and in Europe. Academic journals such as *Ethics* (January 1978), *Philosophy* (October 1978), *Inquiry* (Summer 1979) and *Etyka* (1980) have published special editions on the moral status of animals. Indeed, animal liberation is possibly unique among liberation movements in the extent to which it has been led and inspired by professional philosophers; rarely has a cause been so rationally argued and so intellectually well armed. Albert Schweitzer had once complained that philosophy had ignored the question, playing 'a piano of which a whole series of keys were considered untouchable'. Yet this modern revolution in thought, which experienced a remarkable surge after the *annus mirabilis* of 1969 (see chapter 11), was heralded by the philosophers themselves.

Our moral argument is that species alone is not a valid criterion for cruel discrimination. Like race or sex, species denotes some physical and other differences but in no way does it nullify the great similarity among all sentients – our capacity for suffering. Where it is wrong to inflict pain upon a human animal it is probably wrong to do so to a nonhuman sentient. The actual killing of a nonhuman animal may also be wrong if it causes suffering or, more contentiously, if it deprives the nonhuman of future pleasures. The logic is very simple.

Geneticists tell us that humankind is physically closer to a chimpanzee than a horse is to a donkey. Surely if animals are related through evolution, then we should all be related morally? The species gap is not an unbridgeable gulf, even physically; some species, such as lions and tigers, can interbreed naturally and produce fertile offspring. Even primate species can do so and, in the laboratory, species can now be mixed like cocktails. One day, if human apes are interbred with other apes, will it be justifiable to hunt or eat or experiment upon the hybrid child, or should he or she be sent to school?

In order to produce cheaper meat, pigs have already been born who contain human genes. Yet surely this makes a nonsense of our speciesist morality? Is it not partial cannibalism to eat such a humanopig? How many human genes are required to make a creature human in the eyes of the law? The Oxford Group has been warning of such genetic developments since the early 1970s.[9] In the 1980s transpecies fertilization became a reality and in April 1988 the US Administration awarded to Harvard University the first patent for a new animal species – a cancer-prone mouse containing a human gene.[10]

The findings of a scientific RSPCA committee under Lord Medway[11] in 1979 to the effect that there now is strong scientific evidence that all vertebrate classes can suffer because all have been found to possess in their bodies those biochemical substances known to mediate pain, supplemented the older biological, neurological and behavioural evidence which pointed in the same direction. Furthermore, we have seen the scientific definition of nonhuman suffering widen to include disease, starvation and mental states such as fear, despair, and those arising from the deprivation of exercise, companionship or stimulation, or from the frustration of other psychological needs.[12]

As if to assert our superior moral status it is sometimes claimed that Homo Sapiens is the only altruistic species. But this may not be accurate, for there are authenticated cases of elephants and cetacea trying to assist ailing individuals of their own species, and reports exist of dolphins allegedly trying to help humans. There are also many instances of symbiosis in nature, where one species depends upon another; a predatory fish, for example, allowing cleaner-fish of a different species to cleanse his or her scales in safety. Perhaps our greater toleration of nonhumans may have similar survival value for ourselves, in terms of physical, ecological or even moral benefits. But even if it were true that humans are the only unselfish species, how could this justify our exploitation of other sentients? Should it not reinforce our sense of duty towards them?

The answer to the question 'But isn't it *natural* to be speciesist?' is that it may *not* be, and that even if it is, speciesism and selfishness are still wrong; rape and murder, after all, can spring from 'natural' impulses, but this consideration does not transform rape or murder into virtuous behaviour. We are not slaves to our genes; genetic tendencies can, to a large extent, be overcome through education and by the restraints of civilization.

Other excuses have been used by humans to justify our speciesism, for example, that we are the only tool-using or tool-making species, or that we are the only animal capable of language. In recent decades, all such distinctions have been eroded by science. Other apes, in particular, have been found to be tool-makers capable of learning human sign-language.

One is left in the startlingly simple position, already stated, that whatever is morally wrong in the human case is probably wrong in the nonhuman case as well. When faced with a particular type of exploitation one can apply some such 'human test'. *Veal calves:* would it be right to separate babies from their mothers while still suckling? *Laboratory rats:* would it be right to inflict severe electric shocks upon unwilling men and women? *Bullocks:* would it be right to castrate boys and fatten them to be eaten? *Foxes:* would it be right to chase vagrants across the countryside and to encourage hounds to tear them apart?

The implications of such a revolutionary conclusion are inconvenient, yet they remain entirely rational. What holds for humans, especially for such categories as the mentally handicapped and infants, should also apply in the case of nonhumans.

Self-deceptions

Powerful classes have often rationalized their exploitation of weaker beings by minimizing the latter's capacities for suffering or denying them entirely. African slaves, being of a different race, were barely sensible of their harsh conditions, or so it was sometimes argued by their exploiters; indeed, in 1799, the Duke of Clarence claimed that the slave trade had the virtue of rescuing negroes from savagery.[13] Similarly, a whole host of self-deceiving tactics have been used to defend speciesism, ranging from pragmatic arguments through to more subtle psychological deceptions.

If, as I consider to be the case, all human beings experience some sympathy with other animals, then do we all feel some guilt when we exploit them? Guilt can be suppressed, denied or reduced by various means: we can blame others for what is done; we can distance ourselves from the bloody act; we can attempt to shut it out of our mind or we can try to convince ourselves that the victim of our exploitation deserves to die or feels no pain. When these defences are stripped away, tell-tale anger can erupt, or 'necessity' — 'the argument of tyrants' as Pope reminds us — is defiantly proclaimed and exaggerated.

The exaggeration of the need for meat, for example, has been a feature of Western cultures for several centuries, and over the last hundred years scientists have exaggerated the importance of their scientific research on animals, just as Alderman Newman exaggerated the value of the slave trade two hundred years ago: 'If it were abolished altogether, he was persuaded it would render the City of London one scene of bankruptcy and ruin.'[14] Of the revolutionary proposal to prevent orphan boys being made to climb chimneys, Sir John Yorke warned that the only alternative was the use of brushes which would destroy the mortar in the chimneys and thus cause devastating and uncontrollable fires.[15]

The fierceness of wolves was once exaggerated just as the 'verminous' natures of dingoes, coyotes and foxes are today. Emotive words worthy of the best propagandist are deployed against nonhuman sentients in order to stifle compassion – 'pest', 'vermin' and 'trash'.

Just as men in battle find it easier to kill at a distance without seeing the suffering of the enemy or getting to know him intimately, so people distance themselves from the nonhumans they exploit. They arrange for those who have not known the cows or pigs or sheep to do the slaughtering, or they give numbers or contemptuous names to their laboratory animals.

In general, with the exception of individually motivated cruelty, the greater the intimacy with an animal the harder it is, psychologically, to abuse or exploit it. Even aboriginal hunter-gatherers, who may show no compunction about cooking wild animals alive, would not dream of eating their pets – they are treated as members of the family. In some Amerindian cases such peoples will not even eat the eggs laid by the domesticated fowl they keep.[16]

Exploiters use many stock excuses to reduce their sense of guilt. Serpell has found that, in Britain, hunters claim to be conservationists and may take pride in following certain rules of 'fair play', pest-controllers blame their employers for their work or attribute deliberate wickedness to the pests they kill, farmers blame consumers for the demand for cheap meat and scientists claim that their experiments on nonhumans are done highmindedly for human benefit.[17] Similarly, veterinarians blame the need to keep good relations with their clients and the latter's legal rights of ownership for their reluctance to take firm action to protect animals under their care.[18]

Those who exploit directly are sometimes shunned as being inferior, as slaughtermen are in some societies; in Japan, for example, meat and leather goods traditionally have been processed only by the Untouchable caste. Alternatively, animal exploiters can be ritualistically elevated so as to counteract the underlying guilt and to put them 'above' blame: scientists and 'sportsmen' are thus glorified.

Language has been pressed into the service of exploitation. Bland euphemisms or even self-aggrandizing quasi-religious terms have evolved:

scientists 'sacrifice' their animals, the hunter 'accounts for' a fox, the slaughter-house becomes a 'packing factory'. Special words are used to conceal the true animal origins of products: skin becomes 'leather', cow becomes 'beef', pheasant becomes 'game', deer becomes 'quarry', tail becomes 'brush', dogs become 'experimental subjects', screams become 'vocalizations'.

All these defences are used in our institutionalized system of speciesism; abattoirs are hidden away, meat is elaborately packaged, laboratories are locked, foxes are characterized as too evil to be pitied, and language is changed to disguise reality. In the ensuing chapters we shall encounter many more excuses, ranging from the religious idea of 'man's dominion' to Descartes's claim that nonhuman animals feel no pain; from the assertion that speciesism is justified because animals lack immortal souls to more modern economic claims. As each generation has exploded the speciesist myths of previous periods it has tended to look for new arguments to support humankind's exploitation of the other animals.

Power

Humans now have almost total power over other animals, yet sometimes we like to pretend that it is an equal fight. Does power alone justify exploitation? Did it justify the persecution of Jews or would it justify the exploitation of humans by a super-intelligent species of aliens from outer space? Does morality stand only upon a fear that the oppressed may one day retaliate? If so, then why not exploit and experiment upon unwanted babies or the mentally handicapped? They cannot effectively strike back, nor do they exercise duties towards the rest of us; they would certainly produce far more reliable results scientifically. Such a proposition rightly appals.

As C. S. Lewis once put it in an attack upon vivisection:

If loyalty to our own species, preference for man simply because we are men, is not sentiment, then what is? It may be a good sentiment or a bad one, but a sentiment it certainly is. Try to base it on logic and see what happens!

But the most sinister thing about modern vivisection is this. If a mere sentiment justified cruelty, why stop at a sentiment for the whole human race? There is also a sentiment for the white man against the black, for a *Herrenvolk* against the Non-Aryans, for 'civilised' or 'progressive' peoples against 'savage' or 'backward' peoples. Finally, for our own country, party, or class against others. Once the old Christian idea of a total difference in kind between man and beast has been abandoned, then no argument for experiments on animals can be found which is not also an argument for experiments on inferior men. If we cut up beasts simply because they cannot prevent us and and because we are backing our own side in the struggle for existence, it is only logical to cut up imbeciles, criminals, enemies, or capitalists for the same reason. Indeed experiments on men have already begun. We all hear that Nazi scientists have done them.[19]

This is surely true, although far from being the only reason for attacking speciesism. If knowing, as we now do, of the community of pain among animals and of our evolutionary kinship, we still persist in the total subordination of nonhumans, then are we not paving the way for a more callous attitude towards the weak generally, whether nonhuman or the children, the elderly or the handicapped of our own species?

Speciesism is indeed sheer sentiment, and its irrationality is easily exposed, yet despite its profound moral blindness it continues without any real excuse and for a number of reasons: first, there is profit in it; secondly, it is enjoyable; thirdly, it is habit.

Does the habit element derive largely from our own distant past when the struggle with nature was a real one and the threat posed by our vertebrate kindred was like the threat still posed by earthquake, fire and flood? A combative approach towards rival species and dangerous predators was then highly necessary, as it is towards terrorists today, and if there were conditions in which other food was scarce, then there was a need to kill to eat. In much of the modern world humans are no longer in such a condition, yet almost everywhere they continue to treat other animals as rivals, enemies or prey.

A distinction has to be made between the cases of cruelty committed by individuals in their private lives and the large-scale institutionalized cruelties. The former are usually instigated either by human anger or neglect (which is often associated with equal anger or neglect to children and to other human beings). The institutionalized cruelties, on the other hand, ranging from the overworking of horses and dogs in Victorian times to the plight of nonhumans in factory-farms and laboratories today, are motivated usually by greed, ambition and an unthinking adherence to convention.

The experiments begun by Stanley Milgram in the early 1960s demonstrated how strong is the normal human drive to conform, even if conformity is believed to involve the infliction of severe suffering upon other people. Milgram's experiments showed that most people will give apparently agonizing electric shocks to others if they are led to believe that this is part of a scientific experiment. Like Eichmann, and hundreds of soldiers, torturers and executioners throughout the ages, they did what they were told to do. Normal people who are part of an evil system do evil deeds. Is not speciesism such a system?

Although it is true that most people will do terrible things motivated merely by the desire to conform, thus overcoming the natural restraints of compassion and squeamishness, is it wrong to assume that sadism is often an additional motive? It may be that pleasure in dominating another and in inflicting pain is a basic human tendency, albeit much denied and rarely discussed. In the average human it is probably no stronger than many other impulses, but it may be there, nevertheless, perhaps associated with sexual excitement or accentuated by frustration and the spirit of revenge. Its antithesis to civilization makes it a taboo subject and, although disguised in human-to-human relationships, it is sometimes blatant in human-to-nonhuman interactions. The child who cuddles the puppy at one moment can all too suddenly switch to sadistic teasing in the next.

SOME QUESTIONS RAISED

Do any of our speciesist excuses hold water? If not, what drives us to continue our tyranny? Is it just material gain, convenience and habit, or is there also a deep-seated drive to dominate, and if so, is this drive innate or acquired?

On the other hand, why is there a countervailing *concern* for non-humans? Is this streak of compassion learned or spontaneous? Is it linked with that powerful yet ignored feeling of squeamishness at the sight of blood? If we try to deny squeamishness because we think it is a sign of weakness, how far do such 'macho' motives explain our cruelty to nonhuman animals? Does the conflict between compassion and cruelty, often within the same person, explain the remarkable inconsistency shown in the human attitude towards nonhumans?

These are just some of the questions to be addressed as we consider the history of the subject. Other questions concern the rate at which more humane attitudes have developed. Has it been a smooth continuous progress, or were the middle ages less anthropocentric and therefore slightly kinder towards nonhumans than the later Renaissance period? Were our hunter-gatherer ancestors more respectful towards other animals than later agricultural ages? What has affected the development of the animal welfare and animal rights movements? Has it been urbanization or affluence, the effects of religious or secular teaching, or the implications of science and, particularly, of Darwinism? Why, when so many outstanding men and women have sided with the animals, has so little changed? If Christianity has been the most speciesist of all the major religions, why have supposedly Christian countries led the modern animal welfare movement? And why have Protestant countries done better than Catholic ones?

To explore and answer such questions I have reviewed the history of the relationship between humankind and the other animals. In Part I, which deals with events from antiquity up to about 1960, I have arranged the chapters approximately in chronological order. Part II deals with a more personal view of the modern movement. As this covers the period in which I have been closely involved as a campaigner, out of necessity my own role has had to be included, although I hope not egocentrically. In Part III, the philosophical and psychological issues are discussed and summarized.

I have been at least four people while writing this book – campaigner, psychologist and 'ideas man' as well as historian. I have wanted to include my knowledge of the national and international aspects of the movement which come from first-hand experience, while at the same time recording the results of some original library research. Where the research has turned up little-known information I have sometimes given this in the notes. I hope this has worked to produce a readable text for the general reader while offering further information for the academic.

2 The Ancient World

Stone-age cave paintings of animals reveal that the human preoccupation with our fellow creatures is an ancient one, whether or not such paintings were to worship beasts, propitiate them, assist in their capture by means of magic, or to express Homo Sapiens's admiration for their strength, speed and beauty – the Palaeolithic equivalent of a twentieth-century child's doodlings of tanks, aeroplanes and racing cars. One thing is certain: nonhuman animals were among the most important elements in the lives of the people of those times, more than ten thousand years ago.

Two themes stand out in the extraordinary history of Homo Sapiens's relationship to the other animals: first, its perennial *importance* in the human psyche and, secondly, the *ambivalence and inconsistency* of that relationship.

It is in sculpture and pictorial art that we find the earliest records in this story. The cave paintings of Lascaux and Altamira are succeeded by later prehistoric effigies of animals suggesting a religious use. Some portrayals indicate that the gods take on animal forms, other imply that the animal itself is to be worshipped.

The prominent place occupied by bulls in the Palaeolithic cave paintings of Spain, as well as in those of the Neolithic Near East several thousand years later, have suggested the worship of a long-lived bull deity which continued in Crete and as the sacred bulls of Egypt. After the later development of Mithraism in the West, its crowning myth became the killing of the bull by the divine Mithra, portrayed as an idealized human figure. This cult, a rival to Christianity, excluded female participation and appealed to the militaristic mind. Its bull-killing myth – possibly one origin of modern bullfighting – was perhaps an early example of the association of speciesism with manliness; the male human figure being extolled in an act of domination over the bull who, in previous centuries, himself may have been worshipped as the epitome of dominance and strength. Man had conquered Beast.

EGYPT

In ancient Egypt the preoccupation with sacred animal forms reached a high level: the goddess Hathor is often represented as a cow, the moon god Thoth as a baboon or ibis, Bastet as a cat, Anubis as a jackal, Horus as a falcon and the midwife goddess Taurt as a hippopotamus. Mixed human and nonhuman forms are also characteristic and appear in later (Dynastic) periods. In Egypt, these hybrid forms of the deities usually had humanoid bodies with nonhuman heads. Later, it was the other way around when the Greeks gave human heads and torsos to their animal-bodied centaurs, mermaids and harpies, and the Mesopotamian civilizations did likewise. Such hybrids seem to imply a basic assumption of the physical inter-relatedness of humans and nonhumans, as Hindu religious sculpture does to this day. Not that the part-animal nature of the gods would necessarily imply respect for their earthly counterparts.

At some periods in Egyptian history, the hunting of lions, hippos, birds, wild oxen and even elephants were regarded as kingly sports. In the Late Period, 664 to 332 BC, however, the manifestation of gods in individual animals (such as the three sacred bulls, Apis, Minevis and Buchis) was extended so that *every* animal of a species in which the power of a god was revealed was regarded as sacred and therefore protected and accorded ritual burial; extensive ibis, crocodile and cat cemeteries have been recorded.[1] Furthermore, Herodotus, perhaps unreliably, states that in later years *all* wild animals in Egypt were held to be sacred and that their murder incurred the ultimate penalty:

Anyone who deliberately kills one of these animals is punished with death. Should one be killed accidentally, the penalty is whatever the priests choose to impose. But for killing an ibis or a falcon, deliberately or not, the penalty is inevitably death.[2]

Such a draconian and comprehensive wildlife conservation policy has not been seen since. Nevertheless, prohibitions upon the killing of members of totem species have been widespread and continue in some parts of the world to this day.

The cat enjoyed a special status in Egyptian society after its domestication in about 1500 BC. Earlier (about 2500 BC), while still wild, the cat had been proclaimed a sacred animal. The portrayals of cats in Egyptian art are often of great beauty and sensitivity, apparently motivated as much by affection as veneration. Herodotus reports that killing a cat also became a capital offence, and there are stories of a Roman soldier and Greek tourists getting into trouble on this account. Thousands of cat and other animal mummies have been found in Egypt and are signs that an after-life was believed to await them. Other pets included dogs, gazelles, ornamental fish, monkeys and even palace-trained lions, although none of these ever gained the popularity of the cat. The Egyptians gave names to their dogs such as 'Ebony', 'Grabber', and even 'Cooking Pot', and a distinguished government official, Sen-Mut, had his pets ceremonially buried, placing a bowl of raisins in his monkey's coffin as food for the afterworld.

There is no indication, however, that food animals in general were treated with any greater respect than those of today. Meat was an important, if rare, item in the Egyptian diet, and Old Kingdom tombs depict the forced-feeding of oxen, calves, antelope, cranes, ducks and geese, presumably not for their benefit but for that of people who were to eat them. Some creatures, such as flies, rats and scorpions were regarded as pests, but other dangerous species such as crocodiles, lions and snakes were incorporated into religion and worshipped in the belief that the gods had chosen to inhabit the bodies of these animals or, at least, to manifest their power in them.

It is tempting to speculate that, if more written works had survived from Egypt, in the later periods we would find references to the sufferings of animals and exhortations, even laws perhaps, against cruelty towards them. One conclusion we can draw tentatively from Egyptology is that out of a worship of nonhuman forms emerged the first recorded signs of affection for nonhumans. Literature which has survived includes moral tales in which animals play the central roles, as well as poetry rich in animal imagery. But at the same time some animals were being hunted and sacrificed barbarously. The perennial ambivalence of people's feelings for nonhumans is certainly detectable in the Egypt of three thousand years ago, yet the balance favoured the animals more than it did in the Greek and Roman civilizations that followed.

MESOPOTAMIA AND GREECE

In Mesopotamia, laws survive from the beginning of the second millennium BC which list penalties for the theft of animals, and stipulate that anyone killing a hired ox through negligence or blows must replace it. A veterinary surgeon received payment only if he cured an animal; if it died after treatment then he was required to recompense the owner. The Mesopotamians, as much obsessed in their art with dogs as the Egyptians were with cats, also gave them names like 'Spot' and 'Red', but no indication of any real respect for them has been found.

The Greeks, although they thought little of cats, obviously highly regarded dogs, and it is in Greek literature that we find the first written concern for the treatment of animals in the West. Indeed the status of nonhumans and their relation to humans were important concerns of Greek philosophy, as they are in ours today. Four differing schools of thought emerged. We can call these animism, vitalism, mechanism and anthropocentrism. Animism's central figure was the great mathematician

Pythagoras (active around 530 BC) who contended that animals and people have souls that are the same in kind. These souls are indestructible, he said, composed of fire or air, and move from human to animal or human in succeeding incarnations. Pythagoras himself was a vegetarian and advocated strict moral self-examination each evening with three questions: In what have I failed? What good have I done? and What good have I not done? Pythagoras certainly regarded kindness to animals as a fundamental good, and is reported to have bought live creatures from fishmongers and fowlers in order to set them free.

Vitalism similarly recognized a difference between organic and inorganic entities. But unlike the animists, vitalists such as Aristotle (384–322 BC) stressed the interdependence of soul and body. Aristotle did not deny that men and women are animals, but placed them (as the most rational of animals) at the head of a natural hierarchy, and proposed that the less rational exist to serve the purposes of the more rational. Even slaves, although human and capable of feeling pleasure and pain, were considered to be less rational and, therefore, open to justifiable exploitation by the more rational: 'Since nature makes nothing purposeless or in vain, it is undeniably true that she made all animals for the sake of man.'[3] Unfortunately for the animal kingdom, Aristotle's philosophy eclipsed the influence of Pythagoras over succeeding centuries and was influentially revived by Aquinas and the Dominicans in the thirteenth century.

A third view, mechanism, was that people and animals are mere machines. They were thus seen as beings essentially the same but without any 'soul' differentiating them from inanimate matter.

Finally, elements of the Aristotelian view were simplified and popularized by Xenophon and others. Their simple creed was that everything in the world has been made for the benefit of mankind. If Aristotle's more sophisticated arguments subsequently helped to build the pinnacles of Western thought, then Xenophon's crude anthropocentrism was one of its foundation stones. The animists (such as Pythagoras), the mechanists and the vitalists (such as Aristotle) all accepted the similarity in kind between people and animals. Only the anthropocentrists proclaimed the gulf between us which became such an anxious preoccupation in Europe over the succeeding ages.

ROME

The Romans' cruelty to animals in the arena is notorious. Countless thousands of animals, maddened with red-hot irons and by darts tipped with burning pitch, were baited to death in Roman arenas. At the dedication of the Colosseum by Titus, five thousand died in a day; lions, tigers, elephants and even giraffes and hippos perished miserably. Nevertheless there were several remarkable humanitarian writers in later

Roman times who showed compassion for animals. Pliny recounted anecdotes about the alleged intelligence and religiousness of elephants, the medical skill of the hippopotamus and the love that dolphins showed for music and young children.[4] A tender feeling for animals is a distinctive feature of the poetry of Virgil, and Lucretius and Ovid also touch upon it.[5]

As a militaristic society the Romans consciously suppressed, their tender feelings, but they could not cut off entirely their natural springs of pity. In 55 BC, Cicero wrote to a friend that the agonized trumpetings of some elephants, being slowly butchered in the amphitheatre, had excited the compassion of the spectators, who had cursed Pompey for his cruelty. Interestingly, Cicero adds that the spectacle in the Circus had aroused not only pity but a feeling that the elephant was allied with man.[6] There was also the favourite story of the slave Androcles who was recognized by a lion from whose foot he had removed a thorn. The lion greeted Androcles affectionately and declined to eat him. [7] Sometimes even an emperor could show flickerings of mercy. Marcus Aurelius (AD 161−80) did not like the public entertainments; their cruelty repelled him.

The philosophers Porphyry and Plotinus, and the statesman Seneca, all followed a vegetarian diet, but the most outstanding exponent of this habit was Plutarch, the Greek-born philosopher, who lived in Rome around AD 46−120. He wrote that he would never sell an ox who had served him well, and he defended animals in his two tracts on eating flesh and in his 'Life of Marcus Cato'. Unlike Pythagoras, Plutarch did not base his vegetarianism upon the idea of reincarnation, but upon a general duty of kindness to human and nonhuman alike. He argued that much of the world's cruelty arose from humankind's uncontrolled passion for meat:

For the sake of some little mouthful of flesh, we deprive a soul of the sun and light and of that proportion of life and time it had been born into the world to enjoy...let us kill an animal; but let us do it with sorrow and pity and not abusing or tormenting it as many nowadays are wont to do.

In Plutarch's day these gastronomic torments included trampling and inflaming the udders of sows about to give birth, sewing up the eyes of swans and cranes, and skewering live pigs on red-hot spits, allegedly to improve the taste of the meat.

The range of meats eaten by the nobility at banquets in both Antiquity and in the middle ages was probably dictated by more than mere gluttony. It seems to have symbolized humankind's conquest of the 'animal kingdom', as well as the superiority and opulence of the host. Thus, meat-eating became a symbol of social status. Later, and possibly in consequence, arose the erroneous belief that meat was an essential

1   Cave paintings of 15,000 to 30,000 years ago are almost entirely of animals. This one at Altamira in Spain is typical. Most pictures are of large animals such as deer and bison. Were the artists' motives religious, aesthetic or magical? Whatever the answer cavepeople seem to have been preoccupied with animals and with their power and beauty. The artists rarely portray animals being eaten or hunted and some paintings are not even of usual prey species. The painters do not seem to have been keen to depict other humans nor prominent environmental features such as trees or rivers or celestial bodies. This apparent obsession with animals reminds us of the historic importance of the human–animal relationship in our mental history.

Whereas the Egyptians made their gods in the images of animals, the Israelites – their resentful slaves – made God in the image of Man. Part animals have continued to be a much loved theme in art to the present day from the mythological creatures of Greece, the bestiaries of Medieval Europe, the pet dogs of Renaissance art and the works of Paulus Potter, George Stubbs and Edwin Landseer. This artistic fascination with animals can be found the world over from totemic tribal art to the sculptured bulls of India and the brush drawings of the Orient.

© KATZ

part of the human diet. Today both these connotations are in decline, and there is a corresponding decline in meat-eating in some advanced countries.

THE GREAT RELIGIONS

It is tempting to try to trace the origins of Pythagorean morality back to Hinduism or to the other faiths which were quite newly founded in Pythagoras's day. Pythagoras, as a traveller, may have encountered people with knowledge of Zoroastrianism (which advocated the protection of useful animals), Jainism or Buddhism, which probably all began between 500 and 650 BC. As many major religions were founded in this era it seems best to discuss them in this chapter; but this is not to deny their continuing importance.

Based upon the idea of the transmigration of souls and the belief that all living creatures are the same in essence, Hinduism provided an entirely different basis from Christianity on which to build society. Animals, like humans, were arranged in a complex social hierarchy. According to this tradition, to kill a cow was as serious as to murder a high-caste man. Elephants and horses also held elevated status, but the penalty for killing even the despised dog was no less than that for the murder of an 'untouchable' human being.

Buddhism springs historically from Hinduism and shares the belief in the rebirth of the soul in human or animal form. Buddha 'trained himself to be kind to all animate life', taught that it was a sin to kill any living creature[8] and observed that 'the key to a new civilization is the spirit of Maitri, friendliness towards all living things.'

Hinduism and Buddhism quite early in their development abandoned animal sacrifice, and the feeling against unnecessary destruction of life led to widespread vegetarianism in both Hindu and Buddhist societies from the third century BC onwards. Animals were held to possess the same feelings as people, and several kings of ancient India are known to have founded hospitals for old and sick animals. Indeed, Asoka, emperor of India from about 274 to 232 BC, became a Buddhist and a vegetarian and, in accordance with the doctrine of 'ahisma' (nonviolence), suppressed the royal hunts and ordered the curtailment of the slaughter of animals throughout his empire. Among some Buddhists respect for all life is still the central ethic. Modern Hindus are still taught that the human soul can be reborn into other forms such as animals and insects – they are all considered part of the Supreme Being. Those who have lived wicked and selfish lives are more likely to be reborn in nonhuman form, whereas good living can mean eventual escape from the world. Hindus feel a duty to care, therefore, for all living things. Failure to observe this duty is believed to create bad 'karma' which increases the likelihood of rebirth as a nonhuman.

Of all the Eastern religions, Jainism in India carried the respect for life (rather than the avoidance of suffering) to its most radical position. The first vow of the Jain is not to kill. This leads to fastidious care for all living beings; 'vermin' may be removed, but never killed, and the mouth is covered and the path swept before it is walked upon, in deference to insect life.

The strict followers of Mani, the third-century Persian, were also forbidden to kill any living creature. The ordinary secular Manichaeans, however, observed a more relaxed code, and it is doubtful whether a respect for nonhuman life survived this religion's contact with Christianity over the subsequent centuries.

The Shinto religion of Japan, too, displayed a reverence for nature, emphasizing gratitude towards its benevolent forces and appeasing the malevolent; monkeys in particular were revered and depicted in the famous sculptured triplet 'see no evil, speak no evil, hear no evil.'

To this day, humankind's relationship with the other animals is an important part of the world's religions and many still believe in an active and magical kinship between human and nonhuman. Some South American Indians, for example, believe that all living things, including themselves, were created by animal spirits. Some animals, like the Harpy Eagle, are partners of members of the tribe and to kill one of them will mean the instant death of the human partner. For this reason some species of animal are carefully preserved. When an animal is killed for meat, it is feared that its angry spirit may seek revenge upon those who killed or ate it, making them ill. Killing for food thus becomes an action which requires special care. Similarly, in Babylon, priests would whisper in the ears of their sacrificial victims that it was the gods who killed them;[9] such is the guilt people feel about their speciesism.

The Australian aborigines for centuries have seen themselves as brothers and sisters of certain totem species. They believe that they and the totem animals share the same ancestors, who are still magically alive. Although they hunt animals for food, the totem species are never harmed and in some sacred places other animals are also protected. Aborigines feel a duty to care for the land and to preserve water-holes not just for themselves but for the nonhumans also.

Muslims believe that God created both human and nonhuman, although people were created in a special way when God breathed his spirit into Adam. Rather like Jews and Christians, Muslims are taught that God has given people power over the animals, yet to treat animals badly is to disobey God's will. They believe that the world belongs to God and that people are answerable to Him for their treatment of it; it is wrong, therefore, to hunt merely for pleasure, to use an animal as a target, to use its skin, to cause animals to fight each other, to incite them to act unnaturally in entertainments, or to molest them unnecessarily. Muhammad, so it is said, left his coat upon the ground rather than disturb his cat Muezza, who was sleeping on it, and was angry with his followers for capturing young birds, not least because this upset the mother bird. In practice this aspect of the Muslim religion has declined in its observance over the years, probably under Western influence, though several modern Muslim writers, such as Sayyid Abu A'la Maududi and Al-Hafiz Basheer Ahmad Masri have sought to re-emphasize Muhammad's concern for nonhumans.[10]

The Prophet taught that an animal should only be killed out of necessity. To do so unnecessarily was a deadly sin: 'He who takes pity (even) on a sparrow and spares its life, Allah will be merciful on him on the Day of Judgement;'[11] and 'if you must kill, kill without torture'.[12] He urged humane methods of slaughter: animals should be killed by the best means possible, should not be bound at slaughter, and should not be made to wait. When he saw a man sharpening his knife in the presence of the animal he was about to kill, he asked: 'Do you intend inflicting death on the animal twice?' Muhammad is also recorded as telling his followers to ride their camels 'only when they are fit to be ridden and let them go free when it is meet that they should rest'. He was opposed to the mutilation or disfigurement of animals caused, for instance, by cutting of forelocks, manes or tails.[13] He said that a woman would be sent to Hell for having locked up and starved a cat and, conversely, that Allah had blessed a serf who had saved a dog's life – 'there is a reward for acts of charity to every beast alive.'[14]

What is remarkable about Muhammad is his equal concern for saving life and avoiding suffering. Furthermore, as indicated by the stories of the animal seeing the knife being sharpened and at the feelings of the mother bird, the Prophet clearly included mental suffering in his considerations.

In most cases where religions lay down rules affecting human exploitation of nonhumans, however, the emphasis tends to be on restrictions on the *taking of life* rather than the *infliction of suffering*.

The religion which could have changed this emphasis through its principle of Love, Christianity, did not do so, as we shall see, because it magnified the gulf between human and nonhuman, eventually espousing the anthropocentrism of St Thomas Aquinas. Christians certainly believe that God is the creator of all things and that he (or she) cares for what he has made. Most also accept that people are responsible to God for the way in which they treat creation, and some feel a unity between all living things and are aware that they should be loving and caring at all times. Yet, strangely, animals were, and still are, usually omitted as appropriate objects of this Christian charity.

In the first book of the Bible, Genesis, it is stated:

And God said, Let us make man in our image, after our likeness: and let them have dominion over the fish of the sea, and over the fowl of the air, and over the cattle, and over all the earth, and over every creeping thing that creepeth upon the earth.

So God created man in his own image, in the image of God created he him; male and female created he them.

And God blessed them, and God said unto them, Be fruitful, and multiply, and replenish the earth, and subdue it: and have dominion over the fish of the sea, and over the fowl of the air, and over every living thing that moveth upon the earth.[15]

This gift of dominion is the key to the Christian understanding of humankind's relation to the other animals. The humanitarianism of the law of Moses, based as it may have been upon the kindly elements in ancient Egyptian and Babylonian cultures, is quite evident for all who wish to find it. On the other hand, a warped interpretation of the concept of 'dominion' in Genesis has often overridden this in practice.[16] The exact meaning of 'dominion', translated as 'rule' in the *New English Bible*, must of course depend partly upon how a ruler of that day and culture was supposed to behave. What connotations were customarily attached to the idea of dominion? Was tyranny the norm or was there an ideal of stewardship in which the lord and master should care for his subjects as a parent does a child? It is worth noting that the same word for dominion was used to describe God's relationship to humankind. But whatever was originally intended by the word, surely it should not be made to cover the full range of exploitation which it has been used to justify in the case of human dominion over the other animals? What Jewish ruler, for example, merely because he had dominion, would have been regarded as justified in hunting his human subjects, or killing and eating them? Even at the height of Roman cruelty such a state of affairs would hardly have passed without comment!

The Jewish attitude towards nonhumans, as displayed elsewhere in the Old Testament, was quite humane. In the book of Isaiah, for example, who was preaching around 730 BC, we find opposition to animal sacrifice when God says: 'I delight not in the blood of bullocks, or of lambs, or of he goats'.[17] And in the book of Hosea, who was also prophesying at this period, a similar sentiment is found:

And in that day I make a covenant for them with the beasts of the field, and with the fowls of heaven, and with the creeping things of the ground: and I will break the bow and the sword and the battle out of the earth, and will make them to lie down safely.[18]

One of the strongest statements comes from Isaiah: 'He that killeth an ox is as if he slew a man',[19] and in the first chapter of Genesis God instructs man to be vegetarian.[20] It is only after the Flood that God gives Noah permission to eat meat.[21]

These are not the only merciful passages to be found in the Old Testament. Cattle are to be allowed to rest on the Sabbath;[22] oxen treading the corn should not be muzzled; kids should not be cooked in their mother's milk; [23] parent birds should not be taken if sitting on eggs or with their young;[24] and men are enjoined not to yoke together the ox and the ass.[25] Proverbs recognizes that 'a righteous man regardeth the life of his beast'[26] and in Ecclesiastes it is stated that 'a man hath no preeminence above a beast: for all is vanity'.[27]

Even the strict injunctions of the Old Testament against sexual union between human and nonhuman were similar to those against incest; nonhuman animals were in this respect to be regarded rather as relatives.[28]

The decline in nonhuman sacrifice in Europe and Asia over the last two thousand years should not be taken to be a sign of growing respect for nonhumans, but of a belief that the gods were not to be placated in this way. Paradoxically, animal sacrifice works best, surely, when nonhumans are perceived as being kin, and thus qualifying as human sacrificial surrogates.

A LOST EDEN

What *was* the origin of meat-eating? Why are so many people repelled by the sight of blood, and why can so few easily kill and gut an animal until they get used to doing so? This reaction must tell us something about the basic programming of the human psyche. We do not seem to be designed as thorough-going carnivores. Nor do our teeth appear strong enough to tear and chew uncooked flesh. So, if it was not always present, when did our humanoid ancestors start this strange habit? Was it when the Ice Ages encroached slowly upon their fertile habitats, blighting the fruits and nuts upon which they had flourished and leaving vegetation suitable only for true herbivores? Perhaps there was indeed once an Eden in which men and women were all vegetarians because there was no shortage of fruit and vegetables; perhaps this economic, healthy and humane paradise will return.

Animals have been domesticated for thousands of years, kept as sources of food, clothing and services. New archaeological discoveries have pushed back the earliest dates of domestication far further into the past than had previously been recognized. Pigs, cattle and goats were kept as long ago as 6000 BC, dogs and sheep by 8000 BC. Did domestication improve the relationship between human and nonhuman? Some anthropological evidence suggests that modern hunter-gatherers show more respect for wildlife than agriculturalists do for their stock. But opposite cases can be found: the pastoralist Nuer, for instance, show considerable respect for their cattle, whereas some primitive hunters treat their quarry with appalling callousness, as in the case of the Baka pygmies of the Cameroon who use the same word for 'meat' as for 'animal' and see nothing wrong in cooking their prey alive.[29]

Serpell has eloquently asserted that typical hunter-gatherers see wild animals as their 'mental and spiritual equals or even superiors, capable of conscious thoughts and feelings analogous, in every respect, to those of humans'.[30] This is a pleasing idea. It may be true of some hunter-gatherer cultures, but it is doubtful if it is typical, except in the important case of totem species. On the contrary, it is reasonable to suggest that it was only after the domestication of agricultural and pet species that relationships between human and nonhuman could develop. In the absence of fear on either side, the solitary shepherd, for example, might begin to develop the feelings of companionship and protectiveness which this book is all about.

Maureen Duffy takes rather the same line as Serpell in arguing that 'it must have been the introduction of farming which led to the abandonment of respect for other animals and of a perception of humans as one species among many'.[31] The greater control exercised over nonhumans by the farmer indeed may have reduced his or her fear, and hence 'respect' for them. But this does not necessarily imply that it reduced his or her sympathy for nonhumans or increased his or her cruelty towards them. Surely the general rule is that familiarity breeds sympathy. It is easier to identify with a creature one knows, and although on occasions this will also lead to irritation at the other's failings, it at least allows him or her to be included in the moral circle.

Among primitives the moral circle is a small one, including only the tribe or group. Within this group nonhumans *can* be included provided that, as individuals, they are well known. Pet-keeping and even pet-suckling are common practices in hunter-gatherer societies, as Serpell notes,[32] and it is in relationships of this sort (rather than in the hunter–prey relationship) that kindness develops.

Farming comes somewhere between pet-keeping and hunting in the degree of intimacy which usually prevails between human and nonhuman, and typically creates a position for the animal which is on the periphery of the moral circle, closer to the centre of compassion than wild animals but further out than pets. It was probably because peasant Europeans in Antiquity still felt a closeness to other animals that the theologians of later times were so often prompted, as we shall see, to stress the desirability of maintaining a distance between human and nonhuman.

3 The Christian Legacy: Medieval Attitudes

Christianity can be seen as, in part, a reaction against the Roman cult of violence, but its concern was limited to human victims. Perhaps it was as politically unrealistic to try to save the thousands of creatures slaughtered in the Roman games as it would be today for a religious or political group to seek the abolition of football; the games were so central to the Roman way of life that not even emperors dared to interrupt them.

EARLY CHRISTIANITY

Except for his remark about the value of sparrows in the eyes of God, Jesus' own attitude towards animals is simply not known, perhaps because it was considered too unimportant to record, and St Paul – by far the most influential figure in early Christianity after Jesus – failed to include animals in the moral in-group. This is perhaps surprising in view of the revolutionary character of St Paul's teachings and his explicit opposition to prejudice based on class, sex and race.

The New Testament hardly mentions the human–nonhuman relationship. But this silence may have been only because it was conceived largely as a 'crisis document', written hurriedly to prepare people for Christ's return, which was believed to be imminent. The more comprehensive moral teachings of the Old Testament still stood.[2] One possible reason for the early Christian failure to include nonhumans more emphatically within the circle of Christian love, its central principle, is that early Christianity had to overcome pagan religions which included the worship of animals. To make matters worse, some early opponents had actually accused Christianity of donkey-worship, thus, possibly, putting its leaders on the defensive on this subject. Furthermore, the Christian and Jewish god, unlike many others, was explicitly manlike in form, rather than animal-like in any way. According to Lecky, no Christian writings equalled Plutarch's emphasis upon kindness to animals for another seventeen hundred years after his death.[3]

It was, however, Christianity which established the prevailing opinion on animals in the West, based to some extent upon one short remark made by St Paul. When commenting upon the law of Moses which states (Deuteronomy 25:4): 'Thou shalt not muzzle the ox when he treadeth out the corn', St Paul writes (I Corinthians 9:9–10): 'Doth God take care for oxen? Or saith he it altogether for our sakes? For our sakes, no doubt this is written: that he that ploweth should plow in hope.' Although the modern historian, Keith Thomas, has questioned St Paul's meaning, theologians usually did not.[4] They interpreted Paul as indicating quite definitely that God does *not* care for oxen.

Early Christianity continued to flourish in a world of declining civilization. Barbarian invasions from the North and East and the collapse of the Roman empire led to the erosion of law and order and the lowering of educational and administrative standards. Men and women of learning may have felt that human society was slipping back into a state of nature, and, in order to arrest this process it may be that they were further inclined to assert humankind's separateness from the beasts. Men and women definitely were *not* animals, they claimed; they alone were made in the image of God and alone possessed immortal souls.

The differences between human and nonhuman were thus exaggerated. Indeed, humankind's superiority over the other animal creation came to be regarded as almost synonymous with civilization itself, and those who behaved in an uncivilized way were dismissed as beast-like. This attitude continued through to the medieval and Renaissance periods, and, latterly at least, the characteristic view was one of exultation in the 'Empire of Man' and the hard-won conquest of nature.

ST THOMAS AQUINAS AND ST FRANCIS

The ambivalence of Christians in their attitude towards nonhumans is typified by the contrasting attitudes of St Thomas Aquinas and St Francis of Assisi.

Aquinas was born in Sicily in 1225, only a few months before St Francis died, into a world riven by religious dispute. Throughout the south of France and northern Italy at that time the Cathars had replaced Catholicism as the dominant religious influence, teaching that nonhuman animals as well as humans had immortal souls and forbidding the consumption of meat. At the age of nineteen Aquinas joined the austere Order of St Dominic, recently founded to suppress such heresy by the instigator of the Spanish Inquisition. Aquinas was very much influenced by Aristotle,[5] many of whose works had only recently become available to European scholars, and it seems he absorbed from Aristotle the idea that less rational beings, such as slaves and animals, exist to serve the interests of the more rational.

In his *Summa Contra Gentiles* Aquinas wrote:

If in Holy Scripture there are found some injunctions forbidding the infliction of some cruelty towards brute animals...this is either for removing a
man's mind from exercising cruelty towards other men, lest anyone, from
exercising cruelty upon brutes, should go on hence to human beings; or
because the injury inflicted on animals turns to a temporal loss for some
man, either the person who inflicts the injury or some other; or for some
other meaning, as the Apostle expounds Deuteronomy 25:4.[6]

Here he is referring to St Paul's remark about the oxen mentioned above
– 'Doth God take care for oxen?' And in his *Summa Theologica*,
Aquinas states: 'God's purpose in recommending kind treatment of the
brute creation is to dispose men to pity and tenderness towards one
another.'[7]

St Francis had been born forty years before Aquinas in Assisi and,
after a turbulent youth, had experienced visions and voices which led to
his conversion; he renounced material goods and began to preach the
imitation of Christ. Francis saw all nature as a mirror of the creator and
called not only living creatures but also the sun, moon, wind and water
his 'brothers' and 'sisters'; even illness and death were similarly greeted.
Francis was a visionary and a poet more than an intellectual. His
mystical sense of oneness with creation, his all-embracing love and his
frenzied life-style are in total contrast with the reserved, courteous and
scholarly character of Thomas Aquinas. The one was warm and intuitive
almost to the point of mania, the other cool and academic.

A medieval collection of anecdotes tells how St Francis preached to
his 'little sisters', the birds, and how he rescued some wild doves being
taken to the market and made nests for them. On another occasion he
tamed the fierce wolf of Agobio who had been eating people from the
town. St Francis spoke firmly to 'brother Wolf' and made him an offer:
if he would stop eating people then the townspeople would give him
food for the rest of his life. The wolf solemnly shook St Francis by the
hand and agreed. Such charming stories underline St Francis's love of
creation. Yet, as Peter Singer points out, he still accepted the orthodox
anthropocentric view that all creation exists for humankind's benefit.[8]
Indeed, he hardly distinguished between animate and inanimate; nor
is there any record of vegetarianism in the rules of the Franciscan
Order.

The Order did somewhat develop its ideas two centuries later in
the treatise *Dives and Pauper*,[9] written about 1410 and probably of
Franciscan origin, which implies that the commandment 'Thou shalt not
kill' (Exodus 20:13) applies in principle to nonhuman as well as to
human, although *not* applying in certain major cases such as the killing
of noxious animals or for meat and clothing. *Dives and Pauper* goes on
to state that men should not harm animals without cause and that it is a
grievous sin to torment beasts or birds for cruelty or vanity.

EARLIER SAINTS

Although Aquinas's doctrine towards the treatment of nonhumans eventually triumphed in Christian theology, it is important to emphasize that
kindness to animals was a hallmark of saintliness long before St Francis.
Far from being an isolated example, as is sometimes suggested,[10] St
Francis was really the culmination of a long saintly tradition. St John of
Chrysostom and St Basil of Caesaria, for example, both in the fourth
century, had preached kindness to animals. St John of Chrysostom, who
was a powerful influence in the Byzantine Church, is even quoted as
saying 'The Saints are exceedingly loving and gentle to mankind and
even to brute beasts...Surely we ought to show them great kindness
and gentleness for many reasons, but above all, because they are the
same origin as ourselves.'[11]
In the Liturgy of St Basil can be found this prayer:

The Earth is the Lord's and the fulness thereof. O God, enlarge within us
the sense of fellowship with all living things, our brothers the animals to
whom thou has given the earth as their home in common with us. We
remember with shame that in the past we have exercised the high dominion
of man with ruthless cruelty, so that the voice of the earth, which should
have gone up to Thee in song, has been a groan of travail. May we realise
that they live, not for us alone, but for themselves and for Thee, and that
they love the sweetness of life.[12]

Both these texts are remarkable and explicit in their compassion.
Many other saints are portrayed performing individual deeds of mercy
to animals: St Jerome (373−420), like the Roman slave Androcles, is
credited with taking a thorn from the paw of a lion who repaid him by
becoming a vegetarian and serving the monastery until he joined St
Jerome in death. St Columba, so it is told, ordered his monks to care for
an exhausted crane, and his follower, St Walaric, was wont to caress the
woodland birds. Some saints even anticipated the tactics of the modern
Animal Liberation Front: St Neot saving hares and stags from huntsmen,
and the twelfth-century Northumbrian, St Godric of Finchdale, rescuing
birds from snares.[13] St Aventine, who lived around 438 in Gascony,
rescued a stag from the hunters. St Carileff (c.540) protected a bull that
was being hunted by King Childebert, and both St Hubert (646−727?)
and the Roman general St Eustace (died 118), saw visions of the cruci-
fixion between the antlers of stags they were hunting; in the case of
St Hubert this led to his renunciation of the pleasures of the chase.
St Monacella (c.604) in Wales is said to have protected a hare from the
hounds, as did St Anselm (1033−1109) and St Isidore in Spain about a
century later.
In 1159, a monk of Whitby, who was living in Eskdale, rescued a wild

2 *Buddha* (563–483 BC) taught friendliness towards all living things, not only on the grounds of reincarnation but for their own sakes. Although his followers construed a gulf between humans and animals, a respect for all forms of life is still a central issue for many Buddhists. The great Buddhist ruler Asoka (c. 260 BC) banned hunting, encouraged vegetarianism and established animal hospitals in many parts of India.

boar from the hunt. So outraged were the huntsmen at the disruption of their sport by this early hunt saboteur that they attacked and mortally wounded him. The abbot rallied to the support of the hermit who, before he died, forgave his murderers but ordered them, as a penance, to build a breakwater on the beach to prevent erosion of the land. Until the twentieth century this penance was remembered by the driving in of stakes into the sand on each Ascension Day.[14] The hermit of Eskdale surely must rank as one of the first great environmentalists, showing concern for wildlife and for habitat alike.

The remarkable St Cuthbert, too, was fond of wild animals and seems to have felt a sense of unity with them. A seventh-century Scottish shepherd-boy, he was fifteen when he became a monk in Melrose Abbey. Later, he became a hermit, living on Farne Island in a small cell. There he made friends with the birds, giving them his protection from the depradations of men, and, so the story goes, receiving food from them in return, as they shared their meals together.

Whether or not these stories are historical fact, it is true that they were part of Church lore for many centuries. If such compassion for beasts was attributed to the saints, it is clear that many ordinary men and women would have striven to follow their example. Regardless as to what the theologians were saying at the time, kindness to nonhumans must have been widely regarded as a saintly virtue.

In general, perhaps, later Christian theologians have not really faced up to the issue; rather than being actively speciesist they have ignored the problems intrinsic in the human–nonhuman relationship. Yet many in the Catholic Church continued to follow Aquinas's line and, as late as the nineteenth century, Pope Pius IX refused to allow the foundation of a society to protect animals in Rome on the grounds that human beings had no duties towards lower creation.[15]

THE MEDIEVAL RELATIONSHIP

Yet what did ordinary people think and do about the other animals in medieval times? It seems that Aquinas's anthropocentrism did not really percolate down to the masses for several centuries. Although it is evident that the middle ages were no exception to the age-old rule of ambivalence in the human–nonhuman relationship it seems that at least the non-humans were given a place in the community. Keith Thomas, in *Man and the Natural World*, mentions instances of everyday compassion contrasting with the better-known cruelties of the period,[16] and one can dimly discern that many in the medieval era perceived a kindred feeling with the beasts and that the natural impulse of compassion was often felt and acted upon. Nevertheless, the equally elemental sadistic desire to dominate was also present, as displayed in baiting, and the habitual contemporary exploitation of human and nonhuman alike bred an

3 *St John of Chrysostom* – a powerful influence in the early church – emphasised the common origin of animals with humans and pointed out that the saints are "exceedingly loving and gentle" to both. This perceived closeness to the animals probably increased in Europe during the twelfth and thirteenth centuries but was undermined by Thomas Aquinas (1225–1274) when he re-established the Aristotelian view of human superiority. Such speciesism suited the ethos of the Renaissance and, later, was further reinforced by René Descartes (1596–1650). The modern church still forgets that for a thousand years its saints were depicted as caring for animals, communing with them and rescuing them from adversities.

insensitivity to suffering and a thoughtlessness that we have with us to this day.

The record of the medieval relationship between human and nonhuman is, of course, rather sparse. Yet a feeling of kinship seems to have been taken for granted, with both kind and unkind consequences.

Country folk in Britain, after all, frequently slept under the same roof as their livestock until the sixteenth century. Even in towns it was not unusual to find horses, pigs and chickens sharing houses with men and women, rather as today our houses are inhabited by pet dogs, cats and budgerigars. It was not unknown to bedeck animals with bells or ribbons, to speak to them and to call them by name. Their alleged moral or immoral behaviour, or their social standing, could save or condemn them and, to a degree, the human class system was extended to the nonhuman community; falcons, greyhounds, spaniels and thoroughbred horses being regarded as 'noble', ferrets and cats as 'base'; and eagles, whales and lions as 'kings' of their respective orders.

Sometimes the 'social class' of an animal was simply a reflection of the class of human being who exploited it or the use to which it was put. This is clearly exemplified in the case of dogs, divided by Dr John Caius in 1576 (Of English Dogges) into three sorts — a 'generous' kind used for hunting or as pets, a 'rustic' sort used for necessary work, and a 'degenerate' type which included turnspits and stray curs.[17] As with human society, class was determined largely by breeding and partly by occupation.

Even more revealing is the old practice of holding animals responsible for crime, based perhaps upon Exodus 21:28: 'If an ox gore a man or a woman that they die; then the ox shall be surely stoned, and his flesh shall not be eaten: but the owner of the ox shall be quit.' Trials in England seem not to have occurred, although on the continent of Europe and particularly in France they were commonplace. A sow who killed a child in Falaise in 1386, for example, was sentenced to death by strangulation after being mutilated by the executioner, and during the following century sows were executed, usually by hanging, in Meulan, Lavegny and Laon for similar offences; in 1497, in Chavonne, a sow was condemned to be beaten to death for wounding a child, and another was executed in Nancy in 1572. Bulls were usually strangled, as at Moisy in 1314. A dog was hanged in the Netherlands in 1595, the carcass being duly suspended from the gallows to deter other dogs from biting babies, much as some modern gamekeepers will still display the corpses of 'vermin' they have shot.

Affronts to the dignity of the medieval church rarely went unpunished, as some sparrows had discovered in 1499 when they were excommunicated for leaving their droppings on the seats of the pews in St Vincent.[18] The famous Jackdaw of Rheims, who was cursed by bell, book and candle, was clearly not alone.

At least, one might say, nonhuman delinquents in the middle ages had the benefit of due process of law; they were not summarily executed as they are today. They were at least accorded the dignity of being treated, to some degree, as 'people' and not as things. Such trials may have satisfied the human need to 'make sense' of terrible events such as the killing of a child,[19] but it was surely because the medieval mind saw nonhumans as being very much like humans that it could not accept the modern explanation — that the child's death had been an accident caused by a less rational and unculpable being.

Insects often escaped with lighter sentences, most commonly being ordered to move to alternative accommodation. Beetles in St Julien, for instance, were ordered to move away from the vines they had damaged, and some leeches, convicted of killing fish in Lake Geneva in 1431, were excommunicated and banished to another home by the Bishop of Lausanne. Caterpillars in Valence and mosquitoes in Mayence suffered similar fates.

It can be seen that many regarded nonhumans as part of a wider class system, and the relationship between a peasant and his lord was considered similar in kind to that between an animal and his master. In short, the animals were often treated rather like poor relations — with a mixture of contempt and pity. Indeed this feeling of hierarchy was formalized in the popular philosophy of the Great Chain of Being which, as it derived from Aristotle, depicted nature as a huge feudal structure; at the top was God and beneath came archangels, seraphs, angels, man, animals, plants and minerals — in that order. However, the old pagan idea of transmigration persisted too; in medieval England the souls of the unshriven were commonly believed to roam, sometimes taking the form of seagulls or geese, or spectral dogs, and indeed some fishermen until quite recently believed that seals were the reincarnation of their comrades drowned at sea.

Perhaps as a reaction to such folklore, the denial that animals possessed a soul which would survive the death of the body became an important assertion among churchmen and one on which, rather inexplicably, many based their justification for the exploitation of nonhumans. Only a few splendid exceptions, like Cardinal Bellarmine, maintained the more logical opinion that because they lacked an afterlife nonhuman animals therefore deserved special consideration in this one: 'we shall have Heaven to reward us for our suffering, but these poor creatures have nothing but the enjoyment of their present life.'[20]

The large place filled by animals in the psychology of the middle ages can be seen in their heraldry, bestiaries, inn-signs and folk tales. Even their riddles and jokes reveal an often affectionate (and even anthropomorphic) interest in nonhumans:

Question: What day in the year be the flies most a-feared?

4   *Richard Martin MP* (1754–1834) The flamboyance, wit and virility of Martin and his collaborator Lord Erskine (1750–1823) undermined the criticism that a concern for nonhumans was "unmanly" and helped them to negotiate successfully their anti-cruelty legislation in 1822, the first of its kind anywhere in the world. With William Wilberforce and other anti-slavers, Martin went on to establish the Society for the Prevention of Cruelty to Animals two years later, demonstrating, as many have done before and since, that commitments to the welfare of humans and animals are often associated.

Answer: That is on Palm Sunday, when they see everybody have a handful of palm in their hand; they ween [think] it is to kill them with.

Question: Why come dogs so often to the church?

Answer: Because when they see the altars covered, they ween [think] their masters go thither to dinner.

Question: Why doth a dog turn him thrice about ere he lieth him down?

Answer: Because he knoweth not his bed's head from the feet.

Question: Wherefore is it that an ass hath so great ears?

Answer: Because her mother put no biggin [bonnet] on her head in her youth.[21]

Rude Sports

One of the main indications of how humans treated nonhumans in the medieval period is in the sporting record, for throughout the middle ages in Europe, as in classical times, the hunting and fighting of wild beasts were extolled as sports and entertainments. Although in later times Tudor ladies participated, and indeed sometimes delighted, in shooting and cutting the throats of captured animals, these activities were principally pursued in earlier days by men.

Such country sports can be divided into two major types. In the first a wild quarry is sought and killed, while in the second a captive animal is tormented. Both sports probably tap basic instincts — those of searching and bullying. The secondary reasons for these activities are fairly obvious. There were the usual social rewards associated with any sport: the displays of fashion, the conviviality and companionship. Furthermore, the fact that hunting (rather more than baiting) was for centuries the pastime of kings and nobles gave it an aristocratic appeal, and countless thousands of creatures have in consequence died on this altar of snobbery — and, indeed, still do so.

Throughout the middle ages, Europeans indulged in sports of both principal types; connected with both was the widespread idea that they were manly. Both had been founded upon the once essential tasks of the physically strongest and bravest of the tribe or family: the acquisition of food and the defence against predators. In prehistoric Europe, as in some parts of the globe to this day, these tasks had been necessary and dangerous. It did indeed take courage for Stone Age men to attack the mammoth with their primitive spears and to defend their families against the sabre-tooth tiger, but, gradually, as nature was conquered and food became cultivated, the necessity for hunting and conquering dwindled. Yet men did not wish to relinquish the pleasures they had derived from proving their manhood in these ways.

In the twelfth century, John of Salisbury criticized hunters thus: 'By constantly following this way of life they lose much of their humanity and become as savage, nearly, as the very brutes they hunt.'[22] Such early criticisms, however, were rarely recorded, unlike the better-known contemporary resentment towards the draconian laws against poaching which prevented the common man from killing for food.

The Norman kings had claimed a monopoly of hunting over large parts of the country and enforced this through a highly unpopular policy of 'afforesting' other people's land, penalties being imposed upon those who killed game species without authority. Indeed poaching was suppressed with brutality all over Europe for many centuries and, as late as 1537, the Bishop of Salsburg tied a poacher in the skin of a deer and threw him to the hounds to be torn to pieces in the market place.

It appears that hunting, although recognized as primarily a sport, had long been justified on the grounds that it produced food. Indeed, at least from Chaucer's day, the edible hare and deer were acceptable quarries while the fox, like the badger, was not. It was only in the early sixteenth century that fox-hunting became established,[23] and was then justified on the grounds that the fox was the utmost villain.

Cockfighting, according to Lecky, was a favourite sport for children in England as early as the twelfth century,[24] although it was, like football, suppressed for a time by Edward III because it was considered to be diverting men from learning the valued skills of archery. Bull-baiting goes back at least to the reign of King John in the thirteenth century, but in this case again the justification given was a culinary one. Baiting, so it was claimed, was necessary to make the bull's flesh whole-some, and for many years butchers in England were prohibited by law from killing a bull until it had been baited.

4 The Renaissance and its Aftermath

It seems that as the medieval period drew to a close, the human treatment of nonhumans in Europe actually worsened. The influence of the saints faded and the growing anthropocentrism of the Renaissance heralded several centuries of outstanding cruelty. It was at this time that the speciesism of Thomas Aquinas became a useful doctrine in helping to allay any qualms of conscience.[1]

TUDOR AND STUART BRITAIN

Whereas in earlier times hunting in Britain had been associated mainly with the killing of edible species, such as deer and hares, around the end of the fifteenth century this began to change. In 1539 Robert Pye informed Thomas Cromwell that foxes could be got rid of entirely, but the gentry would not allow it because they enjoyed hunting them. Foxhounds, he added, did more damage to farmers' chicken and sheep than did foxes.[2] Nevertheless, fox-hunting gained steadily in popularity throughout the sixteenth and seventeenth centuries. From the fifteenth century onwards hunting practices seem to have become increasingly bloody, the quarry (usually deer) being dismembered and disembowelled on the spot, its less noble portions being thrown to the hounds and blood being ritualistically splashed upon the onlookers. The hapless Henry VI (1421–71), although he hunted, could not bear to see the animals killed.[3]

In England, the scarcity of game after the fifteenth century encouraged the development of parks from which the deer could not easily escape and in which poachers found it more difficult to follow their craft. Seated in a bower surrounded by servants, Queen Elizabeth I, in later years, would shoot deer at close range, rounded up especially for the purpose. On one occasion, in 1591, she shot and killed four out of thirty deer brought to her and, while music played, one of the ladies shot another. On other occasions she hunted in the conventional manner, dismounting to cut the animals' throats. Once she contented herself by cutting off the ears of a terrified hart as 'a ransom' before allowing it to return to the herd. James I, too, would personally dispatch his cornered quarry, and he maintained contact with the latest hunting techniques from France, employing French riding and hunting masters to teach his children.

In many European countries, hunting became a spectator sport involving carefully staged mass executions of confined animals. In Germany, for example, deer were driven through triumphal arches or into lakes to be hacked to pieces with swords by men in fancy dress. Indeed it was towards the end of the sixteenth century that hunting and baiting became barely distinguishable. When Queen Elizabeth visited Kenilworth in 1575 she first watched a hart being killed in the water by hounds, then saw a pack of mastiffs let loose on thirteen bears – 'a sport very pleasant', said Robert Laneham, 'to see the bear...shake his ears twice or thrice with the blood'.[4] In Scotland the animals were driven into especially prepared dykes to be slaughtered, or rounded up in huge herds and then attacked with any sort of weapon that was to hand. James I used to paddle in the resulting gore, convinced that it strengthened the sinews of his somewhat spindly legs.

Baiting became increasingly barbaric and almost any creature unfortunate enough to be taken alive in the fifteenth and sixteenth centuries might be used for this purpose; bears, bulls, monkeys, cats, even horses, were chained to a post and then attacked. Dogs were the usual assailants, but men would also bait tethered bears, provided they had first been blinded. Paul Hentzner, a German tourist in England, reported in 1598 that he saw such a blinded bear scourged:

by five or six men standing circularly with whips, which they exercise upon him without any mercy as he cannot escape because of his chain; he defends himself with all his force and skill, throwing down all that come within his reach and are not active enough to get out of it, and tearing the whips out of their hands and breaking them.[5]

In Tudor times bear-baiting reached its zenith of popularity and herds of bears were maintained throughout England. The most famous beargarden was on Bankside in Southwark, which admitted a thousand spectators at a penny a head to view bears set upon by mastiffs, who would often be so mutilated that they would also die cruel deaths.

In some parts of the country cock-fights were staged in churchyards, and many new cockpits were built in the reigns of Henry VIII and Elizabeth I. The other great bloodsport was cock-throwing. This involved tying a cock or hen to a stake and then hurling sticks at it until it was dead. Turner notes that 'if its leg was broken, rough splints were applied so that it could still stand to receive punishment. Sometimes it was buried in earth with only its head visible; or it might be thrust in an earthen vessel, with head and tail protruding, and become the prize of the first person to break the vessel.'[6] Throwing at cocks was a sport especially indulged in on Shrove Tuesday, although the reason for this is unclear. (A similar sport, involving throwing stones at live rabbits hung on stakes, persists in parts of Spain to this day.)

Despite royal patronage, towards the end of Elizabeth's reign there were signs that baiting was losing some of its popularity and that Londoners, at least, were beginning to prefer the more intellectual pleasures of the theatre. Elizabeth herself deplored this trend and, with the support of the Lord Mayor, she prohibited the performance of plays on Thursdays, which were reserved for baiting.

There seems to be no evidence that this gradual disenchantment with baiting was due to any organized opposition, and especially not on humanitarian grounds; such overt campaigns were only to begin in the following century. So we see the dwindling of a cruel custom without any accompanying reform movement to account for it. Was it just that William Shakespeare was writing such excellent plays? Was it the growing fastidiousness of the new middle classes, or was it the stirrings of conscience?

It is likely that in Britain in the sixteenth century there had been more tormenting of nonhumans just for sport than at any time before or since. But matters did not much improve in the following century. The cruelty of children, in particular, was marked. They would indulge themselves by throwing at cocks, tying pans to the tails of dogs, skinning live frogs, dropping cats from heights, inflating toads by blowing into them through a straw and pushing needles through the heads of chickens.[7] Throughout the Tudor and Stuart periods the long-established view had persisted that animals were given life in order to be of service to humankind, and this opinion was the usual justification given for barbaric sports. Keith Thomas aptly describes the attitude of the preachers of this period as 'breathtakingly anthropocentric'. Every beast was believed either to have a practical function or a moral meaning for human benefit.[8]

The medieval bestiaries, the best known of which was that of the perennial Physiologus, probably the most popular tome after the Bible itself, had been a wonderful mixture of inaccurate observations of animals laced with fantastic and religious overtones. The main intention of the bestiaries was to display virtues and vices in animal behaviour and to exhort the reader to imitate the former and abjure the latter. In some quarters these arguments were carried to extremes and even the most unlikely instances of creation continued to be explained in this way, even into the eighteenth century. Horseflies, according to William Byrd as late as 1728, had been created so 'that men should exercise their wits and industry to guard themselves against them'. The louse was indispensable, the Reverend William Kirby explained, as an incentive to cleanliness. Even horse manure had been given a sweet aroma, George

Cheyne explained in 1705, because God knew that man would often be close to it.[9]

The earlier emphasis upon the Fall and the consequent imperfection of nature was replaced in the late seventeenth century by arguments of this sort, intricately demonstrating the benevolence of the creator. Not only medics, but scientists in general, consciously espoused this position, arguing that the object of their studies was to discover God's benevolence to man through nature.

Post-Renaissance Europe had become exceptionally dependent upon animals as sources of food, motive-power and clothing, and from the seventeenth to the nineteenth centuries England was probably one of the most carnivorous societies of any age, reinforced by the theories of contemporary medicine (in the late twentieth century to be entirely revised) which held that meat was an essential part of the human diet and was of particular value to health.

The Renaissance had ushered in a process of refinement in manners, dress and attitudes, upon which men and women prided themselves. The rough simplicity of the early middle ages was looked down upon, and humankind's 'animal' functions such as excretion, copulation and suckling became increasingly matters for embarrassment — a long-lasting trend which only began to be reversed during the early twentieth century under the influence of Freud. The word 'beast', in common use during earlier centuries, began to be replaced by the more contemptuous 'brute' (literally 'stupid' or 'irrational') from the late sixteenth century onwards.

Middle-class Englishmen of the period were anxious to assert the difference between themselves and the brutes, partly to reassure themselves of their intellectual and social status and partly out of a genuine belief in the process of civilization. The Renaissance was, moreover, about humanism; the claim that man was of prime importance, dignity and potential. This opinion left the 'lower animals' out of the picture and compounded the anthropocentrism already being expounded by contemporary Christian theologians.

From about 1450 till 1700 the situation in Britain was at its blackest for nonhuman creatures. Nevertheless, although as we shall see it was only in the eighteenth century that the humane reaction really took off, the spark of compassion was far from being entirely extinguished by the rampant speciesism of the preceding two centuries.

SIGNS OF COMPASSION

Little is known of Leonardo da Vinci's concern for animals save that it is reputed that he became a vegetarian, that he used to buy caged birds in order to release them, and that he saw humankind as tyrannous.[10]

He is quoted by John Vyvyan as expostulating 'Oh, Justice of god! Why dost thou not wake and behold thy creatures thus ill used?'[11] When he died in 1519, there could have been few other contemporaries who had publicly committed themselves to such a view. But then Leonardo in so many ways anticipated the thinking of later centuries.

It is perhaps a feature of genius to feel sympathy with nonhuman animals. Isaac Newton, for instance, more than a century later, would become noted as a cat-lover, and is reputed to have invented the 'catflap' for his pets; that other great cosmologist, Albert Einstein, would· urge 'widening our circle of compassion to embrace all living creatures', and Albert Schweitzer, in almost identical words, would warn 'until he extends the circle of his compassion to all living things, man will not himself find peace'.

In 1516 Sir Thomas More (1478–1535) published his *Utopia*, and thus qualifies as one of the first writers since classical times, albeit implicitly, to advocate mercy towards nonhumans. He wrote of his Utopians: 'They kill no living beast in sacrifice, nor they thinke not that the merciful clemencye of God had delite in bloude and slaughter, which hath geven liffe to beastes to the intent they should live.' They also despised the 'foolyshe pleasures' of hunting and hawking: 'Thou shouldest rather be moved with pitie to see a selye innocente hare murdered of a dogge: the weake of the stronger, the fearefull of the fearce, the innocente of the cruell and unmercyfull.'[12]

William Shakespeare's writing reflects the perennial ambivalence of human towards nonhuman. Throughout his plays animals are referred to in allegory and metaphor and dogs, for example, are depicted as figures of contempt. Yet the author reveals a humanitarian attitude in several instances. Isabella, for example, in *Measure for Measure*, claims that

> the poor beetle, that we tread upon,
> In corporal sufferance finds a pang as great
> As when a giant dies.

In *As You Like It* the First Lord describes Jacques in the Forest of Arden watching:

> A Poor sequester'd stag,
> That from the hunters' aim had ta'en a hurt,
> Did come to languish; and, indeed, my Lord,
> The wretched animal heav'd forth such groans
> That their discharge did stretch his leathern coat
> Almost to bursting, and the big round tears
> Cours'd one another down his innocent nose
> In piteous chase.

5 *John Stuart Mill* (1806–1873) argued that the ethical position of animals was similar to that of children and he urged legislation to protect them. The other great Utilitarian, Jeremy Bentham, had already pointed out in 1789 that in considering the rights of animals "the question is not can they reason? Nor can they talk? But *can they suffer?*"

King Henry VI, in the play of the same name, is made to say:

> As the butcher takes away the calf,
> And binds the wretch, and beats it when it strays,
> Bearing it to the bloody slaughter house;
> Even so, remorseless, have they borne him hence:
> And, as the Dam runs lowing up and down,
> Looking the way her harmless young one went,
> And can do naught but wail her darling's loss,
> Even so myself bewail good Gloster's case...

In *Cymbeline*, the Queen proposes to experiment upon animals in order to test poison:

> I will try the forces
> Of these thy compounds on such creatures as
> We count not worth the hanging but none human,
> To try the vigour of them, and apply
> Allayments to their act, and by them gather
> Their several virtues and effects.

But she is warned off by Cornelius:

> Your Highness shall from this practice but make
>   hard your heart;
> Besides the seeing these effects will be
> Both noisome and infectious.[13]

One or two other thinkers of the sixteenth century are believed to have shown some compassion for animals. Tycho Brahe (1546–1601), the great Danish astronomer, is reputed to have been an animal-lover, as is Pierre Charron (1541–1603), the French theologian whose friend, Michel de Montaigne (1533–92), published his essay *Of Cruelties* in 1588. Montaigne has been hailed by Singer as the first since Roman times to condemn cruelty to animals as wrong in itself. Montaigne certainly does this, although his grounds appear emotional rather than reasoned:

Amongst all other vices, there is none I hate more, than crueltie, both by nature and judgement, as the extremest of all vices. But it is with such an yearning and faint-hartednesse, that if I see but a chickins necke puld off, or a pigge stickt, I cannot chuce but grieve, and I cannot well endure a seelie dew-bedabled hare to groane, when he is seized upon by the houndes...As for me, I could never so much as endure, without remorse and griefe, to see a poore, sillie and innocent beast pursued and killed, which is harmelesse and void of defence, and of whom we receive no offence at all. And as it commonly hapneth, that when the Stag begins to be embost, and finds his strength to faile-him, having no other remedie left him, doth yeeld and bequeath himselfe unto us that pursue him, with teares suing to us for mercie, was ever a grievous spectacle unto me. I seldom take any beast alive, but I give him his libertie.[14]

Montaigne repeatedly quotes Plutarch and Pythagoras rather than holy scripture. His sympathy for animals is clearly a 'gut' reaction and the texts he uses for support are pagan rather than Christian. Although himself a sceptic, he does produce one religious argument in support of his compassion:

Divinitie it selfe willeth us to shew them some favour: And considering, that one selfe-same master (I meane that incomprehensible worldframer) hath placed all creatures in this his wondrous palace for his service, and that they, as well as we, are of his household: I say, it hath some reason to injoyne us, to shew some respect and affection towards them.

Montaigne, like St Francis, goes on to express a feeling of:

respect, and a generall duty of humanity, which tieth us not only unto brute beasts that have life and sense, but even unto trees and plants. Unto men we owe Justice, and to all other creatures that are capable of it, grace and benignity. There is a kinde of enter-changeable commerce and mutuall bond betweene them and us. I am not ashamed nor afraid to declare the tendernesse of my childish Nature, which is such, that I cannot well reject my Dog, if he chance (although out of season) to fawne upon me, or beg of me to play with him.

He roundly rejects the anthropocentric view. He sees human and non-human animals as being qualitatively the same and therefore on the same level morally:

We are neither above nor under the rest: what ever is under the coape of heaven (saith the wise man) runneth one law, and followeth one fortune... Some difference there is, there are orders and degrees: but all is under the visage of one-same nature.[15]

Although Montaigne's works were promptly translated into English and were read by many, probably including Shakespeare, their message had already been somewhat anticipated in England by Philip Stubbes in 1583. Stubbes (1555–1610) was of a very different mould from the gentle but worldly Montaigne. A Puritan theologian, he attacked cock-fighting and hunting partly on the grounds that these sports tended to be accompanied by swearing, brawling, drinking and whoring: 'I never read of any in the volume of the Sacred Scriptures that was a good man and a hunter.' Stubbes's principal argument was that it is an insult to God to abuse his creatures. Yet one can also detect some genuine sympathy for the animals themselves:

What Christian heart can take pleasure to see one poor beast to rent, tear and kill another, and all for his foolish pleasure? And though they be bloody beasts to mankind and seek his destruction, yet we are not to abuse them for his sake who made them and whose creatures they are...[16]

Even the great Protestant reformers, Martin Luther (1483–1546) and John Calvin (1509–64) showed feelings of compassion for the beasts, although both reinforced the anthropocentric view of creation. Calvin wrote that God 'will not have us abuse the beasts beyond measure, but to nourish them and to have care of them'. Man still comes first, but a beast is 'a creature of God' who gave man dominion 'with the condition that we should handle them gently'.[17]

At the end of the sixteenth century, at the height of British speciesism, the humanitarian spark still glows dimly, fanned partly by secular compassion and partly by religious feeling, epitomized by Philip Sidney's (1554–86) gentle injunction: 'Thou art of blood, joy not to make things bleed. Thou fearest death; thinke they are loath to die'.[18]

In Catholic states, too, there were signs of compassion: in 1588 an anonymous Spanish officer on board one of the ships of the Armada noted the pitiable plight of horses thrown overboard into the sea, and in 1567 Pope Pius V prohibited bull-fighting and the baiting of wild beasts, and denied Christian burial to bullfighters killed in the ring. The motives are unclear, but his Bull states that such exhibitions are 'contrary to Christian duty and charity'.[19]

A trickle of arguments in favour of the nonhumans slowly appeared during the seventeenth century. The fashionable writer Francis Quarles, for example, expostulated in 1641:

> The birds of the aire die to sustain thee;
> The beasts of the field die to nourish thee;
> The fishes of the sea die to feed thee.
> Our stomacks are their common sepulcher.
> Good God! With how many deaths are our poor lives patcht up!
> How full of death is the life of momentary man![20]

Quarles demonstrated a practical and down-to-earth sort of decency towards animals which remains part of British culture to this day: 'Take no pleasure in the death of a creature; if it be harmless or uselesse, destroy it not: if usefull, or harmefull destroy it mercifully.'[21]

A significant figure of this period was the Chief Justice, Sir Matthew Hale (1609–76), who worried about eating flesh, yet assumed that it was necessary. He wrote, in about 1662: 'I have ever thought that there was a certain degree of justice due from man to the creatures, as from man to man.'[22] Sir Matthew abhorred cruel sports and saw all cruelty as 'tyranny' and 'a breach of that trust under which the dominion of the creatures was committed to us'. It was said of Sir Matthew that the only occasion on which he was known to be thoroughly angry was when a servant allowed a pet bird to starve.

The distinction falls to the remarkable Gloucestershire shepherd, Thomas Tryon (1634–1703), to be the first to introduce the word 'rights' in the nonhuman context, when he made the 'fowls of heaven' complain, in about 1683:

But tell us, O Man! we pray you tell us what injuries have we committed to forfeit? What law have we broken, or what Cause given you, whereby you can pretend a Right to invade and violate our part, and natural Rights, and to assault and destroy us, as if we were the Agressors and no better than Thieves, Robbers and Murtherers, fit to be extirpated out of the Creation?[23]

Tryon, who was a vegetarian, wrote extensively about diet and was an active opponent of slavery. Later, he wrote in his *Wisdom's Dictates* in 1691: 'violence and killing either Man or Beasts is as contrary to the Divine Principle as light is to darkness...Man's Soul nor Body can never be at rest or peace, until he do suffer the inferior creatures to have and enjoy that Liberty and quiet they groan to be delivered into.'[24]

During the early seventeenth century Puritan opinion began to come round to the view that animals did indeed have souls. John Milton, Robert Fludd and the Leveller Richard Overton were of this opinion. In the following century, Joseph Butler, John Hildrop and Richard Dean concurred. Nevertheless, Puritans during the Civil War decided that the best way to stop bear-baiting, souls or no, was to kill the bears. Cromwell himself ordered this to be done when, upon entering Uppingham, he found a bear-bait in progress on the sabbath: the bears were tied to a tree and shot. General Ireton acted similarly, and in 1635 Colonel Pride shot the bears at Southwark – an action which plagued his conscience on his death-bed. How far the Puritans were acting out of compassion is debatable. Later historians such as Hume and Macaulay were certain that it was the spectators' pleasure and not the bears' pain to which they objected.[25]

Baiting, like other blood sports, had become associated with the Royalist cause and with the rough hedonistic side of Old England. The Puritans were thus acting politically in their suppression of these kingly pleasures. They disliked the accompanying crudeness and immorality which attended them, and in addition may have had grounds for fearing that these sports were a breeding ground for Royalist sympathy or a pretext for Royalist gatherings.

At the Restoration, however, baiting did not experience the revival that some may have anticipated for it. The theatre, which had threatened to usurp the affection felt for baiting in the previous century, had also been suppressed by the Puritans, and after 1660 its popularity soared, along with that of horse-racing, while baiting continued to languish.

Two other figures of the seventeenth century must be mentioned: Henry More and John Locke. More (1614–87) had studied philosophy at Cambridge; although he put humans far above the other animals, he told Descartes that his doctrine that nonhumans were unconscious was 'murderous'. More tended to the view that animals, like men, had immortal souls, and in 1655 he wrote that animals had been created to enjoy themselves as well as to be of service to man, and that to assert otherwise was sheer pride, ignorance and 'haughty presumption'.[26]

John Locke (1632–1704), the great English philosopher, was another who could see through Descartes's contention. The idea that animals had immortal souls had caused some people considerable anxiety, Locke suggested, and this was the real reason why they argued that animals were unfeeling machines. He considered it wrong to waste any food that might sustain wild animals or birds. Locke argued that compassion was natural and cruelty unnatural, and in his *Thoughts on Education* he wrote: 'Children should from the beginning be bred up in an abhorrence of killing and tormenting any living creature...and indeed, I think people from their cradle should be tender to all sensible creatures.'[27]

EARLY LEGISLATION

The first modern laws to protect animals appear to date from the seventeenth century, one in a Puritan setting, the other originating from a more Royalist source. Thomas Wentworth, Earl of Strafford (1593–1641), a powerful and ambitious English statesman, was made Lord Deputy of Ireland in 1631, and as part of his 'civilizing' and 'anglicizing' reforms in that country, passed a law in 1635 prohibiting the pulling of wool off sheep and the attaching of ploughs to horses' tails; one of the two reasons for this law being given as 'the cruelty used to the beasts'. This is probably the earliest legal reference to this concept in the English language.[28] Strafford's motives are unknown. He seems an unlikely candidate to be a pioneering humanitarian, being better known for his arrogant pursuit of power, which eventually led him to the scaffold in 1641. If such a measure meant no more to him than being part of an accepted 'anglicization', it may reveal that by the early seventeenth century, condemnation of cruelty to animals was becoming part of English culture.

The other example of seventeeth-century legislation comes from the other side of the Atlantic where, in 1641, the Puritans of the Massachusetts Bay Colony printed in their first legal code 'The Body of Liberties':

OFF THE BRUITE CREATURE. LIBERTY 92.
No man shall exercise any Tirranny or Crueltie towards any bruite Creature which are usuallie kept for man's use.

LIBERTY 93.
If any man shall have occasion to leade or drive Cattel from place to place that is far of, so that they be weary, or hungry, or fall sick, or lambe, It shall be lawful to rest or refresh them, for a competent time, in any open place that is not Corne, meadow, or inclosed for some peculiar use.

These liberties were framed by Nathaniel Ward (c.1578−1652), who had been born in Haverhill in England and had graduated in law from Emmanuel College, Cambridge. Ironically, it was Strafford's friend Bishop Laud who had driven him from England in 1634 for heresy.

Of course, there had been some far earlier precedents. Besides the commands to be found in the Old Testament, Lecky records that for a time among the Greeks and early Romans it had been a capital offence to kill an ox. This is typical, suggests Lecky, of societies in which legislators are trying to establish agricultural habits among a warlike and nomadic people. He also cites Quintillian's first-century account of a child being put to death for cruelty to birds.[29] Among the Egyptians it had been a capital offence to kill almost any wild animal, and Asoka in India had similarly decreed (see chapter 2).

In other words, legislation in this field was not new. However, in the English-speaking world, the statutes of Thomas Wentworth and the Reverend Nathaniel Ward are the earliest records so far discovered. Yet for a hundred years after the passing of Martin's Act in 1822 (see chapter 6) this was believed to be an unprecedented step. Only in the last few years have the statutes of the seventeenth century been rediscovered, and so it may well be that others of even earlier date are yet to be found.[30]

THE VIRTUES OF BEASTS

The seventeenth century also saw a revival of interest in stories about the alleged virtues and abilities of beasts. These had been common themes in later Roman literature, as we have seen (chapter 2), and in stories of the saints in early medieval times (see chapter 3).

By the early seventeenth century animals were being promoted on several counts: first, it was claimed that they were almost as clever as men and perhaps wiser; secondly that they were morally superior. It was pointed out that animals did not tell lies, get drunk or wage war,[31] and Montaigne himself used such arguments to bolster his claims for their fairer treatment. Indeed these themes prepare the ground before almost all the major advances in humanitarian legislation. We find them in the late sixteenth and early seventeenth centuries in the fifty years prior to the first legislative protection of Strafford and the Puritans. They also are a feature of the movement at the end of the eighteenth century before Martin's legislation of 1822, and again in the middle of the nineteenth century prior to the Cruelty to Animals Act of 1876 (see chapters 5 and 7). In a more sophisticated form in such works as Desmond Morris's *The Naked Ape* (1967) and in the celebration of the intelligence of whales, dolphins and apes, these themes reappeared in the 1960s and 1970s. In each century, it seems, humans go through a period of reminding each other that the chasm between themselves and non-humans is not so wide. This process often anticipates political campaigns and legislative reforms, although all too often these have been postponed during periods of war, as for example, in the cases of the Napoleonic wars and the two World Wars in the present century.

John Locke himself postulated that animals share some mental processes with human beings. Sir Matthew Hale thought that many displayed sagacity. The Dean of Winchester in 1683 agreed that animals showed the capacity for reason. Indeed by this date this was orthodoxy in some circles, as is noted in the very revealing comment made by W. Howell in 1679: 'That there are some footsteps of reason, some strictures and emissions of ratiocination in the actions of some brutes, is too vulgarly known and too commonly granted to be doubted'.[32] It has been suggested that the scientists, whose experiments began to reveal the general similarity between the physiology of animals and themselves, were responsible for narrowing the gap. Up to a point they were, for the more they searched for the seat of the soul in the hearts or pineal glands of men and animals, the more it became clear that the physical differences between the species were more of degree than kind. It was not, however, the scientists themselves who drew the obvious moral conclusions from this. Sheltering absurdly and selfishly behind Descartes, they left it to the men of letters to call for justice for the animals.

DESCARTES AND VIVISECTION

Towards the end of the seventeenth century there seems to have been a rapid increase of interest in the practice of vivisection. Anyone could do it and almost everyone with intellectual pretensions did: princes and charlatans, serious scientists and quacks, all jumped on the bandwagon. No sooner did the rude sport of baiting begin to lose support than this new and even more frightful form of torture swept into vogue.

As E. S. Turner puts it:

In France fashionable ladies who used to attend the disembowellings of dead criminals for the frisson now watched living dogs turned inside out. There was no attempt to coordinate research, if research it could be called; anyone who could think of an audacious or amusing experiment proceeded to carry it out. Nor was it always pretended that the overriding object was to save human suffering, or to improve the human lot. For every experiment conducted to elicit new information, a score were performed to demonstrate what was already well known, or to show off the manipulator's skill...the new intellectual pursuits were dismembering, poisoning, drowning, suffocating, gutting, burning, impaling, draining, starving and injecting.[33]

Whereas the two great diarists of the seventeeth century, Samuel Pepys and John Evelyn, condemned baiting as 'rude' and 'butcherly', they both enthusiastically attended vivisections, Evelyn showing only minor twinges of concern.

During the middle ages vivisection was almost unknown. It was Renaissance Italy which had revived the practice established in classical times by Galen (AD c.130–201). In the sixteenth century, the anatomist Realdus Columbus of Cremona (1516–59) had dissected living animals; so also had Paracelsus (1490–1541) and Andreas Vesalius (1514–64). Later, William Harvey (1578–1657) had conducted research on deer in the parks at Hampton Court and Windsor, put at his disposal by Charles I, although it has been alleged that Harvey's initial postulation of the circulation of the blood arose not from such experiments but from his observation of valves in the blood vessels of dissected human cadavers,[34] and Robert Boyle himself related that Harvey had told him this.

Whether the influential contribution of René Descartes (1596-1650) helped to expand the practice of vivisection, as some such as John Vyvyan, suggest,[35] or whether his argument that animals do not feel pain was an attempt to justify an expansion which had already occurred and in which he participated, is not easy to ascertain. Certainly Descartes's fatuous assertion that animals do not feel pain helped to ease the consciences of many experimenters in the years to come.

Descartes, a neurotic young man, had peeled away the concretions of superstition and the other unprovable cultural beliefs that he had accumulated and found inside only one statement of which he could be sure: *Cogito ergo sum* ('I think, therefore I am' or, to parapharase Spinoza's rendering, 'I am conscious, therefore I exist'). Descartes's very fundamental sense of personal uncertainty led him to put great store upon the one thing of which he *was* certain – his consciousness. For the same reason he espoused a faith in mathematics 'because of the *certainty* of its proofs', and the definiteness of the new science of mechanics similarly attracted him. But Descartes also clung to his Christianity, although his faith seemed to be in conflict with his belief that the bodies of men and women are machines. He solved this problem by emphasizing the importance of the human soul (which, he said, does not have its origin in matter) and by equating this immortal soul with consciousness. As only men and women have immortal souls, he argued, then it follows that animals cannot have consciousness; they are machines only and experience neither pain nor pleasure. When burnt with a hot iron or cut with a knife their writhing and screaming are like the creaking of a hinge, no more. He proceeded to alienate his wife by experimenting upon their dog.

As Singer points out, Descartes was aware that such an argument had several other advantages, moral and practical. In the first place it helped avoid the assumption that people are like animals in that they can expect no after-life – an error that could lead to immoral conduct.[36] Secondly, Descartes's line of argument solved the theological problem of why a good God should allow animals to suffer, since they were not responsible for Adam's original sin. Finally, as Descartes put it in a letter to Henry More dated 5 February 1649: 'My opinion is not so much cruel to animals as indulgent to men...Since it absolves them from the suspicion of crime when they eat or kill animals.'[37]

Two outstanding British scientists of the period seem not to have taken Descartes too seriously. Both Robert Boyle (1627–91) and Robert Hooke (1635–1703) experimented on animals, but did so knowing the suffering they caused. Indeed both declined to repeat cruel experiments on the same animal and, in their correspondence, discussed the use of opiates to reduce their subjects' pain.[38] Most thoughtful people, then as now, probably remained convinced that nonhumans *do* feel pain, but the fact that the so-called 'father of modern philosophy' should make such an extraordinary claim remained a refuge for many subsequent vivisectors who were haunted by guilt or attacked by humanitarians.

An eye-witness account by Nicholas Fontaine (1625–1709) survives, which illustrates the attitude of contemporary Cartesians:

They administered beatings to dogs with perfect indifference, and made fun of those who pitied the creatures as if they felt pain. They said the animals were clocks; that the cries they emitted when struck were only the noise of a little spring that had been touched, but that the whole body was without feeling. They nailed poor animals up on boards by their four paws to vivisect them and see the circulation of the blood which was a great conversation.[39]

Fontaine was clearly critical, and so was the Parisian Jesuit, Gabriel Daniel (1649–1728), who mocked Cartesianism in his *Voiage du Monde de Descartes* in 1690. In England Descartes's view that animals feel no pain continued to be received with scepticism over the ensuing years and, writing in 1742, the Reverend John Hildrop remarked chauvinistically: 'Surely nothing but the Vanity of a Frenchman could ever expect that so absurd a scheme could pass upon a learned world for sound Reason and true Philosophy. For my own part, I could as soon expect to see Gallantries between a couple of amorous Clocks or Watches, or a Battle betwixt two quarrelsome Windmills.'[40]

As early as 1665 vivisection had been opposed on grounds of cruelty by the Irish physician Edmund O'Meara (c.1614−81), who had also pointed out that the subject's agony might well distort the results of the experiment.[41] Nevertheless, the practice continued to have a relatively free run until the turn of the century, before intellectuals in any number began to voice their criticisms. The darkest age of speciesism was then passing.

5 The Age of Enlightenment: The Eighteenth Century

By the eighteenth century there was no monopoly on compassion. The Quakers, and especially George Fox (1624–91), were noted for their concern for animal life. So were the Methodists, whose founder John Wesley (1703–91) opposed cruel sports, and thought it probable that animals had souls and that children should not be allowed to cause them needless harm. Anglicans and sceptics were equally committed to the cause.

MEN OF LETTERS

In the early years of the century, however, it was the secular writers who began to outnumber the theologians in their support for 'brute' nature. Some witty magazine articles are worth noting, written by Richard Steele in the *Tatler* of 1709, Joseph Addison in the *Spectator* in 1711 and Alexander Pope in the *Guardian* in 1713.

Richard Steele attacked the continuing practice of cock-throwing on Shrove Tuesdays and also the violence portrayed in the contemporary theatre, describing the unnecessary killing of animals as 'a kind of Murder'.[1] Joseph Addison (1672–1719) referred to 'a very barbarous experiment' on a dog and attacked it as 'an instance of cruelty'.[2] He believed that 'True benevolence, or compassion, extends itself through the whole of existence and sympathises with the distress of every creature capable of sensation.'[3] Alexander Pope (1688–1744) referred to the writings of Plutarch, Ovid, Montaigne and Locke, and concluded that 'there is certainly a Degree of Gratitude owing to those Animals that serve us.'[4] Like Addison, he narrowed the gap between men and beasts, seeing all creatures as 'but parts of one stupendous whole'; and in attacking vivisection he asked: 'how do we know that we have a right to kill creatures that we are so little above, as dogs, for our curiosity or even for some use to us?'[5]

Pope went out of his way to criticize the doctrine that animals are created for the benefit of humankind — 'is it for thee the lark ascends and sings?' He disliked the shooting of animals for sport[6] and, echoing Locke, urged that children should be taught kindness: 'I cannot but believe a very good use might be made of the fancy which children have for birds and insects.' The whole tenor of these early eighteenth-century writings is the awareness that humans themselves are animals. This is also made clear by Bernard de Mandeville in his *The Fable of the Bees*, published in 1714. For these sophisticated members of the intelligentsia there seemed no need to assert otherwise; their sense of their own civilized status was sufficiently secure.

French and German Writers

It should not be assumed, as it too often is, that England was the only country whose literate classes began to attack cruelty. Nearly all European countries had their humanitarians. Philipp Camerarius of Nuremburg advocated 'gentleness towards brute beasts' as early as 1621, and in France there was the priest, Jean Meslier (1664–1729), whose horror at human cruelty to nonhumans was so intense that he lost his faith; he deplored even the killing of insects.[7]

Voltaire (1694–1778), a Frenchman who lived in England between 1726 and 1729 and was a member of the same literary circle as Pope, subsequently attacked vivisection, pouring scorn upon Descartes:

How pitiful, and what poverty of mind, to have said that the animals are machines deprived of understanding and feeling...

Judge (in the same way as you would judge your own) the behaviour of a dog who has lost his master, who has searched for him in the road barking miserably, who has come back to the house restless and anxious, who has run upstairs and down, from room to room, and who has found the beloved master at last in his study, and then shown his joy by barks, bounds and caresses. There are some barbarians who will take this dog, that so greatly excels man in capacity for friendship, who will nail him to a table, dissect him alive, in order to show you his veins and nerves. And what you then discover in him are *all the same organs of sensation that you have in yourself*. Answer me, mechanist, has Nature arranged all the springs of feeling in this animal *to the end that he might not feel*? Has he nerves that he may be incapable of suffering?[8]

Voltaire, citing the compassion of Isaac Newton for the 'lower animals', went on to claim that compassion is not merely an acquired trait, but an instinct.[9]

Another great Frenchman, Jean-Jacques Rousseau (1712–78), also spoke out. In 1755 he wrote: 'It appears, in fact, that if I am bound to do no injury to my fellow creatures, this is less because they are rational than because they are sentient beings.'[10] In *Emile* in 1762 he claimed that animals could form ideas rather as men do, and went on to attack meat-eating on the grounds that it is bad for the character, as well as unnatural:

One of the proofs that the taste of flesh is not natural to man is the indifference which children exhibit for that sort of meat, and the preference they all give to vegetable foods, such as milk-porridge, pastry, fruits etc. It is of the last importance not to de-naturalise them of this primitive taste and not to render them carnivorous, if not for health reasons, at least for the sake of their character. For, however the experience may be explained, it is certain that great eaters of flesh are, in general, more cruel and ferocious than other men.[11]

In Germany, too, humanitarians were active. As early as 1684 a man had been pilloried in Sagan for cruelty to his horse, and in Leipzig, in 1765 and 1766, there had been imprisonments for inhumane behaviour.[12] Although Immanuel Kant (1724–1804) argued that we have no direct duties toward animals and that they exist to serve humankind, he recounts how the philosopher Gottfried von Leibnitz (1646–1716) had stressed the continuity between human and nonhuman, and would carefully replace a worm upon its leaf after observing it 'so that it should not come to harm through any act of his'.[13]

But the mid-eighteenth-century German scientists such as Christlob Mylius and Albrecht von Haller, rather like Hooke and Boyle in England before them, at least saw that vivisection posed a moral dilemma and admitted that they were causing pain. In general they justified their researches on the grounds of possible medical progress and by pointing to the routine killing of animals for meat. In the following century their fellow-countryman, Arthur Schopenhauer (1788–1860), in 1841 would fulminate against cruelty to animals: 'The assumption that animals are without rights, and the illusion that our treatment of them has no moral significance, is a positively outrageous example of Western crudity and barbarity. Universal compassion is the only guarantee of morality.'[14]

FLESH-EATING

The late seventeenth century provides the first modern evidence of revulsion at the slaughter and eating of animal flesh, and many distinguished men such as Milton, Pope and Isaac Newton began to commend a vegetable diet. Voltaire in 1736 attacked 'the barbarous custom of supporting ourselves upon the flesh and blood of beings like ourselves', although he remained a carnivore. Similarly, Jean-Jacques Rousseau in 1762 attacked meat-eating. In England, Thomas Tryon was a vegetarian on moral grounds, and wrote at length about diet.[15] In 1741 David Hartley argued that flesh-eating was unnecessary, and that 'taking away the lives of animals, in order to convert them into food, does great violence to the principles of benevolence and compassion.'[16]

William Paley, although justifying meat on religious grounds, emphasized in 1785 that it was not necessary and was poor economy: 'A piece of ground capable of supplying animal food sufficient for the subsistence of ten persons, would sustain, at least, the double of that number with grain, roots and milk.'[17]

John Oswald, the Scottish atheist and soldier-poet who died for the French Revolution in 1793, commented that:

The tender-hearted Hindoo would turn from our tables with abhorrence. To him our feasts are the nefarious repasts of Polyphemus; while we contemplate with surprise his absurd clemency, and regard his superstitious mercy as an object of merriment and contempt.[18]

Indeed, by the end of the eighteenth century the inconsistency in eating animals while advocating their rights began to worry some humanitarians. As Oliver Goldsmith remarked drily, 'they pity and they eat the objects of their compassion.'[19]

Vegetarianism was the main subject of George Nicholson's 1797 anthology of writings against cruelty.[20] He argued that humankind had been vegetarian for 1,600 years before the deluge and is not by natural inclination carnivorous. Nicholson cited medical sources such as Dr Cheyne's *Essay on Health* of 1725 to the effect that a vegetable diet renders 'the circulation more free and the spirits the more lightsome, that is, the better the health be'. He quoted a Dr Buchan's opinion that meat 'induces a ferocity of temper' and a Dr Graham's even more dire warning:

Do not degrade and beastatize your body by making it a burial place for the carcases of innocent brute animals, some healthy, some diseased, and all violently murdered. It is impossible for us to take into our stomachs putre-fying, currupting, and diseased animal substances, without becoming ob-noxious to horrors, dejections, remorse, and inquietudes of mind, and to foul bodily diseases, swellings, pains, weaknesses, sores, curruptions, and premature death.[21]

Finally, Nicholson argued on grounds of justice and compassion, and asserted that 'there exists within us a rooted repugnance to the spilling of blood; a repugnance which yields only to custom...'[22] Surely, Nicholson had a point. This question of natural repugnance or squeam-ishness is a fascinating one, which will be explored in later chapters.

A CRUEL NATION

Often the impression is gained that England was regarded by others as the cruellest country in Europe. In the *Tatler* of 1709, Richard Steele had remarked that foreigners were shocked by the pastime of cock-throwing: 'Some French writers have represented this Diversion of the Common People much to our Disadvantage...as they do some other Entertainments *peculiar to our Nation*, I mean those elegant Diversions of Bull-baiting, and Prize fighting, with the like ingenious Recreations of the Bear Garden.'[23] Pope reiterated this view in the *Guardian* in 1713.[24] In 1751 Lord Kames remarked that 'the bear garden, which is one of the chief entertainments of the English, is held in abhorrence by the French and other polite nations,[25] and Rousseau condemned the English as 'coarse'.[26] In 1756 Adam Fitz Adam, writing in the *World*, was sorry to have to record that in the streets of London there are to be seen 'more scenes of barbarity than perhaps are to be met with in all Europe besides'. Arthur Broome noted that in 1768 the King of Denmark, on a visit to England, was shown a bull-baiting, but 'retired with expressions of abhorrence'. James Granger in 1772 saw England as 'the Hell of Horses'. In 1798 Thomas Young thought 'that the English have more of cruelty to animals in their sports in general, than any of their neighbours'.[27] Susanna Watts in the early nineteenth century could still argue in her *Animals' Friend*:

It is a very striking fact, that though the present age is boasted as highly enlightened, refined, and as far removed from barbarism as science, art, and literature can make it, no nation which we call savage, practices more degrading cruelty towards animals than the people of Great Briatin. The inhuman amusements of bull-baiting, cock-fighting, pigeon-shooting, etc. followed with such indefatigable ardor by the great and little vulgar, certainly contradict the vaunt of polish and refinement.[28]

An occasional sport at country fairs was the eating of live cats. The *Sporting Magazine* records several instances, one at Beverley in 1777 and another at St Albans in 1788. Earlier in the century it had been claimed that a man had eaten five live fox-cubs for a wager. Biting the heads off sparrows, beating rams to death and tying cats together by the tail were contemporary schoolboy games.

E. S. Turner describes how aristocrats in England, often following the example of the uncouth 'Butcher' Duke of Cumberland, would seek to stage various bloody encounters between animals. Yet towards the end of the century this crudeness was in retreat. In 1772 Dr Charles Burney was disgusted to see an advertisement in Vienna for the baiting of bears, boars and bulls which he felt was 'hardly fit for a civilised and polished nation to allow'. (It was stopped in 1791.) When Nelson was taken to a bull-fight in Cadiz in 1793 he felt sick and wondered if he could sit it out.[29]

Thus we see the beginnings of English criticisms of foreign behaviour on the very same grounds on which they themselves had been criticized – an attitude which persists to the present day. Goose-pulling, that is to say horsemen attempting to pull off the heads of live greased geese suspended upside down, currently continues in Spain and is roundly attacked by British and American organizations. Yet it was a favourite sport in Britain, and especially in Scotland, until the eighteenth century.

THE HUMANE REACTION

Perhaps it was partly because Britain had been the cruellest nation in Europe that it led the humane reaction over the next two centuries.

In 1742 John Hildrop published what appears to be the earliest example in Britain of a book devoted almost entirely to the subject of humankind's relationship with animals. Besides ridiculing the ideas of Descartes, he stressed the closeness of animals with uneducated humans. Animals, wrote Hildrop, were made to be happy, and it is an injustice to deprive them of this except for our own happiness.

Anonymous contributors to staid organs such as the *Gentleman's Magazine* were quite frequently attacking cruelty by mid-century. In April 1749 one such writer composed the dying speech of a hen martyred at the stake on Shrove Tuesday:

Perhaps the legislature may not think it beneath them to take our sad case into consideration or if the Government (taken up with great affairs of the nation) should think poultry below their regard; who can tell but some faint remains of common sense among the vulgar themselves, may be excited by a suffering dying fellow creature's last words, to find out a more good natured exercise for their youth, and idle fellows, at this holy season, which tends not to harden their hearts, and taint their morals?[30]

The same magazine recorded in May 1754 that a butcher had cut out the eyes of an unruly sheep. This had caused indignation in all who saw it, 'except the executioner'.[31]

In eighteenth-century England the unorthodox compassion of previous centuries rapidly became the established view among artists, poets, theologians and other leading intellectual figures. Even the popular scientist, James Ferguson (1710–76), criticized the 'agonies' of animals used in air-pump experiments, and in his public demonstrations he employed instead a model utilizing a bladder to simulate lungs. Ferguson must go down in history as the pioneer of humane alternatives to the use of animals in research.[32]

6 *Charles Darwin* (1809–1882) emphasised the mental similarities between humans and other animals. Although he abhorred cruelty Darwin was nervous about upsetting his scientific colleagues on the question of vivisection. The development of the Victorian animal welfare movement preceded Darwin and campaigners did not perceive him as being an ally. His central message, that the species are related through evolution, was not widely recognised as being of ethical importance in this context until the 1970s. The moral implications of Darwinism concerning our treatment of members of the other species, are only now being fully realised.

By mid-century the relatively mild exhortations of Rousseau's friend, the philosopher David Hume, to the effect that people should show 'gentle usage' to the animals, began to sound out of date.[33] The more robust views of Dr Samuel Johnson (1709–84) were more typical of the age; he chastised the 'race of wretches' who perform experiments on animals:

It is time that a universal resentment should arise against those horrid operations, which tend to harden the heart and make the physicians more dreadful than the gout or the stone. Men who have practised tortures on animals without pity, relating them without shame, how can they still hold their heads among human beings?[34]

Boswell recorded Johnson's fondness for animals, and in particular for his cat Hodge, for whom Johnson was in the habit of buying oysters. In

1776 Johnson remarked that there was 'much talk of the misery which we cause the brute creation' and indeed the references to animals and the injunctions against cruelty became numerous in the final third of the century.

Richard Dean, writing in 1767, referred approvingly to the earlier work of Hildrop. But for Dean the animals' sentiency is the main reason for treating them kindly: 'As Brutes have sensibility, they are capable of pain, feel every bang and cut and stab, as much as he himself [the reader] does, some of them perhaps more, and therefore he must not treat them as stocks or stones or things that cannot feel.' That this new, almost revolutionary, fashion in thought was limited chiefly to urban intellectuals is suggested by the reaction received by the Reverend James Granger from his rural Oxfordshire congregation when he preached a sermon at Shiplake on 18 October 1772 entitled 'An Apology for the Brute Creation or Abuse of Animals Censured'. He notes in a postscript: 'the foregoing discourse gave almost univeral disgust to two considerable congregations. The mention of dogs and horses, was censured as a prostitution of the dignity of the pulpit, and considered proof of the Author's growing insanity.'[36] His sermon was, however, more kindly reviewed by the literary press.

Religious thinkers of all denominations matched secular writers in their new concern for nonhumans. The Quaker John Woolman (1720–72), for example, in his journal in 1740, argued against 'cruelty towards the least creature' as a contradiction of the love due to God, and in 1772 he opposed any lessening of the 'sweetness of life in the animal creation which the Great Creator intends for them under our government'.[37]

Perhaps the most outstanding of all theological contributions of this period was that published by Dr Humphry Primatt in the year 1776. God would require a strict account from man for the creatures entrusted to his care, Primatt warned. Yet, despite this somewhat archaic imprecation, Primatt's book is otherwise remarkably modern in tone and entirely comprehensible to the animal liberationist of the twentieth century: 'Pain is Pain, whether it be inflicted on man or on beast; and the creature that suffers it, whether man or beast, being sensible of the misery of it whilst it lasts, suffers Evil.'[38] Primatt, like Tryon before him and Wilberforce afterwards, was also active in attacking the slave trade and frequently drew the analogy between racism and the exploitation of nonhumans: 'The white man...can have no right, by virtue of his colour, to enslave and tyrannise over a black man...for the same reason, a man can have no natural right to abuse and torment a beast.'[39]

Primatt's was an important work for the additional reason that it was read (and republished) by the Reverend Arthur Broome who, nearly half a century later, in 1824, was to help found the society which became the RSPCA. Interestingly, Primatt's Old Testament references, cited to support his thesis, outnumbered those of the New Testament by about five to one, and the RSPCA's educational tracts of the 1860s show a similar ratio. Primatt anticipated Jeremy Bentham's opinion in many ways:

Now if amongst men, the differences of their powers of the mind, and of their complexion, stature and accidents of fortune, do not give to any one man a right to abuse or insult any other man on account of these differences; for the same reason, a man can have no natural right to abuse and torment a beast, merely because a beast has not the mental powers of a man. A brute is an animal no less sensible of pain than a man. He has similar nerves and organs of sensation.[40]

Primatt went on to regret that cruelty to animals was inadequately controlled by law in the England of his day and unreproved from the pulpit. As G. H. Toulmin noted in 1780, the common view was still that 'everything is created for our practical use',[41] and although the sophisticated opinion of the London coffee-houses was now overwhelmingly on the side of the animals it is clear from Primatt's sarcasm that general public opinion was still far from sympathetic:

I am well aware of the obloquy to which every man must expose himself, who presumes to encounter prejudices and long received customs. To make a comparison between a man and a brute, is abominable; to talk of a man's duty to his horse or his ox, is absurd; to suppose it cruel to chase a stag, or course a hare, is unpolite; to esteem it barbarous to throw at a cock, to bait a bull, to roast a lobster, or to crimp a fish, is ridiculous.[42]

The gluttons of the eighteenth century indeed had much to answer for. Pope described 'kitchens covered with blood and filled with the cries of creatures expiring in tortures'. The whipping to death of pigs, in the mistaken belief that this improved the meat, was to continue in England until the following century. Turkeys were very slowly bled to death suspended upside down from the kitchen ceiling. Salmon were crimped (cut into collops while still alive), living eels skinned, and the orifices of chickens were sewn up, supposedly to fatten them. Geese repeatedly were plucked of their feathers while alive in order to provide writing quills, and many were nailed to boards for their entire lives, some with their eyes put out, while they were subjected to forced-feeding.

Meat was cheap in England at this time and its consumption continued to be gargantuan. Receipts for large houses indicate that it was ordered by the stone rather than the pound, and include details of the typical contemporary menu – lambs' tails for the first course for example, tongues and udders for the second, followed by ox palates with cheese-cake for the third.[43]

William Hogarth depicted some of the common cruelties of his day.

Although his strongly expressed objection to such activities was partly on the grounds that cruelty to beasts could lead to cruelty to people, it is clearly the case that he was also concerned for the well-being of the animals themselves. Animals were important to Hogarth, and in many of his pictures dogs appear as symbols of sincerity, contrasted with human affectation and hypocrisy. In 1750 he published 'The Four Stages of Cruelty', a series of prints depicting not only cruelty to animals but murder, in part the outcome of the former. Hogarth wrote of these prints: 'The four stages of cruelty were done in the hopes of preventing in some degree that cruel treatment of poor Animals which makes the streets of London more disagreeable to the human mind than anything whatever, the very describing of which gives pain.'[44] When told that his prints were much admired, he replied:

It gratifies me highly, and there is no part of my works of which I am so proud, and in which I feel so happy because I believe the publication of them has checked the diabolical spirit of barbarity, which, I am sorry to say was once so prevalent in this country...I had rather, if cruelty has been prevented by the four prints, be maker of them than of the [Raphael] cartoons.[45]

Trinity College, Cambridge, produced two Fellows of this period who applied their pens to the animals' cause: Thomas Young, who wrote *An Essay on Humanity to Animals* in 1798, and the Reverend C. Hoyle, whose 'Ode to Humanity' was published as its preface. Young marshalled all the usual arguments against cruelty to animals – that it renders people cruel to others of their own species, that it is opposed to the will of the creator who wishes to see the happiness of his creatures, that it is sometimes inconsistent with mankind's pecuniary interest, that it creates a bad impression socially and that it is contrary to scripture. He went on to describe the robbing of birds' nests as the commonest cruelty committed by contemporary schoolboys: 'we shall be sensible of this if we only reflect how many thousand boys make this their principal diversion during the greater part of spring.'

Indeed, the unbridled cruelty of young males is frequently remarked on. At Eton the annual clubbing to death of a hamstrung ram provided by the local butcher had been notorious from about 1687 until it was stopped in 1747. The tying of a duck to an owl and the hunting of the struggling pair over water, as well as the baiting of bulls, badgers and cats, and the fighting of dogs, continued to be regular public-school pastimes, approved by the educational authorities in the eighteenth century. Young cited bull-baiting, cockfighting and throwing at cocks as the principal sports common to men and boys, of which the most prevalent was still cockfighting, despite attempts from some magistrates to suppress it by refusing licences to publicans who allowed it on their premises. He also noted that in 'many large and respectable towns' cock-throwing had been banned by proclamation.

Forms of cockfighting included the 'battle royal', in which an un-limited number of birds were pitted, the last survivor being proclaimed the victor. In the Welsh Main form of the sport sixteen pairs of cocks were fought; the sixteen victors then were pitted a second time; the eight victors a third time; the four victors a fourth time; and then the two victors were pitted in the final. In such an event thirty-one cocks, said Young, 'are sure to be most inhumanely murdered for sport and pleasure'. Young referred to 'the Rights of Animals', and his philosophy was that of the applied Utilitarian:

A man who has made a tolerable progress in humanity, will adopt, and ever bear in mind, the principle of increasing, as far as lies within his power, the quantity of pleasure in the world, and diminishing that of pain: he will establish this to himself as a constant and inviolable rule of action, and in carrying it into practice he will not overlook one created thing that is endowed with faculties capable of perceiving pleasure and pain.[46]

Naturally enough, Young was also strongly opposed to the chase.

THE POETS ARISE

Among poets, cruelty was ardently decried in the eighteenth century. For his contemporaries it was the Scotsman James Thomson (1700–48) who was seen as the outstanding poetic inspiration of the humanitarian movement, as he attacked 'the steady tyrant man' who 'for sport alone pursues the cruel chase...to joy at anguish and delight in blood'. Thomson was especially critical of hunting by the female sex, fearing that it would 'stain the bosom of the british fair'.[47]

In his *Canterbury Tales* Chaucer had written that his prioress 'wolde weepe if that she saw a mous caught in a trappe', yet subsequent medieval verse and the great body of Elizabeth and Jacobean poetry is almost silent on such matters. Only when we get to Andrew Marvell (1621–78) do the poets begin to catch up the theologians. Marvell's 'Nymph complaining For the Death of her Faun' bemoaned:

> The wanton troopers riding by
> Have shot my fawn, and it will die.
> Ungentle men! They cannot thrive
> Who killed thee.

'Nothing', wrote Marvell, 'may we use in vain; ev'n beasts must be with justice slain...'

After Pope and Thomson came Oliver Goldsmith (1728–74) and William Cowper (1731–1800), closely followed by William Blake (1757–1827) and Robert Burns (1759–96), all showing a tenderness for nonhuman life. They were part of a society in which the cultivated mind had adopted a far more romantic view of all nature; no longer was it something simply to be subdued. Gardens which had previously been regimented and in which flowers and shrubs had been tamed with an almost military discipline were now allowed to unfold naturally. Animals, too, began to be regarded as lovely in themselves.

Cowper, who kept a pet hare, attacked hunting as a 'detested sport, that owes its pleasures to another's pain' and added: 'I would not enter on my list of friends (though graced with polish'd manners and fine sense, yet wanting sensibility), the man who needlessly sets foot upon a worm.'[48] Burns roundly condemned the hunter who wounds the hare:

> Inhuman man! Curse on thy barbarous act,
> And blasted be thy murder-aiming eye.[49]

He was another who saw man as tyrannizing the animals:

> Man; your proud usurping foe,
> Would be lord of all below:
> Plumes himself in Freedom's pride,
> Tyrant stern to all beside.[50]

Burns claimed kinship with a mouse[51] and Blake with a fly: 'Am not I a fly like thee?'

Towards the end of the eighteenth century, into a society in which cruelty was being routinely condemned in educated circles were born the poets William Wordsworth (1770–1850), Samuel Coleridge (1772–1834) and Robert Southey (1774–1843); all three defended nonhuman animals. Wordsworth, in his elegy on the legend of the hunted deer which leapt to its death near Richmond in Yorkshire, warned 'never to blend our pleasure or our pride with sorrow of the meanest thing that feels'.[52] Southey, in his poem 'The Dancing Bear', revealed the state of average opinion in 1799:

> We are told all things were made for Man:
> And I'll be sworn there's not a fellow here
> Who would not swear 'twere hanging blasphemy to
>   doubt that truth...
> And politicans say...that thou art here
> Far happier than thy brother bears who roam
> O'er trackless snow for food.
> Talk of thy baiting, it will be replied
> Thy welfare is thy owner's interest...[53]

Much of the poetic concern with cruelty at this period was not centred upon baiting, nor on culinary tortures, nor on vivisection, but continued the attack on hunting with hound or gun. Besides Burns and Cowper, other poets also reviled themselves for having indulged in such sports.[54]

Byron (1788–1824) wrote a moving epitaph to his dog Boatswain in 1808:

> to mark a friend's remains these stones arise;
> I never knew but one – and here he lies.[55]

Percy Bysshe Shelley (1792–1822), besides criticizing the chase, was one of the first to record being moved by the plight of ordinary farm animals:

How unwarrantable is the injustice and barbarity which is exercised towards these miserable victims. They are called into existence by human artifice that they may drag out a short and miserable existence of slavery and disease, that their bodies may be mutilated, their social feelings outraged. It were much better that a sentient being should never have existed, than that it should have existed only to endure unmitigated misery.[56]

It is believed that in 1816, while living in Wales, Shelley put out of their miseries several diseased or dying sheep belonging to neighbouring farmers. This so incensed local opinion that three shepherds attacked Shelley one night, firing three pistol shots at him. Shortly afterwards, the Shelleys fled to England. Shelley advocated vegetarianism out of respect for our 'kindred' the animals, who 'think, feel and live like man',[57] and in 1819 in *Prometheus Unbound,* he wrote: 'I wish no living thing to suffer pain.'

In America the poets were awakened in the early nineteenth century. Henry Wadsworth Longfellow (1807–82) wrote:

> Among the noblest of the land,
>   Though he may count himself the least,
> That man I honor and revere,
>   Who, without favor, without fear,
> In the great city dares to stand
>   The Friend of every friendless Beast.[58]

Oliver Wendell Holmes (1809–94) pitied the caged lion – 'poor conquered monarch'[59] ('To A Caged Lion') – and Ralph Waldo Emerson (1803–82) extolled the titmouse and the bumble-bee.

THE PARAGON OF ANIMALS

Long before Darwin's day, man had been regarded as an animal. In classical literature, Epicureans and writers such as Lucretius, Cicero, Diodorus Siculus and Horace had suggested that humankind had only slowly developed from the animal condition, gradually forming language and civilization. Aristotle viewed man as being at the top of the natural hierarchy, superior in reasoning to any other animal, but not different in kind. Shakespeare, through Hamlet, had seen man as 'the paragon of animals'. Yet, as we have seen, the full awareness of humankind's animality by many people was intermittent and discouraged by the Church; most behaved as if Homo Sapiens was a creature of an altogether different order, 'made in the image of God'.

Perhaps it was at opposite ends of human society that the consciousness of animality was least clouded. The medieval peasant, and later the poor townsman, living with beasts under the same roof, could not escape noticing the similarity in bodily functions and behaviour between themselves and their animals. Indeed the common assumption that sexual intercourse with animals was the cause of human deformity and handicap indicates some sense of underlying awareness that human and nonhuman were of a kind, despite the Inquisition's fierce opposition to such views.

At the other end of the scale, scholars and thinkers often had the time to reflect and the intelligence to realize the zoological facts of life. Whereas the common man might sometimes feel his social status threatened by his closeness to the brutes, and would react by emphasizing his dominion over them, the more elevated members of human society, sure of their social standing, could sometimes risk a more liberal view. The theologians disliked such liberalism, but could not entirely prevent it.

The discovery of the great apes made it more difficult than ever to deny the similarity between men and beasts. In 1613 the first reliable descriptions of the great apes were published by Andrew Battell – 'hairie all over, otherwise altogether like men and women'. In 1661 Samuel Pepys saw an ape exhibited, 'so much like a man in most things'. In 1653 John Bulwer reported the contemporary opinion that man 'was at first but a kind of ape or baboon'. Scientists like Edward Tyson in 1699 noted the resemblance of ape and human anatomy. Sir Thomas Browne remarked in 1643 that in the brains of people he could find no organs not also discoverable 'in the crany of a beast'. By 1700 it was acknowledged that the nervous system mediated feeling and it was accepted that animals had nerves similar to those of humans.[60]

In 1735 the Systema Naturae of Carolus Linnaeus (1707–78), the great Swedish naturalist, was published. In it, Linnaeus classified man as part of the Primate order which also included, he said, apes and bats. Indeed, Linnaeus even put man into the same genus as the orang-utang.

This view was opposed by other zoologists, most notably by Georges Leclerc, Comte de Buffon (1707–88), although his translator, William Smellie, placed man in the class of mammalia: 'Man is arranged with them, because he nearly resembles them in structure and organs, though', Smellie adds cautiously, 'raised in reality far above them by the possession of superior intellectual and moral powers.' Smellie thus enforced the view that man is an animal and, specifically, a mammal.[61]

Of all eighteenth-century pronouncements on this subject, those of the eccentric Scotsman James Burnet, Lord Monboddo, caused the greatest sensation. In 1774 he asserted that Jean-Jacques Rousseau was correct in identifying orang-utangs as a race of men who had not yet acquired the art of speech. With training, Monboddo claimed, animals could be educated. He could produce evidence, he said, to prove that a school-teacher in Inverness had a tail six inches in length which was only discovered after his death. The gulf between men and beasts disappeared under Monboddo's sturdy rhetoric.[62]

At the time that Monboddo was using such arguments to elevate animals, others were using them to lower the status of men – or at least certain races of men. Edward Long in 1774, for example, argued that the orang-utang was closer to the negro than the negro was to the white man.[63] Joseph Ritson, writing in 1802, could assert that man could properly be 'arranged under the monkey kind; there being the same degree of analogy between the man and the monkey, as between the lion and the cat'. The apes, said Ritson, were intermediate between man and monkey. 'Man, therefor, in a state of nature, was, if not the real ourang-outang of the forests...at least an animal of the same family.'[64] Ritson goes on to relate many amusing travellers' tales about the intelligence, language and sensitivity of apes.

Eighteenth-century writers from Rousseau onwards also recounted stories of wild children and adults found living in the woods with wolves, bears or other animal companions. These reports were often used to illustrate the closeness of mankind to nature, and to show that civilized behaviour was not spontaneous but learned.

By the eighteenth century, horses, cattle, sheep and dogs were all being bred with scrupulous care, so the fact that their physical and behavioural characteristics could change radically over the generations had become a self-evident truth; this was helping to prepare the ground for the acceptance of Darwin's ideas on Evolution.

In northern Europe it had become fashionable for country curates, gentlemen and ladies to be keen naturalists, although such a pastime did not develop so much in southern European countries. In England the libraries of country houses were filled with contemporary zoological best-sellers from authors such as Oliver Goldsmith, William Mavor, John Hill, William Smellie, Thomas Pennant and William Bingley. Although earlier writers had categorized animals according to their

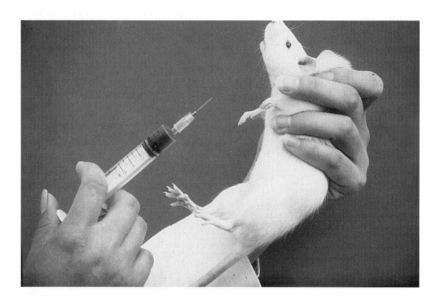

7 *Animal Experiments* Millions of animals die every year in laboratories around the world. Vivisection, as it used to be called, was the object of vigorous opposition in Victorian Britain and again, after the publication in 1975 of *Victims of Science* and the *Smoking Beagles* story. These publications helped to provoke an outcry which led eventually to new European and British legislation controlling such research in 1986.

The successful modern campaign in Britain has emphasised three aspects of research. First, that much of it causes animals *pain and distress*, either directly or as a result of long incarceration in bleak cages. Secondly, that many experiments on animals are for trivial or *nonmedical purposes* such as the testing of cosmetics for toxicity or the development of weaponry. Thirdly, that *humane alternative* techniques not using animals, such as tissue cultures, do exist and should be further developed. The scientific community is increasingly accepting these points and is pursuing the so-called 'three R's' of reduction, refinement and replacement.

usefulness for man or their edibility, gradually such criteria shrank in importance as interest grew in the nonhuman animals themselves.

By the end of the century, therefore, not only the poets but the scientists, too, albeit more or less unwittingly, had done much to remove the human species (although not themselves) from a self-established pedestal.

PREPARATIONS FOR LEGISLATION

We have seen that by the 1780s pain had clearly emerged as the main matter for concern in humankind's treatment of the other animals. Earlier worries about the welfare of the oppressor's character and pre-occupations about the intelligence of animals, their capacity for language or the quality of their souls, if any, were finally swept away by the philosopher Jeremy Bentham (1748–1832), who wrote in 1780:

The day may come when the rest of the animal creation may acquire those rights which never could have been withheld from them but by the hand of tyranny...a full-grown horse or dog is beyond comparison a more rational, as well as a more conversable animal, than an infant of a day, or a week or even a month old. But supposed the case were otherwise, what would it avail? The question is not, can they reason? Nor, can they talk? But *can they suffer?* Why should the law refuse its protection to any sensitive being? The time will come when humanity will extend its mantle over everything which breathes...[65]

Bentham, like Montaigne and Johnson, is another example of a cat-lover who has contributed significantly to the history of the animal protection movement. His favourite was a cat called Mr Blackman who, because of his solemn demeanour, was progressively promoted to being addressed as Dr Blackman and, finally, the Reverend Dr Blackman.[66] Bentham's biographer, John Bowring, himself an advocate of humanity to animals, records that Bentham, as a boy, had burnt some earwigs in a candle flame and had been reprimanded for this cruelty by a servant called Martha.[67] His uncle also had occasion to rebuke him for teasing his dog Busy. Bentham never forgot these two experiences. Bowring also recalls Bentham's claim that he had been impressed by the fondness for animals shown by Cowper, George Wilson and Romilly. The philosopher had shown affection for 'a beautiful pig at Hendon' and 'a young ass of great symetry and beauty' at Ford Abbey, and his genuine feeling for animals is most convincingly displayed in his relationship with mice:

I became once very intimate with a colony of mice. They used to run up my legs and eat crumbs from my lap. I love everything that has four legs: so did

George Wilson. We were fond of mice, and fond of cats; but it was difficult to reconcile the two affections.[68]

Bentham opposed hunting, fishing and baiting, but for him it was the infliction of pain, and not death, that was the main evil. In line with this principle, he saw no objection to dispatching a cat who had become 'despotic' and 'clamorous', sending him 'to another world':

It ought to be lawful to kill animals, but not to torment them. Death, by artificial means, may be made less painful than natural death: the methods of accomplishing this deserve to be studied and made an object of policy. Why should the law refuse its protection to any sensitive being? The time will come, when humanity will extend its mantle over everything which breathes. We have begun by attending to the condition of slaves; we shall finish by softening that of all the animals which assist our labours or supply our wants.[69]

Thus, by the end of the eighteenth century in England the basic principles of the modern animal welfare position were established. These are that nonhumans, like humans, can suffer pain, and that pain entitles them to legal as well as moral rights. Pain had emerged as the central evil and, as Walter Savage Landor later put it − 'cruelty is the chief, if not the only sin.' The old preoccupations with the immortality and intelligence of nonhumans were dismissed as quibbles. Indeed, if animals, unlike men, had 'no mind to bear them up against their sufferings', as Thomas Chalmers (1780−1847) had it, and no hope of everlasting peace, then their torment surely would be the greater.

Cruelty to animals remained quite a major subject of interest in certain circles right through to the end of the century and beyond. And those circles were widening. For example, John Oswald, the soldier mentioned above who was carried off by a cannon-ball in 1791, wrote on the topic, and recommended vegetarianism.[70] Soame Jenyns (1704−87), an influential and popular Member of Parliament, could see that much customary cruelty was the result of force of habit and of the loss of sensitivity caused by habituation to the normally repugnant sight of blood; he described this with memorable metaphor: 'The butcher knocks down the stately ox with no more compassion than the blacksmith hammers a horse-shoe; and plunges his knife into the throat of the innocent lamb with as little reluctance as the taylor sticks his needle into the collar of a coat.' In 1794 Thomas Paine briefly urged kindness to animals in his radical classic *The Age of Reason*. In 1797, George Nicholson, a printer living in Manchester, published what is probably the first anthology of writings on the subject (also mentioned above). He strongly advocated vegetarianism and attacked some appalling cruelties in his home town, recording the state of the law at the time, which

8   The killing of seals in Canada was opposed skilfully by Brian Davies of the International Fund for Animal Welfare and this led to a ban on all imports of baby seal products into Europe in 1982. After this setback, the seal industry has, more recently, been revived by the selling of seal penises to China and hundreds of thousands of seals are again being slaughtered annually. Nevertheless, wildlife welfare, usually working in alliance with conservation interests, is enjoying growing support and the treatment of fur bearing animals, whales and elephants are issues that are rising on the international political agenda.

permitted cruelty on the grounds that animals were mere property:

In November, 1793, two butchers of Manchester were convicted in the penalty of twenty shillings each, for cutting off the feet of living sheep, and driving them through the streets. The sheep were not their own property or, we suppose, they might with impunity have been allowed to dissect them alive.

A butcher in the same town has been frequently seen to hang poor calves up alive, with the gambril put through their sinews, and hooks stuck through their nostrils, the dismal bleating of the miserable animals continuing till they had slowly bled to death. Such proceedings frequently struck the neighbourhood with horror. Attempts were made to prevent the hellish nuisances caused by this man, but in vain, for he did but torture his own property! Such are the glaring imperfections of the laws of a civilised, a humane, a Christian country![72]

He concluded:

We have said that animals should be protected by the legislature, but there exists no statute which punishes cruelty to animals, simply as such, and without taking in the consideration of it as an injury to property.

Nicholson's anthology in its first edition in 1797 was dedicated to the 'generous, enlightened and sympathising few'. However, such was the demand for his book that he published the fourth edition in 1819, noting that 'the few have increased to a numerous and decided body.'
    A writer in the *Gentleman's Magazine* of January 1789 provided a revealing description of contemporary cruelty:

The infant is no sooner able to use its little limbs, than they are exercised in procuring diversion by torturing every animal that comes within its reach, and which it is able to master: and the pleasure it manifests in these malevolent employments is such that the tender parents generally provide the pretty innocent with a constant supply of insects, birds, kittens, and puppies, to keep it in good humour. As years and strength increase, tearing flies piecemeal, sticking crooked pins through the tails of cockchafers to make them spin to death; misusing, laming, and killing, all the animals they are supplied with...they then prowl about to rob innocent birds of their nests, for the pleasure of destroying their eggs, and killing the unfledged brood. They catch dogs, tie old lanterns or faggot-sticks to their tails, and then drive them away with shouts, to be hunted to madness and death by all who meet them. They set dogs upon stray cats with the utmost glee, and enjoy their struggles while they are worried to death; and the hanging of a dog or a cat collects all the children in the neighbourhood as eagerly as the execution of a criminal, or a fire, draws together their fathers and mothers. They will tie two cats together by the tails and then throw them over a line, for the luxury of seeing them tear each other's eyes out. They will tie a string to a rat's tail, pour spirit of wine over it, set fire to it, and betray the most rapturous joy at seeing the unhappy animal run about covered with flame till it expires under this refinement in barbarity. The most agreeable sports of youth have for their common object a delight felt at the sufferings of animals appropriated to our diversion: thus harmless fowls and pigeons are set up to be knocked down with sticks: ducks are hunted in ponds by dogs; an owl is tied on the back of a duck, and both thrown into the water; while this glory of the creation, with the stamp of divinity on his mind, is worked up to extasy in contemplating their mutual distresses.

The writer, who signed himself only as 'Mr Humanus', concluded:

It is hard that there should be no law for brute animals, when they carry so large a proportion of representatives to every legislative assembly.[73]

To a certain extent cruelty to animals had become, by the end of the eighteenth century, a mark of distinction between the refined and the vulgar, between the uneducated and the cultivated. Many of the latter felt it was time to curb cruelty with legislation, and it seems to have been the public spectacle of cruelty to horses and farm animals in the street, and their witnessing of bloodsports which prompted this move.

Most humane eighteenth-century writers, including Pope, Jenyns, Nicholson, and Bentham, were explicitly critical of hunting, shooting and angling, and although his ambivalence on fox-hunting, is not typical, perhaps the most influential (besides Bentham) in this secular group of writers was gentleman-farmer John Lawrence, who proposed 'The jus animalium, or the rights of beasts to the protection of the law, on the ground of natural justice in the first intance, and in sequel, on that of expedience, regarding both humanity and profit.'[74] He published prolifically on sporting and agricultural topics, invariably advocating the duty of humanity. Like Young, he gave currency to the idea that animals have rights. 'Life, intelligence, and feeling, necessarily imply rights', Lawrence claimed, and he applied this principle in defence of human and animal rights alike. After his death in 1839 in his eighty-sixth year, he was almost entirely forgotten until forty years later, his writings were rediscovered by E. W. B. Nicholson. There is a copy of his *Philosophical Treatise* in the Bodleian Library, Oxford, into which Nicholson said he transcribed annotations made by Lawrence during the years 1835 to 1837; among these is the note: 'Mr. Martin M.P. for Galway, subsequently took up this cause on my recommendation, and got the animal protection bill with much difficulty thro' Parliament. Mr. M. and myself had many conferences on this subject.' Lawrence's political importance stands largely on this claim.

Apparently ashamed of his addiction to hunting, Lawrence published his book *British Field Sports* in 1818 under the pseudonym of William Henry Scott. His favourable view of certain forms of hunting and cockfighting – he condoned animals fighting if they did so voluntarily, and the hunting of ferocious (rather than timid) animals who, he believed, feel no fear — lays him open to the familiar charge of inconsistency. Nevertheless, Lawrence admitted that the cruelties perpetrated by drovers and other members of the lower orders were in no small part due to their emulation of the habits of the gentry: 'Since the most exquisite pleasure is supposed by their betters to be derived from hunting, worrying, and tearing the living members of the most harmless and timid animals, why not hunt bullocks as well as hares and deer?'[75] Lawrence was particularly concerned about the welfare of horses, who, he claims, were being 'literally whipped and goaded to death'. In a later edition of his book, Lawrence noted in 1812 that in the hot July of 1808 many stage-horses had died upon the roads and 'on the great road to Edinburgh fourteen or fifteen were killed in one day.' He drew an analogy between defending the cruelties committed by carmen and postilions and defending the African slave trade, and repeatedly called for comprehensive legislation to protect animals.

Lawrence paid tribute to a number of politicians for their humane interest in animals, among them Lord Erskine, Sir Charles Bunbury, Sir Samuel Romilly, Sir Richard Hill and the black Haitian leader, Toussaint L'Ouverture.

Although literate opinion was by now on the side of the animals, this had little effect upon the postilions and cowherds — 'The misfortune is the writings of an Addison are seldom read by cooks and butchers', regretted Adam Fitz Adam.[76] It was clearly time that the law should play its part in persuading the illiterate.

6 Time for Action

Gradually, naturalists, educators, politicians and campaigners had rejected the old view that nonhumans had been created to serve humankind. The time had come to take action. As soon as the Napoleonic wars were over, great advances were made towards putting into effect the ideas of the humanitarian writers of the eighteenth century.

The cultivated section of society felt it their duty to civilize the less educated. Three hundred years earlier the elite had been anxious to enlarge the conceptual gap between human and nonhuman; now the process was in reverse. The early nineteenth century saw a surge of activity which included the publication of numerous humane educational works for children, the foundation of the RSPCA in Britain, the first signs of organized vegetarianism, and a successful campaign to introduce effective legislation.

Under the so-called 'Black Act' of 1723 it was a capital offence, under some circumstances, to destroy the property of others – and this included their animals. In 1749, for example, two men at Gloucester had been convicted of killing a mare to spite its owner, and one had received sentence of death. On the other hand, a Quaker was convicted at Sussex Assizes in 1806 of pouring sulphuric acid on a dog, causing its intestines to fall out through the wound in its belly, and the court was able only to award compensation of £5 to be paid to the dog's owner for damage to property.

THE FIRST ATTEMPT: BULL-BAITING

John Lawrence noted that some magistrates, especially in London, had been trying to take a firmer line on cruelty during the last few years of the eighteenth century. They were, however, handicapped by the lack of appropriate legislation. Cruelties to dogs, horses and meat animals, notably those being driven to the Smithfield Market in London, were all contemporary causes of concern, but it appeared that among the 'softest' targets for legislation was bull-baiting. Few members of the upper classes still subscribed to the sport and it was widely regarded as vulgar and disreputable. In addition, it could become a public nuisance. In 1756 Adam Fitz Adam, for example, had complained that such cruelties 'frequently run me into great inconveniences', and it was certainly true that bull-baitings could severely disrupt the ordinary business of a town, especially when ancient custom or covenant decreed that bulls should be run through the streets before baiting. Usually the bulls were disinclined to fight and had first to be maddened. Various methods were used, ranging from pepper or gunpowder in the nostrils, fireworks under the tail, soap in the eyes, or tail-breaking. 'We have heard of a hot iron being thrust up the animals' fundament', Henry Alken recorded in 1821.[1]

Most infamous of all were the bull-runnings and baitings at Stamford in Lincolnshire. Bulls were let loose in the blocked-off streets, chased by men and dogs, beaten with cudgels and thrown off the bridge into the river before being baited. Despite attempts by the Earl of Exeter and the mayor to stop these customs, they continued. On one occasion the mayor called in dragoons, but they refused to intervene and joined in the sport.

The first Bill designed to put down bull-baiting was introduced into Parliament on 18 April 1800 by Sir William Pulteney, an independent-minded Scottish MP and an old friend of David Hume. He was tortuously opposed by William Windham on several grounds, not least that the Bill was an attempt by the rich to interfere with the sports of the poor. 'Why should the butcher be deprived of his amusements anymore than the gentleman?', Windham demanded. Besides, bull-baiting helped to cultivate the sterling qualities of both dogs and men.

John Lawrence, angered by Windham's sophistry, subsequently wrote in *The Sportsman's Repository*:

That man had in an eminent degree the gift of the gab; and at the same time, the pre-eminent art of confounding every subject beyond all possibility of its being developed and comprehended either by himself or others. He was the very Hierophant of confusion and his mind the chosen Tabernacle of that goddess. He had in truth been so much in the habit of shaking up right and wrong in the bag together that he had long lost the faculty of distinguishing one from the other.

Windham, however, was aided by George Canning, who thought the Bill absurd, and despite support from Rowland Hill, Richard Martin and Richard Sheridan, the Bill was narrowly lost by forty-three votes to forty-one. Windham was toasted in ale-houses all over the country and bulls, bears and badgers were subjected to celebratory baitings. *The Times* of 25 April 1800 supported Windham; its editorial fulminated against 'undue interference with private life', proclaiming that 'whatever meddles with the private personal disposition of a man's time or property is tyranny direct.'

In 1801, at Bury St Edmunds, a baited bull broke loose. As punishment, its hoofs were hacked off and it was again baited. An editorial in the *Sporting Magazine* expostulated: 'God of Nature, in what country am I? The bull of St Edmund's Bury is tormented for the amusement of Christian savages who take delight in inflicting torture. Can the philosophic Windham, the champion of Christianity and Social Order, stand up in Parliament and vindicate such amusements?'[3] He did, and repeatedly.

The Bill against bull-baiting was eventually reintroduced by a Mr Dent, and although he was supported by William Wilberforce – 'wretched indeed must be the condition of the people of England if their whole happiness consisted in the practice of such barbarity' – the Bill was again defeated.

THE EFFORTS OF THOMAS ERSKINE AND RICHARD MARTIN

In 1809, a new champion of the animals, Lord Erskine of Restormel, entered the arena by introducing into the House of Lords his Bill designed to prevent any 'wanton cruelty' to animals. This stipulated that any person maliciously wounding or cruelly beating any horse, mare, ass, ox, sheep or pig should be found guilty of a misdemeanour and sentenced, on first offence, to not less than one week and not more than one month in prison. Once again it was the drovers and others of the lower classes who were seen to be threatened by such legislation.

Thomas Erskine (1750–1823), had been born in Edinburgh and had risen to become Lord Chancellor in the years 1806 and 1807. Before he took up law, he had served as a young officer, first in the Navy and then in the Army. His success at the bar was rapid and spectacular, and by the 1780s he had become rich from his practice.

In Parliament he generally followed Fox and supported Whig policy, advocating the emancipation of slaves with a conviction that grew over the course of the years. He was well known as an admirer of animals, and his pets included a dog, a goose and even two leeches. He is reputed to have been an amiable and witty man and a great lover of puns. When he met Dr Johnson in 1772, he impressed Boswell with his 'vivacity, fluency and precision'. A little later he had become a friend of Jeremy Bentham, and it is possible that Johnson's and Bentham's views on animals were impressed upon him at this early stage in his career. Once aroused, his enthusiasm for a cause could lead him to forget the conventional dignity of his position. It is said, for example, that one day on Hampstead Heath Erskine saw a carter beating a horse. On remonstrating with the man he received the familiar reply: 'Can't I do what I like with my own?' 'Yes', replied Erskine, striking the carter, 'and so can I – this stick is my own.'

In his speech on the Second Reading of his Bill on 15 May 1809, Erskine complained:

Nothing is more notorious than that it is not only useless, but dangerous, to poor suffering animals, to reprove their oppressors, or to threaten them with punishment. The general answer with the addition of bitter oaths and increased cruelty, is 'What is that to you?' If the offender be a servant, he curses you, and asks 'Are you my master?' and if he be the master himself, he tells you that the animal is his own. The validity of this most infamous and stupid defence, arises from that defect in the law which I seek to remedy. Animals are considered as property only. To destroy or abuse them, from malice to the proprietor, or with an intention injurious to his interest in them, is criminal, but the animals themselves are without protection; the law regards them not substantively; they have no rights.

On 9 June the Bill was passed by the Lords. Sir Charles Bunbury, with William Wilberforce once more in support, then tried to pass it through the Commons, but it was defeated by thirty-seven votes to twenty-seven, much to the disgust of the *Gentlemen's Magazine,* whose editorial stated: 'Surely few subjects in the whole compass of moral discussion can be greater than the unnecessary cruelty of man to animals which administer to his pleasure, his consolation and to the very support of his life!'

It was another thirteen years before any reforms on behalf of animals finally became law. In 1821 Erskine joined forces with Richard Martin MP, and these two men qualify as the first people, anywhere in the world, to succeed in legislating against cruelty to animals by means of parliamentary procedure.

Richard Martin (1754–1834) was a similarly robust character and in his early years he had gained a reputation as a duellist. In 1781 George 'Fighting' Fitzgerald, a provocative eccentric, had deliberately and cold-bloodedly shot dead an Irish wolfhound belonging to Lord Altamont. Martin, friend of both dog and owner, was so angered at its death that two years later he fought a duel with Fitzgerald in which both men were injured. Educated at Harrow and Cambridge, Martin was the owner of vast estates in Galway. He sat in the House of Commons from 1801 till 1826, where he actively supported Catholic emancipation and championed such humane causes as the abolition of the death penalty for forgery, and the establishment of legal aid at the state's expense for those charged with criminal offences who could not themselves afford to employ counsel. Such attitudes show that Richard Martin cared as much for human as for nonhuman beings. Indeed he provided shelter for the

9   The Committee for the Reform of Animal Experimentation (CRAE) was the key to the modern reform of British (and European) law protecting laboratory animals. Here, its members are on the steps of the Home Office after presenting the Houghton/Platt memorandum to the Home Secretary on 4 August 1976.

Left to Right: Clive Hollands, Lord Platt, Dr Kit Pedler, Bill Jordan, Lord Houghton and the author.

homeless at his own castle, and his life-story is sprinkled with anecdotes that illustrate his kindness towards his own species, which earned him the nickname 'Humanity Dick' from his friend, King George IV.

From about the beginning of 1821 Martin was in touch with John Lawrence. Both men of the land, they had much in common. Together with Erskine, they planned the new legislation. On 18 May Martin printed his Bill, proposing:

that if any person or persons having the charge, care or custody of any horse, cow, ox, heifer, steer, sheep or other cattle, the property of any other person or persons, shall wantonly beat, abuse or ill-treat any such animal, such individuals shall be brought before a Justice of the Peace or other magistrate.

By preserving the rights of owners of animals to 'do as they liked with their own' Martin no doubt reduced the opposition to his Bill. Its targets, too, could be seen to be the drovers and carters of the London working classes rather than anyone with political connections. The Bill was amended in committee to include mares, geldings, mules and asses, and then triumphantly passed through the Commons on 1 June 1821, by forty-eight votes to sixteen. In the Lords, however, Lord Erskine's influence was not enough and the Bill was defeated.

Undismayed, Martin and Erskine reintroduced their Bill the following year, and it was passed in both houses. On 22 July 1822, it finally received the royal assent and became the first national law anywhere in the world, passed by a democratically elected legislature which dealt specifically and entirely with cruelty to animals.

Entitled 'An Act to Prevent the Cruel and Improper Treatment of Cattle', it quickly became known as Martin's Act. Over the next four years, until he was unseated in 1826, Richard Martin continued to present Bills to protect animals. His main targets were bull-baiting, slaughter-house conditions, dog-fighting and the general protection of cats and dogs (who were not included in the species protected under his Act of 1822). Martin was a determined parliamentary tactician. On several occasions he succeeded in bringing up his Bills late at night before a thinly attended chamber well stocked with his friends. However, all these efforts at further reform were narrowly defeated, either in the Lords where he lacked the skilled support of his old friend Erskine, who had died in 1823, or in the Commons, where Martin encountered persistent opposition from Sir Robert Peel.

Some time shortly after the passing of his Act, Martin himself brought the first prosecution. A costermonger, Bill Burns, was charged with cruelty to his donkey. It is alleged that Martin, as usual never afraid to flout convention, insisted that the donkey be brought into court so that his wounds could be seen. This episode created quite a lot of publicity, which was probably Martin's intention. The occasion was celebrated by a popular song entitled 'If I had a donkey that wouldn't go', and commemorated by a print bearing the legend:

> Bill's Donkey then was brought into Court
> Who caused of course a deal of Sport.
> He cock'd his ears and op'd his jaws,
> As tho' he meant to plead his own cause.[4]

On 11 August 1822, Martin brought a case against Samuel Clarke and David Hyde for savagely beating tethered horses at Smithfield. Both men were fined twenty shillings. Martin was determined that his legislation should be enforced and he methodically brought a number of such prosecutions; anxious to educate rather than punish the poor too harshly, he frequently paid the fines himself.

There is little doubt that Martin and Erskine succeeded where men of milder temper would have failed. In an age when sexual stereotypes were even more pronounced than they are today, a concern for animals' welfare might well have been discounted as effeminate. The subject was still regarded by many as essentially ludicrous, yet few could argue, when faced with these two virile firebrands, that it was womanish. The Celtic vigour of the Irish Martin and the Scottish Erskine spiked the guns of those, like Windham, who tried to argue that opposition to cruel sports was unmanly. It was said of Martin that 'he lets drive at the House like a bullet and the flag of truce is instantly hung out upon both sides.' The same source added: 'he holds the House by the very test of the human race, laughter, and while their sides shake, their opposition is shaken and falls down at the same instant'.[5]

Martin was a flamboyant witty figure; eccentric, quick-tempered, yet kind. With his extensive holdings in Ireland he had also been bequeathed debts of an equal magnitude and, hounded by creditors, he was to end his days as a refugee in Boulogne in 1834, mourned by the poet Thomas Hood as:

> Thou Wilberforce of hacks!
> Of whites as well as blacks,
> Piebald and dapple grey,
> Chestnut and bay —
> No poet's eulogy thy name adorns!
> But oxen, from the fens,
> Sheep in their pens,
> Praise thee, and red cows with their winding horns![6]

His Act of 1822 did not specifically mention bulls; the bull-baiters therefore continued their sport. Martin's Act sought to prevent the cruel and improper treatment of horses, mares, geldings, mules, asses, cows, heifers, steers, oxen, sheep and other cattle. Martin failed in 1823 and 1826 to outlaw bull-baiting specifically, but nevertheless tried to apply his Act to this sport, arguing that the phrase 'other cattle' clearly covered bulls, and in 1825 he vainly attempted to have convicted two baiters from Hounslow Heath.

CALL IN THE CAVALRY

Much agitation was caused by a lion-bait at Warwick in the summer of 1825, the first for some two hundred years. The lion, Nero, had been bred in captivity. Like some lions of the Roman theatre, Nero was disinclined to fight. Instead of biting the dogs who were set upon him, he politely pushed them away with his paw; when that failed, he rolled upon them. Eventually, after Nero had been severely bitten, the bait was stopped. Later in the show another lion, named Wallace, was baited with similar disappointment for the spectators.

The Times, now on the side of reform, attacked the events as 'a disgusting exhibition of brutality'. Baiting continued to wane in popularity, under growing middle-class disapprobation. Not until 1835, however, was it finally outlawed under an Act introduced by Joseph Pease MP. This legislation prohibited 'wantonly and cruelly ill-treating or torturing any horse, mare, gelding, bull, ox, cow, heifer, steer, calf, mule, ass, sheep, lamb, dog or any other cattle or domestic animal.' It also banned the keeping or using of 'any house, room, pit, ground or other place for running, baiting or fighting any bull, bear, badger, dog or other animal (whether domestic or wild) or for cock-fighting.'

But the battle was not quite over. At Stamford the traditional bull-baiting assumed almost revolutionary significance, as some of the 'lower orders' continued to defy not only the law, the mayor, the magistracy, and the local aristocracy, but subsequently the London police, the Home Secretary and the Dragoon Guards as well. At times the bull-baiting mob, swollen by outsiders, was estimated to be four thousand strong. In November 1836, the annual Stamford bull-running and baiting took place as usual and a subsequent prosecution was brought by the newly established Society for the Prevention of Cruelty to Animals (SPCA), resulting in two defendants being bound over under Pease's Act. (For an account of the founding of the SPCA see below.) The following year two hundred special constables, abetted by local magistrates, declined to enforce the new law.

In 1838 Lord John Russell, then Home Secretary, at the request of the SPCA, drafted in a force of Dragoons and police who guarded the only two available bulls. But in the afternoon a bull calf, recently sold by Lord Spencer and *en route* to its new owner, was seized by the crowd and briefly run before it was recaptured by the Dragoons. In 1839 it was a similar story, the bull again being saved by the cavalry. Finally, the cost of the forces of law and order became too much for the citizens of Stamford and they themselves ensured the end of the sport.

Attitudes certainly had changed, and one can discern a pattern of development. The prevailing anthropocentric view of the intelligentsia during the Renaissance, which had emphasized the chasm between human and nonhuman, had been challenged during the sixteenth and seventeenth centuries. Dissent then became the established view of the literati in the eighteenth century. The masses at first resisted this change, but gradually, the growing middle classes, motivated by a desire to seem civilized and respectable as well as by genuine humane feeling, came to accept the new opinions. At this time politicians began attempts at legislative reform, motivated not by a desire for popularity, but by the same sincere sympathetic feelings that had driven several of them to become opponents of the slave trade. Although the Evangelical element was pronounced, it is striking that animal welfare reformers came from all sects and from none: Catholics, Puritans, Quakers, Methodists, Anglicans, Tories, Whigs, Utilitarians, atheists and cynics all contributed to the movement, their common motivation, it seems, being a sense of compassion.

THE FOUNDING OF THE SPCA

The British instinct for forming committees and societies had led to the formation of the Society for the Suppression of Vice in 1802, one of this Evangelical committee's aims being the abolition of animal-baiting. In Liverpool in 1809 the short-lived Society for Preventing Wanton Cruelty to Brute Animals was established; its two main concerns appear to have been the treatment of hamstrung sheep being driven through the streets of Liverpool, and cruelty to horses. It was not until 1824, however, that a society was formed which survived its first few gatherings. On 16 June 1824, a meeting was called in Old Slaughter's Coffee House, St Martin's Lane, London, at which Fowell Buxton MP, the active anti-slavery campaigner, took the chair. The Society for the Prevention of Cruelty to Animals was launched at this meeting, and the Reverend Arthur Broome, subsequently to be described as the society's founder, was appointed its first secretary. Two committees were set up. One was to 'superintend the Publication of Tracts, Sermons, and similar modes of influencing public opinion' and consisted of the Utilitarian Sir James Mackintosh MP, A. Warre, William Wilberforce MP, Basil Montagu, the Reverend Arthur Broome, the Reverend G. Bonner, the Reverend G. A. Hatch, A. E. Kendal, Lewis Gompertz, William Mudford and Dr Henderson. The other committee was 'to adopt measures for Inspecting the Markets and Streets of the Metropolis, the Slaughter Houses, the conduct of coachmen etc.', and consisted of Fowell Buxton MP, Richard Martin

MP, Sir James Graham, L. B. Allen, C. C. Wilson, John Brogden, Alderman Brydges, E. A. Kendal, E. Lodge, J. Martin and T. G. Meymott.

Of the twenty-one people mentioned in the first minutes, three were clergymen and five were Members of Parliament. Three were already well-known humanitarians − Wilberforce, Buxton and Mackintosh. All were established figures but none, at this stage, were titled aristocrats. There were no women members, although the publications committee, which got off to a cracking start, decided at its third meeting on 25 June to publish 'a tract on cruelty to brutes by Mrs. Hall'. It also decided, at the same meeting, to publish a sermon on compassion as well as the late Lord Erskine's speech on the introduction of his Bill of 1809.

It was not until 1829 that women were again mentioned in the society's minutes. It was then decided to establish a ladies committee, initially to consist of Mrs Thompson, Mrs Fenner, Mrs Tattersall, Miss Milne and Mrs L. Gompertz. The heyday of the ladies committee came under the presidency of Baroness Burdett-Coutts (1814−1906), the outstanding humanitarian, although until 1886 ladies were not considered sufficiently business-like to be allowed to join the general committee governing the society's affairs.[7]

The Reverend Arthur Broome (1780−1837), who became so important in the SPCA's history, had gone up to Balliol College, Oxford, in 1798. In 1803 he was ordained in the Church of England and became curate at Brook and Hinxhill in Kent. From 1820 he was vicar at St Mary's, Bromley (now Bromley-by-Bow), in London, until he resigned his living in 1824 to devote himself entirely to the society's affairs as its secretary. In 1822 and 1831 he published abridged editions of Humphry Primatt's work *A Dissertation on the Duty of Mercy and Sin of Cruelty to Brute Animals,* with extensive footnotes.

Initially, the society was funded by donations, not least from Broome himself (although he was not a wealthy man). By January 1826, however, the society was in debt to the tune of nearly £300, and the committee sadly contemplated its closure. At that juncture, however, a legacy of £100 was received from the estate of the novelist Mrs Ann Radcliffe. This saved the society, but did not prevent Arthur Broome from being thrown into prison for the society's remaining debts, from which he was quite quickly rescued by the redoubtable Richard Martin (himself heavily in debt) and the ingenious Lewis Gompertz.

Early in 1828 Gompertz was appointed to succeed Broome as secretary, though the reasons for the change are not clear. A minute indicates that Broome had 'not been attending to the duties of his office', nor been present at meetings. Nevertheless, the committee's attitude remained one of respect rather than censure. Perhaps Broome had been made despondent by the society's financial problems and his own imprisonment.

In its first few years the society had, nevertheless, been a success. In

1824 alone it had brought nearly 150 prosecutions, mainly of drovers and others involved in the Smithfield Market. At Broome's expense the society had employed its first inspector, a Mr Wheeler, to gather evidence of cruelties, and the publication of tracts had begun in earnest. By the end of 1828 Gompertz had succeeded in putting the society on a sound financial footing, for which he was awarded the society's Silver Medal four years later, along with Inspector Wheeler. Gompertz, who was a practising Jew, had the reputation of being an eccentric, albeit an effective one. He was also a writer and an inventor, and among some thirty-eight inventions one, the expanding chuck, has proved to be of lasting value. It is clear that he was a man of 'advanced principles', for he not only was a vegetarian, but he also refused to ride in horse-drawn carriages because of his opposition to animal exploitation of any sort. In 1824 he wrote *Moral Inquiries on the Situation of Man and Brutes,* in which his argument for animal protection was based on 'the similitude between man and other animals'. In 1852 he published *Fragments in Defence of Animals* in which he attacked cruelties to horses and cattle, hunting, vivisection and the 'barbarity of whale fishing'.

How this radical man related to the hunting Martin and the shooting Buxton is not recorded, but, for whatever reason, he fell out with two other members of the committee, Dr John Fenner and the Reverend Thomas Greenwood. Fenner and Greenwood attacked Gompertz on three grounds: first, because he used 'informers' (i.e. the society's inspectors) to prosecute offenders; secondly, for his professed 'Pythagoranism', by which was meant his advocacy of a vegetarian diet; and thirdly, because he was not a Christian. In the summer of 1832 the SPCA committee resolved to suspend the inspectorate and insisted that 'the proceedings of this Society are entirely based on the Christian Faith and on Christian Principles.' Gompertz resigned, giving as his reason his opposition to behaviour 'inimical to the institution' on the part of one of the society's leading members.

So, within eight years of its foundation, the society had lost both its founder and its first saviour. Even before Princess Victoria's association with the society, therefore, which began in 1835, it seems that its conservative character had become established. We cannot attribute this with certainty to Martin, Wilberforce or Buxton, since these three men, all establishment figures in their fashion, had by this time ceased to be actively involved with the society. In the years 1833 and 1834 the character of the society became increasingly aristocratic, although quite how this came about is unclear, and it seems that those responsible for alienating its outstanding first two secretaries were otherwise men of little significance in the history of the movement. Although Broome and Gompertz are today honoured by the RSPCA, it appears that they were the first victims of the society's tendency to reject its more controversial and effective figures.

After his departure, Gompertz founded the Animals' Friend Society, with the aim of continuing 'those operations which the Society for the Prevention of Cruelty to Animals, when United, so successfully performed'. He ran this society with considerable success, and apparently with the approval of Richard Martin, until 1848, when he gave up because of ill health.

In 1840 Queen Victoria granted the prefix 'Royal' to the SPCA, thereby marking the final arrival of animal welfare as an entirely respectable concern. The first great golden age of reform in this field was over, but the royal patronage and prefix assured its continued advance during the remainder of the century.

EDUCATION

Shortly before the politicians started their attempts at reform, and at the height of the serious eighteenth-century outpourings on the subject of animal protection, there had been an increase in the number of educational books for children which, following the advice of Locke and Pope many years earlier, began to refashion nursery attitudes on the topic. Nearly all, until the end of the nineteenth century, were by women – such as Dorothy Kilner, Sarah Trimmer, Mrs Charles Bray, Edith Carrington, Charlotte Elizabeth, Emily Cox, Arabella Argus, Mary Turner Andrewes and Susanna Watts. Writers were not only continuing to use animals as mouth-pieces and exemplars of virtue, as 'disguised humans'; they were also beginning to teach children kindness to the nonhumans themselves.

In one of the first books of children's fiction in English, *Goody Two-Shoes,* published in 1765, the heroine was depicted as taking great pains to care for mistreated animals, and in 1783 Dorothy Kilner's *The Life and Perambulations of a Mouse* was the first children's book to stress kindness to nonhumans as a moral duty;[8] the author pretends to have been asked by a moralizing mouse to take her under her protection and to write her history of callous treatment at the hands of humans. But it was Sarah Trimmer's story, three years later, which was destined to become the classic in this field. Sarah Trimmer (1741–1810) was a noted educationalist who, as a young woman, had met and become a friend of Dr Johnson. Her first work was her *Easy Introduction to the Knowledge of Nature,* published in 1780, which was shortly followed by the remarkably enduring and most popular of her books – *The History of the Robins* in 1786.[9] This famous work continued in print until about 1911. It concludes with the words:

Happy would it be for the animal creation if every human being consulted the welfare of inferior creatures, and neither spoiled them by indulgence nor injured them by tyranny! Happy would mankind be, if every one acted in conformity to the will of their Maker, by cultivating in their own minds, and those of their children, the Divine principles of general benevolence.

Mrs Trimmer established a trend which continued for several generations after her death, and, for a century after the *History of the Robins*, publishers like Griffith and Farran, the Religious Tract Society, and S. W. Partridge produced numerous publications of this sort, explicitly aimed at inculcating kindness to animals.

Among the first to follow Mrs Trimmer was the pioneer feminist Mary Wollstonecraft (1759–97), whose *Original Stories from Real Life*, published in 1788, told of a kindly Mrs Mason who commented to some children upon her reluctance to kill insects: 'You are often troublesome – I am stronger than you – yet I do not kill you.'

Later, she advised them to 'Be tender-hearted…it is only to animals that children *can* do good. Men are their superiors.' Obviously Wollstonecraft's concern for women's rights cannot be separated entirely from her concern for nonhuman animals. Her famous feminist work *Vindication of the Rights of Woman* was published in 1792, shortly before her death after giving birth to Mary, who was to become the creator of Dr Frankenstein and second wife of the anti-speciesist Percy Bysshe Shelley. Ironically, her feminist views were subsequently ridiculed by Thomas Taylor, the contemporary philosopher, in an anonymous satirical work entitled *A Vindication of the Rights of Brutes*.

Early educational publications argued strongly against bloodsports and angling, as in the anthropomorphic *The Hare, or Hunting Incompatible with Humanity: Written as a Stimulus to Youth Towards a Proper Treatment of Animals*, which was published by John Gough in 1799 and was followed by similar injunctions in the *Youth's Magazine* of 1813, *The Picturesque Primer* published by W. Fletcher in 1837, and *Holiday Amusements* by William Belch, published around 1828. The latter work also argued strongly against birds-nesting. Some authors adopted a religious tone, as did Susanna Watts in *The Animal's Friend*, arguing that humanity to animals is a religious duty. Others wrote pseudo-autobiographical pleas for kindness from horses, dogs, mice or donkeys, as in *The Adventures of a Donkey* (1815) and *Further Adventures of Jemmy Donkey* by Arabella Argus; *The Life and Perambulations of a Mouse, Keeper's Travels in Search of his Master* (1850) and *Tuppy* (1860). Most famous of such books was to be Anna Sewell's humanitarian classic *Black Beauty*, published in 1877. In the anonymous *The Escapes, Wanderings and Preservation of a Hare*, published about 1820, and *The Hare, or Hunting Incompatible with Humanity* of 1799, hares recount to their human rescuers the hunting and deaths of members of their families. These were perhaps the first books devoted entirely to attacking bloodsports. A famous series which ran to numerous editions throughout the second half of the nineteenth century was entitled *A*

Mother's Lessons on Kindness to Animals and published by S. W. Partridge. The chapter headings exemplify the typical themes of the period: 'Don't Whip them, Coachee', 'A Boy Reproved by a Bird', 'Sagacity of a Horse', 'Birds and their Nests', and 'The Progress of Unrestrained Cruelty'. Another popular work was *Our Duty to Animals* (c.1870) by Mrs Charles Bray, who, although opposed to killing for sport, explicitly condoned meat-eating on the grounds that it is natural and that unless the dead carcasses of animals were consumed disease would become rampant. This is essentially the same line as had been taken by Mrs Trimmer nearly a century earlier, when she had accepted that 'The world we live in seems to have been principally designed for the use and comfort of mankind, who by the Divine appointment, have dominion over the inferior creatures', and that:

Some creatures have nothing to give us but their own bodies; these have been expressly destined by the Supreme Governor as food for mankind, and He has appointed an extraordinary increase of them for this very purpose; such an increase as would be very injurious to us if all were suffered to live. These we have an undoubtful right to kill; but should make their short lives as comfortable as we can, and let their deaths be attended with as little pain as possible.[10]

The other eighteenth-century work of note is *Pity's Gift: A Collection of Interesting Tales to Excite the Compassion of Youth for the Animal Creation.* Its tales of Kind-Hearted Henry and Tender Amelia are said to have been selected by an anonymous lady from the writings of a Mr Pratt. In her Preface she writes:

Everyone must have noticed, in most children, a tyrannical, sometimes a cruel, propensity to torment animals within their power, such as – persecuting flies, torturing birds, cats, dogs, etc. Some friends of mine joined me in thinking that a collection of humane facts, and arguments, in favour of these suffering creatures, might be of considerable use if brought into view, not only to our own offspring, but if made public, to youth in general.[11]

It has been claimed that these early educationalists were concerned not about the welfare of animals but for the character of the children. This is debatable. Admittedly, a concern for the reader's character is often expressed, but in most cases this seems to be offered by way of justification, being intended to persuade the more speciesist parent or teacher that kindness to animals is indeed a subject fit for serious concern.

The reforming streak found in some earlier educational works had all but vanished by late Victorian times. Kindness to favoured animals, even sentimentality, by then had become so much a part of polite society that the sense of urgency had almost disappeared from the educational literature.

THE NATURALISTS

As we have seen, during the late seventeenth and throughout the eighteenth centuries the naturalists had been moving away from the Renaissance anthropocentric view of nature. It began to be clear to them that animals were *not* made solely for the service of mankind. Thomas Bewick (1753–1828) wrote about nature fondly and, fairly, putting the human race into a context with the other creatures, and the Reverend Gilbert White (1720–93), showing a similar respect and sensitivity for all living beings, planted four lime trees at Selbourne to block his view of the butcher's yard opposite. White's *Natural History of Selbourne* remained a favourite for over a hundred years.

Nor did the old division of animals into benevolent and malevolent seem to be quite so clear-cut. Creatures like toads and snakes, previously regarded as repulsively ugly, came to be treated more rationally by the early 1800s. People also began to realize that some animals, in the past considered to be dangerous, could be quite unthreatening unless provoked; even the wolf, renowned in folklore for its wickedness, began to receive kinder portrayals.[12]   Keith Thomas cites John Ray, writing in the seventeenth century, as being the first English naturalist to break away from the Aesop and bestiary traditions which had portrayed nonhuman animals emblematically, describing them in terms of imagined virtues, vices or other symbols of alleged significance to humankind.[13] Certainly, by the nineteenth century there is, among naturalists, a general respect for the animal kingdom *per se* which sometimes becomes distinctly humanitarian, especially in books for children such as *Gleanings in Natural History* by Edward Jesse, published in 1861; the popular writings of the Reverend J. G. Wood in the 1870s and Mrs Brightwen's *Wild Nature Won by Kindness* of 1893. All these are aimed at the older child and are far more concerned to 'excite kindly feelings' in the reader than are similar biological textbooks from about 1900 onwards, which too often reek of the arrogance of science.

Even insects are shown respect, as, for example, in *Insects and their Habitations*, which was published in 1833 under the aegis of the Society for Promoting Christian Knowledge. Although this book still harks back to an earlier generation of texts in its tendency to urge the reader to 'reflect upon the lessons of wisdom and virtue which they [insects] teach', it also enjoins kindness:

It is a sin against that God who created both them and you, to inflict unnecessary suffering upon any of His creatures. Ask yourselves too, how you would like such treatment, from one stronger than yourself. If you meet a beetle or a caterpillar, step aside, and do not wantonly crush it. And should you see a poor earth-worm, lying in the dusty path, parched with the sun, and too much exhausted to regain his home, extend a kind hand to help him, and place him on the nearest cool and moist ground. He is a harmless little creature, though not pleasing to the eye or agreeable, but he is God's workmanship; and while you are thankful for being endowed with reason, and with an immortal soul, let the inferior creatures enjoy their little lives while they may.[14]

VEGETARIANISM ESTABLISHED

As we have seen, a few exceptional people have questioned the slaughter of animals for food over the centuries. Some, like Leonardo, kept their views private, while others have spoken out, like Richard of Wyche (1197–1253), Bishop of Chichester, when he observed animals being killed for food: 'you, who are innocent, what have you done worthy of death?'[15] Joseph Ritson, the antiquarian, was one of the first to devote a whole book in English to vegetarianism. *His Essay on Abstinence from Animal Food as a Moral Duty* was published in London in 1802. In it, Ritson argued against meat-eating on the grounds that it is unnatural, unnecessary, unhealthy and immoral. He repeated the notion that meat 'is the cause of cruelty and ferocity' among those who devour it, and drew attention to the widespread existence of vegetarian cultures. He quoted the eighteenth-century zoologist, William Smellie, who wrote:

Of all rapacious animals, man is the most universal destroyer. The destruction of quadrupeds, birds and insects is, in general, limited to particular kinds: but the rapacity of man has hardly any limitation. His empire over the other animals which inhabit this globe is almost universal.[16]

Medieval prohibitions on the consumption of useful animals such as oxen continued in some Mediterranean countries until the seventeenth century. But by this time Europe had become far more carnivorous than most of the rest of the world and England probably had a greater density of food animals than any other country save the Netherlands. By 1700 oxen were no longer regarded as draft animals in England and the country became notorious for its ravenous consumption of beef. Strangely, the decline in the agricultural use of horses and dogs in the present century has not led to a corresponding increase in their consumption, presumably because of their enhanced sentimental status.

Around 1790 an American sect in Vermont, the Dorrilites, prohibited the wearing of clothes derived from animals and the eating of meat, and in 1809 William Cowherd in England made vegetarianism obligatory in his Bible Christian Church based near Manchester. This was the start of the organized modern vegetarian movement. One of Cowherd's followers, William Metcalfe, emigrated to Philadelphia and became a founder of vegetarianism in America.

From about 1812, Percy Bysshe Shelley advocated vegetarianism and, during the nineteenth century, abstinence from animal flesh gradually became established among a minority of the middle class. Slaughtering and slaughter houses began to be concealed from public view, and the animal origin of meat dishes became obscured, as recognizable carcasses were less frequently served at table. The word 'vegetarian' appeared in 1842 and came into widespread use after the establishment of the Vegetarian Society in England in 1847 by secular followers of Metcalfe.[17] At the end of the century the cause received a considerable boost from Howard William's *The Ethics of Diet* (1883) and from the writings of Henry Salt, himself inspired in part by advocates of vegetarianism such as Shelley and Henry Thoreau (see pp. 125–8).

Perhaps some children have always disliked meat; it may be this is especially true among those who realize the connection between meat and animals before they are addicted to flesh-eating. One may speculate on the use of Norman words for meat derived from animals who are called by their Saxon names. By calling cow-meat 'beef' and pig-meat 'pork', many an infantile eater is deceived. Words like 'chicken' and 'lamb' can, however, suddenly give the game away. It was in the first half of the nineteenth century that vegetarianism, thanks to the influence of Gompertz, Ritson, Shelley, Cowherd, and others, first became an established minority fashion in Britain. Today young children who refuse meat spontaneously are being allowed this dietary freedom by more permissive twentieth-century parents: they like animals and therefore, quite logically, decline to eat them.

7 Victorian Consolidation

The Victorian era was a period of active consolidation for animal welfare in Britain, and the reign saw numerous campaigns to reduce the miseries of food animals being driven to slaughter through the streets of London and other cities, to improve the methods of slaughter, to stop the export of worn-out old horses to Belgian abbatoirs, to protect performing animal in circuses and to outlaw the use of dogs for the drawing of carts. Some of these agitations only bore fruit in the following century − such as the ban on the export of live horses for slaughter in 1914, and the effective prohibition of the cruel bearing-rein for horses under the restrictions of the major Protection of Animals Act of 1911. The legislation of 1835 had outlawed cockfighting and dog-fighting, but this encouraged rat-fighting, which continued until it was also made illegal under the 1911 Act.

These campaigns have already been well written about[1] and will not be discussed here in detail. By far the two most controversial welfare issues of the era, however, were the killing of birds for sport and millinery, and the use of nonhumans in vivisection. A closer examination of these cases illustrates the degree to which the ideals of animal welfare had become part of British culture by the end of the nineteenth century, and how this had occurred through two principal channels − nursery education and the influence of the aristocracy.

THE ELEVATION OF THE RSPCA

The aristocracy had, no doubt, noticed the example set by the young Princess Victoria, who had honoured the SPCA with her patronage in 1835 and, after she became Queen, with the royal prefix in 1840. These were momentous developments, for they put the cause of animal welfare on the way to the international and fashionable respectability which would guarantee its progress.

Who planned this ennoblement of the RSPCA? It may have followed quite naturally from the involvement of Victoria, but little is known about how she became involved. The only record is of Robert Batson, one of four members of the SPCA committee attending its monthly meeting on 6 July 1835,[2] reporting that 'at the suggestion of several Ladies he had presented a Report of the Society and a letter to their Royal Highnesses the Duchess of Kent and the Princess Victoria with a request that they would honor [sic] the Society by becoming Ladies Patronesses.'[3] Sir John Conroy, the Duchess of Kent's close friend, had presented the request of 2 July to the Duchess and her daughter, and had replied two days later to Batson that 'Her Royal Highness very readily acceded to your request that her name and that of the Princess Victoria be placed on the List of Lady Patronesses.' The Committee resolved that Batson write letters of thanks to their Royal Highnesses and to Conroy.

Who the 'several ladies' were remains unknown. But to them and Robert Batson much credit is due for this initiative, which did much to further the cause of animal welfare. It was certainly very timely; once she had become Queen in 1837, it might have been too late to expect Victoria's involvement as a Patroness. The Earl of Carnarvon had consented to be the SPCA's president in 1834, and from then on until the next century the society's president and vice-presidents tended to be titled. In 1850 it was the turn of the Duke of Beaufort to be president, in 1854 the Marquess of Westminster, in 1861 the Earl of Harrowby, in 1878 Lord Aberdare, in 1893 HRH the Duke of York (the future King George V), in 1910 the Marquess of Cambridge and in 1918 the Prince of Wales. By 1887 the society could boast no less than twenty royal and four ducal patrons, and thirty-four titled vice-presidents (including Field Marshall Lord Wolseley). The Church connection was maintained by an archbishop, five bishops and Cardinal Manning as vice-presidents.

When, after the First World War, royalty and aristocracy drifted away from the RSPCA, its prestige and effectiveness declined. Traditional aristocracy was, for several decades, replaced not by the 'modern aristocracy' of bankers, industrialists and intellectuals but by people of little influence.

In the Victorian era, however, the endorsement of animal welfare by the Crown and aristocracy in an upward-looking and class-conscious society had the undoubtedly beneficial effect of making the cause fashionable and effective. The emulation of the upper classes, after all, was a central preoccupation in the lives of thousands of Victorians. But there were disadvantages. Certain aristocratic exceptions and inconsistencies had to be accepted. The aristocratic pastimes of hunting and shooting animals, for example, could not be included in the campaign for reform, their importance in the web of British upper-class ritual being too great. Some of the cruelties associated with horse-racing, game-fishing, meat-eating and agriculture also had to be tolerated. Predominantly working-class cruelties were, however, to be fair game and the RSPCA played an important part in the suppression of bull-baiting and cockfighting. Indeed, in 1838 the society's then secretary, Henry Thomas, and two inspectors of the society, visited Hanworth in Middlesex after hearing of a proposed cock-fight. There they were set upon by the cock-fighters and badly injured. Shortly afterwards one of the inspectors, James Piper, died in St Thomas's Hospital, although the post-mortem stated that the cause of death had been tuberculosis.

This double-mindedness in the RSPCA, a willingness to attack working-class cruelty while condoning that of the upper crust, provoked some objections. John Stuart Mill, for example, wrote to the society's secretary on 26 July 1868 declining any closer association with the society 'while it is thought necessary or advisable to limit the Society's operations to the offences committed by the uninfluential classes of society.'[5] He cited pigeon-shooting exhibitions as an example of a cruel sport which ought to be opposed. In retrospect it appears most unfortunate that Mill, one of the greatest of political philosophers, should have been alienated in this way. Following the Bentham line, he had strongly argued that nonhumans should be included in efforts for reform. Writing in *The Principles of Political Economy* in 1848, Mill had made this quite clear:

The reasons for legal intervention in favour of children apply not less strongly to the case of those unfortunate slaves and victims of the most brutal part of mankind – the lower animals. It is by the grossest misunderstanding of the principle of liberty that the infliction of exemplary punishment on ruffianism practised towards these defenceless creatures has been treated as a meddling by government in things beyond its province; an interference with domestic life. The domestic life of domestic tyrants is one of the things which it is the most imperative on the law to interfere with.

The RSPCA had certainly played a part in promoting legal changes, building on the pioneering work of Martin's 1822 Act. That Act was amended after the passing of a Bill put forward by Joseph Pease MP (himself a member of the RSPCA committee) in 1835 to prevent 'fighting or baiting any bull, bear, badger, dog, cock or other kind of animal, whether of domestic or wild nature'; in 1854 legislation was passed prohibiting the use of carts drawn by dogs; in 1869 wild birds received some protection. In 1876 it was the turn of laboratory animals; in 1878 animals in transit; and in 1900 even wild animals were legislated for to a very limited degree. By the end of the century the RSPCA's handbook listed a score of such statutes.

PROPAGANDA AND PROSECUTION

Within the RSPCA there was a debate as to whether to emphasize education or prosecution as the society's chief instrument of reform. But from 1857 onwards, with the co-option of two government school inspectors to the society's staff, and with the appointment of John Colam in 1860 as secretary of the society (a post he held until 1905), it was education which was paramount. Early RSPCA tracts dealt with cruelty to donkeys, post-horses, race-horses and dogs and were religious and rather patronizing in tone:

> A man of kindness to his beast is kind,
> But brutal actions show a brutal mind;
> Remember he who made thee made the brute;
> Who gave thee speech and reason, formed him mute.
> He can't complain — but God's all-seeing eye
> Beholds thy cruelty — he hears his cry.
> He was designed thy servant, not thy drudge:
> And know that his creator is thy judge.[6]

Quotations from the Bible, especially the Old Testament, were used profusely: 'A righteous man regardeth the life of the beast' is frequently found, as is 'God delighteth in mercy.' Cruelty to animals was depicted as 'unnatural and abhorrent to the original constitution of human nature' and as 'the direct road to cruelty to our fellow [human] creatures and to its final reward — the gallows'. In its educative drive the RSPCA exhorted donkey-drivers to withold 'the merciless whip', butchers to show 'humanity', schoolboys to desist from birds-nesting, cabmen to remember that 'fair play is an Englishman's motto', and drovers to show 'kindness' to their sheep and cattle:

Remember the extreme agonies they endure from hunger and thirst, cold and heat, want of rest, stiffened limbs, bleeding feet, wounds from blows and dogs; never forget the heart-sickening, unnumbered cruelties awaiting them at those places of dreadful torture, THE MARKETS AND SLAUGHTER HOUSES.[7]

In 1860 the RSPCA published *The History of William Brown, or Cruelty to Animals Punished,* which relates how William graduates from torturing flies and worms to dropping a kitten from high places and thence to bull-baiting. When whipping a horse one day, he misses, and so severely injures his own leg that it has to be amputated without anaesthetic. In contrast, another pamphlet relates how the kindly Charles Jones makes friends with a mouse who obligingly wakes him when the house catches fire; Charles saves his employer's family and is duly rewarded.

The publication and use of numerous educational works on animals continued until the First World War. Broadly, these taught that it is wrong to inflict cruelty wantonly and that it is right to put wounded or diseased creatures out of their miseries by killing them humanely.

As an extra spur to influence their readers the RSPCA often included in their pamphlets detailed reports of the convictions they had obtained. Despite the emphasis upon education, prosecutions continued to increase, approximately doubling in each decade between 1830 and 1900. Probably this was a reflection not of increasing cruelty but of growth in the number of inspectors (or 'constables') employed by the society. In 1832 there had been two; by 1855 there were eight, by 1878 forty-eight and by 1897 one hundred and twenty.

From 1856 onwards the inspectors were invariably uniformed. Antedating the establishment of the police by a few years, the society's inspectors in England found that the police tended to regard the enforcement of the cruelty laws as chiefly the concern of the society, rather than their own. In the late twentieth century such an expectation of a charity seems somewhat anomalous, but it continues, encouraged by a cost-conscious state, and inspectors and police are in some respects still mutually dependent. In the nineteenth century the society often recruited ex-policemen, and the police themselves occasionally would solicit assistance from RSPCA inspectors in the enforcement of law and order unrelated to the treatment of animals. Inspectors were based in London, but would travel around the country attending to complaints and information received. They were expected to be respectable and disciplined, although Colam was entirely opposed to 'the autocratic military style' which became more prominent after his retirement in 1905.

John Colam's greatest achievement seems to have been to preserve the society's social eminence while at the same time maintaining its campaigning vigour. 'Wily he certainly was', said the author Henry Salt (see chapter 8), but Colam's prudence was combined with strict adherence to principle, as, for example, in his steadfast objection to any infliction of pain in animal experiments. He could also show personal bravery and was sometimes in direct and vigorous action, as when he stopped a Spanish bull-fight staged in London in 1870 by personally jumping into the ring.

Colam not only edited the RSPCA's journal *Animal World*, he often conducted the society's prosecutions himself, and with great skill. Under his guidance, the RSPCA established a special relationship with government, giving advice which was usually heeded, and using its very high-level contacts to influence the introduction and implementation of legislation. Only when such tactics failed would the society use publicity as a means of pressure, but when it felt this was necessary it did not shrink from doing so.

Many radicals, then as now, called upon the RSPCA to take a more extreme line. But instead of treating them as enemies, Colam helped and encouraged them with their work and sometimes prompted them to establish independent organizations. Even Frances Power Cobbe, the formidable leader of the anti-vivisectionists (see below), has nothing but praise for Colam in her autobiography.

Perhaps the main criticism to be made of the RSPCA under Colam is that it failed to join forces with the new wave of thinkers on the subject. Nor did Colam's RSPCA attract the great social reformers as it had done earlier in the century, when it had received support from men like T. F. Buxton, Lord Ashley (later Shaftesbury) and even Jeremy Bentham (who had donated to it in 1831). As we have seen, the philosopher J. S. Mill, who had given money before Colam's appointment, also became alienated. By the end of the century the remarkable union of Utilitarian and Evangelical which had characterized its foundation had been lost; the more intellectual, and even more intelligent, among the animal reformers now chose to remain independent of the RSPCA.

The radical John Bright, although he signed several anti-vivisection 'memorials' and described humanity to animals as a 'great point'[8] had no real connection with the society. Lord Shaftesbury became disillusioned with it and so did Frances Power Cobbe. Charles Dickens, although opposed to animal experiments, never became actively involved with the RSPCA. Not even the campaigning Duchess of Hamilton (see chapter 8) in the Edwardian era was to support it, nor her colleague Louise Lind-af-Hageby. Towards the end of the century, few of the literary figures who sympathized with animals – Shaw, Salt, Galsworthy, Carroll, Browning or Ruskin, for example, were involved in any way with the RSPCA. Perhaps some of these writers were considered by the RSPCA to be too extreme; what Victorian worthy, after all, could take the poet Christina Rossetti (1830–94) seriously when she claimed:

> The tiniest living thing
> That soars on feathered wing,
> Or crawls among the long grass out of sight
> Has just as good a right
> To its appointed portion of delight
> As any King.[9]

Rossetti was not an activist in the movement, but, like so many other poets and writers of the age, she so easily might have been if the RSPCA had sought to enlist her services. Although the RSPCA owed much of influence to its aristocratic support and, above all, to the Queen, its preoccupation with established respectability caused it to lose touch with the more progressive and inspirational elements in the animal welfare movement.

For a time, this division among campaigners did not undermine the promotion of reform, but, when Lord Aberdare took over from Lord Harrowby as the society's president in 1878 and began to water down the RSPCA's opposition to vivisection, the split between the 'radicals' and the 'traditionalists' widened.

VIVISECTION

After the seventeenth-century fad for experimentation on living animals had died down, the practice had continued among a small fraternity of scientists. After William Harvey (see chapter 4) and the surgeon John Hunter came nineteenth-century physiologists like Charles Bell and Marshall Hall, who practised this approach. France, to a large extent, became the centre of vivisection, François Magendie (1783–1855) Claude Bernard (1813–78) and Louis Pasteur (1812–95) being three of its most prolific proponents. Magendie was, according to Claude Bernard, the founder of experimental physiology. He was, however, an experimenter in the hit-and-miss sense of the world, lacking the modern concern for precision and the control of variables. John Elliotson, afterwards professor of medicine at the University of London, attended some of his demonstrations in Paris and was appalled at the clumsy savagery of 'Dr Magendie, who cut living animals here and there with no definite object, but just to see what would happen'.[10] Magendie used huge numbers of animal subjects, including some old army horses who had survived Waterloo. An eye-witness account of one of Magendie's demonstrations brings home the unpleasantness of such work:

Magendie, alas! performed experiments in public, and sadly too often at the Collège de France. I remember once, amongst other instances, the case of a poor dog, the roots of whose spinal nerves he was about to expose. Twice did the dog, all bloody and mutilated, escape from his implacable knife; and twice did I see him put his forepaws around Magendie's neck and lick his face. I confess – laugh vivisectors if you please – that I could not bear this sight.[11]

There is no doubt that Magendie's callousness was outstanding even for the age he lived in, and shocked some of his contemporary physiologists. Even Hooke and Boyle had shrunk from experimenting upon the same animal twice 'because of the torture of the creature'.[12] John Elliotson wrote that 'In one of his [Magendie's] barbarous experiments, which, I am ashamed to say I witnessed, he began by coolly cutting out a large round piece from the back of a beautiful little puppy as he would from an apple dumpling.'[13]

All of Magendie's experiments, and nearly all of those carried out by his successors, including Claude Bernard, were of course without any form of anaesthesia or analgesia. Moreover, each of these experiments and demonstrations went on for some time and the agonies of the subjects must have been both intense and prolonged. We know from Claude Bernard that dogs were cut open in preparation 'an hour or more' before the actual demonstrations took place. We also know that they were not destroyed immediately afterwards, but if still alive were available for further operations by students.

Twenty years after Magendie's death Dr Francis Sibson (Consultant Physician at St Mary's Hospital) testified to the first royal commission investigating vivisection in 1876 that 'Magendie might have made his experiments with much greater consideration for his animals...I do not think that the idea entered his mind that he had a suffering being under him.' Another witness before the commission was Dr William Sharpey, who had also seen Magendie at work. 'He put the animals to death in a very painful way. The consequence was that I never went back to that course of demonstrations.'[14]

When Magendie died in 1855 he was succeeded in the chair of Experimental Physiology by Claude Bernard. Bernard had begun his medical studies in 1834, taking his degree in 1843. During these nine years he had studied under Magendie and in 1841 took up his first appoinment, as *préparateur* in Magendie's laboratory at the Collège de France. From an early stage in his training as a scientist, Bernard rejected the view common in France at the beginning of the century that the functioning of living organisms is determined in an entirely different way to that which determines inanimate matter: 'We therefore conclude, without hesitation, that the dualism between brute matter and living bodies, which is affirmed by the vitalist school, is entirely contrary to science itself. Throughout the whole domain of science, unity reigns.'[15] Bernard would not, like Descartes, have separated the human organism from the rest of creation. He was, however, entirely determined to ignore the sufferings of his subjects. He had no interest in the practice of medicine, in the healing of the sick or the comforting of the dying. For Bernard, a hospital training was a necessary step towards the medical laboratory, no more; research, and not the patient, was the priority. Indeed, he felt a slight contempt for the medical practitioner and the healer. Bernard's famous remark about biology suggests an extraordinary sense of purpose: 'If I were to look for a simile that would express my feelings about biological science, I should say that it was a superb salon resplendently lit, into which one may only enter by passing through a long and horrible kitchen.'[16]

If Bernard had ever had any feelings of compassion they had been soon dispelled:

The physiologist is not an ordinary man: he is a scientist, possessed and absorbed by the scientific idea that he pursues. He doesn't hear the cries of the animals, he does not see their flowing blood, he sees nothing but his idea, and is aware of nothing but organisms which conceal from him the problems he is wishing to resolve.

Dr George Hoggan worked under Bernard, and subsequently wrote to the *Morning Post* (2 February 1875):

We sacrificed daily from one to three dogs, besides rabbits and other animals, and after four years' experience I am of the opinion that not one of those experiments on animals was justified or necessary. The idea of the good of humanity was simply out of the question, and would be laughed at, the great aim being to keep up with, or get ahead of, one's contemporaries in science, even at the price of an incalculable amount of torture needlessly and iniquitously inflicted on the poor animals... I think the saddest sight I ever witnessed was when the dogs were brought up from the cellar to the laboratory... they seemed seized with horror as soon as they smelt the air of the place, divining, apparently their approaching fate. They would make friendly advances to each of the three or four persons present, and as far as eyes, ears and tail could make a mute appeal for mercy eloquent, they tried it in vain.

Like Descartes's wife, Bernard's, too, was fond of animals and detested her husband's work. After years of dissension she left him. During his last years, however, Bernard gained the fame and admiration he had always yearned for, and his example encouraged the setting up of animal research laboratories all over Europe.

The other outstanding Frenchman whose work contributed to France's reputation as the country of vivisection was Louis Pasteur (1822–95), whose life-long advocacy of germ-theory led him to experiment upon many animals, infecting them with various fevers, anthrax and rabies. His work on rabies was the subject of constant attack by anti-vivisectionists in the 1880s,[17] not only on grounds of cruelty but because it was claimed that his rabies vaccine was a danger to his patients. Indeed opposition to vaccination became closely associated with the anti-vivisection movement from this time until the First World War.

German scientists were also contributing to the new experimental physiology, but it was these three Frenchmen, François Magendie, Claude Bernard and Louis Pasteur, who were mainly responsible during the first eighty years of the last century for turning vivisection into an everyday scientific practice throughout much of Europe and America. They also ensured that it would become the outstanding animal welfare issue of the second half of the century.

ANTI-VIVISECTION AND FRANCES COBBE

In 1824, Magendie had visited London and provoked a considerable outcry after public demonstrations of his physiological experiments on rabbits, frogs, dogs and cats. A few months later, pioneering legislator Richard Martin raised the subject in the House of Commons (24 February and 11 March, 1825) on hearing that Magendie was planning a return visit. Magendie, although defended by Sir Robert Peel, seems to have had second thoughts about his lecture tour.

In 1846 the Reverend David Davis had petitioned the French authorities to suppress the practice of vivisection at the veterinary college at Alfort near Paris, but in 1857 reports reached the RSPCA that horrendous cruelties were being continued there and the society petitioned for an audience with the French emperor, which eventually took place in April 1861. The experiments, however, persisted. *The Times* of 8 August 1863 reported that 'At the Veterinary College of Alfort a wretched horse is periodically given up to a group of students to experimentalise upon. They tie him down and torture him for hours, the operations being graduated in such a manner that sixty and even more may be performed before death ensues.' These operations included dissection of eyes and viscera and the removal of hooves. British veterinary surgeons signed a mass protest and sections of the French press joined in the campaign for reform. Even the *British Medical Journal* attacked the French vivisectors. Indeed it went much further: 'It has never appeared clear to us that we are justified in destroying animals for mere experimental research under any circumstances; but now that we possess the means of removing sensation during experiments, the man who puts an animal to torture ought, in our opinion, to be prosecuted.'[18]

Among those members of the British public who felt revulsion at the Alfort revelations was the writer and welfare-worker, Frances Cobbe, destined to become the most doughty and effective anti-vivisectionist of the nineteenth century. Frances Power Cobbe (1822–1904) was born in the year that Richard Martin's Act was passed. The daughter of wealthy Anglo-Irish parents, at an early age she showed an independence of spirit by questioning and, for a time, rejecting the Evangelical religious conventions in which she had been instructed. In their place she developed her own personal brand of Christianity, addressing her prayers to the Unknown God and even to the 'possibility of God'. In 1855 she published a treatise on Kantian ethics entitled *Essay on the Theory of Infinitive Morals*. For a while she joined Mary Carpenter, the pioneer social worker, teaching children in the slums of Bristol. An injury to her ankle, however, put an end to this work after three years, and while temporarily crippled, Frances again took up writing.

Public opinion in Britain was profoundly shocked by the Alfort revelations. Frances Cobbe's contribution to the debate was an article 'The Rights of Man and the Claims of Brutes', published in the November issue of *Fraser's Magazine* (which was reprinted in *Studies Ethical and Social* two years later). The purpose of this essay was, she said, to find 'a definition of the limits of human rights over animals'. Although animals are 'subordinated' to mankind, Cobbe argued, we nevertheless have a duty to consider their pains and pleasures.

10 Members of the Oxford Group protest against an otter hunt in Buckinghamshire, June 1970. The philosophers Stanley Godlovitch (extreme left) and Roslind Godlovitch (second from right) were, with John Harris, the editors of *Animals Men and Morals* published in 1971. This was the first book written in the twentieth century devoted to a serious philosophical treatment of the ethical issues arising out of the human-animal relationship. The author (centre), who was a contributor to this book, continued to organise protests until the hunting of otters was suspended. It was finally made illegal to kill otters in England and Wales in 1978.

During the month that the article was published, Frances Cobbe travelled to Florence and there happened to hear of the activities of the physiologist Moritz Schiff. In particular she was impressed by the evidence of a Dr Appleton from Harvard Univesity who 'told us that he himself had gone over Professor Schiff's laboratory, and had seen dogs, pigeons, and other animals in a frightfully mangled and suffering state'.[19] Those in the neighbourhood of Schiff's laboratory had begun to complain about the disturbance caused by the 'cries and moans of the victims'. Frances Cobbe decided to channel this feeling into a 'Memorial' addressed to the professor, urging him to spare his animals as much pain as possible. The memorial was signed by 783 people, including many eminent and aristocratic Florentines. Among the English signatures was that of the author, Walter Savage Landor, who, according to Frances Cobbe, 'added some words so violent that I was obliged to suppress them'.[20] This document probably constitutes the first instance of organized opposition to the cruelty of vivisection. Although it had little immediate effect upon Schiff, it started a tradition of opposition to his laboratory which led ten years later to the formation of the Florentine Society for the Protection of Animals by Contessa Baldelli. The activity of this society and the continuing lawsuits and complaints against Schiff contributed to his eventual departure to Geneva in 1877.

Frances Cobbe had returned to her life as a professional and successful journalist in London. For another ten years after the Alfort affair and the memorial to Schiff, her main concern continued to be with the rights of human beings rather than animals. One cause on which she often wrote was that of women's rights; in 1862 she was scoffed at for advocating university places for women.

In response to the Alfort affair, the RSPCA offered a £50 prize for the best essay received on the subject of vivisection, with special reference to the question of its necessity. Two essayists, Dr Markham, physician to St Mary's Hospital, London, and Mr Fleming, veterinary surgeon to the Third Hussars, won prizes, and their essays recommending the use of anaesthetics in experiments, were published by the RSPCA in 1866.

Four years later, the British Association for the Advancement of Science published four recommended rules by which vivisection should be controlled: experiments should not be performed for the mere purpose of obtaining greater operative skill; they should always be performed by qualified experts properly equipped; they should be under the influence of anaesthetic wherever possible; and no demonstrations to an audience should ever involve the suffering of pain.

In 1874 the habits of French vivisectors once again caused an outcry in Britain. At a Congress of the British Medical Association held at Norwich, Eugène Magnan, an erstwhile pupil of Magendie, shocked some of his British medical colleagues by publicly operating on some dogs in order to demonstrate the effects of alcohol and absinthe which he injected into them. The meeting was abandoned after strenuous objections from two Irish scientists, Samuel Haughton and Jolliffe Tufnell. The RSPCA instituted proceedings against Magnan, and Sir William

Fergusson (Sergeant-Surgeon to the Queen), called as a witness, described the 'ghastly scene', the 'groaning of the dogs' and 'their writhing agony'.

The action brought by the RSPCA was under the amended form of Richard Martin's Act of 1822. Magnan swiftly withdrew to his own country and the prosecution failed. Nevertheless these events caused some important publicity, and it was in the ensuing public agitation that Frances Cobbe was once more drawn into the issue, on this occasion by personal contact with Mrs Luther Holden, the wife of a surgeon at St Bartholomew's Hospital in London. Frances Cobbe drew up another 'memorial' expressing general concern over the increasing number of experiments being performed in Britain, alluding to the Magnan affair in particular. This memorial was signed by seventy-eight medical practitioners, by many peers and bishops, and by such illustrious Victorians as Cardinal Manning, Lord Shaftesbury, W. E. H. Lecky, the Reverend B. Jowett, John Bright, Major-General Sir Garnet Wolseley, Thomas Carlyle, Alfred Tennyson, John Ruskin and Robert Browning. 'This I know', wrote the latter, 'I would rather submit to the worst of deaths as far as pain goes, than have a single dog or cat tortured on the pretence of sparing me a twinge or two.'[21]

It was while Frances Cobbe was working on her memorial, in June 1874, that the president of the RSPCA, Dudley Ryder, the second Earl of Harrowby, received a letter from Queen Victoria's private secretary expressing the Queen's concern over the treatment of animals in science and enclosing a donation to the society's funds. If the society needed any further encouragement, then here it was. This influential letter was a further indication of the Queen's heartfelt concern.

This was not to be the only occasion upon which the Queen recorded her disquiet on the issue of vivisection. Although unable, for constitutional reasons, openly to patronize a reform movement, she made sure that eminent scientists and her ministers knew her views on the subject. In 1875 she wrote to Joseph Lister, the eminent surgeon, asking him to oppose vivisection, and in March 1876 she urged her prime minister, an initially apathetic Disraeli, to legislate against it. In April of 1881 her secretary wrote to Gladstone, then prime minister:

The Queen has seen with pleasure that Mr. Gladstone takes an interest in that dreadful subject of vivisection, in which she has done all she could, and she earnestly hopes that Mr. Gladstone will take an opportunity of speaking strongly against a practice which is a disgrace to humanity and Christianity.[22]

It was probably such pressure from the Queen that persuaded home secretaries to administer the 1876 Act particularly vigorously in its early years.

The opinion of the ruler of the empire having been made known to the RSPCA, it was hardly surprising that the society was fairly well disposed to receive the advances made by Frances Cobbe and her friends. In January 1875 their memorial was presented to the council of the RSPCA under the chairmanship first of Prince Lucien Buonaparte, nephew of Napoleon, and subsequently of Lord Harrowby. A sub-committee was immediately appointed and the diligent John Colam set about collecting extensive evidence of painful experiments from accounts published in scientific journals. It was at this point that the letter from Claude Bernard's old student, Dr George Hoggan, appeared in the *Morning Post* of 1 February 1875 (see above, p. 107), making a further profound impact upon public opinion. When it came to decisive action, however, the RSPCA dithered. Richard Hutton, editor of the *Spectator*, accused the society of dragging its feet.[25] Prepared to delay no longer, Frances Cobbe joined forces with Hoggan and, with support from various parliamentarians and others, among them Robert Lowe (Home Secretary 1873−4) and Lord Chief Justice Coleridge, and with the approval of the government, a Bill for Regulating the Practice of Vivi-section was introduced into the House of Lords by Lord Henniker on 4 May 1875.

On the 12th of the same month, however, a weaker Bill was read in the House of Commons by Dr Lyon Playfair MP, instigated by scientists such as John Burdon Sanderson and T. H. Huxley, who wished to maintain almost complete freedom of research.

Because the two Bills were contradictory, the government decided to appoint a Royal Commission of Enquiry in June 1875 under the chair-manship of a vice-president of the RSPCA, Edward Cardwell. Another RSPCA vice-president who was appointed to the commission was W. E. Forster MP, and at least one of the other commissioners, the journalist Richard Hutton, also was known to be sympathetic to the animals. The scientific community was represented by Professors Eric Erichsen and T. H. Huxley.

Among the witnesses who testified before this commission were several eminent men of science, and, although some attempted to justify vivisection, it is striking that most seem to have expressed general concern over the unnecessary cruelties being perpetrated in animal laboratories. For example, Professor Henry Acland, FRS (Regius Pro-fessor of Medicine at Oxford University), spoke of 'experiments of a revolting and grave nature'. Sir William Fergusson, FRS (Sergeant-Surgeon to the Queen) was not impressed by the value of many experi-ments being performed; Dr Alfred Taylor, MD, FRS, cited 'purposeless cruelty'; Professor George Rolleston (Linacre Professor of Anatomy and Physiology at Oxford) warned that 'vivisection has special and distinctive liabilities and amenabilities to abuse; for it does act on our emotiono-motor nature in a particular way.' This last witness main-tained, in effect, that vivisection can sometimes liberate a blood-lust or a sadistic impulse, just as 'soldiers will tell you that the sight of blood upon the gauntlet, that white glove which Dragoon regiments wear, to use their plain language, "wakes up all the devil in them".'[24]

Even staunch supporters of the vivisection *status quo* in England were ready to admit in their evidence that things had gone too far in France. Professor J. Burdon-Sanderson, FRS (Professor of Human Physiology at University College, London), said that 'there are certain things done in connection with research, which ought not to be done on humanitarian grounds, if I may be excused for using the word'; and Dr John Anthony testified that some experimenters gave no thought for animals as sentient beings: 'the continual sight of animals being acted upon, particularly if the observer has any enthusiasm for the pursuit, in a very short time blinds the man's sense of humanity.'

The staunch supporters of experimentation did not do their cause much good. The honest answers of Dr Emanuel Klein, lecturer in histology at St Bartholomew's Hospital, disgusted even Huxley, and convinced the commissioners that there was indeed a strong case for legislation:

Question: When you say that you use [anaesthetics] for convenience's sake, do you mean that you have no regard at all for the suffering of the animals?
Klein: No regard at all.
Question: You are prepared to establish that as a principle which you approve?
Klein: I think that with regard to an experimenter, a man who conducts special research and performs an experiment, he has no time, so to speak, for thinking what will the animal feel or suffer. His only purpose is to perform the experiment, to learn as much as possible and to do it as quickly as possible.
Question: Then for your purpose you disregard entirely the question of the suffering of the animal in performing a painful experiment?
Klein: I do.[25]

This stunning exchange has reverberated down the decades, being frequently quoted as an example of scientific callousness, most recently in the House of Lords by the Earl of Selkirk a century later, during a debate on the Animals (Scientific Procedures) Bill on 12 December 1985. Klein went on to state that British physiologists had the same attitude as those on the Continent towards the suffering of animals, but that there was 'a great deal of difference' in the attitude of the British public compared with abroad.[26]

The commission duly reported (with a short minority report from Richard Hutton seeking to prohibit experiments on dogs and cats entirely) that a total ban on vivisection would be unreasonable, since such research sometimes mitigates human suffering and, furthermore, it would result in scientists emigrating to Europe, so producing no real benefit to animals. Nevertheless they found a case for state licensing both for original research and for teaching demonstrations. After the publication of the report, on 8 January 1876, both sides of the argument set about drafting new Bills.

Frances Cobbe, disappointed by the RSPCA's ineffectual response, had in the meanwhile founded, in November 1875, together with Dr George Hoggan and Richard Hutton (editor of the *Spectator*), her own anti-vivisection society. Originally named the Victoria Street Society, it eventually became the National Anti-Vivisection Society. Hutton shared Cobbe's disgust with the RSPCA, writing in the *Spectator*: 'If they do not show a little more courage and a little more zeal, some other Society will grow up in their place which, by boldly doing the work from which they shrink, will succeed in their popularity and influence.'[27] By 1884, the Victoria Street Society boasted more than a score of titled vice-presidents, including a duke, a duchess and three marquesses. It also had the support of nine bishops, several privy counsellors and MPs, Lord Chief Justice Coleridge, Cardinal Manning, Tennyson and Browning. The president of the new society was Anthony Ashley Cooper (1801–85), seventh Earl of Shaftesbury, the outstanding philanthropist of the age who had earlier been, for a short time, a supporter of Dr Playfair's rather pro-vivisection Bill. After a life-time spent in the service of his fellow humans, in old age he had, like Wilberforce before him, turned his attention to the welfare of dumb animals. By the time he became actively involved in the anti-vivisection cause he had already made major contributions to reforming the legislation dealing with the treatment of the insane, the conditions of the workers in mills and factories, the employment of children in mines and as chimney-sweeps, to measures to improve the housing and education of the poor. He wrote of vivisection: 'the thought of this diabolical system disturbs me night and day.' There is little doubt that his timely intervention in the cause did much to hasten the legislation controlling vivisection.

Shaftesbury several times chaired the meetings of the Victoria Street Society, and he led an important delegation from the society to see the Home Secretary on 20 March 1876. This deputation, which included Cardinal Manning, was favourably received and invited to submit suggestions for legislation. These were swiftly drafted into a Bill which was introduced into the Lords by the Colonial Secretary, the Earl of Carnarvon, and received its second reading on 22 May. Frances Cobbe wrote of this Bill:

No experiment whatever under any circumstances was permitted on a dog, cat, horse, ass or mule; nor any on any other animal except under conditions of complete anaesthesia, from beginning to end. The Bill included licences, but no certificates dispensing with the above provisions.[28]

11 *Peter Singer* (right) with the author in Oxford in 1980. A decade earlier, it was the Oxford Group (see page 00) which rekindled the international interest in animal rights with the publication of papers, leaflets such as Ryder's *Speciesism* (1970) and *Animals Men and Morals* (1971). Singer's review of the latter led to the publication of his classic *Animal Liberation* in 1975 which took to America the intellectual revival of interest in the subject.

The Bill received support from the RSPCA and had a good reception in the press. It proposed to implement all the recommendations of the royal commission (except that proposing an appeal procedure against the revocation of licences) and went further in several respects, including incorporating Hutton's minority report's recommendations. Unfortunately Lord Carnarvon was, at this juncture, called away from London because of his mother's serious illness (she died on 26 May). Despite a letter of condolence from the Queen referring to 'horrible, disgraceful and un-Christian vivisection' and urging Carnarvon to continue his work, Carnarvon was absent long enough to give the scientists an opportunity which they seized.[29]

THE CRUELTY TO ANIMALS ACT, 1876

The General Medical Council, armed with the signatures of some 3,000 members of the medical profession, hurriedly made representations to the Home Secretary, Richard Assheton Cross, petitioning him to modify the Bill. Lord Salisbury, later Prime Minister, gave his support to Professor Burdon-Sanderson and his allies, who now included Ernest Hart, editor of the *British Medical Journal*. The British Medical Association also supported the experimenters' lobby. Apparently this 'active maliginity of the scientific men', as Shaftesbury subsequently described it in a letter to Frances Cobbe, persuaded the hard-pressed Home Secretary to give way, despite a counter-deputation from the RSPCA led by its President, Lord Harrowby, and including the Bishop of Gloucester and Cardinal Manning. Harrowby, in uncharacteristically bellicose style, threatened that if the Bill was thrown out the RSPCA would 'kindle a flame of indignation against vivisection even in the remotest hamlets in this kingdom'.[30]

On 10 August Cross, the Home Secretary, introduced the new Bill, which received the royal assent only five days later. So was born the Cruelty to Animals Act of 1876 which, while making numerous worthy restrictions on animal experimentation, allowed nearly all those restrictions to be annulled by means of special certificates issued to experimenters by the Home Office. Its clumsy and inadequate form suggests, as Sir George Kekewich MP pointed out thirty years later, a rush-job hurried through an ill-attended Parliament at the end of a session. The reformers felt they had been cheated by this Act and with some cause, for it allowed the vivisector, now armed with licence and certificates, to continue to inflict severe pain upon his experimental animals.

The RSPCA, alternately blowing hot and cold, and by now thoroughly unpopular with the anti-vivisectionists in the Victoria Street Society, weakly criticized the new law as being a protection rather more for the scientist than for the animal and describing it as 'very unsatisfactory as a means for the discovery of offences'. In 1881, Cardinal Manning stated that the reformers had realized too late that they had been 'hoodwinked' by the Bill.

Further vain attempts were made to introduce more stringent legislation in every subsequent year till 1884 but, although no further reforms were achieved, the opposition to vivisection continued, not least in the old universities.

SCIENCE AND RELIGION

In some quarters science was viewed with suspicion in the nineteenth century. In literature, Dr Frankenstein had made a monster and Dr Jekyll had liberated the evil Mr Hyde.[31] Richard French has rightly asserted that the great controversy over vivisection was not only about cruelty to animals; it also reflected the tensions surrounding the roles of medicine and science in Victorian society: 'Victorian England was profoundly shaken by the emergence of science as a major influence and a leading institution. The concern was multidimensional: what was the appropriate cultural role for science, what were its religious implications and its institutional perquisites?'[32] French concludes that the Victorian anti-vivisection movement, half unconsciously, was protesting about the declining humanity of the medical profession and 'the cold, barren, alienation of a future dominated by the imperatives of techniques and expertise.'[33] This is surely true, but it should in no way detract from the role played by the spontaneous sense of compassion for the animals in the movement, which explains not only its fervour but the striking social heterogeneity of its membership.

If there is a political point to be made in considering the events of 1876 it is, as French puts it, that the politicians revealed an 'awe of science' and a deference towards it which resulted in 'a measure ultimately administered to protect experimental medicine rather than restrict it, under which research upon living animals prospered as never before.'[34]

Socially, it was a skirmish between the forces of science and religion. But it was also, to an extent, a battle between the old and the new elites; between, on one hand, the aristocracy and the Church, as the old leaders of society, and, on the other, the upstarts of science. The experimental approach in physiology, which came quite late to Britain, was to bring medicine into line with science. This was one of the aims of T. H. Huxley, James Paget and other leading pro-vivisectors. Their colleagues in France and Germany not only saw science as progress but as part of the new order challenging the traditional land-owning ruling class.

CONTROVERSY IN OXFORD

At Oxford, Charles Dodgson (Lewis Carroll) had joined in the controversy in 1875 by publishing an attack on vivisection in the *Fortnightly Review* which he entitled 'Some Popular Fallacies about Vivisection'. His biographer S. D. Collingwood records that:

Mr Dodgson had a peculiar horror of vivisection. I was once walking in Oxford with him when a certain well-known professor passed us. 'I am afraid that man vivisects' he said, in his gravest tone. Every year he used to get a friend to recommend him a list of suitable charities to which he should subscribe. Once the name of some Lost Dogs' Home appeared in this list. Before Mr. Dodgson sent his guinea he wrote to the secretary to ask whether the manager of the Home was in the habit of sending dogs that had to be killed to physiological laboratories for vivisection. The answer was in the negative, so the institution got the cheque. He did not, however, advocate the total abolition of vivisection − what reasonable man could ? − but he would have liked to see it much more carefully restricted by law.[35]

We will never know for certain who was the well-known professor that Dodgson passed in an Oxford street, but it may have been Burdon-Sanderson, who had been appointed Waynflete Professor of Physiology at Oxford in 1882. Burdon-Sanderson had been a keen supporter of vivisection when it was opposed in the Convocation of the University of London in 1874. Furthermore he was the editor of a *Handbook of the Physiological Laboratory* which had been discussed in some detail by the royal commission in 1875. It was admitted before the commission that the book contained descriptions of painful experiments and John Colam, secretary of the RSPCA, had pointed out that the Preface stated that the book was aimed at instructing beginners in research. The chairman of the commission had read from its descriptions of experiments on animals paralysed with curare: 'Rabbits...die before the end of the first day. Dogs live longer; often two or three days.' Burdon-Sanderson had been forced to confess to the commission that the use of anaesthetics whenever possible 'ought to have been stated much more distinctly at the beginning of his book'.

Burdon-Sanderson's appoinment of 1882 began a series of protests and arguments among Oxford scholars. The two chief supporters of the new professor were Sir Henry Acland, Regius Professor of Medicine from 1857 till 1894, and the Very Reverend Henry George Liddell, the Dean of Christ Church. The leading opponents of vivisection in Oxford became Charles Dodgson, John Ruskin and H. P. Liddon, the Bishop of Oxford, aided, later, by Bodley's Librarian E. B. Nicholson and Professor E. A. Freeman.

Charles Dodgson (1832−98) was not only the famous author of *Alice's Adventures in Wonderland* and *Through the Looking Glass*; he was also a mathematician, and it was on logical, rational grounds that he attacked vivisection. Collingwood records a letter he received from Dodgson dated 29 December 1891, in which Dodgson criticized an attempt by Collingwood to justify 'killing animals for the purpose of scientific recreations', not by commenting on his conclusions, but by shooting holes in the logic of the 'poor little essay'.[36] Earlier Dodgson had written to the *Pall Mall Gazette* on the subject: 'Is the anatomist, who can contemplate unmoved the agonies he is inflicting for no higher purpose than to gratify a scientific curiosity, or to illustrate some well-established truth, a being higher or lower in the scale of humanity, than the ignorant boor whose very soul would sicken at the horrid sight?' In 1875 Dodgson expressed his fear that a new breed of scientist was coming to the fore: 'a new and more hideous Frankenstein — a soulless being to whom science shall be all in all'.[37]

The interest that the subject aroused in Oxford can, perhaps, be gauged by the attendance at successive Convocations where grants were to be voted for the new professor. In 1883 the vivisectors were 88 against the anti-vivisectors' 85. In 1884 it was 188 to 147. Three years after Burdon-Sanderson had got his chair the arguments about granting funds for vivisection reached a climax. Dodgson noted in his diary for 10 March 1885: 'A great Convocation assembled in the theatre, about a proposed grant for physiology, opposed by many (I was one) who wished restrictions to be enacted as to the practice of vivisection for research. Liddon made an excellent speech against the grant, but it was carried by 412 to 244.' This result precipitated the most dramatic of all the anti-vivisection protests at Oxford: John Ruskin's resignation as Professor of Art.

Ruskin had been apointed Slade Professor of Art at Oxford University in 1869. On 9 December 1884, Bishop Liddon held a meeting of the new Oxford branch of the Victoria Street Society at which Professor Ruskin attacked vivisection. For him, he declared, the object of education was the teaching of gentleness to the students: 'their noblest efforts and energies should be set upon protecting the weak and informing the ignorant of things which might lead them to happiness, peace and light, and above all other things the relation existing between them and the lower creation in this life.' On 17 March 1885, a week after the university had voted further funds for the setting up and equipping of the phy-siology laboratory, Ruskin wrote in his diary: 'A lovely and delightful day, yesterday, getting Lilias' and Goodwin's sketches and doing quan-tities of good work myself, but put in a passion by Acland's speech on vivisection after dinner and slept ill, waking at two to think whether I would resign professorship on it.'[38] Five days later, on 22 March, the melancholic Ruskin resigned his chair. In his opinion vivisection experi-ments 'were all carried on in defiance of what had hitherto been held to be compassion and pity and of the great link which bound together the whole creation from its Maker to the lowest creature'.

It has been alleged that the Vice-Chancellor declined to read Ruskin's letter of resignation to Convocation as Ruskin had asked him to do, that the *University Gazette* refused to publish the reasons for his resignation and the rumour was deliberately put about that Ruskin had resigned on account of age.[39] It is clear that feelings were running high at Oxford over the vivisection issue. The principal antagonists had known each other for years and most had connections with the same college — Christ Church — where Dean Liddell's influence had for so long been paramount. Charles Dodgson's friendship with Liddell's daughter Alice had been part of the inspiration for his famous stories.[40]

THE REPERCUSSIONS OF THE 1876 ACT

One of the remarkable developments after the passage of the 1876 Act was the firmness of control exercised by the first two home secretaries responsible for its administration. The Conservative Richard Cross refused to license seven established scientists in three years, while the Liberal William Harcourt refused six in his first twelve months. They also refused certificates. Indeed the overall refusal rate was approximately 15 per cent of all applications, and was chiefly on two grounds — either that the proposed research involved too much pain or that it lacked 'utility'.[41] Yet prosecutions under the new Act proved difficult.

In 1881, the Victoria Street Society prosecuted Professor David Ferrier for allegedly experimenting upon the brains of two monkeys without a licence. In his defence, Ferrier successfully claimed that the operations were in fact carried out by a licensee, Professor Gerald Yeo, despite reports to the contrary in academic journals. The case brought together several scientists concerned to protect their right to vivisect, and in 1882 Yeo, Burdon-Sanderson, Sir William Gull, Sir James Paget, Joseph Lister, Sir William Jenner and others formed the Association for the Advancement of Medicine by Research. From 1882, when the Home Secretary, Sir William Harcourt, wrote to Jenner offering to avail himself of their advice, until 1913, the AAMR entered into a clandestine liaison with the Home Office which in effect allowed the scientists themselves to control the administration of the Act.[42] So began a long tradition of co-operation between government and vested interest which today is practically universal in this field. In America, too, the battalions of science united to block any further attempts by humanitarians to restrict their activities by legislation. Conscious and successful attempts were made to promote the image of the scientist as a heroic, even messianic figure. Governments, as well as many of the lay public, came to accept the view that the 'scientists knew best.'

THE PROTECTION OF BIRDS

Anti-vivisection, of course, was not the only great campaign of the animal welfare movement during Victoria's reign, although it created by far the greatest and most prolonged controversy. Some other campaigns resulted in measures to protect animals which seem to have slipped through almost without effort and with relatively little comment: examples are the general consolidating Prevention of Cruelty Act of 1849 and, much later, the Wild Animals in Captivity Protection Act of 1900. But an issue which was both prolonged and controversial was the crusade to protect birds, which began in mid-century, at a time when the bird populations all over Europe were coming under increasing attack from gun, lime and net. Slaughter had reached a new order of magnitude, so that sometimes the distinction between sportsman and poulterer became blurred. One such, the Marquess of Ripon, shot over half a million creatures in his life-time, including 112,598 partridge, 79,320 grouse and 222,976 pheasant. In England song-birds were being devoured by gourmets, and fashion designers decreed that ladies should be clad in feathers. Schoolboys robbed birds' nests, weekenders shot seagulls at the seaside and gamekeepers, anxious to destroy any threats to their employers' pheasants, killed almost anything that fluttered.

In the 1860s the shooting of sea birds for sport reached such proportions that sailors approaching the shores of Britain began complaining that they were no longer receiving their accustomed warnings of approaching land. Evidence that shipwrecks were on the increase was used to support such contentions, and in 1869 Christopher Sykes, MP for the East Riding, persuaded Parliament to pass the Sea Bird Protection Act, which protected sea birds during the nesting season but did not stem their mass slaughter at other times. Indeed the feather trade grew during the 1880s and 1890s, and the European and American millinery markets demanded the deaths of millions of birds worldwide – humming-birds, parrots, kingfishers, birds of paradise, herons, canaries and egrets. Ladies of fashion appeared in dresses covered entirely with plumage and on occasions, and much to the disgust of Bernard Shaw whose night at the opera was once ruined by it, wearing whole birds in their hair. Some three hundred million dead birds were imported into Europe each year in the 1880s, and about twenty-five million of them into Britain.

In 1889 Mrs W. Williamson of Didsbury founded the society which was to become the Royal Society for the Protection of Birds. One of its aims was to curb the trade in song-birds, and another was to stop the escalating destruction of birds caused by the proliferation of breech-loading and double-barrelled shotguns.

John Ruskin was among those who objected: 'Very earnestly I ask you, have English gentlemen, as a class, any other real object in their whole existence than killing birds?'[43] He was not alone in claiming that average 'experts' maimed almost as many birds as they killed. When Lord Walsingham in 1888 dispatched 1,070 grouse in fourteen hours and eighteen minutes, he used 1,510 cartridges. Could such a marksman have entirely missed with the unaccounted for 440 shots? After a shoot organized by the flashy Lord Burnham at Hall Barn in 1913, in which 4,000 pheasant were left in twitching heaps on the ground, King

12   Probably the first Prime Ministerial meeting at Downing Street with animal
welfarists, arranged by the Political Animal Lobby (PAL) in 1992.

Left to Right: Gloria and Brian Davies, John Major and
the author (then director of PAL).

George V remarked to the Duke of Windsor: 'Perhaps we went a little
too far today, David.'

Pigeon-shooting from traps had also become a popular sport in mid-
century and consisted of shooting at half-tame and sometimes blinded
pigeons released from boxes. In parks all over London, and especially at
Hurlingham, guns blazed as bets were made and well-dressed ladies
looked on admiringly. Under attack from *The Times* and lukewarm
disapproval from the RSPCA, this so-called sport flourished, despite a
Bill introduced by George Anderson MP in 1883. With the support of
Lord Randolph Churchill, who described the sport as 'the most horrible
and repulsive sight possible to imagine', the Bill passed the Commons
but failed in the Lords. It was only with the persistent support of Queen
Alexandra that the pigeon massacres at Hurlingham were eventually stopped
in 1906.[44]

WILD ANIMALS

Despite the great agitations to protect birds and laboratory and farm animals, wild animals remained largely untouched by Victorian reforms. Old ideas about the countryside and the unending war between 'man' and 'beast' persisted, tied up as they were with the ownership of land and the seemingly unassailable rights of the landed gentry to treat 'their' wildlife as they saw fit. It has been claimed that during the nineteenth century hostility to hunting was based mostly upon class envy,[45] but this was hardly true of E. A. Freeman, Professor of History at Oxford, whose articles in the *Fortnightly Review* in 1869 and 1870 on 'The Morality of Field Sports'[46] put the case very clearly. Freeman attacked the inconsistent attitudes, current then as now: 'To chase a calf or a donkey either till it is torn in pieces or till it sinks from weariness, would be scouted as a cruel act. Do the same to a deer and it is a noble and royal sport.' Freeman saw fox-hunting as no better than, and probably a little worse than, bull-baiting, asserting that it is wrong 'to inflict and to seek pleasure in inflicting, needless suffering'.

Far from fox-hunting fading away during the nineteenth century, the introduction of the railways and the popular tendency to emulate the gentry had helped to keep it very much alive. Organized opposition appears to have begun only when Henry Salt and Howard Williams founded the Humanitarian League in 1891 (see chapter 8).[47]

During the Victorian era the idea that humans had a duty of kindness towards nonhumans became generally established. Birds, farm animals and laboratory sentients had all benefited to a degree by the end of the century, and the growing exploitation of nonhumans had begun to be restricted by a small amount of red tape. The climate of opinion had changed decisively, albeit selectively, and much progress remained to be made.

8 Edwardian Vigour and Post-War Apathy, 1900–1960

The end of the nineteenth century and the succeeding Edwardian era in Britain was a time of intense activity by animal welfarists. Indeed the forty years up to 1914 represent the most vigorous period in the movement's history until then, comparable with the periods of about 1770–98 and 1822–54. All three periods were interrupted by wars which broke the momentum for a while. In general, influential writings heralded the practical and legislative advances. In the twentieth century, the Second World War succeeded the First World War before the movement could re-establish itself and, as we shall see in part II, it was only from about 1969 that it fully regained its momentum.

An analysis of Henry Salt's bibliography of 1894, for example, shows two major clusters of serious publications about animals rights: one in the last quarter of the eighteenth century preceding the Napoleonic wars, and the other at the end of the nineteenth century. The latter was to be extended by Salt's own writings, eight of which appeared before the end of the First World War. There is even a lesser cluster of publications between 1824 and 1846, just before the Crimean War. After outbreaks of war there are clear-cut gaps from 1798 to 1824 and from 1846 to 1873.[1]

The Edwardian phase of the movement was notable for the intellectual calibre of Henry Salt and his friends George Bernard Shaw and Sir George Greenwood. This was matched by the political enthusiasm of the first mass campaigning of the movement, organized in London by the Swedish ladies Louise Lind-af-Hageby and Leisa Schartau, supported by their British colleagues the Hon. Stephen Coleridge and Nina, Duchess of Hamilton.

THE INTELLECTUAL CONTRIBUTION: HENRY SALT AND FRIENDS

Henry Salt was an influential thinker and leading campaigner for animal rights; it is worth looking into the background and lives of such people in order to round out our picture of the period's developments. Henry was the son of an austere Indian Army Officer whom he rarely saw, and was reared largely in England by his mother and her relatives in Shrewsbury. He grew up as an outgoing and sensitive boy who enjoyed his sojourn at Eton and went on to take a First Class degree in Classics at Cambridge. He then returned to Eton as a master, but left after his advocacy of the poetry and philosophy of Percy Bysshe Shelley began to raise the eyebrows of the orthodox. After marrying Kate Joynes, the daughter of his old tutor at Eton, Henry decided to give up conventional upper-class life and to settle in rustic simplicity at Tilford in Surrey. Here the Salts proceeded to scratch a living from their vegetable garden and from Henry's writings.

Kate and Henry had become socialists, but, more importantly for them, they also developed their own philosophy of trying to live in harmony with nature, showing respect and compassion for all sentient creatures. Among their sources of inspiration were Henry Thoreau and Edward Carpenter. The latter, known affectionately as the 'Noble Savage', had abandoned an academic career to live the life of a shoemaker, overtly confessing his homosexuality. He became both friend and frequent visitor.

George Bernard Shaw was another early associate and shared with Kate a love of music; he wrote passionately against vivisection, bloodsports and meat-eating, describing the latter to Ellen Terry in the summer of 1900 as 'cannibalism'. In a society heavy with moral rectitude and hypocrisy, the Salts and their circle became an oasis of open-mindedness, rarely discussing politics, preferring to practise and communicate their ideals rather than campaigning to have them translated into legislation. Shaw wrote shortly before his death: 'We were Shelley-ans and Humanitarians...my pastime has been writing sermons in plays, sermons preaching what Salt practised.'[2]

Among Salt's many friends and admirers were George Meredith, John Galsworthy, G. K. Chesterton, Ralph Hodgson, W. H. Hudson, Ramsay Macdonald, Havelock Ellis, William Morris and Bertram Lloyd. For Carpenter's seventieth birthday in 1914, Salt composed a statement of humanitarian principles which was signed by, among others, Rabindranath Tagore, Bertrand Russell, H. G. Wells, G. M. Trevelyan, Prince Kropotkin, W. B. Yeats and Sidney and Beatrice Webb. This intellectual circle was widely influential in the development of modern social thought.

Socialism for Salt was not an end but a means, a way to 'love, beauty and humanity in our daily lives'. He lived to be disillusioned with the British Labour Party which, when in power, showed little interest in the humanitarian reforms that he yearned for. Salt's life was to a large extent a reaction against the pretensions and stoicism of Victorian society. He was part of an intellectual group which attacked the contemporary convention which equated compassion with weakness: 'The longer I live', said Galsworthy (referring to solitary confinement), 'the more constantly I notice that hatred of suffering, abhorrence of cruelty, is called sentiment by those who have never fathomed or truly envisaged the nature of that particular suffering or cruelty.'[3] Yet Salt undoubtedly had an influence upon events. For example, in 1890 he published *The Life of Henry David Thoreau* and in 1917 *David Henry Thoreau: A Centenary Essay*. Years later, Gandhi wrote to Salt from prison to tell him that he came to his policy of peaceful non-cooperation by reading these books. Salt may have played a part in persuading Ramsay Macdonald to invite Gandhi to England for the Round Table Conference in 1931, and Salt and Gandhi certainly met at this time and at Gandhi's suggestion.

Salt was a prolific author, although never a best-seller. Of some forty-six titles including revisions, four were poetry, two advocated vegetarianism, one was about socialism, two were classical, two were on wild flowers, six were on Shelley and ten were to do with the rights of animals. Indeed, animal rights was the subject on which Salt concentrated the largest number of his published works, although this fact has been rather overlooked by his biographers. He founded the Humanitarian League in 1891, yet Salt was not closely allied with most animal welfare campaigners of his era. Although of different generations, Cobbe and Salt were of the same social class, but incompatible politically; Cobbe does not mention him in her autobiography, nor do the two secretaries of the RSPCA who published accounts of animal welfare covering this period. As Salt noted sadly, zoophilists and socialists too often feared one another, and it would be another half-century before the political Left became fully part of the animal protection world.

The four members of the Humanitarian League who were most active politically in the animal rights cause were the Liberal MP George Greenwood, Ernest Bell the publisher, Edward Carpenter and the mystic Edward Maitland. For Salt, the word 'humanitarian' was defined to mean respect and kindness towards all sentient life. Humanitarianism, was not to be confused with philanthropy (love of mankind) nor with zoophily (kindness to animals). It embraced both. Salt fought and debunked the speciesist clichés of his age – the allegation against animal defenders that they were 'sentimental' and the claim that the 'instincts' of animals were entirely different from the 'reason' of men. He proclaimed 'the kinship of all sentient life', and in his sarcastically entitled autobiography, *Seventy Years Among Savages*, he castigated as barbarous and ignorant the attitude of his fellow men and women towards their nonhuman kin, reminding them in a jingle that:

> The motive that you'll find most strong,
> The simple rule, the short-and-long,
> For doing animals no wrong,
> Is this, *that you are one.*

For Salt, the 'creed of kinship' was the greatest religion, and he acknowledged Thoreau, Shelley and Bentham as its recent prophets and before them Seneca, Porphyry and Plutarch. In his major work, *Animals' Rights Considered in Relation to Social Progress*, published in 1894,[4] Salt cites such diverse authors as Humphry Primatt, the Reverend J. G. Wood and Schopenhauer. Salt approved the latter's horror at the English habit of referring to nonhuman animals as 'it', as if they were inanimate objects, and he politely chided Frances Cobbe for asserting that animals have 'no moral purpose'. Such ideas, said Salt, were purely arbitrary; sentience and individuality are what matter. This book was reprinted several times, sometimes with revisions, for the last time during Salt's life on the centenary of Martin's Act in 1922. This edition includes a letter from Thomas Hardy, dated 1910:

Few people seem to perceive fully as yet that the most far-reaching consequence of the establishment of the common origin of all species is ethical; that it logically involves a readjustment of altruistic morals, by enlarging, as a necessity of rightness, the application of what has been called 'The Golden Rule' from the area of mere mankind to that of the whole animal kingdom... While man was deemed to be a creation apart from all other creations, a secondary or tertiary morality was considered good enough to practise towards the 'inferior' races; but no person who reasons nowadays can escape the trying conclusion that this is not maintainable.

LITERARY TRENDS

The enthusiastic attitude of the 1890s is epitomized by the adventure stories of Ernest Seton-Thompson, in which the heroic content is combined with a serious concern for the many animal personalities who fill his pages. Writing in New York on the last day of the old century, Seton-Thompson had proclaimed his commitment to the underlying ethic:

A moral it would have been called in the last century. No doubt each different mind will find a moral to its taste, but I hope some will herein find emphasised a moral as old as Scripture – we and the beasts are kin. Man has nothing that the animals have not at least a vestige of, the animals have nothing that man does not in some degree share. Since, then, the animals are creatures with wants and feelings differing in degree only from our own, they surely have their rights. This fact, now beginning to be recognised by the Caucasian world, was first proclaimed by Moses and was emphasised by the Buddhist over 2,000 years ago.[5]

The literary co-operation between the British and American humane movements had reached a peak towards the end of the century. Ernest

Bell and Edith Carrington published in London in 1895 the stories written for the American Humane Education Society by Harriet Beecher Stowe and Mrs Fairchild Allen, under the title *The Animals on Strike*. Although the tone of the Humanitarian League's publications was indeed sometimes sentimental and anthropomorphic, the commitment to the animal rights ideal was strong and explicit.

Bell, who later became president of the Vegetarian Society, published several animal rights books of his own, among them *Fair Treatment for Animals* and *The Wider Sympathy*. He also published *The Animals' Friend*, a series of pamphlets for the Animals' Friend Society, many written by himself and some by other authors including Sir George Greenwood, Professor E. A. Freeman (a reprint of his famous essay *The Morality of Field Sport*), Jerome K. Jerome (*The Cruel Steel Trap*), Andrew Lang (*On Otter Hunting*) and John Galsworthy (*For Love of Beasts* and *Treatment of Animals*).

Beatrix Potter's anthropomorphic little stories at the start of the century rapidly became classics. Later in the century moralistic writers such as C. S. Lewis continued to use nonhuman animal characters to make their point (such as the lion, Aslan, in his Narnia stories). Hugh Lofting in *The Story of Dr Doolittle* of 1922 shows his hero as someone who not only can communicate with his nonhuman friends but who sets about righting the wrongs done to them. Later again, nonhumans would be depicted as morally superior to the humans, as in Erich Kästner's *Animal Conference* of 1955 and Robert O'Brien's *Mrs Frisby and the Rats of NIMH* of 1971.

Some of the most famous writers of their times are on record as concerned for the relationship between nonhumans and humans. D. H. Lawrence castigated himself for throwing a log at a snake: 'Immediately I regretted it. I thought how paltry, how vulgar, what a mean act! I despised myself and the voices of my accursed human education', and Albert Schweitzer wrote in 1923: 'until we have drawn the animal into our circle of happiness, there can be no world peace.' In discussing his motives for writing *Animal Farm*, George Orwell stated: 'Men exploit animals in much the same way as the rich exploit the proletariat.'[6]

The illustrated monthly magazine, *The Animals' Friend*, was started in 1894 under the aegis of Frances Cobbe's Victoria Street Society; its editor was Sidney Trist, who also edited a paper called *The Animals' Guardian* and, in 1913, a book of essays on animal cruelties entitled *The Under Dog*, to which he contributed the chapters on wounded war horses, pit ponies, vivisection and trapping. Trist repeatedly quoted John Ruskin's words drafted as a rule for the Society of St George: 'I will not kill nor hurt any living creature needlessly, nor destroy any beautiful thing; but will strive to save and comfort all gentle life, and perfect all natural beauty upon the earth.' Trist was a close colleague of Stephen Coleridge,[7] and it was Coleridge's two works, *Vivisection* published in 1917 and *Great Testimony* in 1918, which mark, together with Salt's last works, the end of the era.[8] While the horrors of the war turned the survivors' attention to rebuilding human society, the animal welfare movement sometimes made itself appear trivial. For example, a popular contemporary book for children, *The Law of Kindness*, addressed itself in mincing tones to the members of 'Dumb Animals' Leagues and Dicky-Bird Societies'. Adam and Charles Black brought out a series of 'animal autobiographies' in 1904 which continued in vogue during the war years; written by several authors, they told the life stories of a dog, a cat, a rat and several other animals, all narrated in the first person. C. H. Claudy's *Tell me Why Stories about Animals*, published in 1915, carried the whimsy to its extreme. The mud and blood of Flanders could not have been further removed from precious tales such as these. The stark contrast of reality at its most hellish with the cosy world of Edwardian nursery stories was, sadly, to leave the latter looking discredited. Many serious people could no longer take the subject seriously.

The RSPCA somewhat changed its public face during this period. Its monthly magazine, *Animal World,* so dignified in the 1880s and 1890s, gradually altered during the Edwardian years, growing smaller and less formal. The embossed portrait of the Queen on the cover gave way first to a Cecil Aldin picture of two puppies and then to a Harry Rountree one of a dozen ducklings, as the society's contingent of eighteen royal patrons of 1901 dwindled over the next generation until it had halved by the 1920s.

SIR GEORGE GREENWOOD AND THE 1911 ACT

Whether the criterion used is the number of new societies formed, the number of books published or the number of actions taken for libel, the Edwardian era was clearly a heyday for animal welfare. Its crowning achievement in England was the passage in 1911 of the Protection of Animals Act. From 1822 to 1835 British legislative attention had centred on baiting, from 1839 to 1854 on banning dogs used for draught, in the 1870s on the protection of birds and vivisection, and in 1887 it had been the turn of pit-ponies to receive very limited protection. From the end of the century onwards the pace had accelerated, with legislation being passed to protect captive wild animals in 1900, to ban the pole trap in 1904, to give some protection to stray dogs in 1908 (prohibiting their transfer by the police to laboratories), to stop the hooking of birds in 1908, and to restrict the transportation of horses in 1910 (strengthened in 1914).

Sir George Greenwood MP deserves the credit for the passage of the major legislation of 1911. Greenwood, a friend of Salt, was Liberal MP for Peterborough from 1906 till 1918, and the Bill was drafted by him and the Reverend W. E. Bowen. The latter was not opposed to hunting, and in order to avoid too much opposition to the Bill, its drafters exempted any ban on bloodsports. The Liberal Party had a majority in the House, a fact that aided the passage of the Bill.[9]

The Bill was introduced by Greenwood on 15 February 1911, and received its Second Reading without debate on 8 March. On 30 June Greenwood put forward, and the House approved, a number of amendments at its Third Reading, and the Act became law on 18 August. Besides raising the maximum fines for cruelty, the new Act consolidated the previous legislation, repealing the Cruelty to Animals Acts of 1849 and 1854, and defined 'animal' as 'any bird, beast, reptile or fish'. This rendered illegal the use of living fish as bait, the gutting of live eels and the scaling of live fish, as additional offences to those already on the statute book.

The desirability of all-party support for such measures led Greenwood to obtain assistance from Sir Frederick Banbury MP and Colonel Mark Lockwood MP (later Lord Lambourne), who were Conservatives, and from George Lansbury, the Labour MP, when in the same year he vainly attempted to legislate to improve slaughtering conditions. He was more successful, also in 1911, when, with the support of Keir Hardie MP and Harry Lauder, the famous comedian, he secured regulations under the Coal Mines Act to give greater protection to pit-ponies.

As early as 1906 Greenwood had tried unsuccessfuly to restrict the export of live horses to Belgium, and in 1910 he had introduced the Diseases of Animals Bill which achieved some control over the trade. This was after the well-publicized arrival at Antwerp from Hull of a ship which had encountered heavy storms on the way and in which thirty horses had died or had to have their throats cut at sea.

In the years 1912 and 1913, Greenwood, by this time a member of the RSPCA council, sought to widen the Geneva Convention to cover veterinary surgeons, in order to promote better care for wounded horses on the battlefield. He was also particularly concerned about animal experimentation and, besides supporting Louise Lind-af-Hageby's campaigns, he actively participated in the RSPCA's prosecution of Dr Warrington Yorke in 1913 for cruelty to a donkey left in a field in a suffering and 'mangled' state after experimental surgery. The charge was dismissed on the grounds that Dr Yorke was an experimenter licensed under the 1876 Act.

Greenwood was also responsible for a steady stream of Parliamentary questions on animal welfare, and he put the Home Office on its toes over the administration of the 1876 Act when, in 1915, he revealed that it had been delaying publication of the returns until the statutory six-month period for prosecutions had elapsed.

Throughout the First World War good work was done by the RSPCA and other societies to protect, as far as possible, the thousands of horses being used by the Allied armies. Special shelters and horse ambulances were supplied by the RSPCA and in 1915 the society's chief secretary, Captain E. G. Fairholme, received a temporary commission in the Royal Army Veterinary Corps. In France alone, 725,216 horses were treated by the corps during the course of the war.

BIG GAME AND LITTLE GAME

In 1914 the Humanitarian League published a collection of essays critical of bloodsports entitled *Killing for Sport,* edited by Salt and assisted by George Greenwood. In his preface, Shaw wrote provocatively:

I know many sportsmen; and none of them are ferocious. I know several humanitarians; and they are all ferocious. No book of sport breathes such a wrathful spirit as this book of humanity. No sportsman wants to kill the fox or the pheasant as I want to kill him when I see him doing it...Bloodsport affects me much as the murder of a human would affect me rather more than less; for just as the murder of a child is more shocking than the murder of an adult (because, I suppose, the child is so helpless and the breach of social faith therefore so unconscionable), the murder of an animal is an abuse of man's advantage over animals...[10]

It seemed to Shaw that the plea of the humanitarian had become a plea for widening the range of fellow feeling:

The time will come when a gentleman found amusing himself with a gun will feel as compromised as he does now when found amusing himself with a whip at the expense of a child...Surely the broad outlook and deepened consciousness which admits all living things to the commonwealth of fellow-feeling, and the appetite for fruitful activity and generous life which come with it, are better than this foolish doing of unamiable deeds by people who are not in the least unamiable.

Amusing himself with his gun was precisely what R. Gordon Cummings did in 1850 when he described wounding a large elephant in Africa. Instead of killing it at once, he proceeded to 'light a fire and make a cup of coffee. Having admired the stricken elephant for a considerable time he proceeded to 'make experiments'; that is to say he took pot shots at the wounded giant, observing the effects in a leisurely kind of way until the poor creature, with 'large tears' trickling from his eyes, eventually rolled over and died.[11]

The popularity of big-game hunting had increased during the nineteenth century and into the next. Yet the memoirs of big-game hunters began to reveal an ambivalence about their actions: on the one hand the burning desire to conquer and on the other their growing qualms of conscience – the eternal conflict between the lust for power and the equally innate twinges of compassion.

As I have suggested elsewhere, the motivation for hunting and shooting is both learned and innate. That some of its several components are almost certainly instinctive is hardly surprising for, until the last few thousand years, nearly all humankind has depended to a greater or lesser extent on such activities. But in modern times so many other factors also contribute to their popularity: the pleasures of adventure, of exercising a skill, of observing a tradition, of open-air exercise, and of congenial company. Yet most of these are pleasures which today can be found in alternative modern sports from rock-climbing to hang-gliding. Snobbery, too, can be indulged in other, less harmful ways. Yet there are three other more peculiar motives which lurk just below the surface. These are power, sex and machismo; one or several of these are often present as motives in bloodsports. By 'power' I mean natural self-assertiveness and aggressiveness, especially in the male which, when it is exaggerated by the *culture* so as to become a cult, I call 'machismo'. Anger is, of course, not the same, being an emotional reaction to frustration or insult which nevertheless makes it another common motive for violence towards nonhumans. Sadism, another but far more furtive motive for cruelty, is something different again, being the linking of the infliction of pain or dominance with sexual excitement. Maureen Duffy, controversially, has described the sexual parallels of the hunt in some detail; it has, she writes, 'like masturbation fantasies, two parts: the hunt and the kill; the build up and the orgasm'.[12] Hinting at some partly conscious sadistic feeling, Sir Henry Seton-Karr asked in 1904: 'Why is it, by the by, that the size and beauty of wild stags and other big game arouse in certain individuals this lust to kill?'[13] The same author, in *In Praise of Bloodsports* (1906), suggested that, anxious to cleanse himself of unmanly weakness, the hunter would find his sport 'a healthy natural antidote to the enervating refinements of modern life'. Captain J. T. Newall in his *Hog-Hunting in the East* (1867) revealed, in unguarded and pre-Freudian innocence: 'that was the first pig I ever dipped steel into, and I felt elated at flashing my maiden spear, though I had yet to learn the triumphant delight and rapture of taking a first one' (i.e. literally being the first hunter to draw blood).

Certainly, the language of love and that of hunting had for centuries been partly interchangeable, and lovers frequently might use hunting metaphors: 'Some Cupid kills with arrows, some with traps.'[14] It is also true that hunting and shooting boomed during a period of sexual repression in European society, and it is highly likely that these sports served, in many cases, as releases of libidinous tension. Yet sexual motivation, sadistic or more simple, is surely only one of several which account for the fascination of bloodsports.

At the turn of the century, the fierce discipline in British private schools was followed by a highly structured way of life for those born into the upper classes; not only was the sexual drive likely to be frustrated, so also was general self-assertion. Young Victorians and Edwardians, entering upon their careers, would have felt inhibited in many ways, and the one certain result of this frustration was anger — an anger which could not always be vented with gentlemanly propriety against one's own species. There is little doubt that this thwarted and displaced anger was sometimes discharged down the barrel of the big-game rifle or shotgun. Sir Robert Baden-Powell, the founder of the Boy Scouts, unashamedly illustrated this aggressive component in his *Pig-Sticking or Hog-Hunting* (1889), when he eulogized the sport as 'manly and tip-top', and offering 'a task of the brutal and most primitive of all hunts — namely the pursuit, with a good weapon in your hand, of an enemy whom you want to kill...you rush for blood with all the ecstasy of a fight to the death.' The death was, of course, only rarely the hunter's. Less passionately, bloodsports were also (and still are) motivated by the Victorian cult of machismo, by which I mean the high cultural evaluation of the so-called 'manly virtues'. Professor A. E. Freeman, writing in 1869, criticized this in the following terms:

the risk of these sports, and the supposed manliness of facing that risk, is generally put forth as one of their merits. Now I may be very blind and very mean-spirited, but the manly sport of foxhunting seems to me not to be manly at all, but to be at once cowardly and fool-hardy. It is cowardly as regards the cruelty practised on a victim which cannot defend himself by tormentors who, as far as the victim is concerned, are perfectly safe. It is fool-hardy as risking men's lives for no adequate cause. It is manly, it is something much better than manly, when a man sacrifices or risks his life in a good cause. But I can see nothing manly, nothing in any way praise-worthy, in a man risking his life in a bad cause or in no cause at all.[15]

Trophy-hunting also became an important component of blood-sports, and taxidermists were called upon to stuff especially large fish, notably 'gallant' foxes, or the heads of deer and moose. Tiger skins bedecked many a Victorian drawing room, and elephant's feet acted as umbrella-stands in the hall. A Victorian gentleman decorated his house with bits of slaughtered animals in much the same way that a latter-day athlete crowds his or her mantelpiece with cups and medals. Even favourite pets and horses were transformed post mortem into ashtrays, waste-paper bins, piano-covers or hat-racks, perhaps as part of the Victorian fascination with death. In many ways the camera was eventually to replace the gun in 'capturing' moments of the past and as a way to record achievements and adventures.

Henry Salt's Humanitarian League, founded in 1891, made the Royal Buck Hounds one of its early targets. This was an organization which hunted half-tame 'carted' deer and was ridiculed not only because its ribbon-bedecked quarry would sometimes wander into barns and railway stations, but also because of its following of obvious social climbers; hunting then, as now, attracted more than its fair share of those who imagined that such antics lent credibility to their social pretensions. According to Lord Randolph Churchill, the Royal Buck Hounds consisted of 'the counter-jumpers of London'.

In reply to a letter from the Reverend J. Stratton in 1891, Buckingham Palace replied that 'the Queen has been strongly opposed to stag-hunting for many years past.' It was not, however, until after her death that the Royal Buck Hounds were actually disbanded by King Edward VII.[16] Even then, the hunting of carted deer continued in other parts of the country.

The Humanitarian League also turned its attention to the hunting of hares with beagles, in particular to the beagles of Henry Salt's old school, Eton. The campaign was scarcely assisted by the RSPCA, whose ranks had been joined by the Headmaster and Provost of the school, both keen supporters of the sport. The Suffragettes, however, rushed to the hares' defence, protesting vehemently on hearing that quarries were sometimes pregnant. Twenty-four women, including Christabel Pankhurst, wrote to the headmaster in 1906:

It seems that the hunting of a creature so timorous and defenceless as the hare is at best but little calculated to foster those qualities of manliness and courage which it is so desirable to develop in the youth of our nation; but to hunt the female hare at a time when she is handicapped by the burden which Nature imposes on her would seem to be not merely contrary to the spirit of true sportsmanship but positively demoralising and degrading to all who consciously participate in it.

The RSPCA's record was one of inaction. In 1891 the Reverend J. Stratton complained that the RSPCA had never made a persistent stand against bloodsports, and in 1908 a motion passed at the society's AGM to campaign for the abolition of otter-hunting produced no further action. By 1926 the society had become so cautious that it actually refused a bequest of £10,000 which had been made conditional on its opposition to vivisection and bloodsports.

In 1924 two RSPCA rebels, Henry Amos and Ernest Bell, founded the League for the Prohibition of Cruel Sports (later to become the League Against Cruel Sports), and by 1927 some 500 members had joined. According to author Richard Thomas these were mostly 'disgruntled RSPCA supporters' dissatisfied by the RSPCA's failure to take a stand against the cruel sports of the upper classes. The League's early opposition was the *Shooting Times*, which extolled bloodsports as a bulwark against decadence. In 1930, after six years of propaganda from the League, worried bloodsportsmen joined together to set up the British Field Sports Society.

During the 1930s several up-and-coming Labour MPs voiced their support for the League's campaigns; Chuter Ede and Tom Williams were among them. When Labour came to power in 1945, however, despite the pleadings of Labour MP Anthony Greenwood, a fear of losing rural votes caused the Labour front bench to change its mind and in 1949 both Williams, then Minister of Agriculture, and Ede, then Home Secretary, voted against a Bill to ban hare-coursing and stag-hunting. This 'defection' by Labour MPs was a repetition of what had occurred in the case of vivisection twenty years before, and was to be repeated in 1986.

After an internal row, all too typical of the animal welfare scene, Bell, together with the League's president, the Hon. Stephen Coleridge, had resigned from the League in 1932 and set up the National Society for the Abolition of Cruel Sports. But neither organization achieved much progress. After the failure of the 1949 Bill and the disappointing recommendations of the Committee of Enquiry chaired by J. Scott-Henderson KC, which reported in favour of permitting coursing and hunting in 1951, both societies went through a lean decade.

The National Society for the Abolition of Cruel Sports enjoyed the support of distinguished people such as Bertrand Russell, J. B. Priestley and H. G. Wells in the 1930s and of Patrick Moore, Lord Soper and Iris Murdoch later. But, despite its respectability, it achieved little after the publication in 1965 of Patrick Moore's widely reviewed *Against Hunting*.[17]

ANIMALS FOR AMUSEMENT

One particular Edwardian anxiety was the condition of animals kept in zoos and circuses. Earlier, Charles Dickens had criticized the public feeding of live creatures to zoo animals – once a favourite spectator sport at the Tower menagerie and a practice which continued surreptitiously in the Regent's Park zoo which opened in 1829. By the end of the century, voices were being raised about the grim conditions of incarceration in traditional zoos and circuses.

Teaching animals to perform tricks had undergone a boom in the nineteenth century, owing largely to the growing public fascination with the 'sagacity' of animals. Unscrupulous showmen cynically cashed in on this friendly curiosity not with kindness but with hidden cruelty. Based on the age-old idea that wild animals, and especially dangerous ones, could only be trained by being 'broken', the circuses became schools of sadism, where animals were bound and beaten not only as punishment but merely to reduce them to psychological pulp. One of the most outstanding exponents of these techniques was the American lion-tamer Isaac van Amburgh, whose tools included the iron crowbar and the red-hot ramrod. Tigers, bears, monkeys, elephants and hyenas all succumbed to van Amburgh's persuasive methods. Any that would not cower with fear were dispatched. In his defence, van Amburgh quoted Genesis – man had been given dominion. 'The subduing of wild beasts, as men have learned from van Amburgh, is merely the result of merciless thrashing when they are young', stated *The Times* of 24 August 1869.

Towards the end of the century, trainers such as Carl Hagenbeck reacted against such cruel techniques and showed that the laborious use of rewards and kindness were, in skilful hands, just as effective. A campaign to give legal protection to performing animals gained some success in 1900 when the Cruelty to Wild Animals in Captivity Act was passed; this measure outlawed in Britain the abusing, infuriating and teasing of captive animals.

Conjurors also came under suspicion in the early part of the century. Rabbits and doves appeared and disappeared mysteriously, leading to understandable fears about their well-being. A Parliamentary Select Committee discovered that special collapsible canary cages were being sold which disappeared up the conjuror's sleeve when he waved his wand, unfortunately crushing the cannary in the process. The Performing Animals Defence League was founded in 1914, and in 1925 the Per-forming Animals (Regulation) Act was passed, which required the regis-tration of circus trainers and gave access into training areas for local authorities, but failed to prohibit the use of cruel appliances.

The RSPCA, as too often in its history, was hampered by individuals in its upper echelons who had a vested interest, in this case in the person of Lord Lonsdale, the president of Mills Circus, and the society was widely accused of dithering ineffectually on the side-lines on this issue.

A new form of entertainment using animals arrived after the First World War, namely the cinema. Early silent films showed confined crocodiles being slaughtered by gunfire, horses plunging over precipices or being felled by tripwires at full gallop, and lions and tigers in mortal combat. It is certainly easier to stop new abuses than to end established ones, and the RSPCA in this case did well to approach the newly appointed film censor in 1913.[18] After a long campaign Sir Robert Gower MP, the RSPCA chairman, enhanced the society's record by shepherding through Parliament in 1937 the Cinematograph Films (Animals) Act, prohibiting the production or exhibition of films involving cruelty to animals.

HUMANE SLAUGHTER

Seeking improvements in slaughter-house conditions was another great objective for humane campaigners. As we have seen, as early as 1835 Joseph Pease MP, a member of the RSPCA committee, had introduced the first humane controls over slaughter houses. These had had to be licensed since 1785, but after 1835 the licence could be revoked on evidence of cruelty and all horses and cattle had to be slaughtered within three days of arrival, being fed and watered in the interim period.

In 1901 a competition offering prizes for the invention of humane killers was announced in Germany, and a prize was awarded in 1903 to Hugo Heiss, who predicted the development of the 'captive bolt pistol'. The following year an Admiralty committee under the chairmanship of Arthur Lee MP recommended that all animals for slaughter should be stunned before blood was drawn. In 1906 Major Derriman, the new RSPCA secretary, designed a successful long-handled humane killer which fired a large-calibre soft-nosed bullet, and in 1911 this was followed by the introduction of German-made captive-bolt pistols which fired a steel bolt. A year later Christopher Cash and J. G. Accles improved the captive-bolt design and the RSPCA stepped up its long campaign to persuade reluctant slaughtermen to adopt these new techniques. The society was assisted by two eminent authors, John Galsworthy and Thomas Hardy, who wrote in support of the cause. Finally, in 1933, owing largely to the efforts of Sir Thomas Moore MP, the Slaughter of Animals Act was passed, requiring the pre-stunning of cattle. This protection would be completed when the Earl of Selkirk finally ` per-suaded the House of Lords to include pigs in the pre-stunning requirement of the Slaughter of Animals (Scotland) Act in 1949 and when, in 1954, the Slaughter Houses Act would extend protection to include animals slaughtered elsewhere than in a licensed slaughter house. With the major exception of ritual slaughter, which is still exempted from these humane requirements, animals slaughtered in Britain after this date have all, in theory, been rendered unconscious before being bled, although the findings of the government's Farm Animal Welfare Council in the 1980s would cast serious doubt on the efficacy of some of the techniques in use.

Why was there so much resistance to such an obvious reform? Why did it take half a century before slaughtermen on both sides of the Atlantic would accept the ways of mercy with good grace? The economic arguments surely were little more than pretexts. Was it not also that men inured to bloodshed can become curiously addicted to it – 'bloodied' and therefore an elite? Was inhumane slaughter not another instance of cruelty being confused with manliness?

VIVISECTION AGAIN

Lind-af-Hageby

In 1897 Frances Power Cobbe had approved the appointment of Stephen Coleridge as secretary of her National Anti-Vivisection Society. A driving character and the son of a Lord Chief Justice, Coleridge began to take a more moderate line than Cobbe's, calling for legislation that did not seek immediate prohibition. At a council meeting on 9 February

1898, Cobbe and her friends were defeated, and sadly left the society which they had founded. Later the same year Cobbe started a new body, the British Union for the Abolition of Vivisection. After she died in 1904 the union was to become dominated by a highly qualified medical man, Dr Walter Hadwen, who maintained its pure abolitionist stance.

Cobbe had never married and had shared forty years of her life with her close friend, the Welsh sculptress Mary Charlotte Lloyd. Shortly before Cobb died, she was visited by two young ladies from Sweden. Louise Lind-af-Hageby and Leisa Schartau had met at a ball in Stockholm where they had begun their life-long friendship; in so many ways, among them the intensity of their relationship with someone of the same sex, these two women were to carry on the lives of Cobbe and Lloyd.

In the year 1900 Schartau and Lind-af-Hageby had innocently visited the Pasteur Institute in Paris and been appalled by the ways in which animals were being used there. Back in Sweden, they had contacted the Swedish Anti-Vivisection League which had been founded by Adolf Nordvall and Princess Eugenie in 1882. They then resolved to register as medical students in England in order to prepare themselves for work as anti-vivisectionists, and for two years they attended lectures and demonstrations at King's and University Colleges in London. In 1903 they published a book, *The Shambles of Science*, giving details of what they had seen. It was a bombshell, receiving widespread attention and acclaim, including more than two hundred reviews in four months, and running to five editions before the First World War.

In the first edition of the book, Schartau and Lind-af-Hageby described the case of a brown dog who had been used for four separate procedures at University College, London, over several months in the years 1902 to 1903. An early reader of this description was Stephen Coleridge, who referred to the dog at a meeting in St James Hall in May 1903; in consequence, a libel action was brought against him by Dr W. M. Bayliss, one of the experimenters mentioned. Although it was admitted in court that regulations had been broken, the jury found Coleridge guilty of defamation and Bayliss was awarded £2,000 damages. Nevertheless, Coleridge's ordeal served to turn the spotlight once again upon vivisection, and press and public opinion veered to his support and that of the Swedish women.

Eighteen months later, in 1906, Lind-af-Hageby founded her own organization, the Animal Defence and Anti-Vivisection Society, and in the same year, the International Anti-Vivisection Council, with the consent of Battersea Council, erected a bronze statue of a dog in Battersea Park, with the following inscription:

In memory of the brown Terrier Dog done to death in the laboratories of University College in February 1903 after having endured vivisection extending over more than two months and having been handed over from one vivisector to another till death came to his release. Also in memory of the 232 dogs vivisected in the same place during the year 1902. Men and women of England: How long shall these things be?[19]

A year after it had been unveiled by the Mayor of Battersea, the bronze statue of the brown dog was damaged by medical students of University College. Summonses, angry meetings and further disturbances ensued. Pressure was brought on the Battersea Borough Council to have the statue removed or the inscription deleted; stalwartly they refused to do either.

Demonstrations were large and violent. On 10 December 1907 about a hundred medical students attempted to remove the memorial, and from five o'clock in the afternoon until midnight they were opposed by growing numbers of local citizens who successfully defended their statue. Finally, a large body of mounted police managed to disperse the mob, arresting ten demonstrators who were fined £5 each on the following day. Two days later a mob of about a thousand students and their supporters surged along the Strand shouting slogans in support of Professor Starling, the brown dog's chief tormentor. Medical students were joined by veterinary students in pro-vivisection demonstrations over the ensuing weeks, and some violently invaded a women's suffrage meeting in Paddington held by Millicent Fawcett, the leading Suffragette, as well as a meeting held by Miss Lind-af-Hageby in Acton. Although the London students failed to enlist much support from colleagues at Oxford and Cambridge, they continued to cause trouble for the hundreds of police detailed to guard the statue. Parliament, the Battersea Borough Council, and public opinion generally, sided with the brown dog.

Suddenly, in the spring of 1910, the statue disappeared, never to be seen again. A protest meeting in Trafalgar Square was attended by several thousand people including representatives of five trade unions, and was addressed by Lind-af-Hageby.[20] To some extent it had been a battle between the sexes and, more particularly, between machismo and feminism. Although the brown dog had gone, in the seven years since its death it had become a martyr and had gained more publicity for the humane anti-vivisection point of view than had ever been previously received. The speeches and meetings and the riots stimulated considerable discussion in the press, and the widespread popular reaction demonstrated once again that whenever the issue is clearly presented to the public, majority British opinion is overwhelmingly opposed to the infliction of unnecessary suffering in the name of science.

While all this was happening, and perhaps influenced by the widespread sympathy shown for the little brown dog, the second Royal Commission on Vivisection (1906–12) was sitting to consider the practice, and the administration of the law relating to it. The commission's main recommendations led to the attachment to licences of a 'pain condition' as well as the establishment of the Home Office's advisory committee on the administration of the 1876 Act.

The royal commission had heard some startling evidence from the Hon. Stephen Coleridge, who charged Home Office officials with 'having placed themselves in improper confidential relations with a private society composed of supporters of vivisection'. The society to which he alluded was the Association for the Advancement of Medicine by Research, founded in 1882 to protect the interests of vivisectors (see p. 120). Under cross-examination by the commission, the Home Office Chief Inspector, Mr Byrne, admitted that his department had been in continuous consultation with this organization, from which it had regularly accepted advice 'in regard to applicants for licences and certificates'. Stephen Coleridge had done some good detective work.

In 1909 two large international congresses were held in England; the first under the auspices of Lind-af-Hageby's society and the second organized by the World League Against Vivisection. The former advocated the gradualist approach supported by, among others, Sir George Kekewich, Stephen Coleridge, the theosophist and social reformer Annie Besant, the leading suffragette Charlotte Despard, the two women from Sweden and Henry Salt. The latter congress, notably under the influence of Dr Hadwen of the British Union for the Abolition of Vivisection, proposed nothing short of total and immediate abolition. This rift in the anti-vivisection movement sapped much of its energies until the outbreak of the Second World War, and may have been responsible for alienating some people from the cause.

Lind-af-Hageby's Animal Defence and Anti-Vivisection Society had maintained the aristocratic image; no fewer than 48 titled persons were vice-presidents of her society, in addition to half a dozen foreign princesses. The church appeared to be less involved, although over 50 MPs, including George Greenwood, were enlisted, and 175 members of the French Chamber of Deputies had pledged their support. The society was founded 'on the principle that the cause of humanity to animals is not a side-issue but a vital part of civilisation and social development', and was given considerable financial and moral support by Nina, Duchess of Hamilton. The Duke, for many years an invalid, was the premier peer of Scotland and both he and the Hamiltons' close friend, Admiral Lord Fisher, gave rather cautious public backing to the Duchess in her humanitarian efforts.

During the First World War the Animal Defence and Anti-Vivisection Society (later abbreviating its title to the Animal Defence Society) set up three veterinary hospitals for wounded and sick horses, and campaigned against chicken batteries, fur-trapping, cruelty to performing animals, bloodsports, the transportation of live animals and the use of pit-ponies in the coal mines. In 1909, and again in 1927, the society organized large and successful congresses in London, and for the 1927 one erected a £40,000 model abattoir at Letchworth to demonstrate humane slaughter techniques based in part on those they had observed in operation in Berne in 1922. In 1926 the three ladies tried to introduce humane killers into abattoirs in France. In 1928 the society held an exhibition in Geneva, which was attended by George Bernard Shaw. Later, the Duchess, together with Lind-af-Hageby and Schartau, established the Ferne Animal Sanctuary in Somerset at a country house belonging to the Hamilton family. All these activities were in addition to their main drive against vivisection. Throughout its history the majority of the society's active members were female, and by the early 1920s only one male, the vegetarian Howard Williams, remained on its executive council. Far from being embarrassed by this imbalance of the sexes, the society's journal on occasion emphasized it.[21]

Eminent Supporters

As we have seen, the cause of anti-vivisection has always been well supported by some of the most eminent men and women. In later nineteenth-century Britain, Tennyson and Carlyle (who were both vice-presidents of the National Anti-Vivisection Society), Browning, Bright, Ruskin, Cardinals Manning and Newman, as well as Shaftesbury, were all involved. In the early years of the twentieth century, writers as different from one another as John Galsworthy, Ouida, Thomas Hardy, Sarah Grand, Marie Corelli and Colette expressed their conviction that kindness to others should mean kindness to all sentient creatures, not only to our fellow men and women. Artists and actors such as Sir Edward Burne-Jones and Sir Henry Irving concurred, and Walter Crane designed and presented to Hageby's society a dramatic frontispiece for its journal depicting a knight in armour, shield emblazoned with the words 'The Rights of Animals', defending some frightened dogs from the grasping hand of a cloven-hooved vivisector, which was used from 1912 onwards.

A few medical people, such as Walter Hadwen, dared to follow Dr George Hoggan in voicing open criticisms of the system; yet to do so at that time was to court censure from the profession. Even Sir William Fergusson, FRS, Sergeant-Surgeon to Queen Victoria and president of the British Medical Association, had been posthumously denigrated for questioning the validity of much of the animal research that was being performed a generation earlier.[22] One surgeon who had continued to support Fergusson's point of view was Robert Lawson Tait (1845–99), a well-known specialist of his day, a pioneer of aseptic methods and several new and successful techniques in abdominal surgery.[23] His independence of mind enabled him to question contemporary ortho-doxies and he was closely associated with the movement to allow women admission to the medical profession on equal terms with men. He outspokenly opposed vivisection on four grounds – moral, political, religious and scientific.[24] He respected the moral view 'that we have no right to inflict sufferings on others that we ourselves may benefit'. After the turn of the century one voice in particular joined in eloquently on the side of the laboratory animals. Shaw, in his *May Lectures,* in the preface to his play *The Doctor's Dilemma,* and in his *The Adventures of the Black Girl in Her Search for God* puts the humanitarian argument very strongly. His earliest brush with the vivisectionists appears to have been when, with jocular gallantry, he attacked Professor Sir Victor Horsley for calling Frances Cobbe a liar: 'I at once took the field against Horsley. "The question at issue", I said, "is not whether Miss Cobbe is a liar, but whether you as a vivisector are a scoundrel." Horsley's breath was taken away. He refused to debate what seemed to him a monstrous insult.'[25]

In 1927 Shaw's old friend H. G. Wells wrote a defence of vivisection in the *Sunday Express.* Wells, to his eternal discredit, put forward the old cliché that because vivisection was not, in his opinion, the greatest cruelty inflicted by mankind, it was thus justified − the 'two-wrongs-can-make-a-right' argument. Shaw replied in the *Sunday Express* of 27 August 1927:

But Mr Wells has another shot in his locker...'There is a residuum of admittedly painful cases, but it is an amount of suffering infinitesimal in comparison with the gross aggregate of pain inflicted day by day upon sentient creatures by mankind.'

This defence fits every possible crime from pitch-and-toss to manslaughter. Its disadvantage is that it is not plausible enough to impose on the simplest village constable. Even Landru, and the husband of the brides in the bath, though in desperate peril of the guillotine and gallows, had not the effrontery to say: 'It is true that we made our livelihood by marrying women and burning them in the stove or drowning them in the bath when we had spent their money; and we admit frankly and handsomely that the process may have involved some pain and disillusionment for them; but their sufferings (if any) were infinitesimal in comparison with the gross aggregate of pain inflicted day by day upon sentient creatures by mankind.' Landru and Smith knew what Wells forgot: that scoundrels who have no better defence than that have no defence at all...

Between the wars, other men of letters were to join Shaw in attacking the practice of experimenting on animals. Prominent among these was John Cowper Powys, who made the subject central to his novel *Morwyn or The Vengeance of God.*

The Changing Social Climate: Feminism, Socialism and Sentiment

Stephen Coleridge's doughtiest adversary was Stephen Paget, the secretary of the Association for the Advancement of Medicine by Research.

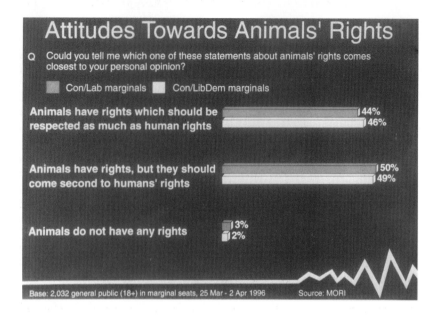

Attitudes Towards Animals' Rights

Q   Could you tell me which one of these statements about animals' rights comes closest to your personal opinion?

■ Con/Lab marginals   ■ Con/LibDem marginals

Animals have rights which should be respected as much as human rights
44%
46%

Animals have rights, but they should come second to humans' rights
50%
49%

Animals do not have any rights
3%
2%

Base: 2,032 general public (18+) in marginal seats, 25 Mar - 2 Apr 1996   Source: MORI

13 *Opinion Polls* indicate that animal welfare enjoys massive and international public support. British adult opinion, as measured by MORI in 1996, is even overwhelmingly in support of the concept that animals have *rights*. Indeed, less than 3% were found to disagree with this proposition and, even more remarkably, about 45% considered that animals have rights which should be respected as much as human rights. These results are despite a sustained campaign by vested interests to create an artificial distinction between "animal welfare" and "animal rights" and to castigate the latter as an extreme minority view.

The proposal that rights be given to animals is frequently opposed by the argument that animals cannot have rights because they can observe no duties. This strange doctrine, if true, would also deny rights to many invalids, children and the severely handicapped.

The dislike of the word "rights", probably due partly to the historic reason that it was used by American and French revolutionaries in the eighteenth century, has led to a misunderstanding of the Rights Theory position, portraying it as invariably fanatical and opposed to gradual reform. There has also been some muddle about the word "rights" itself with opponents confusing passive with active rights, and legal with moral rights. What most campaigners mean by "animal rights" is simply a far greater respect for individual animals and for their moral right not to be caused pain.

Since the publication of Paget's *Experiments on Animals* in 1900, the vivisectors had appeared increasingly the more rational in comparison with their opponents. Gradually the image of science had improved, as knowledge derived from animal experimentation was accumulated and applied.

Since the 1880s scientists had tried to smear the anti-vivisection movement, and eventually the mud began to stick.[26] Paget denounced the anti-vivisectionists as quarrelsome and ineffective, while portraying the scientists as serious and high-minded.

The Victoria Street Society had long dominated the anti-vivisection movement; while Frances Cobbe was in command she had taken pains to keep out extremists like the visionary Anna Kingsford (see p. 168–9) and had been overtly hostile towards vegetarianism. Just as Martin's and Erskine's robust personalities had given the campaign credibility many years earlier, so had Cobbe's at the end of the century. Futhermore, Cobbe's formidable character had also prevented the infiltration of the Victoria Street Society by vivisectors – a fate which had befallen French and German animal protection societies in the 1880s. Whereas in Germany scientists were venerated in the late nineteenth century, in Britain the aristocracy were still the leaders of society and it was they who had decorated the letterheads of Victorian and Edwardian anti-vivisectionism.

The emergence of socialism in Britain after the 1914–18 war was to be a further disappointment to anti-vivisection and to animal protection generally. Although Salt, Shaw and Carpenter saw animal protection and socialism as part of the same humanitarian movement, the leaders of the new Labour party, once in power, were not interested. Carpenter in 1895 could portray animal experimentation 'as the irrelevant and cruel means by which capitalists sought to cure diseases resulting from their own firms' pollution and disruption of the human environment'.[27] In 1909 Sir George Kekewich could enthuse: 'A new party, the Labour Party, has arisen in Parliament; and every member of that party is on our side.' Indeed, four future Labour cabinet ministers – Ramsay Macdonald, Philip Snowden, Arthur Henderson and J. R. Clynes had attended the World League Against Vivisection Congress in the same year. But when these men came to office twenty years later in the first Labour government, they did nothing to honour their pledge to help nonhuman animals. The British working class had not yet taken animal protection to its bosom, and far from seeing nonhumans as an exploited proletariat they tended to view them as a preoccupation of the sentimental rich. This situation was only to change in Britain in the 1970s.

Another feature of the late Victorian and Edwardian scene was that animal protection had become associated in the public mind with the campaigns of women rather than men; after the departures of men like Shaftesbury and Colam the public stage had been left chiefly to the female sex. Five of the major 'stars' of the movement were Cobbe,

Kingsford, Lind-af-Hageby, Schartau and the Duchess of Hamilton; only one of the principal parts was played by a male — Stephen Coleridge. For Cobbe and Kingsford the anti-vivisection campaign was consciously recognized as having the subsidiary aim of improving the social and political position of women, but by cleverly associating her feminism with an aura of respectability and moral conservatism, Cobbe had made it harder for her opponents to discredit her. After she was gone it was easier to play upon male prejudice and to portray the concern for animal welfare as being womanly. The French physiologist Elie de Cyon had gone further in insinuating that involvement in animal welfare was an outlet for frustrated 'old maids'; in Catholic countries such spinsters took to convents, he said, but in Protestant societies they directed their 'disordered minds' towards anti-vivisection. In the first few decades of the century, the divisions within the now predominantly female movement had given it a reputation for 'hysteria', and the cause lacked intellectual and practical leaders to refute the contemporary charge of 'sentimentality'.

While anti-vivisection was the most public and publicized element of the animal protection cause, other elements had made quieter but more solid progress. Trist's book on cruelties to animals of 1913, one of the first to be assisted by the use of horrific photographs, could recount undeniable achievements in the campaigns against the feather trade, the export of worn-out horses, the use of the bearing-rein and the treatment of pit-ponies.

STAGNATION: THE MID-TWENTIETH CENTURY

After the carnage of the First World War the movement seemed to stagnate. In the stunned silence following the last barrage of the war, survivors turned their attention to the welfare of their own species. The animal welfare organizations, dominated by middle-class women, continued their good work, but without the mass support which they had enjoyed before the war. To some of those who had endured the Somme they began to appear faintly ridiculous. The few effective campaigners who remained took great pains to appear moderate and sensible, striving to restrict rather than to prohibit the cruelties they opposed. The Second World War was a further setback and it seems that the period from the mid-1920s until the 1960s represents a gap in the progress of the movement.

In 1926 Major C. W. Hume MC founded the University of London Animal Welfare Society, which later became, more simply, the Universities Federation for Animal Welfare. It was a product typical of the post-war era in its almost fanatical determination not to be fanatical. Hume wrote: 'UFAW helps to compensate the harm done to the cause of animal welfare by animal-lovers of the unbalanced kind, and to form an intelligently humane body of public opinion.'[28] So anxious was he to appear reasonable that on occasions the federation seemed more cerebral than practical. Membership of the Universities Federation for Animal Welfare was limited to those with a university training, and any discussion of animal experimentation was prohibited at its meetings. It was decreed that its approach had to be 'with a maximum of sympathy but a minimum of sentimentality': instead of seeking to ban whaling it initiated scientific experiments with the aim of making whaling more humane; instead of trying to outlaw the fur trade it issued a 'white list' of furs obtained by allegedly ethical means; it researched into less painful methods of killing unwanted domestic pets; and instead of urging a ban on experiments it published a detailed handbook on the care of laboratory animals.

The federation's greatest achievement, however, was its thirty-year campaign to prohibit the use of the leghold gin trap in Britain. In 1935 Viscount Tredegar introduced a Bill to ban steel-toothed leghold traps of this type, reminding the House of Lords that such devices for catching human beings had been banned in 1827. The federation estimated that 1,800,000 birds, 124,000 cats and 35,000,000 rabbits were being caught annually in gin traps, as well as other animals including farm livestock. The Bill was, however, successfully opposed by the British Field Sports Society, and another world war intervened before the Parliamentary Scott-Henderson Committee of 1949, describing it as 'a diabolical instrument which causes an incalculable amount of suffering', encouraged the gin trap's eventual demise under a 1958 amendment to the Pests Act of 1954.

Although much credit must go to Hume for this achievement, and to his colleagues such as Dr Jean Vinter, their argument that the best way to abolish gins was through the promotion of poison gas and other methods as alternative ways of killing rabbits, was unheeded at the time and strikes the modern campaigner as repugnant. At the same time as the federation's members were advocating such tactics, other university scientists in Britain were perfecting the rabbit plague, myxomatosis, which was deliberately introduced in Australia and Europe in the early 1950s, causing horrifying deaths for countless millions of animals. Sightless, swollen and almost hairless, rabbits battered themselves against walls, and corpses littered the roads and fields all over England. With the approval of Winston Churchill, the government agreed to Dr Horace King's demand that the deliberate spreading of this disease be outlawed and the Pests Act was duly amended.

Bodies similar to the Universities Federation for Animal Welfare were established in Germany by Dr Wiema von During and in America by Dr Robert Gesell. Throughout the Western world, however, the forty years after 1918 were a barren period in the evolution of the animal rights ethic; basic speciesism was accepted as common-sense necessity and dissent was dismissed as eccentricity. In Britain, the RSPCA ticked over inoffensively, rescuing, homing and killing thousands of unwanted animals each year, raising money to pay the salaries of two hundred or so uniformed inspectors, cautiously prosecuting only the most flagrant cases of cruelty, and avoiding controversy. Gradually the society had lost its sense of urgency and settled for the status quo. After John Colam retired in 1905, he was followed by stalwarts such as Captain Edward Fairholme and Arthur Moss; loyal dependable men but lacking the drive and initiative of the true reformer. Although as late as 1924 Edward Fairholme and Wellesley Pain's historical account of the society was graced with a foreword from Edward, Prince of Wales, the link with royalty had faded away gradually after Queen Victoria's death in 1901. At the same time the large numbers of aristocrats on the RSPCA council, conservative but often sophisticated in outlook, had slowly given way to the even more conservative middle classes whose less secure social positions sometimes made them even less prepared than the upper classes to criticize the cruel habits of professionals or gentry. With a few exceptions, such as its pre-war chairman Lord Lambourne (Colonel Mark Lockwood), who died in 1928, and Sir Robert Gower MP, the RSPCA came to lack figures of stature. Gower's successful introduction of a Bill banning rodeos in 1934 and the Cinematograph Films (Animals) Act of 1937, prohibiting cruelty to animals in filming, were among the society's few innovative achievements of the period. The RSPCA maintained its position as a household word, but it was no longer peopled by those in positions of great influence; what potential for reform it retained remained under-utilized and, for some, its un-doubted respectability had become an end in itself.

Not only the RSPCA but the whole animal welfare campaign had become bureaucratized; this gave it some durability but restricted its movement forward. What few sparks of inspiration there were came from independent individuals rather than from the organizations: Dr Harry Lillie of Dundee, for example, studiously avoided committees of any sort and, working on his own, used modern technology in the form of a motion picture camera to bring to restricted audiences in the 1950s and 1960s horrific evidence of the cruelties inherent in whaling, trapping, the killing of seals in Canada and the use of animals in research. Lillie's pioneering work sowed the seeds for the rejuvenated campaigns of the 1970s. Through his agency hundreds, rather than a handful, saw the protracted sufferings of whales impaled by explosive harpoons, the clubbing of baby Harp seals and the agonized day-long deaths of animals trapped in the fur trade.

Air Chief Marshall Lord Dowding, too, continued doggedly through-out the apathetic 1950s and early 1960s to plead the animals' cause in speech after speech on twenty-seven separate occasions in the House of Lords. As the man whose policies had saved the country in the Battle of

Britain in 1940 he was given a hearing but little more. His interest in spiritualism unfairly helped his opponents to stereotype him as an eccentric. As we shall see in later chapters, his wife, Muriel, made significant progress in these unsympathetic years by setting up the Beauty Without Cruelty organization and in her direction of the National Anti-Vivisection Society.

What a strange era it was; moving from the sense of progress and confidence of the late Victorian and Edwardian periods through the First World War to stagnation beyond the Second. As far as humankind's attitude towards nonhumans was concerned it saw a transition in Northern Europe from strong sentiment and idealism to excessive caution, practicality and a decline in serious interest.

9 Why Britain? Pain, Evolution and Security

Why did the Victorians lead the way in restraining humankind's exploitation of the other species? Why did the pressure for reform happen when it did?

This chapter considers various possible answers to these questions, looking at the changing attitudes towards pain, the increasing sense of kinship culminating in the theory of evolution, and in social changes which may have given humans the confidence to be magnanimous towards nonhumans. We shall also consider the development of scientific psychology at the end of the century.

THE INDUSTRIAL REVOLUTION

One idea put forward, for example by James Turner, is that Britain's 'urbanisation and industrialisation in some way helped to generate the new concern for beasts'.[1] Up to a point this may be true, for both processes (in which Britain led the rest of the world) certainly removed humans, to an extent, from direct and visible economic dependence upon nonhumans and allowed people to mature in the absence of the sort of desensitizing subculture typical of a rural community which is committed to speciesist exploitation; subcultures which surely train most children to suppress their natural sympathies for nonhumans. Yet it must be remembered that some of the worst cruelties towards nonhumans in Victorian Britain were inflicted by urban-dwellers in the pursuit of objects that were neither agricultural nor sporting: vivisection, the fashion industry and the daily abuse of horses are three major examples. Furthermore, although the animal welfare movement in America was largely an urban phenomenon, in Britain this was not so true; many of the movement's leaders, for instance, were country clergymen or landowners (admittedly often with business in London) such as Martin, Shaftesbury and Lawrence; indeed the industrial middle class played little part in the British animal welfare crusade.

Turner, even more contentiously, argues that it was the incompatibility of bloodsports with the new system of regular and longer working days in the factory that determined the change in attitudes. Certainly there were some mill-owners and other employers who disapproved of sports such as bull-baiting because they could 'affect the regular progress of working and carrying on the Mines and Manufactures of the county',[2] but the importance of this factor was not paramount, nor was the loss of some large open spaces suitable for bull-baiting of any real significance, as Turner alleges was the case,[3] for many other spaces remained available.

QUEEN VICTORIA

It has often been said that the Englishman's dream is to be a country gentleman, and it is certainly true that by the early twentieth century, caricatures of the English would include three features explicable in terms of such an aspiration – a love of gardening, an obsession with the weather and an enthusiasm for keeping animals. Paradoxically, whereas some cruelties (such as bloodsports) were encouraged by this dream, others (such as vivisection) almost certainly were not, and it is still common to find fox-hunters and factory-farmers who are passionately opposed to animal experiments. But above all it was the role played by the RSPCA, and the Queen's patronage from the 1830s onwards, which influenced the attitudes of the established and aspiring upper classes in Britain. Increased wealth meant that more were looking to their social superiors for models of behaviour, and among these they found the new sense of duty towards animals. Unlike France, where revolutionary changes had undermined the influence of royalty, nobility and Church, Britain was still an upward-looking society in which academics were not the unchallenged leaders of opinion.[4]

Indeed, it can be said that animal welfare had become a British upper-class preoccupation by mid-century. As well as commanding some respect from all sections of society, this gave animal welfarists access to the political establishment. Were the upper classes merely emulating the Queen? Probably to a large extent they were. It was known that she had written to scientists and statesmen condemning vivisection (see p. 111), and in her Jubilee address of 1887, in commenting on the spread of enlightenment among her subjects, she noted in particular 'with real pleasure, the growth of more humane feelings towards the lower animals'.[5] This was not mere lip-service – it was real commitment on her part.

But was not the growing interest in animal protection also an effect of the increasing stability of society and the extension of affluence? Never before had so many felt economically and socially secure. They could afford to show some compassion for the underprivileged, both human and nonhuman. Moreover, there was no longer the feeling that they ought to prove their superiority over the brute creation, for the latter

	BASIC CRITERION IS PAIN	SOME INDIVIDUAL TRADE-OFFS ALLOWED	AGGREGATION OF PAIN/ PLEASURE AMONG MANY	AGAINST SPECIESISM
Peter Singer (Utilitarianism)	✔	✔	✔	✔
Richard Ryder (Painism)	✔	✔	✘	✔
Tom Regan (Animal Rights)	✘	✔	✘	✔

14 Professional philosophers have played a prominent role in leading the modern revival of interest in the treatment of animals. Furthermore, their concern with animal abuse has helped to develop modern theories of ethics in general. Peter Singer, a Utilitarian, has become one of the best known of all ethical philosophers and has given considerable currency to Ryder's concept of speciesism. Tom Regan, the leading US philosopher in the field, has championed a Rights Theory view.

This table shows how three philosophical positions, all sympathetic to the animals, can nevertheless differ in significant detail.

The author's own position, *painism*, is that the suffering of each painient individual is what matters morally. Pain, in all its manifestations, is the essential evil. Our prime moral concern should always be to reduce the pain of the greatest sufferers, regardless of their sex, race or species. This may justify the causing of lesser pain to another individual. It makes no sense, however, to aggregate the pains or benefits of *several* others because it is the boundaries of the individual which are also the boundaries of consciousness.

was no longer intuitively considered, as it sometimes had been in medieval times, a part of the same social hierarchy. Furthermore, for a hundred years after Waterloo, Britain was not threatened by war. In the previous century the country had, on several occasions, felt threatened by France. In the seventeenth century it had been riven by civil war and in the sixteenth the threat of invasion had come from Spain. For nearly a century after 1815 however, the civilian British felt fairly safe from armed attack. The Queen herself, on the throne from 1837 till 1901, became a symbol of that security. Perhaps this unprecedented affluence and security gave many the chance to reflect upon the condition of the less fortunate. And at the same time attitudes towards pain were changing.

PAIN AND STOICISM

In 1799 Humphrey Davy had described the anaesthetic properties of nitrous oxide; in 1842 Crawford Long used ether to produce surgical anaesthesia; and William Morton publicly demonstrated its use in 1846. In 1832 chloroform was produced, and in 1847 it was first used as an anaesthetic by Sir James Simpson in Edinburgh. In 1899 aspirin was discovered.

In some quarters there was resistance to the use of such anaesthetics and pain-killers on religious grounds. This resistance was strongest against their use in childbirth: 'In sorrow thou shalt bring forth children' (Genesis 3:16) was the much-quoted text. But the opposition declined after chloroform was administered by John Snow to Queen Victoria during labour in 1853. After mid-century, civilized men and women knew that pain, at least theoretically, could be controlled.

Among Victorians, the fear of pain became somewhat more open. Earlier generations, without effective anaesthetics and pain-killers, had been more stoical; pain which could scarcely be avoided had to be endured and the less said the better. Nevertheless it was the pronounced horror of pain in others, including nonhuman sentients, that was the common factor shared by most outstanding reformers; this explains why they came from non-religious backgrounds as well as from every religious sect and from all shades of political opinion. Opposition to pain, and not religious scruple or political doctrine, was their principal motive.

Perhaps it was those who were particularly prone to pain who led the campaigns against it. Wilberforce was not the only humanitarian of the nineteenth century who continuously took opium to dull the aches and pains of living; indeed he advised his friend the first Earl of Harrowby to do likewise for his headaches.[6] Shaftesbury, too, to use his own word, felt 'tortured' by the thought of suffering.[7]

The Victorians were, of course, more accepting of death. The conventional attitude towards nonhumans therefore became one of tolerance of killing, provided trouble was taken to make it 'a clean kill'. In the later twentieth century, as will be discussed in later chapters, at a time when death had become almost a taboo, the animal rights movement would argue as strongly against killing as against inflicting pain.

Paradoxically, in England and Germany in the nineteenth century there was also a strong stoical streak, perhaps typical of imperialistic cultures, which glorified the endurance of pain. In British public schools boys of twelve and over were deliberately subjected to harsh regimes of exhausting physical exercise, rough sports and corporal punishment. They were taught to disregard injury and to make light of pain. To make a fuss was to court the contempt of other boys and teachers alike.

Is it a coincidence that Britain and Germany, two of the most stoical cultures of the period, should also have been the most advanced in social reform and humane attitudes to animals? Those who suffer are often hardened into apparent callousness, but there are others who emerge from suffering as pain's deadliest foes.

Science, however, as it developed, became linked with stoicism and the idea that the head ought to rule the heart. For many years the British were taught that their feelings had to be kept under control, and in this period displays of affection and even compassion could be taken to be indications of weakness or effeminacy. The British macho image was colder and less swaggering than the Latin original, but just as important for the national character. The unflinching *infliction* of pain upon others, provided it was done in the line of duty, was considered no less admirable than the equally unflinching *suffering* of pain; both qualities were regarded as manly and desirable in an Empire-building master race. So, vivisection, a practice which expanded very rapidly during the final decades of Victoria's reign, became a symbol, not only of material progress but also of masculine hard-headedness. Science proudly proclaimed itself to be the antithesis to sentimentality, effeminate emotion and superstition.

Writers like Primatt towards the end of the eighteenth century had already isolated pain as the great evil and the Utilitarians under Bentham formalized this concern by making pain and pleasure the main criteria of morality; if an event increased the total sum of happiness (animal as well as human, Bentham argued) then it was good; if it reduced happiness (or increased pain) it was bad. The mathematics of Bentham's 'calculus of happiness' pose many problems, but the elevation of the importance of pleasure and pain as motives and as moral criteria remains valid. This was to some extent a revival of the ideas of Epicurus and other altruistic hedonistic classical thinkers, and such criteria went on to form cornerstones of both Freudian theory and experimental psychology. In the former, the 'pleasure principle' is seen as the basic human motivation, just as in modern scientific psychology the concepts of reward and punishment, applied to human and nonhuman alike, are regarded as the fundamental determinants of learned behaviour.

There is little doubt that the avoidance of pain and the seeking of pleasure (defined widely) are the main objects common to all sentient creatures. Pain and pleasure can be 'mental' as well as physical, and each act may be determined by complex combinations of pains and pleasures. Bentham's extension of this biological fact into an ethical theory brought together nature as it is and as it ought to be, and despite the obvious difficulty (although not impossibility) of quantifying such concepts, the main ethical problem is Bentham's proposal to calculate the goodness or badness of an act by adding the pains and pleasures of *all* the individuals affected by it. That it makes no sense to do such a sum across the boundaries of sentience between individuals did not seem to bother Bentham.

Bentham's significance for our subject, as I have already argued, is twofold: first, he had brought animals into the moral fold, and secondly he had put the spotlight on what really mattered: 'the question is not can they *reason*? Nor, can they *talk*? But can they *suffer*?'

The growing movement for the protection of nonhumans can be seen as part of a general trend in nineteenth-century Britain, against pain and suffering. Prison inspectors were introduced in 1835 and the pillory done away with in 1837. The slave trade had been abolished in 1807 and slavery in the British Empire in 1833. Help for the deaf and blind, and Shaftesbury's great reforms for lunatics, factory children, working women and chimney-boys ensued. In 1832 and 1837 the number of capital offences was drastically reduced; death sentences (mostly commuted) fell from 1,549 in 1831 to 116 in 1838.

As we have seen, in many cases the same people who were involved in helping human beings were also active in the humane movement to protect nonhumans from suffering. William Wilberforce and Lord Shaftesbury were the two most striking examples; but there were also T. F. Buxton (the anti-slaver) and 'Humanity Dick' Martin. There was Angela, Baroness Burdett-Coutts, who established a home for 'fallen women', battled for sanitary reforms, pioneered model housing and numerous other humanitarian ventures and was also an active member of the RSPCA from 1839 almost until her death in 1906. Frances Power Cobbe herself had worked as an early social worker.

The anti-vivisection campaigners, Dr Lawson-Tait and Lord Chief Justice Coleridge (the father of Stephen) were also noted feminists, and Charlotte Despard and Annie Besant, campaigners for the rights of women, were also supporters of the anti-vivisection movement. Lewis Gompertz was also a feminist, as was John Stuart Mill. Later, Maria Dickin, the pioneer social worker, turned her attention to animals and founded the People's Dispensary for Sick Animals of the Poor in 1917.

One psychological factor common to bull-baiting, vivisection and indeed all forms of cruelty to animals is that they teach people to overcome their natural scruples against inflicting pain and drawing blood; a useful qualification in fighting men. Such a process was sometimes acclaimed as an advantage and the idea was used, for example, by Windham when defending the 'old English character' as displayed in 'manly sports' such as baiting. The scientist's oft-voiced castigations of anti-vivisectionists as 'emotional' and 'sentimental' have similar connotations, in that they imply that overcoming a natural reluctance to inflict pain is a sign of rationality and manliness. Lord Coleridge had to protest that anti-vivisectionists were 'surely not weak or effeminate',[8] and a twentieth-century scientist, Professor Miriam Rothschild, has far more recently stated: 'I know several zoologists who have admitted that they suffered from the fear of being dubbed 'unmanly' and struggled to overcome their dislike of causing animals pain, or killing them.'[9]

As long ago as 1675 Benedictus de Spinoza had remarked that a concern over killing animals was based upon 'womanish pity',[10] and this irrational argument has been used for centuries to dismiss the seriousness of the reformers' case. It is similar to the claim that because opposition to cruelty is sometimes 'emotional' it is therefore invalid: as if opposition to Nazi atrocities, for example, should not have been accompanied by anger or pity. Emotion should imply neither ignorance nor wrongness; on the contrary, its absence in the context of cruelty could well be a sign of personality disorder. (This point is discussed further in the final chapter.)

The nineteenth-century conflict between vivisectors and anti-vivisectors took on the aspect of a conflict between an old and a new religion; the latter, powerful but amoral, and making sense of the world in a new way. This conflict slotted conveniently into the battle which already raged between religion and science, and between the theories of creation and evolution.

If the three basic psychological ingredients of a religion are its moral code, the meaning it gives to life and the 'magical' power it bestows, then science qualified brilliantly on the last two. But strangely, and terrifyingly for the Victorian moralists, it offered no moral code; morality was dismissed as just another form of behaviour which had evolved through natural selection. Science's only moral code appeared to consist of a narcissistic and arrogant self-worship; whatever promoted scientific progress was right, whatever opposed it wrong. So science meant power without principle, and for this reason remained suspect in the eyes of many Victorians; in so many ways it was itself the monster irresponsibly created by that symbolic nineteenth-century figure Dr Frankenstein – the blasphemy of man playing God.

Paradoxically, although science stood for a hard-headed attitude towards nonhumans, its discoveries about the reduction of pain had encouraged a less fatalistic attitude towards the sufferings of humans and nonhumans alike. As we have seen, lay people began to feel that something could now be done about it. But to what extent did British science, through its promulgation of the idea of evolution, inadvertently encourage the bridging of the gap between Homo Sapiens and the other animals?

EVOLUTION

The theories and attitudes of Charles Darwin have such an important bearing upon the human−nonhuman relationship that they will be looked at in some detail. In November 1859 Darwin published his great work *On the Origin of Species*; this was followed in 1871 by *The Descent of Man*, which demonstrated the evolutionary kinship of all animals. Yet, strangely, Darwinism had very little immediate effect on the way in which humans treated their newly discovered relatives. Darwin himself remained weak and ambivalent on the question of kindness to non-human animals and, in particular, on the morality of vivisection. His natural compassion and concern over pain would often prompt him to make a sympathetic statement, but this would be followed by an apparent contradiction, probably motivated by his reluctance to upset his scientific colleagues, particularly T. H. Huxley.

As we have seen, Darwin had dropped out of medical school because he hated dissection; the operating theatre horrified him. Yet, although his squeamishness and sensitivity about pain may have been intense, he did not, like Wilberforce or Shaftesbury, devote his life to reducing suffering. Instead, or so it seems, he tried to discount such sensitivity. His uncharacteristically shrill attack on the anti-vivisectionist Richard Hutton as 'a kind of female Miss Cobbe' may be a clue that Darwin saw his own concern about pain as effeminate.[11] Yet on occasions it could get the better of him and, according to his son Francis, his anger at cruelty would break through.[12]

Darwin argued that humans and nonhumans were not just physically, but also mentally similar:

We have seen that the senses and intuitions, the various emotions and faculties, such as love, memory, attention and curiosity, imitation, reason etc., of which man boasts, may be found in an incipient, or even sometimes in a well-developed condition, in the lower animals...There is no fundamental difference between man and the higher mammals in their mental faculties...The difference in mind between man and the higher animals, great as it is, certainly is one of degree and not of kind.[13]

There is some evidence that the scientific advocates of vivisection successfully manipulated Darwin to their political advantage. When testifying before the royal commission in 1876 he was confronted with some leading questions suggesting that he had participated in the pro-vivisection initiative of the British Association in 1871, and in the preparation of the Scientists' Bill presented to Parliament by Dr Lyon Playfair. Darwin denied that he had participated in preparing the British Association resolution:

Darwin: No, I had nothing to do with that.

Then he qualified this by saying that nevertheless he approved of the resolution. As to Dr Playfair's Bill, he agreed that he had helped in its preparation, but added mysteriously:

Darwin: But the Bill itself did not exactly express the conclusions at which after consultation with several physiologists we arrived; I apprehend that it was accidentally altered.

Question: But in the main you were an approving party?

Darwin: In the main.

Darwin went on to confirm that he had never been directly or indirectly connected with the performing of experiments upon living animals. However, although not a physiologist, he believed that experiments on animals were necessary for physiology and that physiology in the future would 'confer the highest benefits on mankind'. Nevertheless it was his belief that most experiments could be performed while the animal was insensible to pain, and should be so performed. The minutes of evidence conclude with a final question and answer:

Question: Now with regard to trying a painful experiment without anaesthetics, when the same experiment could be made with anaesthetics, or, in short, inflicting any pain that was not absolutely
necessary upon any animal, what would be your view on that
subject?

Darwin: It deserves detestation and abhorrence.[14]

In these exchanges Darwin's position remains ambiguous, partly, one feels, because of the complex and loaded questions from the royal commission's chairman, but also, perhaps, because of his own conflicting feelings – the clash between his love of science and his anger at cruelty. Nevertheless, his general detestation of pain emerges clearly. Darwin says he does not understand the objection (except when held by a Hindu) to killing an animal, but he abhors inflicting pain upon it. One gains the impression that Darwin is uneasy in giving his evidence;

perhaps this was because he was in the presence of scientific friends, including Huxley, who were far more fanatical than he in their devotion to the vivisector's cause. In public he felt obliged to give support. In his private notebooks, however, can be found statements indicating that he linked the exploitation of nonhumans with slavery: 'Animals — whom we have made our slaves we do not like to consider our equals. Do not slave holders wish to make the black man other kind?'[15]

Darwin is, perhaps, the prime example of humankind's inconsistency in relation to nonhumans. He spotted the kinship with them, but, like his pupil George Romanes, continued to shoot them for sport. Unfortunately, Darwin's co-discoverer of evolution, Dr Alfred Russell Wallace, was not summoned as a witness. His views are unequivocal:

I have for some years come to the conclusion that nothing but *Total Abolition* will meet the case of vivisection. I am quite disgusted at the frequency of the most horrible experiments to determine the most trivial facts...evidently carried on for the interest of the 'research' and the *reputation* it gives...[16]

The *Origin of Species* had made an immediate impact, the whole first edition being sold out on the day of issue. Controversy ensued, reaching a climax with a famous debate in Oxford in 1860 between Bishop Samuel Wilberforce and Huxley as the champion of Darwinism. Darwin believed that morality itself is the result of evolution, and he was disturbed by 'the horribly cruel works of nature', rejecting the idea of any divine purpose in the arrangements of the universe. Such views only intensified the conflict between his theories and conventional religion.

For the intelligent lay person, however, Darwinism had three implications of fundamental importance for the relationship between human and other animals.

First, Darwinism appeared to imply (although not necessarily) a lack of divine purpose. In doing so, it tended to undermine the assertion of a special relationship between man and God, as well as the biblical idea that God has given man dominion over the other species for man's benefit. Secondly, and perhaps conflictingly, Darwinism's concept of natural selection suggested that those who are 'fittest' survive best, and this was taken by some to imply that *stronger* individuals, classes and species have a right to dominate and destroy the weaker. Thirdly, and surely most importantly, Darwinism underlined the *kinship* between human and other animals.

The detailed evidence for the last assertion was to accumulate over the final years of the nineteenth century. Yet its moral implication, that what is considered wrong in the treament of human beings ought also to be wrong for the treatment of our nonhuman sentient kin, was not immediately accepted. Although the scales fell from the eyes of some, such were the colossal implications of evolutionary kinship for the day-to-day comforts and convenience of men and women, and for their commercial dealings, that the full message was unacceptable.

By 1870 Darwinism had been generally accepted on both sides of the Atlantic, yet this made little difference to the intensity or content of the animal welfare debate. A few animal welfare writers used the Darwinian idea of kinship, such as E. B. Hamley in *Our Poor Relations* published in Boston in 1872, Bertram Lloyd in *The Great Kinship* of 1921 and Henry Salt, particularly in his late works *The Creed of Kinship* (1935) and *The Story of my Cousins* (1923); but others, such as Frances Power Cobbe, were alarmed at Huxley's and Darwin's agnosticism and their view of morality . So in general evolution had remarkably little effect on the campaign and, paradoxically perhaps, Huxley became a key advocate of speciesism.

The view that nonhuman animals were quite like humans had been gaining ground for many years before the *Origin of Species*. Indeed, tales of the sagacity of brutes, their loyalty, altruism and parental devotion were as old as the hills, and had again been popularized throughout the first half of the nineteenth century. The corollary, that people were sometimes quite brutish, had also been supported during the preceding two centuries by the increasing volume of travellers' tales of wild and primitive savages in newly explored lands. Were all these creatures, some allegedly ape-like in appearance, truly human, or were some the missing links between men and monkeys? These questions were re-inforced rather than answered by the earliest anthropologists.

Darwinism was thus unveiled at a moment when some human beings had already begun to close the conceptual gap between the species. Nevertheless, bursting as it did upon the highly mannered life-style of the mid-Victorian era, where perceived differences even between social classes were huge and highly exaggerated through modes of dress, speech and etiquette, the idea of kinship with animals was certain to ruffle a few feelings and upset well-bred sensibilities; indeed, there may have been a larger number of people living in Victorian London than at any other time before or since who genuinely found it hard to conceive of themselves as a species of animal.

Furthermore, the sexually repressed and over-controlled middle-class culture of the time caused many to feel alienated from their own 'animal instincts'. For many, the word 'animal' still rang alarm bells about their own unacceptable sexual feelings and excretory and other bodily functions. If Darwin had published *Origin of Species* before Victoria's time, or after Freud's, then its reception might have been less explosive.

It is clear from Huxley that the popular reaction of indignation to Darwinism was based on the assumption that it 'degraded' the human being. In 1863 Huxley wrote:

On all sides I shall hear the cry – 'We are men and women, not a mere better sort of ape, a little longer in the leg, more compact in the foot, and bigger in brain than your brutal Chimpanzees and Gorillas. The power of knowledge – the conscience of good and evil – the pitiful tenderness of human affections, raise us out of all real fellowhip with the brutes, however closely they may seem to approximate us.

To this he replied:

I have endeavoured to show that no absolute structural line of demarcation, wider than that between the animals which immediately succeed us in the scale, can be drawn between the animal world and ourselves; and I may add the expression of my belief that the attempt to draw a psychical distinction is equally futile, and that even the highest faculties of feeling and of intellect begin to germinate in lower forms of life.[17]

Yet, while denying that Darwinism would in any way reduce 'our reverence for the nobility of manhood', Huxley did not say that evolutionary theory logically should extend this sense of reverence to the other species. Instead, he went on to stress that: 'No-one is more strongly convinced than I am of the vastness of the gulf between civilised man and the brutes; or is more certain that whether from them or not, he is assuredly not of them.' Such an inconsistent view indicates that Huxley could not or would not face up to the full implications of Darwin's theory. He went so far as to refer to man as 'The only consciously intelligent denizen of this world'.

Such sentiment singles out Huxley from other students of Darwin such as George Romanes and the banker-scientist Sir John Lubbock and even from his master, Darwin. Of far sterner stuff, for example, was the Darwinian Dr Lauder Lindsay, who wrote in 1879:

In truth, the psychical difference between certain animals and certain men is much less obvious than between different individuals, classes and races of man himself. Thus the difference is not more striking between different ages, sexes, and other conditions of man than between the lowest savage races of man and the anthropoid apes, the dog, or even the ant...Man's claim to pre-eminence on the ground of uniqueness of his mental constitution is as absurb and puerile, therefore, as it is fallacious. His overweening pride or vanity has led to his futile contention with the evidence of facts. He has trusted to a series of gratuitous assumptions.[18]

Lindsay, a medical man, claimed that nonhumans are capable of reason as well as religious and moral sense, and went on to argue that since the lower animals 'are unquestionably our fellow-creatures and fellow-mortals' then man is bound to show them kindness: 'In general terms, the treatment of the lower animals by man is to be conducted on the same principles as that of his fellow man, or of the child by his parent or instructor. This is the only rational system or mode of treatment.' This was more in line with Darwin himself, who had argued in *Descent of Man* that the history of man's moral development has been a continual extension in the objects of his 'social instincts and sympathies'. Originally each man had regard only for himself and those of a very narrow circle about him; later, he came to regard more and more 'not only the welfare, but the happiness of all his fellow men'; then 'his sympathies became more tender and widely diffused, extending to men of all races, to the imbecile, maimed, and other useless members of society, and finally to the lower animals...'[19]

The paradox, that scientists simultaneously wanted, for their own experimental convenience, to put nonhumans outside the moral pale while also affirming their physical similarity with human beings, was already a matter for comment. A. Armitt wrote in 1885:

It is, indeed, the scientists themselves who have proved to us the close relationship existing between man and animals, and their probable development from the same origin. It is they who instruct us to cast aside the old theology which makes men differ from the beasts of the field, inasmuch as he was created in 'the image of God', and yet would arbitrarily keep, for their own convenience, the line of division which such a belief marked out between man and animals.'[20]

Later, Sir John Lubbock warned against treating animals 'too much like mere machines'. For Lubbock, even ants had minds – 'all our recent observations tend to confirm the opinion that their mental powers differ from those of men, not so much in kind as in degree.'[21]

MODERN PSYCHOLOGY

It is in the 1890s, however, that modern experimental psychology was born, and with it the more rigorous scientific view that psychologists should not attribute unnecessary 'human' qualities to the behaviour of animals. If ants crowded together on a pebble and touched one another with their antennae, asked Wilhelm Wundt in 1892, why should the observer assume that they 'sported' or were 'saluting their queen?' Such descriptions, said Wundt, were 'due to the imagination of the observer'.[22]

So began the hardening of the psychologist's attitude which led to a widespread contempt for so-called 'anthropomorphism', a word previously reserved to describe the attribution of human characteristics to the deity. During the twentieth century the pendulum would swing so far in the other direction that it became fashionable for scientific psychologists to ignore almost any subjective experience.

Scientific psychologists of the American and British schools, embarrassed by the popular appeal of the unprovable and (in their opinion) improbable theories of Freud, Adler and Jung, became absurdly objective and quantitative in their approach to behaviour, tending to ignore consciousness not only in nonhuman but also in human subjects. The view that animals are living machines tended to cause some scientists to behave as though living creatures could not be both mechanical (in the sense that they followed observable regularities of behaviour which depended upon the physical state of their nervous systems) and also, at the same time, conscious.

The words 'anthropomorphism' and 'sentimentality', both widely used in twentieth-century Britain to disparage those who treated nonhuman animals in ways considered to be only appropriate to humans, were unheard in this context until after Darwin's day. Is it too fanciful to suggest that they were the animal exploiter's defences against the logical implications of Darwinism? If they were, they were certainly effective, casting doubts, as they did, on both the manliness and the intellectual calibre of those they were used against.

Edward Thorndike and J. B. Watson in America and Romanes's student, C. Lloyd Morgan in Britain followed Wundt in condemning the anthropomorphic approach to the study of animals. Together they steered psychology away from the study of the mind and to the objective aspects of behaviour. Inevitably this led to the increasingly cold-blooded study of laboratory animals under more and more rigorous scientific conditions. In 1894 Lloyd Morgan enunciated his famous canon: 'In no case may we interpret an action as the outcome of the exercise of a higher psychical faculty, if it can be interpreted as the outcome of one which stands lower in the psychological scale.'[23] In 1927, Ivan Pavlov went further. Animals should be studied as 'physiological facts, without any need to resort to fantastic speculations as to the existence of any possible subjective states'.

All this was really a version of the philosophers' 'principle of parsimony', which states that when several explanations are equally satisfactory then the simplest should be used. But where behaviourists, and others fanatically opposed to 'anthropomorphism', have gone wrong is that by ignoring the great *similarities* between human and other animals they have used theories which are *less* explanatory than valuable and valid human analogies would have been. Their reasons for making this mistake may lie in their guilt over the misuse of nonhumans and in their reluctance to face up to the fact that most laboratory species feel fear and pain much as they do.

Unlike so many hundreds of his followers who were to inflict terrible sufferings upon nonhumans in their psychological experiments, Lloyd

Morgan, however, had some feeling for them. As early as 1891 he had counselled: 'Sympathy is one of the great and beautiful bonds of life to life. Without sympathy you cannot study even a humble-bee aright.'[25]

CONCLUSIONS

In conclusion it has to be admitted that the theory of evolution played suprisingly little part in the quickening of anti-speciesism in nineteenth-century Britain. It should have done so, but it did not. Perhaps this was because the animal welfarists of the time saw evolution as an invention of the enemy: science. Some of the arch-vivisectors, after all, were keen exponents of evolutionary theory. It would be only in the following century that the moral implications of evolution would help to inspire the cause of animal liberation.

As for the industrial revolution, it increased affluence and created a large middle class; it may have liberated some minds to ponder the plight of nonhumans. But surely this tendency was augmented by the fact that Britain in the nineteenth century enjoyed an almost unprecedented period of peace which stretched, interrupted only by the Crimean and colonial campaigns (which never, of course, produced any fear of invasion) from 1815 till the end of the century. After the 1830s the upper and middle classes felt relatively safe; few external threats distracted them from considering the sufferings of others. Pain, too, had come out into the open as a fashionable preoccupation, and the discovery of anaesthetics created in some minds the optimistic view that pain had been conquered and could, if only anaesthetics were used, be easily banished from the vivisection laboratory.

The power of Queen Victoria's example should not be underestimated as a cause of Britain becoming the leading animal welfare nation in the nineteenth and early twentieth centuries. The aristocracy followed her lead by supporting the RSPCA, and some of their number, such as Shaftesbury and the Duchess of Hamilton, became leaders of the movement. The affluence and security of the Victorian upper classes, their new conviction that something now could and should be done about pain, and the example of genuine concern which they emulated in their Queen, had all played their parts.

10 The Revival of the Movement after 1960

This chapter describes how Britain led a revival in the animal protection movement in the decades of the 1960s and 1970s. It began with the
escalation of protests against the RSPCA's failure to oppose bloodsports
and was followed by the formation of the Hunt Saboteurs Association
in 1963 and the appearance of groups of young people directly confront-
ing fox- and deer-hunts in the south of England. Ruth Harrrison's attack
on factory-farming (1964) and Brigid Brophy's restatement of the animal
rights ideal (1965) came next, to be followed by the formation of the
Oxford Group (1969) (see p. 6). In the 1970s the RSPCA Reform
Group forced the society to adopt a modern approach; a major campaign
to restrict experiments on nonhuman animals was launched; Peter Singer
gave the movement new intellectual leadership (1975); the established
British animal welfare organizations were revitalized; the RSPCA successfully extended its influence to the rest of the European Community
(1978); and, by the end of the decade, with Lord Houghton's assistance
nonhuman animals in Britain were 'put into politics', the major parties
for the first time formulating their own official animal protection policies
(1979).

But what was the background to these undoubted advances?

After the First World War the animal welfare movement in Britain,
almost paralysed by its fear of appearing sentimental or extreme, had
become increasingly preoccupied with the day-to-day care of stray dogs,
unwanted cats and the declining number of tradesmen's horses. Campaigning against the institutionalized exploitation of animals faded.

Those cruelties in the public eye, such as the abuse of animals in the
new film industry, the condition of animals in circuses and zoos, and the
steadily increasing number of sea birds being found on the beaches
covered in oil, were issues on which the RSPCA took worthwhile action.
But the hidden cruelties went almost unchallenged: between 1920 and
1940 licensed animal experiments increased from 70,000 to around one
million annually, and factory-farming expanded on a huge scale.

RADICALS AND TRADITIONALISTS: THE RSPCA

In earlier days the split between the RSPCA's progressive and conservative elements, and the society's slowness to come to terms with new cruelties, had been masked by its undoubtedly great achievements in other areas. After 1918, however, the clash between radicals and traditionalists had become public and damaging. Whereas the deliberate social elevation of the RSPCA in the nineteenth century had been highly effective as a means of achieving social and legislative reform, in the present century it became, at best, a mixed blessing. By 1945, the RSPCA council had become composed chiefly of those who had little or no political, social or financial influence. True, there was Sir Robert Gower MP, who was chairman in the 1920s and 1930s, but he was an exception. Senior RSPCA staff, such as Arthur Moss in the 1950s, had felt held back and frustrated by the lack of drive and imagination of their council.[1]

The RSPCA, however, remained by far the most prestigious animal welfare organization in Britain and, probably, in the world. As a charity, its many thousands of members elect an unpaid council which determines its policies and appoints its senior paid staff. The society's large income, mostly derived from legacies, allows it to employ many hundreds of people, which makes it the largest of all professional animal welfare bodies. It receives no funding from the state, but is widely, although wrongly, regarded as a government agency. Several hundred animal welfare organizations around the world are affiliated to the RSPCA, and it is increasingly international in its operations, being especially influential in Europe and in the nations of the Commonwealth.[2]

As we have seen in chapter 8, during the stagnation of the post-war years the pattern, all too often repeated, was that the critics expostulated for a year or two against the RSPCA's failures before being intolerantly expelled from the society by a complacent council, dropping out to form their own independent organizations or giving up the fight entirely in a mood of bitter disillusionment. By 1970, at least a hundred animal welfare bodies existed in Britain, some active and some not, but the majority in principle committed to greater change than the RSPCA appeared to favour. Only in the late 1960s were the radicals to show the persistence necessary to achieve a significant change in the RSPCA itself. It was in this decade that the whole movement began to regain its intellectual power.

THE WIND OF CHANGE

The development in the 1960s and 1970s of the philosophical concern with the status and treatment of nonhuman animals, and the more general public concern has been described in the Introduction. There were other contributions to the debate. In 1964 Ruth Harrison published her book *Animal Machines*, an important attack on the cruelties inherent in certain forms of 'factory farming'. She called for new legislation to ban battery-hen cages and to prohibit the keeping of veal calves permanently tethered or in darkness or on deficiency diets. The book was widely acknowledged and helped alter permanently the public perception of intensive husbandry.

The following year Brigid Brophy's article in the *Sunday Times* caused much interest.[3] Probably not since the First World War had a serious paper given so much space to this all-but-forgotten subject. Brophy, influenced by the writings of Bernard Shaw, had been a vegetarian for ten years and thought it was time she told people 'without apology or embarrassment'. Her motivation was 'revulsion from cruelty, distaste for hypocrisy and double think'.[4] She had not been aware of any significant animal welfare movement during the 1950s and certainly was not part of it.

In 1970 two other authors, Monica Hutchings and Mavis Caver, published *Man's Dominion* – a devastating catalogue of human cruelty which argued the moral case strongly but in the language of the past.[5] This book failed to gain the publicity it deserved and was not, I believe, widely read by the new young activists just emerging. Nevertheless it made a deep impression upon some of the older generation.

BLOODSPORTS

Since Henry Salt drafted his Bill in 1893 attempts to curtail bloodsports have led to Bills being introduced into the British Parliament on more than thirty occasions. Latterly, many were successfully defeated by Conservative MP Marcus Kimball's use of parliamentary tactics, the basic one being to talk at length on the parliamentary business preceding the antihunting Bill so that when the Bill was debated, it failed through lack of time. (The official curtailment of filibusters is considered acceptable only on Bills which are part of a government's published programme.[6])

Nevertheless one Bill passed all its stages in the Commons in 1970, but it did not proceed through the Lords because a general election supervened. The 1975 Bill came even closer to success, but the British Field Sports Society (BFSS) on the advice of Lord Denham, managed to ensure that the Bill was sent to a specially set up select committee which persuaded the House of Lords not to proceed with it. This select committee was assisted not only by a scientist who argued that prey-species may not dislike being coursed, but also by advice received from an eminent law lord, the late Lord Diplock, to the effect that the Bill would be impracticable and difficult to enforce. Diplock did not reveal to the select committee at the time that he was a life-long supporter of bloodsports, nor that he was closely in touch with the BFSS and had written articles for the society in the 1930s.[7] Four out of the seven members of the committee were Conservatives, and these were the four who voted that the Bill should not proceed.[8]

A survey conducted by Richard Thomas in 1977 found that whereas 45 per cent of Masters of Foxhounds actually belonged to the Conservative party (20 per cent being activists) and 81 per cent said they would vote Conservative in the general election, only one MFH said he would vote for the Liberals, and none chose Labour.[9] In contrast, politics were not found to be a central part of the lives of members of the Hunt Saboteurs Association, only 7 per cent saying they were members of the Liberal party, 5 per cent of the Conservative party and 3 per cent of the Labour party; 29 per cent said they would vote Liberal, 23 per cent Labour and 18 per cent Conservative. Thomas, in his excellent study, summed up the two groups:

The evidence from the questionnaires shows that MFHs are a relatively homogeneous group of mainly middle-aged and middle or upper class country dwellers. Hunt saboteurs on the other hand are much more heterogeneous, being a more equal mixture of classes and age groups. They are also more evenly divided between the sexes and between urban and rural dwellers. From the evidence of this study, it is apparent that MFHs are essentially tough-minded conservatives and that saboteurs are radicals, although some are tough- and some are tender-minded.

He concludes that the two groups share almost no common ground: 'The HSA is firmly on the side of freedom and the MFH is strongly on the side of order.' There is also evidence that whereas MFHs were very often following in a family tradition, saboteurs were not. Indeed the latter were sometimes departing from their usual life-styles through their activities in defence of animals – driven very often, it seems, by an overwhelming sense of indignation and compassion.

More than any other aspect of animal welfare, the bloodsports issue in Britain had become party political by 1970. In general, the Conservative party supported these sports, the Labour party opposed them and the Liberals occupied the middle ground. As early as 1967 Eric Heffer had introduced a Bill against bloodsports and by the 1980s the anti-bloodsports campaign in Parliament had become part of the programme of the extreme Left. In his 1982 book *The Hunt and the Anti-Hunt*, Philip Windeatt quoted several well-known public figures of the Left: Tony Benn – 'bloodsports degrade us all'; Arthur Scargill – 'how anyone can inflict unnecessary pain on innocent and defenceless animals is beyond my understanding'; and Dennis Skinner – 'it is unjustified murder'. Yet it is doubtful whether, twenty years earlier, all such pillars of socialism would have expressed this conviction. The change in attitude was probably due partly to the effect the Hunt Saboteurs Association had had upon the image of animal welfare generally.

Direct Action

In 1963 the new chairman of the League Against Cruel Sports, Raymond Rowley, had begun to steer it away from confrontational protest at a time when some members wanted to step it up. These people proceeded to form the autonomous Hunt Saboteurs Association, the aims of which were 'to save the lives of hunted animals by legal, nonviolent, direct means and to bring to the attention of People and Parliament the barbaric cruelties involved in the hunting of animals until such time as these practices are banned by law'. The nonviolent approach was endorsed in the Rules of the Association.[10]

John Prestige, a Devon journalist, appalled when he found himself working on the story of a pregnant hind who had been driven into a village and killed by the Devon and Somerset staghounds, said to a colleague that 'someone ought to sabotage the hunt.' So, with a group of friends, Ken Wanstall, Leo Lewis and members of the Cebo family among them, he fed meat to the South Devon Foxhounds in order to sabotage their meet in Torquay on Boxing Day 1963. His motives, he says, were 'disgust' and 'a feeling that nothing was being done to stop it – the League Against Cruel Sports was ineffective at the time.' He has denied any party political element in his thinking.[11]

Retaliation was brutal. On 2 May 1964 'nearly 300' members of the Culmstock otter-hunt surrounded a car-load of saboteurs, whipped the car, turned it over, dragged Leo Lewis out of it and broke his jaw with an otter-hunting stave. Axminster magistrates in due course imposed small fines upon four hunters and bound over Lewis and Prestige to keep the peace.

Undeterred, Prestige and his friends continued a campaign of weekly sabotage against stag-, otter- and fox-hunting which lasted for three or four years, centred upon Somerset and Devon and using aniseed and hunting horns to divert the pack. They were shortly followed by a London group which began to confront fox-hunts in South and East England.

Using his contacts in the media, Prestige gained a great deal of sympathetic publicity in the years 1964 to 1967. Then, 'disillusioned by the strength of the entrenched system' which he was fighting and because of his dislike of the minority who, he says, wanted to demonstrate chiefly because they were 'anti-establishment', Prestige gave up. The Hunt Saboteurs Association underwent a temporary decline before being revived under the new London-based leadership of David Wetton in 1969.

I had confronted the Bucks and Courtenay Tracy Otterhounds on the family estate around Wytch Farm in Dorset in the summer of 1969, and, although never a member of the Hunt Saboteurs Association, with the support of Wetton and friends from the Oxford area I proceeded to wage a five-year campaign against otter-hunting in the South and West of England which received widespread local and national publicity. The objections to the sport were that it was cruel and that otters were an endangered species in English rivers. I then continued the campaign at the political level until otters became legally protected in England and Wales in 1978.[12]

During the early 1970s Hunt Saboteurs Association members rapidly increased and by 1977 the Association claimed a membership of nearly 3,000, mostly in and around university towns. By 1982 the association's mailing list had grown to around 4,000. Thomas's survey of 1977 showed that members were mostly male and youthful, 46 per cent being under the age of twenty-five. Highly significantly, however, they came from all socio-economic classes, not overwhelmingly from the middle class; for the first time in the history of the animal rights movement, a large number of the working-class young had publicly declared their support. No less than 38 per cent had incomes of less than £1,500 a year. Many were, however, well educated, 19 per cent of the HSA members being students and 59 per cent having had tertiary education.

On some occasions indignant hunting people, some of whom appeared to find it hard to believe that compassion alone could motivate the interruption of their sport, accused the protesters of being professional troublemakers hired by mysterious political godfathers. Lord Houghton, as chairman of the League Against Cruel Sports, angrily rebutted one such 'rent-a-mob' accusation:

If Princess Anne wants to know who is paying the demonstrators of Hunt Saboteurs Association the answer is − no one. They are dedicated young people who risk insult and injury from brutal huntsmen because they are passionately opposed to hunting foxes with hounds for pleasure. And so am I.

The crowd of several thousands of young people who demonstrated in Trafalgar Square against the appalling slaughter of baby seals in Canada at this time of year were not being paid either.

It is a hopeful sign for the future of mankind that so many young people now reject inhuman and unenlightened attitudes and practices towards animals which have become ingrained in society by centuries of greed, vanity and sport.

It is an impertinence for Princess Anne to ask them 'who's paying you?' We may well remind her of who's paying her![13]

The methods of the HSA in its earlier years were both peaceful and legal. Dave Wetton's anti-violent and good-humoured approach pervaded the organization as he strove, primarily, to protect the quarry rather than to antagonize the hunter. On some occasions, however, his skilful use of the hunting horn would lure the pack in entirely the wrong direction across a river, leaving apoplectic whippers-in trumpeting impotently on the other bank while the quarry made good his or her escape. Other tactics included scaring away the quarry in advance of the hunt or spoiling the scent. Aniseed having proved disappointing, our Oxford clique had introduced the use of 'anti-mate' bitch sprays in 1970, and with some success. Oxford University chemists had suggested methyl mercaptan as one of the strongest smells known to man but, after tests on the Berkshire Downs, this substance, although not known to be illegal or toxic, was abandoned in case it might prove to have detrimental effects on humans, hounds, wildlife or the environment generally. Rotten herring, on the other hand, proved irresistibly diverting to otter-hounds and terriers alike, although somewhat philosophically inconsistent and highly unpleasant to use.

Hardly surprisingly, the reactions of huntsmen and coursers to such pungent opposition was sometimes violent. Their sports were often more to them than mere pastimes, being in some cases a central part of their lives and an important element in their sense of identity. To interfere with such sports struck deep. If, in addition, protests stirred uneasy consciences, then the emotional reaction was compounded.

The infiltration of hunts by anti-hunting protesters requires some courage. Nevertheless, Michael Huskisson in the late 1970s masqueraded as a hunt supporter for two years, obtaining film in the process, and subsequently publishing his observations amid passionate condemnation of his conduct from genuine hunters.

The behaviour of magistrates, too, sometimes reflected an emotional quality, and at the expense of justice. In 1977, for example, Mrs Valerie Waters was called by the police as a prosecution witness in a case concerning alleged violence by some supporters of the Atherstone Hunt.[14] When the huntsmen had been bound over, the magistrates proceeded to bind over Mrs Waters although she had only been a witness, on the grounds that she was a well-known member of the Hunt Saboteurs Association. When Waters refused to be bound over, she was sent to prison for a month where she was treated as a criminal. The fines of the guilty huntsmen having been paid for them by the British Field Sports Society, the Master of the Hunt declared: 'I'm very glad she's in prison. She was a bloody nuisance.' In the same year thirty-one saboteurs were bound over for protesting against a coursing meeting. The Association's request for legal aid was refused even though some defendants were students or unemployed. The judge who refused their application for legal aid did not reveal at the time that he was a member of the British Field Sports Society, with one son a former MFH and another a local hunt secretary. When the Association eventually succeeded in appealing to another judge, the case was dismissed.[15]

Such waywardness in the legal process embittered many in the animal rights movement and helped to escalate the levels of violence. Justice too often had not been seen to be done. The network of apparent interest between hunters, lawyers and government appeared to many to be oppressive and conspiratorial. Their traditional alliance with farmers, however, began to crumble. With fewer free-range hens, farmers by the 1970s had begun to realize that the fox, far from being a pest, was probably doing them a service by keeping down rats, rabbits and slugs; at least it was quite obvious that the fox did less damage to crops than a lot of jodphured gents on horseback. Tensions grew between hunts and farmers and there were some nasty incidents, as when, for example, a Devon farmer shot five hounds of the South Devon Hunt at Christmas 1986.[16]

Undoubtedly, all sides on occasions have been provocative. Violence has provoked counter-violence and injustice has provoked extremism. The desecration of the graves of two well-known huntsmen, John Peel and the Duke of Beaufort, have been bizarre instances of this extremism; the attempted disinterment of the corpses by the self-styled Hunt Retribution Squad in 1977 struck most members of the public as a revolting anachronism, and did much to discredit the whole movement.

REFORM OF THE RSPCA

It was in an anti-hunting context that ginger-group activity emerged within the ranks of the RSPCA. One of the main areas of disagreement within the society, and the one seized upon to the exclusion of almost all others by the media, was this question of bloodsports. The British Field Sports Society had long dreaded the outright opposition of the RSPCA to fox-, stag- and otter-hunting, hare-coursing, deer-stalking and other country sports. Paradoxically, the RSPCA's notorious conservatism meant that its opposition was even more to be feared.

The RSPCA certainly had supporters of bloodsports among its members. But such infiltration was not always deliberate, for the classes that led the RSPCA had many animal-lovers among their ranks, who nevertheless hunted or shot for sport, or who, although not participants themselves, had friends, relatives or acquaintances who were. Furthermore, fox-hunting had the same 'snob' appeal as the RSPCA itself, and so those who joined the RSPCA wholly or partly, consciously or barely consciously, in order to enhance their social standing, might equally admire the world of fieldsports and for similar reasons.

In Victorian times, for those with social aspirations, it had been possible to see vivisecting scientists as threats to the old order in society or to look down on them as foreigners or anti-religious intellectuals. Conceivably, it had been possible to view agricultural and other forms of cruelty as being 'tainted by commerce' or springing from peasant ignorance. But to attack bloodsports, and fox-hunting in particular, struck at the core of the British class system and the nation's traditional fantasies about country life. For nearly two hundred years the English middle classes had dreamt of being country gentry and believed that fox-hunting was one of its principal qualifications. The fact that many established country gentlemen and aristocrats never hunted, and that some regarded the hunt as bourgeois, boorish and a damned nuisance, did not register in the public mind. When, therefore, in the 1960s, some members of the RSPCA challenged fox-hunting head-on, it was an occasion for much publicity.

On 8 April 1960, an extraordinary general meeting of the RSPCA was called by three anti-hunting members of the society, Patrick Moore (the distinguished astronomer), Howard Johnson (Conservative MP for Kemp Town, Brighton) and Gwendoline Barter. But their anti-hunting motion failed to attain the necessary three-fifths majority. Similar motions were put and defeated at the AGM in June and at a further EGM in 1961. On each occasion opposition came from senior members of the RSPCA council and, later that year, Howard Johnson and Gwendoline Barter were expelled from the society.

In 1960 Captain Robert Churchward, a former joint Master of the South Shropshire Hunt, after thirty years in the saddle, published an outspoken attack upon the hidden cruelties of fox-hunting, revealing that it was, in his view, 'specifically designed to maintain the present artifically high level of the fox population'.[17] Churchward's book motivated an RSPCA member, Vera Sheppard, to stage a number of solitary protests against fox-hunts and to raise the question of bloodsports at RSPCA meetings in 1962 and 1963, supported by Patrick Moore. At its meeting in 1965, together with Richard Chapman, she proposed a motion that the society 'deplores the killing of wild animals in the name of sport and calls upon the responsible Hunt authorities to substitute drag hunting instead'. In the relevant issue of *Horse and Hound* the editor of the huntsmen's journal advised his readers to attend the RSPCA's meeting 'to see that the proposed motion is soundly defeated'. Hunters arrived in force, among them the Duke of Beaufort, who was then president of the British Field Sports Society, and Marcus Kimball MP its chairman. The meeting was chaotic; at it, three anti-hunting members of the RSPCA council, Rose and Charles Birkett and Edward Whitley, alleged that at least four fellow members of the council supported live hare-coursing and that several supported both hunting and vivisection. The motion was emasculated by an amendment, and approximately two hundred hunting sympathizers immediately left the meeting in triumphant mood.

In 1967 bloodsports were again debated in Parliament, and an attempt was made by William Price, Eric Heffer and other MPs to outlaw hare-coursing. But, under opposition from RSPCA member Marcus Kimball, the Bill was talked out. At the ensuing RSPCA AGM, Sheppard, Whitley, the Birketts and other anti-hunters attempted to pass a motion to expel Kimball from membership of the society. The RSPCA had been prepared a few years earlier to expel the two members who had attacked the society's equivocation on bloodsports; it showed a reluctance to act likewise against Kimball.

Nevertheless, the society's chairman, Lieutenant-Colonel J. C. Lockwood, and the society's council, shifted their position significantly at this time, and public statements were made indicating that the RSPCA did at least consider that cruelty to wildlife was within its remit and that the hunting of otters was a matter for concern. Senior officers of the British Field Sports Society lunched with Lockwood in an attempt to persuade him to recant. They failed, and subsequently instructed some of their members to attend the 1968 RSPCA meeting, where the RSPCA's annual report was tactically rejected and a motion against hunting was rowdily defeated by 448 votes to 197. This contrasted with a postal ballot of the RSPCA membership at this time which showed a majority of four to one opposed to bloodsports.

One reason for this disparity was undoubtedly the RSPCA's practice of holding its annual meetings on a weekday, thus making it harder for ordinary working people to attend. When this situation was reversed in 1970, so that meetings were held on Saturdays, it became the turn of the traditionalist faction to complain, albeit less logically, that the meetings disproportionately favoured the radicals.

During 1969 supporters of hunting continued their pressure. In a letter to *Horse and Hound* published on 17 January, Sir Robert Grant-Ferris MP urged friends of hunting to join the RSPCA and to support leading council-member John Hobhouse.

The annual RSPCA council elections became highly charged. Conservative MP Harold Gurden publicly lobbied against candidates who were known to be opposed to hunting. After a particularly acrimonious AGM, the council ousted its chairman, who was replaced by John Hobhouse, and co-opted, as vice-chairman, Frederick Burden, a Conservative MP who was also president of the Kent Wildfowlers Association. At the subsequent annual meeting in 1970 Sheppard, Whitley and the other anti-hunters were effectively silenced when microphones were switched off, and the meeting itself ended in uproar as protesters were forcibly removed from the platform.[18]

The RSPCA Reform Group

In the same year, a new ginger-group was formed. RSPCA members who were opposed to hunting and dedicated to trying to modernize the society came together as the RSPCA Reform Group. Their leaders were Brian Seager (no relation of Major Ronald Seager, the society's chief officer – then styled secretary but later executive director), Stanley Cover and John Bryant. One of its first actions was to protest in January 1971 against a fox-hunt for children in Warwickshire, organized by someone who was both a huntsman and a member of the RSPCA. A few days later Vera Sheppard was summonsed to appear before the RSPCA council to face expulsion on a charge that by her protests against hunting she had behaved in a manner 'prejudicial to the interests of the Society'. When she arrived at the society's Jermyn Street headquarters accompanied by Edward Whitley, she was met by a crowd of supporters waving placards carrying statements such as 'The RSPCA has *never* expelled a Blood Sportsman.'

In her defence Sheppard alleged a long-standing conspiracy by bloodsportsmen to control the RSPCA, quoting letters published in the sporting press to support her allegation.[19]

In the event, the RSPCA council decided not to expel Vera Sheppard. The RSPCA Reform Group felt that the major reason for the decision was fear of further adverse publicity. History, however, would certainly repeat itself and many others who criticized have found themselves faced with expulsion merely because they *have* criticized the society; indeed a pattern emerged in which outstanding reformers have been expelled, often by those within the society whose contribution to the movement has been negligible.

By 1969 some pro-hunting members had discovered a new weapon. They threatened that if the RSPCA did not cease all campaigning against bloodsports a complaint would be made to the Charity Commissioners arguing that the RSPCA should lose its charitable status because it had become 'too political'. Such a loss of status would mean the loss of tax exemptions, and cost the society many thousands of pounds a year. This threat, believed by many and cynically exploited by a few, severely hampered reform of the society for most of the ensuing decade, making the radicals' task even harder.[20]

The following year, the Reform Group supported a number of sympathetic candidates for the annual RSPCA council elections, five of whom, including Bryant and myself, were elected. Nevertheless, the dominant faction on the forty-six-strong council fought back vigorously and in early 1973 it even attempted to expel from the society the tenacious Reform Group chairman, Brian Seager. Once again the attempt failed when the national publicity surrounding the affair began to escalate.

Concerned about the general running of the society, the Reform Group then mounted a campaign for an extraordinary general meeting to examine the state of its administration. As a counter-move the council proposed, and the Annual General Meeting in June 1973 passed, a resolution to set up an independent inquiry to report on the society's constitution, rules, conduct and management. The three-man inquiry, under the chairmanship of Charles Sparrow QC, started work in August

1973 and reported the following year, after months of lurid publicity as allegations, some wild and some accurate, were aired in its public hearings of witnesses.

The first of Sparrow's thirty-eight recommendations was that the society must have a new chairman. The report also recommended halving the size of the council and urged the need for more council members with expert knowledge; co-option to the council should only be for 'true cases of persons with special qualifications'; the value of the inspectorate was emphasized and the council was reminded that its own function should be limited to 'questions of principle and policy', leaving routine administration to the paid staff. At the council meeting on 21 November 1974, I proposed that the report's recommendations (except that affecting the chairman) should be accepted. Against considerable opposition, but with the support of Lord Houghton, a recent Labour cabinet minister who was, for a short period, a member of the council, this motion was eventually carried, and the whole RSPCA council voluntarily resigned.

Reform Group candidates did well again in the following postal elections to the smaller council of twenty-three, and under its new chairman Michael Kay, an accountant from Leeds, the RSPCA began its slow and belated journey into the modern era. Kay, however, failed to be re-elected in the 1975 council elections and was succeeded as chairman by Roy Crisp, a Suffolk antiquarian.

Neither Crisp nor Kay, both moderates, had been Reform Group members, yet, although the old supporters of the now disbanded Reform Group were still in a minority on the new council and still deeply mistrusted in some quarters, their policies gradually became acceptable to some older members. Indeed, although the Sparrow report had been highly critical of the Reform Group, some of the report's recommendations and most of its consequences were in line with the Reform Group's long-published ideas. Although almost every reform proposed was fiercely resisted by the old guard, enough of the middle ground on the council changed its mind in the succeeding years to allow my election as vice-chairman in 1976 and chairman in 1977.

SOME CHANGES IN THE RSPCA: THE 1970S

The eight years from 1972 to the end of the decade were a period of rapid changes within the RSPCA, initiated by its reforming minority on the council. The first surprise for the new members who joined the council in 1972 had been the discovery that the RSPCA had no written policies. Such as it was, policy consisted solely of half-recalled council resolutions and the *ad hoc* pronouncements of senior officers. A huge staff, some five hundred strong, lacked the basic guidelines that a written policy could provide. Often confused and insecure in the midst of the society's then tumultuous affairs, with policy at the whim of one faction or another, staff understandably played safe. Afraid to take new initiatives which might provoke criticism from council members, they preferred to be cautious. This situation aggravated the society's already powerful inclination toward inertia and blandness.

While many of the branches of the RSPCA had carried on vigorously with routine welfare work, mostly involving domestic pets and strays, certain areas of cruelty and exploitation had received scant attention from the national body for some fifty years. Intensive farming had been allowed to expand and develop with minimal opposition from the one organization prestigious enough to have checked it. Laboratory animals and wildlife had been neglected and their exploitation and abuse had escalated. It seemed that the RSPCA was at this time actually lagging behind public opinion rather than leading it on cruelty issues. It was completely out of touch with the philosophical revival and mass protest against animal experimentation and the exploitation of wildlife of the 1970s (see chapters 12 and 13).

Under RSPCA Reform Group influence the council began reform in 1972 by setting up expert advisory committees on cruelty in animal experimentation and farming. The former committee, under the secretaryship of Bill Jordan and chaired by Dr Kit Pedler (one of the creators of the television series *Dr Who* and *Doomwatch*, the latter being a dramatized attack on pollution and the dangers of uncontrolled science), fast established itself as a radical and effective committee. The farming committee on the other hand, tightly controlled by the RSPCA's then chief veterinarian (considered by some, rightly or wrongly, to be a covert friend of the farming industry), initially did little more than postpone firm action by commissioning research.

Under its new chairmen (the term of office for this position was, after 1975, limited to two years), the council set about formulating policies across the board. Some forty areas of cruelty were considered and the society's basic policy upon each was decided, based usually upon wordings drafted by the society's education officer, David Paterson, and myself. An analysis of the council's minutes in these years will show that nearly all the new thinking came from the Reform Group minority, and that it was consistently opposed by the votes of traditionalists led by Sir Frederick Burden MP. As part of this programme of policymaking, the contentious issue of hunting came up and, remarkably, in a meeting on 25 February 1976, the council of the RSPCA voted without opposition that the society should 'oppose all hunting with hounds'. After fifteen years of bitter wrangling, the supporters of bloodsports within the society had quietly accepted defeat. Strangely, when the policy was restated nine years later, in 1985, it provoked a strong reaction from the hunting community: *Horse and Hound*, ignoring the fact that by this time more traditional figures were once again in control of the society, announced that the policy was due to 'entryism by extremists' whose real aim was 'social change, not animal welfare' (3 January 1986). The *Daily Telegraph* reiterated such inaccuracies and the British Field Sports Society retaliated with leaflets using the RSPCA logo. (In July 1986 they were forced in the High Court to destroy all these leaflets and to pay the RSPCA's legal costs.)

The next step taken by the reformers in the late 1970s was to insist that *priorities* should be decided.[21] Within the wide spectrum of the policies it was resolved that the four major areas – the treatment of farm animals, wildlife, domestic animals, and laboratory animals – would be given equal priority. This move represented a major step away from the society's almost total preoccupation with stray and unwanted pets, which had taken up most of its resources for at least fifty years.

In a complete reorganization of the council's committee structure in 1975, the number of committees was drastically reduced. A council subcommittee continued to deal with the management of domestic animal matters, while the expert advisory committees (now numbering three, after the formation of a Wild Animals Advisory Committee) offered technical advice on the other priority areas.

Trying to alter the direction of the RSPCA was like trying to turn around a huge ship: it took time. By November 1976 little change in the society's animal welfare performance was noticeable to John Bryant. In exasperation he circulated a satirical document to fellow council members ('With the Greatest Respect and So On, while 400,000,000 Animals Suffer') describing what he saw as typical RSPCA council meetings at that time, with lengthy discussions of minor issues, fierce arguments between the factions, the failure to make changes, to face up to facts, to take firm decisions or to use the society's huge resources effectively. Bryant went on to reiterate the view that the society's role should be changed to tackle the mass modern cruelties through education and campaigning. At the most generous estimate, he wrote, the society could not have helped more than two million animals that year, although 'in terms of our own policies, there are in any one year in this country, 400,000,000 animals suffering cruelty. These include 370,000,000 victims of 'over-intensive' farming and 5,500,000 victims of vivisection.' In other words, so Bryant claimed, the RSPCA was squandering its resources on being 'part of the state law enforcement machine' and was helping only half of one per cent of the animals in need – 'What about the other 99½ per cent?' he asked. Looking at the society's account, he reckoned that 87 per cent of the money (over £2 million annually at that time) was spent on the half of one per cent of animals, including the cost of destroying annually over 100,000 unwanted *healthy* dogs and cats.

Traditionally, the RSPCA had destroyed colonies of feral cats. But the so-called radicals at this time backed Celia Hammond's alternative plan to neuter such cats and return them to site. After long resistance from the RSPCA establishment this approach eventually proved practicable and became RSPCA policy.[22]

Over the following two years, against constant opposition, the reforming group on the council did manage to achieve some redistribution of the society's effort and expenditure to cover the neglected areas, and, before the end of my term of office as chairman, the society had established for the first time professional staff departments to campaign in each of the three new priority areas (cruelty to wildlife, laboratory and farm animals) and to service the recently established expert advisory committees.

Collaboration with Other Agencies

Although the RSPCA, in the mid-twentieth century, had been reluctant to collaborate with other animal welfare organizations, the new council members successfully urged RSPCA co-operation with three joint committees that were established during the 1970s. The first, JACOPIS (the Joint Advisory Committee on Pets in Society), set up by the veterinarian Peter Mann and sponsored largely by the pet food industry, brought together the veterinary profession and the welfarists.[23] It quickly adopted the proposal of Ruth Plant and myself that the country's huge unwanted dog problem (and dog pollution problem) should be dealt with by raising the dog licence fee (for more than a century fixed at 37½p) and funding a statutory nationwide service of dog wardens trained to enforce the law and to educate the irresponsible dog-owner. JACOPIS, initially under the chairmanship of Lord Houghton and later Lord Listowel, was not a charity and so had the advantage of being able to act totally unfettered as a pressure group on the government. Houghton pressurized government direct and we had meetings with senior government ministers on several occasions, vainly urging our reforms.

The RSPCA also gave support to the Farm Animal Welfare Coordinating Executive (FAWCE) and the Committee for the Reform of Animal Experimentation (CRAE), both formed in 1977.[24] The latter, established by Lord Houghton, Clive Hollands and myself, had frequent meetings with officials and ministers (including Home Secretaries Merlyn Rees and William Whitelaw) in pursuit of our intention to reform the law controlling animal experimentation. For a few years, until the end of the decade, these three joint committees involved most of the leading campaigners and the major animal protection organizations in the country.

In other ways, too, the RSPCA reformers sought to make the society collaborate with other organizations and individuals travelling in the same direction. It gradually became a little more gracious towards other campaigners. Although the RSPCA had always been generous with awards to its own senior personnel, it had nothing to give to independent animal welfare workers. We managed to rectify this by creating two new top awards for this purpose in 1978 – the Richard Martin and Lord Erskine Awards – Lord Houghton becoming the first recipient of the former. We also created an RSPCA media award to recognize those reporters and television directors who had helped the cause.

Publicity and Pressure Group Activity

Having established policies, priorities, specific legislative goals, and the corresponding new committees and departments, the RSPCA reformers saw that it was necessary to help the society change gear, so that the new machinery could begin to work properly. This meant a creative use of the media, a revival of the society's nineteenth-century role as a proselytizing pressure group and, under David Paterson, the vigorous deployment and expansion of the society's Education Department. The reformers were also quick to initiate a 'consumerist' approach and Paterson was instructed to draw up a list of cruelty-free cosmetics which was made available to members.

The society's very bad publicity throughout the 1960s and early 1970s had compounded the council's natural fear of the media. By the time that Reform Group members arrived on the council in 1972 they found that the shutters were down; the council was attempting to keep all its deliberations secret. Almost every council document was labelled 'Strictly Confidential' and meetings were held in an aura of conspiratorial self-importance.

It was indeed difficult to persuade the society to regard the media not as the enemy but as potential allies in the campaign against cruelty. The appointment of creative press officers and the setting up of an appropriate committee were clearly necessary steps. Later, a staff Campaigns Department was established, and for a short while showed that a positive attitude towards publicity was far better than a purely defensive one.

Another major problem encountered by the more radical RSPCA council members was that many members of the council and staff opposed any approaches to government in the pursuit of legislative reform. Since the 1940s the society's role as a service charity, prosecuting cruelty cases and dealing with the nation's unwanted dogs and cats, had expanded, while its original role as political pressure group had fallen away to near zero. An ill-defined middle-class dislike of 'politics' was aggravated by the recent deliberately raised fear that the society's charitable status was at risk. In consequence, when I, as newly elected chairman, asked the council to approve my proposals that the society should lobby government in pursuit of its policies, I found it sometimes extremely difficult to carry the majority of the council; even correspondence with ministers was considered to be unacceptable.

The society continued to be cautious to an almost unbelievable degree.

Nevertheless, expansion of the legal staff (hitherto preoccupied with matters such as conveyancing of property) and the appointment of two staff to deal with parliamentary affairs and to lobby Parliament on the society's behalf, were eventually agreed, and, although still hotly opposed, the elementary principle was re-established that the RSPCA should strive for improved legislation. Expert legal and political committees were also set up to encourage a more imaginative prosecution policy and to help plan strategy in the political sphere; in January 1979 the RSPCA staff was persuaded to produce a list of specific legislative reforms sought by the RSPCA. This list cited some thirty amendments to existing legislation in addition to proposals for entirely new law. No doubt, if the reforming element had remained in control, an effective team could have been established to push forward these legislative proposals with greater urgency. But the ground had at least been prepared.

In 1976 we set up an inquiry into shooting and angling under the independent chairmanship of Lord Medway, the distinguished zoologist. His committee reviewed the latest evidence on the transmission of pain and concluded that it was reasonable to assume that all classes of vertebrate, including fish, were capable of suffering. This straightforward scientific finding helped to provide a firm foundation for the campaigns which followed.

The RSPCA was also pushed by the radical minority on its council into organizing an Animal Rights Conference at Trinity College, Cambridge, in 1977, which was attended by nearly all the key figures in the movement of that period, except Peter Singer, who compensated for his absence by writing a foreword to the published proceedings.[25]

The two-day meeting concluded when the Declaration Against Speciesism, which I had written, was signed by 150 people.[26] The Declaration went as follows:

A Declaration Against Speciesism

Inasmuch as we believe that there is ample evidence that many other species are capable of feeling, we condemn totally the infliction of suffering upon our brother and sister animals, and the curtailment of their enjoyment, unless it be necessary for their own individual benefit.

We do not accept that a difference in species alone (any more than a difference in race) can justify wanton exploitation or oppression in the name of science or sport, or for food, commercial profit or other human gain.

We believe in the evolutionary and moral kinship of all animals and we declare our belief that all sentient creatures have rights to life, liberty and the quest for happiness.

We call for the protection of these rights.

This declaration, youthful and idealistic in tone, became the basis for many subsequent charters ratified by local authorities in Britain.

The conference, instigated largely by Andrew Linzey and myself, was not only a novelty for the RSPCA, it was also the first serious conference ever held anywhere which was devoted entirely to the subject of animal rights, and I hope, the last such occasion at which meat was offered to those staying for lunch! RSPCA conferences followed shortly on animal experimentation (in London) and farm animal welfare (in Amsterdam).[27]

In 1978 another extraordinary event occurred. The council decided to stage an RSPCA march through Dover in protest against the cruel export of live food animals from British ports. This was probably the RSPCA's first, and so far only, official mass protest march, and involved over a thousand members of the society.

Our so-called SELFA campaign (Stop the Export of Live Food Animals) had started in 1974, and sought to replace the 'on the hoof' trade with one that was entirely 'on the hook'; it failed to achieve this end, but led to a tightening up of the rules under which animals were transported across Europe.

We met officials at the Ministry of Agriculture and with John Silkin himself, the Minister for Agriculture, in trying to achieve reform. But the power of the industry and its friends within the ministry proved too great, aided by the fact that the RSPCA's publicity campaign was vitiated by constant blimpish attacks from some of the society's own senior staff and council, who continued to feel that publicity and 'embroilment in politics' were somehow beneath the society's dignity. Furthermore, they failed to understand that the minister himself needed (and had privately requested) public pressure in order to overcome the resistance of his own officials; instead, some of our own staff publicly attacked me for unfairly pressurizing him!

The European Sphere

Another highly important step initiated by myself and the RSPCA reformers was the decision to enter the European arena. In 1978 'Mike' Seymour-Rouse was appointed the RSPCA's Director of European Liaison, and in an attempt to coordinate the principal welfare organizations within the EEC we formed a new federation under the title Eurogroup for Animal Welfare – later abbreviated simply to Eurogroup. Almost at once the constructive attitude of EEC officials in Brussels and the growing enthusiasm of members of the European Parliament in Strasbourg were evident, in welcome contrast to the negativity and red tape of Whitehall (see chapter 16). By the 1980s the European Commission was showing as much (or more) interest in animal welfare as in conservation.

International Co-operation

The RSPCA's contribution to the campaign against the killing of seals in Canada was also novel. After an approach from Brian Davies, the founder of the International Fund for Animal Welfare (IFAW), I had arranged in 1977 for the RSPCA to join the campaign on both sides of the Atlantic. In Canada, an RSPCA team comprising Richard Adams, Bill Jordan and Mike Seymour-Rouse undertook a gruelling lecture tour in oppositon to the hunt, and in Europe the RSPCA assisted the Fund in bringing pressure to bear on governments, culminating eventually in the ban of baby seal imports into the EEC in 1983 and its extension in 1985 (see chapter 12). Such an RSPCA campaign would have been unthinkable a few years earlier, demanding, as it did, co-operation with other bodies such as IFAW and Greenpeace, an international and political approach, and a concern for wild animals.

Scottish Seals

One of the most satisfactory campaigns of this period was that initiated by Greenpeace in 1978, when they sent a ship to oppose the killing of grey and common seals by Norwegian sealers off the coast of Scotland. This move created massive publicity during the summer period when news was scarce. Greenpeace, by positioning its personnel near the seals, forced the British government to order the Norwegians to delay the use of their rifles.

The next moves were made by IFAW and the RSPCA. The former placed whole-page advertisements in the British national newspapers depicting a young seal, and carrying the simple injunction 'Write to the Prime Minister'. The result was that James Callaghan received in one week some 17,000 letters opposing the seal hunt — more than any British prime minister had ever received before on a single topic.

Meanwhile, I took an RSPCA delegation to the Secretary of State for Scotland. At this meeting Bill Jordan, then the RSPCA's first Chief Wildlife Officer, produced scientific evidence which cast doubt on the government's estimates on the amount of fish predation by seals.

These three separate tactics were well timed. Shortly afterwards the government announced that the seal hunt had been called off. For another decade the British government refused to license a similar man-oeuvre, and since the government's own research by the Sea Mammal Research Unit eventually supported the RSPCA's view that seals were not responsible for declining fish stocks, the seals were left in relative peace for some years.

This operation usefully illustrates the mechanics of a successful campaign for which no single individual or organization can take total credit. Greenpeace had created the headline publicity; IFAW had mobilized its supporters to bombard the prime minister with letters; and the RSPCA had negotiated with the government directly, providing a science-based face-saver which allowed the minister off the hook. Surely, whenever ordinary diplomatic pressures fail to produce results, a good campaign requires these elements: co-operation among campaigning groups, publicity, the channelling of public opinion and negotiation at a high level. This was how the so-called RSPCA 'radicals' had always hoped to see the animal welfare movement operating.

The RSPCA's role was also significant as the parent society for numerous smaller, and on the whole rather conservatively minded, societies all over the world. In 1960 there had been 47 such affiliated societies overseas which, while remaining autonomous in terms of policies and finance, looked towards the RSPCA in England for support. By 1986 this number had grown to 128. Liaison of a less formal sort was maintained between RSPCA headquarters and some 300 other organizations. In addition, the RSPCA could claim three overseas branches, in Hong Kong, St Helena and Gibraltar.

The RSPCA, however, was to play little part in assisting Georges Heuse's unsuccessful efforts to create a United Nations convention in 1977 or in Bill Clark's International Committee for the Convention for the Protection of Animals which met in Geneva in July 1986; as far as Britain was concerned the main effort for this enterprise was left to John Alexander-Sinclair.

Putting Animals into Politics

The successful campaign to 'put animals into politics' (in Lord Houghton's words) aimed to persuade the major political parties in Britain, for the first time, to commit themselves in official policy to the welfare of animals. This idea was formulated by Houghton, Clive Hollands and myself in 1977 and grew out of our disillusionment with the tradition in British politics of leaving legislative reform in this field to the almost invariably frustrated efforts of individual back-bench MPs. Private Members' Bills rarely achieved results, and we felt we had to upgrade the issue so that legislation would be introduced by governments themselves. We had had enough of the specious argument that such 'matters of conscience' should be shunned by government. Had politics sunk so low that British administrations no longer wished to concern themselves with moral issues?

Early in 1978 we set up a joint committee with this aim, entitled the General Election Co-ordinating Committee for Animal Protection (GECCAP). This venture followed the limited success of Animal Welfare Year in 1976; this had been organized by Clive Hollands, who had found it difficult to secure co-operation between the many animal welfare bodies he involved. After many resignations it fell to Hollands and myself to do a speaking tour of Britain in which some increase in public awareness of the major issues may have been achieved.

One of the hardest battles the radicals fought at this time was to persuade RSPCA council colleagues to agree the funding of the General Election Co-ordinating Committee for Animal Protection (GECCAP).

Once again the threat of loss of charitable status was raised by Frederick Burden MP, and the Charity Commissioners were contacted by those who feared this more politically effective animal welfare approach. In their annual report the following year, the Commissioners went so far as to name the RSPCA and to object to its funding of the GECCAP campaign; but by then the role and efficiency of the Charity Commission itself was under scrunity. Furthermore, the right of charities to pursue political action, provided it was relevant to their objectives but subsidiary to their main functions, was being widely advocated.

In the event, the GECCAP campaign was a success. We persuaded the Labour party to produce a policy background leaflet in July 1978 entitled 'Living without Cruelty'. The Liberals took matters a step further by passing actual policy resolutions proposed by ex-party president, Basil Goldstone, and after approaches from Hollands and myself, the Scottish Nationalists also pledged their interest. Only the Conservative party hung back, and I was assigned the task of persuading them to join the rest; after approaches to William Whitelaw and the party's chairman, Lord Thorneycroft, assistance from the Earl of Selkirk, and a meeting with Conservative party officials, the Conservative Research Department promised to write a leaflet. This was not published, however, until September 1979 – six months after the general election.[28]

In April 1979 all the major parties – Liberal, Conservative and Labour – mentioned animal welfare in their election manifestos for the first time. GECCAP had asked the parties for policy under six headings reflecting the interests of the main constituent bodies on the joint committee – the protection of horses (especially in the meat trade), radical reforms in intensive animal husbandry (affecting pigs, veal calves, and battery chickens), the welfare of dogs (especially as regards the need for dog wardens), experiments on animals (such as the need to control the infliction of suffering, improve training and to restrict the use of animals for non-medical purposes), the protection of wildlife[29] (for example the banning of hare-coursing and otter-hunting), and the substitution of live food animal exports with a carcass-only trade. Although the response of the parties was rather piecemeal, both the Liberal and Labour parties endorsed the GECCAP suggestion that there should be a new permanent statutory animal protection body to monitor and co-ordinate the whole field and advise government on new legislation.[30]

After this, all the major parties continued to include animal protection in their official thinking, although Richard Sayer, the RSPCA Parliamentary Officer, was reporting by 1985 that the greatest grass-roots interest, as gauged by attendance at party conference meetings, was being shown by members of the Alliance parties (Liberal and SDP).[31] The Alliance too went ahead with detailed proposals from the SDP's Katya Lester on how to draw together the administration and enforcement of animal protection legislation under a united Animal Protection Commission rather like the Health and Safety Executive.[32]

REACTION: 1980–1983

Shortly before the 1979 election, the Prime Minister, James Callaghan, had written to me confirming his plan to set up a Council for Animal Welfare; after her victory, Mrs Thatcher, the new Prime Minister, sent a letter reassuring me of her intention to honour her party's manifesto pledges. Almost at once, in 1979, the Thatcher government announced the establishment of a Farm Animal Welfare Council (FAWC) to investigate and advise the Minister of Agriculture. The composition of this committee, however, immediately created alarm among the more go-ahead element on the RSPCA council because it contained a preponderance of those with commercial intersts in farming and the meat trade, one of whom was the director of a company recently convicted of cruelty. What had been hoped for was a committee reflecting a balanced composition between agricultural and welfare points of view. A section of the agricultural press was clearly delighted by 'the skilful way' in which the minister had 'spiked the welfarists' guns'.[33]

When the government proceeded to appoint two of the then top officials from the RSPCA, Julian Hopkins and Philip Brown (one of whom, Brown, accurately or not was suspected by some of having sympathetic connections with the agricultural industry) without even the knowledge, let alone approval, of the RSPCA council, a major row erupted. A narrow majority of the RSPCA council voted against allowing the officials to take their place on FAWC. Certain society members, some deliberately misinformed of the true nature of the dispute, reacted angrily, summoned an extraordinary general meeting early in 1980, and tried to expel from the society the eleven dissenters (who included two recent chairmen – Michael Kay and myself). Tempers were lost at the meeting in Central Hall which was attended by 1,600 members.[34] Two announced that they were factory farmers and proud of it, several proclaimed their membership of the National Farmers' Union and others, without any awareness of their absurdity, accused the dissenters of 'disrespect to one of Her Majesty's Ministers'.

The motion failed after a fierce debate.[35] Nevertheless, this meeting marked the commencement of another unhappy period in the society's history after five years of relative peace. The meeting had been advertised in hunting circles and readers of *Horse and Hound* had been urged to give up a day's hunting to rid the RSPCA of its 'anti element and political opportunists of the extreme left'.[36] Furthermore, most of the members attending this meeting were only partially informed of the facts; some had been carefully primed and organized by traditionalist members of the society's staff and few knew, for example, of Brown's threat to testify against the society if it proceeded in a case involving cruelty to zoo animals, or that following his clumsy and unauthorized killing of scores of cats rescued by the society from OLAC (a laboratory breeding business in Wales), the council was actually in the process of considering his dismissal as the society's Chief Veterinary Officer. Revealingly, perhaps, sections of the farming press[37] as well as that of the veterinary profession[38] continued to support Brown against the so-called 'militant' RSPCA council.

To many it appeared extraordinary that Peter Walker, then Agriculture Minister, could have appointed two members of the RSPCA staff to this committee without seeking the approval of the RSPCA's board, or that Hopkins and Brown could have accepted his offer without asking for such approval; both, in the event, ceased to be society employees within three years, one through ill health. Without any publicity, however, the government gradually improved the composition of FAWC over the ensuing months, and it went on to produce a succession of sensible proposals for reform, before having its composition again changed in the mid-1980s.

The reaction against the RSPCA reformers came principally from a handful of branch workers who feared that the rapid changes within the society would threaten its standing. Wild rumours were circulated, sometimes deliberately, to the effect that the younger group on the council was seeking to dismantle both the society's inspectorate and the branch system itself. In fact neither of these objectives ever had been considered and both would have been strongly opposed by most of the reformers. Some widening of the role of the inspectorate to cover the society's new priority areas had been discussed, and the much-maligned 'radicals', after consultations between myself and Mike Seymour-Rouse, had instigated in 1977 the 'plain clothes' undercover arm of the inspectorate, the Special Investigation Unit, which over the years was to do valuable work. But there had never been any wish to do away with inspectors, only to improve their training and to modernize their role. Nor had the disbandment of the branches ever been contemplated, only a development of the role of branch member to allow those who wanted to campaign to do so with the informal co-ordination and briefing of paid staff.

By 1979 the so-called 'radicals' could see that they had shaken the RSPCA from its slumbers. We had created written policies for the society and selected the priorities within them. We had set up expert committees within the new areas of priority and established new staff departments to service them. We had then sharpened the society's campaigning edge so as to put the new policies into effect through the use of political pressure, prosecution, increased educative effort and creative publicity. Furthermore, we had extended our range of operations into Europe and included an undercover element in our inspectorate. We had tried to build bridges, and if we had not always succeeded, at least channels of communication had been opened with government, with other campaigning bodies, and with the conservation movement, both nationally and internationally. All this had been achieved in the context of improved finance and growing membership.[39] Those who opposed us wished the society to continue its role as the nation's principal homer and destroyer of unwanted cats and dogs. Frequently they alluded to the past as support for their opposition to change, apparently ignorant of the society's original role as a reforming and proselytizing body and unaware that in the nineteenth century the RSPCA had shown very little interest in the fate of pet animals compared with its concern for the treatment of farm and laboratory species and wildlife.

In introducing considerable 'glasnost' and 'perestroika' into the society, we had ruffled too many feathers. Two editorials in the *Daily Telegraph*, a leading conservative national newspaper, outrageously asserted that the RSPCA had been deliberately infiltrated by extreme left-wing conspirators intent on using the society's prestige and funds for ulterior political purposes: 'Hunting, the fur trade and almost any sphere of activity related to animals can be used as a stick with which to beat the free society.'[40] The charge of 'Marxist infiltration' into animal welfare circles was repeated in a further editorial later in the month;[41] despite the editor's admission that the original leader has been 'opinionated' and the hysteria about 'reds under the bed' − a charge frequently flung at anyone who tried to change almost anything in post-war Britain − continued. Indeed an RSPCA council member on the BBC's major *Panorama* programme about the society went as far as to say that she thought some of the RSPCA reformers were part of a 'Communist' conspiracy![43] The old slur was resurrected that the reformers were not interested in nonhuman animals but in human revolutionary politics.

Financial Problems

In this sadly paranoid atmosphere, evidence began to come to light in 1980 that, under the new executive director (Major Ronald Seager had retired on health grounds in 1978 and his successor had been appointed shortly before Christmas of that year), the society's finances were deteriorating seriously. In 1978 and 1979 the society had enjoyed surpluses of approximately £1 million each year, but after 1980 these were turned into large deficits caused chiefly by the employment (unauthorized by the society's council) of an additional 200 staff, taken on between the autumn of 1979 and the end of 1980.

It was the much-maligned 'radicals' who had been the first to spot the trouble and to attempt to put it right. We had called for a special finance committee to be established early in 1980 and, when this had been blocked by traditionalists, we had proposed in April an independent investigation. This too had been overruled. On 21 September 1980 the *Sunday Telegraph* broke the news to the public − and to most shocked members of the RSPCA council as well − that the RSPCA was indeed

£1 million in the red. At about the same time allegations began to be circulated within the RSPCA council insinuating extravagance or worse on the part of one or two of the senior staff. Calls by the 'radicals' on the council to have these allegations independently and confidentially investigated were, however, angrily rejected.

Other channels were tried, and deputations of 'radicals' and concerned senior members vainly approached both the Charity Commissioners and the society's auditors for help. Not only were those who were trying to regularize the society's financial affairs repeatedly rebuffed; they were subjected to lawyers' letters threatening libel action on behalf of senior staff and by official moves, in some cases successful, to have them expelled from the society. Indeed, the pilloried would-be saviours of the society's finances were obliged to employ the services of the distinguished lawyer Sir David Napley to defend their positions.[44] The dismal row rumbled on until March 1982, when the results of investigations by the society's able new treasurer, Rachel Smith, were announced to the council, and the society's executive director and finance controller immediately left the society's employment.

One of the sad aspects of this affair is that had the warnings of the radicals been heeded when they had first been raised, the society could have avoided over two years of bad publicity and saved itself many hundreds of thousands of pounds. Instead, two out of four of the key 'whistle-blowers' in this row were ignominiously forced out of the society. Even after they were proved to have been absolutely right about the mismanagement of the society's finances, they received neither apology nor thanks. On 29 September 1982, Richard Adams had been forced to resign as the society's president, supported by the vice-presidents Lord Houghton, Lady Dowding and Clive Hollands who issued a public statement critical of the society's 'institutional lethargy' and of its unfriendliness 'towards the increasing number of younger members who demand more vigorous action against the growing commercial exploitation of animals'; all had supported the reformers' call for an investigation of the society's finances.

It was perhaps because the row over finances had been seen as a clash between radicals and traditionalists that it had taken an unnecessarily long time to resolve. If the so-called traditionalists themselves had called for the inquiries in the first place the matter might have been over in a few weeks.

Not until Rachel Smith became council chairman in June 1983 did the grievous wounds within the society begin to heal and the factions within its council begin to blur. Although not one of the 'radicals', Smith could see the merit in some of their concerns. Late in the day, the finances at last were overhauled, and gradually the society was put back on the more progressive course it had been on since the mid-1970s. This process was very much assisted by the appointment of Frank Dixon Ward as the society's temporary executive director late in the summer of 1982. A recently retired chief executive in local government, Dixon Ward proved a sound administrator and one who took for granted the reformers' hard-fought-for redefinition of the society's role as being, in part, that of a campaigning pressure group seeking new and improved legislation.

COMING TOGETHER AGAIN: 1983–1989

To what extent was the 'Great RSPCA Row' of 1980–3 of any real significance? In some respects – incompetent management, almost incredible resistance to change, unionization, over-manning and bureaucratic lethargy – the society had been a microcosm of some of the problems of British society in general.

In the event, the society's large deficits had forced the axing of its new Campaigns Department, the reduction of its newly appointed parliamentary staff to one, and the decimation of its once-vigorous Education Department. As usual in such situations it was the new small departments which suffered disproportionately more than the old and inflated ones. By the end of 1982 over 170 jobs had gone and the RSPCA's inspectorate training college was up for sale. Under Rachel Smith such necessary cuts were not used to return the society to its uninspiring role of the 1940s and 1950s. Gradually, the more modern aspects were reinstated and, although the few remaining 'radicals' were firmly kept out of office, their theories of the late 1970s were reapplied. They had, in effect, lost the battle of personalities but won the war of ideas, and had succeeded in dragging the RSPCA, yelping and caterwauling, into the twentieth century.

In general, subsequent events proved the reformers right on all issues of substance, but we had made serious mistakes of style and tactics. Sometimes we had appeared arrogant and confrontational, and we had not explained sufficiently to branch members what it was that we were trying to do. Acting under the constraint of a two-year limit to my term of office as chairman, I had tried to go too far too fast, stirring up resentment among the traditional and unsettling many with the literally scores of innovative motions put before council. Furthermore, the reformers had agreed to several unfortunate appointments among senior staff, including those of the two senior staff members who subsequently had to leave.

The crippling internecine warfare within the RSPCA must have delighted many exploiters of animals who, a year or two earlier, had been worried by the society's more incisive approach. Despite all its bad publicity in the 1960s, early 1970s and early 1980s, however, the RSPCA would emerge in the mid-1980s as still the most potentially influential animal welfare society in the world, with over 600 employees, substantial liquid assets and an income of over £18 million in 1987.[46]

Although recovering its performance under Smith and Dixon Ward, the society sometimes continued at odds, however, with the wishes of members attending its AGMs, most of whom wanted a still more vigorous approach. Furthermore, they could point to the fact that, despite the redefinition of the role of the society, still only about 2 per cent of its expenditure was earmarked specifically for the welfare of the hundreds of millions of farm, laboratory and wild animals – three out of four of its main areas of concern. Nevertheless a series of BBC documentaries about the inspectorate, entitled *Animal Squad* and shown in 1986 and 1987, helped considerably to raise public awareness of the superb routine work done by this arm of the RSPCA, and some of the society's younger staff showed themselves to be vigorous and effective campaigners with a modern outlook.[47] Sadly, such able staff rarely continued long enough in the society's employ.

At its annual meeting in 1986 the members threw out an attempt to increase branch representation on the council (which would have reduced still further the influence of the younger and more go-ahead members) and reinstated the reformers' previous council commitment to phasing out the killing of healthy dogs by 1996. Furthermore, the membership reaffirmed its dislike of the government's new Animal (Scientific Procedures) Act.

By 1987 the society was getting to grips with two major issues: the need to extend the law to cover psychological suffering as well as physical pain, and the desperate need to begin to extend protection against cruelty to animals in the wild. These were among its aims published before the general election of 1987. Others included improving the availability of search warrants, increased fines for dog-fighting and baiting of all sorts, the power to remove any cruelly treated animal from its owner on first conviction, the financing of a national dog warden service, universally effective pre-stunning of all animals in slaughter – including ritual slaughter – the banning of pig stalls, veal crates and hen batteries, the banning of live export of food animals across the sea, and of cruel horse-tethering and the use of snares.

The council's chairman from 1986 to 1988, Joan Felthouse, brought tremendous energy to the job, and the society's new executive director, Andrew Richmond, set about the improvement of its regional structure. Together they began to expand its effectiveness not only as a modern service charity but also as a campaigning organization in accordance with the original vision of its vigorous founders over 160 years before. These improvements continued to be marred, however, by occasional disturbances, as when, for example, in November 1988, a majority of the council ordered the expulsion of five active members of the society on the grounds that they had circulated criticisms of the society's work. This self-styled RSPCA Watchdog group, whose avowed aim was to improve the RSPCA's performance, comprised Margaret House, Richard Farhull, Joan Watson (recently elected to the society's council by the membership), and the two outstanding animal welfare campaigners David Wetton and Angela Walder. These expulsions created bad publicity for the society and illustrated once again the society's failure to deal with criticism in a constructive and democratic way.[48]

VETERINARY INVOLVEMENT

One of the saddest aspects of the worldwide campaign for animal protection has been the part played – or not played – by the veterinary profession. Widely seen by members of the public as being interested in the welfare of animals, with a few glorious exceptions vets have been distinguished by their absence from the great campaigns of the last two hundred years.

Attempts to secure the open support of the veterinary authorities in Britain for RSPCA campaigns in the late 1970s were met with prevarication. The president of one august body explained that such were the vested interests of his members that if he publicly criticized bloodsports or cosmetics experiments on animals or factory-farming he would immediately cease to be president.[49] Another distinguished veterinarian explained that, although veterinary students were sometimes 'starry-eyed animal lovers', such 'sentimentality was soon knocked out of them' by their teachers in preparation for their future roles.[50]

In Britain, members of the Royal College of Veterinary Surgeons make a solemn declaration of loyalty to the college, adding: 'I further promise that I will pursue the work of my profession with uprightness of conduct and that my constant endeavour will be to ensure the welfare of animals committed to my care.'[51] Despite this promise cases have arisen in which veterinary surgeons have been closely involved in practices widely disapproved of in animal welfare circles. A member of the Royal College, for example, published a paper describing how he had repeatedly poured weedkiller down the throats of beagle dogs. After passing blood-streaked faeces and vomiting, several dogs died after days of continued poisoning. Post-mortem examination found that the blood was 'dark chocolate brown' and that the mucous membranes had turned blue.

Even if this research, carried out at a commercial testing establishment, had been for the benefit of veterinary medicine (and nowhere in the paper is this claimed), it is a horrific experiment and it is difficult to see how slowly poisoning dogs to death can be consistent with the oath.[52]

It is, perhaps, hardly surprising that, after the appointment of a hare-courser as the president of Britain's top veterinary body in 1987,[53] some members of the profession have begun to come in for more criticism. Clive Hollands, addressing a British Veterinary Association Congress at Warwick in September 1987, attacked the lack of protest against cruel experimentation from the veterinary profession, their policy of not reporting clients suspected of being involved in organized dog-fighting, and their ambivalent attitude towards the animal welfare movement.[54] Hollands quoted a veterinarian's letter in the national press: 'We vets view the animal welfare/conservationist lobby as motivated by sinister, political, anti-British organisations'[55] and a statement by a veterinary surgeon attending a meeting with local council officials in 1987 to discuss spaying clinics: 'We are in it to make money not provide a social service.'

Reassuringly, Hollands also cited some positive statements of veterinarians, suggesting a growing criticism of their own profession,[56] such as Professor John Webster's statement that 'It was important for practitioners to question their motivation for practice. Were they achieving the right balance between animal welfare and a desire for an adequate income?'[57] In America, vets Neil Wolff and Ned Buyukmichi went further and founded an Association of Veterinarians for Animal Rights.

In April 1988 the columnist Celia Haddon in the *Sunday Telegraph* (17 April 1988) expressed surprise that although 'On television, vets are handsome, cuddly men with a warm, caring attitude towards animals', yet some in reality cut the tails off dogs, work in factory-farms or block the solution of the unwanted dogs and cats problem. She quoted Bill Jordan, himself a veterinarian, as saying that 'their feelings for animals get devalued by too great an interest in science...as science grows so beauty dwindles.'

Perhaps it was the report in June 1988 that 'canned safaris' in Texas, in which clients can shoot caged lions for 2,500 dollars a time, were being run by an American veterinary surgeon[58] which prompted a tirade from Angela Walder at the RSPCA's AGM a few days later, in which she attacked those vets who commercially breed animals for research, carry out experiments on nonhuman primates, block the setting up of cheap neutering clinics, or who are 'more in love with their bank managers than with their animal clients'.[59]

Many veterinary practitioners are indeed caring and conscientious professionals. But if one applies the 'human test' to the actions of certain other members of the veterinary profession – those who breed laboratory animals, experiment on dogs or course hares, for example – then the results are, to say the least, highly disturbing. Imagine the public reaction if members of the *medical* profession were found similarly exploiting their *human* patients.

GROWING SUPPORT

Writing in the *New Statesman*, Jolyon Jenkins remarked in 1986:

Animal rights have probably entered the popular consciousness. According to the most recent poll (Gallup 1985), nearly 1.5 million people have given up meat, though only half for 'moral' reasons — an increase of 23 per cent over the previous year. More specifically, animal liberation is arguably the youth movement of the 80's. Magazines as diverse as *Just Seventeen* and *Class War* discuss it, and a host of rock stars and youth cult figures have announced that they have become vegetarians for moral reasons. The trend has been most marked in women between 16 and 24, 10 per cent of whom are now vegetarians.[60]

Indeed, the extent of support from the contemporary well-known is itself an interesting feature of the movement.[61]

Film-makers, too, have absorbed and strongly reinforced the animal liberation ethic, notably with Franklin J. Schaffner's *Planet of the Apes* series in the 1960s which showed nonhumans experimenting upon humans, Steven Spielberg's *E.T.* (1983), Hugh Hudson's *Greystoke* (1984) and Alan Bridges' screening of Isobel Colgate's 1980 novel *The Shooting Party* (1985) — all brilliant films in their own distinct ways.[62]

Desmond Morris's *The Naked Ape*, published in 1968, was, I believe, a turning-point. Scientific, creative and exciting, it brought home to many the simple reminder that we are animals. The Darwinian message, almost universally accepted on an intellectual level and almost as universally rejected emotionally, morally and politically, began to be driven home. How far Morris's reminder played a part in the formation of the Oxford Group is hard to say; it was not overt or recognized at the time. Yet *The Naked Ape* helped us to face up to our animality and its moral implications.[63] Richard North's *The Animal Report* (Penguin 1983) and Maureen Duffy's *Men and Beasts* (Paladin 1984) have provided very worthwhile documentary comments upon the movement and helped the subject to gain a permanent intellectual standing.

In the 1970s and 1980s British and American academic works began to appear which took into account the welfare of nonhuman animals,[64] the animal liberation movement spawned its own magazines,[65] and serious programmes on British television and radio devoted a good deal of attention to animal liberation in the period 1975–84;[66] in the late 1980s wildlife programmes showing concern for welfare as well as conservation appeared.

EPILOGUE

This chapter has concentrated on the *political* developments of the 1970s and the revival of the RSPCA — still the colossus which dominates the animal welfare scene in Britain and, to an extent, internationally. Much else happened in the 1970s and early 1980s.[67] The seventies saw the philosophical revival (see chapters 1 and 17); the growth in direct action both legal and illegal[68] (see chapters 12 and 15); far more effective political lobbying (see chapters 12, 13, 16 and 17); and the increasing internationalism of the movement (see chapters 10, 12, 16, and 17), all of great importance to the history of the period. Lively new groups, too, were established; for example Animal Liberation in Australia (see chapter 16) and People for the Ethical Treatment of Animals (PETA) in America (see chapter 16). In the UK existing groups such as the British Union for the Abolition of Vivisection and the National Anti-Vivisection Society were revived (see chapter 13), as were the Scottish Society for the Prevention of Vivisection and the League Against Cruel Sports (see chapters 11 and 12). New bodies were founded, such as Compassion in World Farming (see chapter 14), the Hunt Saboteurs Association, the Animal Liberation Front (see chapter 15), and Coordinating Animal Welfare. One of the most charismatic was Animal Aid, founded by Jean Pink in the 1970s, which captured the imagination of the young and radical and spread the word. By 1986 it could claim some 12,000 members under the leadership of John Bryant and Mark Gold.

The 1970s had been a remarkable decade, but in Britain at least the 1980s started badly. The government of Margaret Thatcher did not show an interest in 'green' issues, and resisted almost all radical proposals for reform in animal protection.[69] Yet as the 1990s approached, an underlying mood of optimism in the movement began to be felt again and the summer of 1988 turned out to be highly significant for the whole 'green' movement. Much publicity was given to the attempts to dump in Britain toxic waste sent from Italy in the ship *Karin B*, to artificially caused floods in Bangladesh, human starvation in the Sudan and the plight of thousands of seals dying of a viral infection in the North Sea. Shortly before the September 1988 conference of the Social and Liberal Democrats and the address from their new leader, one of the 'greenest' of Britain's leading politicians, Paddy Ashdown, the Prime Minister herself announced a complete change in the British government's attitude to the environment generally; Britain would, in the future, she said, strive to protect the planet from pollution.[70] Three weeks later, the predicament of three grey whales trapped by Arctic ice in Alaska brought a pledge of unlimited help from President Reagan,[71] and, under the spotlight of the international media, the rescue of two of them was achieved after a symbolic joint operation by Americans and Russians.

At their conference in March 1989 the Social and Liberal Democrats passed my comprehensive animal rights policy resolution. British media attention to all green issues (especially the problems of air and water pollution, acid rain, the 'greenhouse effect', and threats to rain-forests, the ozone layer and the survival of the African elephant) increased sharply during the year.

11 A Wider Perspective

This book is written mainly from a British vantage point. This is not as arbitrary as it may seem since the British have led the way in campaigning and legislating to protect animals in the Western world. This is not because the British have been particularly virtuous, indeed, as we have seen, one reason was that the British during the eighteenth century were especially well known for their cruel exploitation of animals.[1] But it was Britain, in the breakthroughs of the 1820s and 1960s, which had led reform and, around the world it was often the English speakers who set up shelters for strays or lobbied for legislation. Most Northern European countries, however, saw simultaneous, if less publicized, progress. As early as 1766 a postilion in Leipzig had been sent to prison for twelve weeks for riding a horse to death at a time when such an act would have passed unpunished in England, and laws against cruelty were passed in Saxony in 1830, in Prussia in 1838 and in Württemberg in 1839. Pastor Albert Knapp founded the first German animal welfare society in 1837 in Stuttgart; Nuremberg and Dresden followed in 1839, Berlin, Hamburg and Frankfurt in 1841, Munich in 1842 and Hanover in 1844. Earlier still, benevolent German kings had sometimes protected animals in their realms. Frederick the Great once remarked: "Since I know men, I have learned to love animals", and Kaiser Joseph II in 1789 stopped the baiting of animals for sport – forty-six years before it was ended in England. In Germany Arthur Schopenhauer in 1841 attacked

The unpardonable forgetfulness in which the lower animals have hitherto been left by the moralists of Europe. It is pretended that the beasts have no rights. They persuade themselves that our conduct in regard to them has nothing to do with morals or (to speak the language of their morality) that we have no duties towards animals; a doctrine revolting, gross and barbarous . . ."[2]

Later, in 1879, Richard Wagner vigorously opposed vivisection, adding that "in the sympathy evoked (for the animals) I recognise the strongest impulse of my moral being and also the probable source of all my art."[3]

In Switzerland, animal protection societies were formed in Berne in 1844 and in Basle in 1849, and Pastor Philip Wolff founded the Zurich Society in 1856. The first Swiss legislation was in 1842.

Not only Germany and Switzerland, however, produced pioneers in the humane movement. The Scandinavian countries were also at the forefront. The first Norwegian animal-welfare society was founded in Oslo in 1859 by David Graah, apparently inspired by the British RSPCA, and the first Norwegian animal-protection legislation was in 1842. In Sweden, too, the first animal-protection law of 1857 preceded the foundation of formal animal-welfare bodies in Gothenburg in 1869 and in Strängnäs in 1870; the latter begun by the anti-vivisectionist philosopher Adolf Nordvall. In Denmark, the first protective legislation was also passed in 1857.

In the Latin countries of Europe, however, no real legislative progress was made during the nineteenth century. What was it about the Protestant north of Europe that put it ahead of the Catholic south? Was it a different interpretation of the idea of 'dominion', or disillusionment with the notion that earthly pain was part of God's purpose? Or was it not its Protestantism so much as the peace and affluence of the north that affected the issue? Although the Catholic Church had adhered more to Aquinas's view of animals than did Protestantism, it seems that social factors in addition to religious ones account for the difference. Where poverty and insecurity lingered, as in the south of Europe, humans were, perhaps, too preoccupied with their own survival to have time or compassion to spare for nonhumans.

In America similar forces were at work. After the Napoleonic Wars there were peace and growing affluence, and old ties with the British were gradually re-established. In 1828 New York made cruelty to horses, sheep and cattle a misdemeanour. Massachusetts legislated similarly in 1835, and Connecticut and Wisconsin followed in 1838. These laws were rarely enforced and seem to have arisen not out of an active reform movement but from the general consolidation and modernization of state codes which still relied on British precedent. In Boston in 1837, however, the Reverend Charles Lowell preached a sermon against cruelty to animals, and various individuals began to make efforts to protect birds and horses during the 1840s and 1850s. In 1860 S. Morris Waln, a rich Philadelphian, wrote to the RSPCA in London asking for assistance in setting up an organization. At this juncture, however, the Civil War intervened. Once again, war temporarily put an end to animal-welfare reform. In 1865, after the end of hostilities, Henry Bergh, a wealthy New Yorker, attended the annual meeting of the RSPCA in England, where he met Lord Harrowby, the Society's President. An aloof and sensitive man, Bergh had been appalled by the treatment of horses he had witnessed the previous year in St Petersburg. Now he saw the way forward. He would emulate the RSPCA by inviting the cream of New York society to help him to establish a similar organization. With some influential colleagues, he petitioned the state legislature for an Act of Incorporation, and on 22 April 1866 the American Society for the Prevention of Cruelty to Animals (ASPCA) was launched.

Later that year Bergh was visited by Caroline Earle White of Philadelphia, the daughter of a well-known Quaker slavery abolitionist, who proceeded to

15 The welfare of laboratory, pet and wild animals, and of those used in entertainment, are four of the main areas of concern. The fifth, and one of the largest, is the treatment of farm animals, particularly those in intensive "factory farm" systems of agriculture. Here, the author, then RSPCA Council Chairman, leads a massed march at Dover against the export trade in live food animals in May 1978. At the extreme right is RSPCA Council member and leading fashion model Celia Hammond. This was the RSPCA's first, and almost only, official street protest. It helped create a temporary cessation of the trade.

Commercial interests and the rules of free trade have made animal protection measures difficult to obtain. Constant attention is then required to ensure the continuation of any reforms achieved. The unnecessary and invariably cruel transportation of live animals over long distances continues in many parts of the world. This issue is often revived by campaigners but without much permanent success.

canvass support from the wealthy elite of her city. In 1867 she united with Morris Waln and Richard Muckle, who had been working independently along similar lines, and on 21 June 1867 the Pennsylvania SPCA was formed. Two years later, White founded the Women's Branch of the Society, of which she became President.

Almost at the same time as the PSPCA was established, Bergh approached Emily Appleton in Boston, who at once adopted the tactics which Bergh and White had already used. On 25 February 1868 she read a letter in the *Boston Daily Advertiser* from a wealthy Bostonian lawyer, the slavery abolitionist George Angell, expostulating against a recent case of cruelty to racehorses. She contacted Angell and on 31 March they formed the

Massachusetts SPCA and Angell drafted new anti-cruelty state legislation which became law almost immediately. Such was Angell's influence that he was allowed to use the services of seventeen Boston policemen to canvass the city for funds and membership and to distribute copies of the Society's new journal *Our Dumb Animals*. Unlike all the other leaders in the American movement, Angell did not come from a wealthy family; he had made his own fortune as a successful lawyer. Like Bergh, however, he was an Anglophile and an admirer of hereditary wealth and status. Both continued to look to London for guidance, although their influence over their state legislatures achieved results with a rapidity unknown in England.

Within ten years almost every large city in the north east of the United States had an SPCA, and the first on the West Coast, in San Francisco, had been started in 1868. Education and prosecution were their main endeavours. Following the example of the RSPCA they consciously chose to make animal welfare an upper-class and fashionable cause. There were campaigns against the bearing-reign, the beating of horses and the horrors of the long-distance transportation of live food animals.

In 1867 and 1880 Bergh tried in vain to achieve legislation against vivisection.[4] The cause was assisted later by Dr Alfred Leffingwell, who advocated a moderate approach; as a physiologist he had watched Claude Bernard at work and became the leading American proponent of reform over the last twenty years of the century. Leffingwell was not entirely alone as an academic in criticizing vivisection. As in England in the 1860s and 1870s, some distinguished medical figures of the old school regretted the loss of humane sensitivity that was engendered by vivisection. In a memorable statement, quoted by Leffingwell, Henry Bigelow, a professor of medicine at Harvard wrote:

Watch the students at a vivisection. It is the blood and suffering, not the science, that rivets their breathless attention. If hospital service makes young students less tender of suffering, vivisection deadens their humanity and begets indifference to it.[5]

Elsewhere he had written:

There will come a time when the world will look back to modern vivisection in the name of Science, as they do now to burning at the stake in the name of Religion.[6]

In 1877 the American societies federated as the American Humane Association (AHA), with the particular aim of dealing with the abuses associated with the long-distance transportation of livestock across state boundaries. Conditions on the railways were terrible and thousands of animals died *en route* to the slaughter houses of the Mid-West, unprotected from climatic extremes, and often unfed and unwatered.

America lacked a titled aristocracy identical with that which led the humane movement in Europe, but its leaders in America were almost all from the equivalent classes – not only the wealthy elite typified by figures such as Bergh but also other society leaders such as the singer Emma Eames and the actress Minnie Maddern Fiske. Even the eminent psychologist William James indicated his mild approval of the humane effect of anti-vivisection in a letter published in 1909. Generally speaking, as the American campaign came later than the British campaign, the experimenters had more time to plan their tactics and to learn by their mistakes. Perhaps American culture was more accepting of "science" and "progress" than was the British, and the American middle classes were probably less committed to the animals' cause. Also, by the end of the century, more examples of biological and medical advances plausibly attributable to vivisection could be marshalled in its defence. For all these reasons, the American nineteenth-century anti-vivisection campaign largely failed in its objectives. The anti-vivisectionists were successfully discredited by the end of the century and often, as Susan Lederer points out, were ridiculed as women "clothed in the plumage of birds and the skins of exotic mammals".[7]

As in Britain, by 1890 the animal protection movement was predominantly female in membership and, as in Europe, it declined seriously in influence after 1918. The cult of machismo, as strong in America as in Britain, and exacerbated by war, became a potent weapon against reform. After Bergh's death in 1888 his ASPCA gradually ossified. In 1892 it unwisely took over the statutory duty of caring for the stray dogs and cats of New York, and spent the next eighty years preoccupied with this problem. Although its inspectors had police powers throughout the state of New York, these were not used as effectively as they might have been to curb the development of the commercialized cruelties of the modern era. The parallels with the British RSPCA are striking.

The American Humane Association, on the other hand, reached its peak under Dr William Stillman in the early twentieth century and its educational influence spread across the American continent and overseas. Stillman's AHA placed an equal emphasis on preventing cruelty to children and animals, and encouraged a universal spirit of humanitarianism of which Henry Salt must have approved. Stillman also founded the Red Star to aid army animals in a manner parallel to that of the Red Cross for humans. In the nineteenth century, in America as in Britain, philanthropists were often active in both human and nonhuman welfare work. Samuel Gidly Howe, for example, educator of the blind and deaf, became a director of the Massachusetts SPCA, and anti-slavery writers Lydia Maria Child and Harriet Beecher Stowe also wrote on behalf of nonhuman slaves.

In 1874 Henry Bergh had been asked by a social worker, Etta Wheeler, to rescue an abused child. Breaking new legal ground, he persuaded a court to remove Mary Ellen from her adoptive mother, and to convict the latter of assault. Other similar cases followed and Bergh went on to help form the

New York Society for the Prevention of Cruelty to Children in the same year. Through Bergh's association with the RSPCA this idea came back to London, where John Colam and the RSPCA committee set about establishing a similar organization in Britain, later called the National Society for the Prevention of Cruelty to Children. Lord Shaftesbury and Cardinal Manning were involved in this venture and so was Dr Thomas Barnardo. In 1886 the NSPCC was given the use of the RSPCA's boardroom in Jermyn Street in London for their meetings, and for some years Colam was an active member of the NSPCC's committee. The Reverend Benjamin Waugh, usually regarded as the founder of the NSPCC, acknowledged his debt to the RSPCA when he said "Your Society, the RSPCA, has given birth to a kindred institution whose object is the protection of defenceless children." This close connection between the two societies is yet another example of the association of kindness to nonhumans with kindness to humans.

If the RSPCA had somewhat stagnated between the wars, then by 1940 the American Humane Association was in a similar condition. It understood the desirability of sponsoring humane education for children as well as the need to collect stray dogs and cats in the cities, but the monstrous hidden cruelties of the Chicago slaughter houses, as well as those inflicted upon wildlife and in American laboratories, were not effectively criticized. Even the less secret atrocities of rodeos, zoos and the fur trade escaped effective censure. After the Second World War some more imaginative members broke away from the AHA to form the Humane Society of the United States. Under the leadership of Fred Myers, they began to tackle the cruelties entrenched in the mass exploitation of the nonhuman species, just as in Britain, too, disgruntled members of the RSPCA began to desert the Society to set up their own groups to protect those nonhumans whom the RSPCA of the early twentieth century had tended to ignore – farm animals, laboratory animals, and exploited wildlife. One major twentieth-century campaign was against inhumane slaughter-house practices. In America and Canada the meat industry objected vehemently to humane pre-stunning techniques, arguing that they cost them five cents' worth of each steer's brain tissue and were too slow. "We hadn't the time to be humane", a Canadian MP quipped. It was not until after the Second World War, with help from leading figures such as Senator Hubert Humphrey, that the humanitarians of America finally made further progress.

One of the outstanding American reformers of the mid and late twentieth century has been Christine Stevens. After the Second World War the National Society for Medical Research (NSMR) demanded that dogs and cats from humane society shelters be handed over for uncontrolled research. To combat this problem Christine and Roger Stevens decided to found their own organizations, the Animal Welfare Institute in 1951 and the Society for Animal Protective Legislation in 1955. In 1952 the Metcalf–Hatch Act was passed requiring all dog pounds and all humane societies in receipt of public funds to surrender animals to scientific institutions. Most humane organizations, with exceptions such as the ASPCA and the Syracuse SPCA, immediately gave up their pound contracts in order to avoid having to send their animals to laboratories. The ASPCA, however, continued to supply dogs for research until 1971[8] when state animal-seizure laws began to be repealed. Throughout this period Christine Stevens played a pivotal role in lobbying congressmen to introduce legislation to give protection to laboratory animals based upon the principles of the British Cruelty to Animals Act of 1876. From 1960 onwards Bills were introduced and hearings were held. Photographs supplied by Stevens prompted *Life* magazine to publish an article on 4 February 1966 which caused public outrage and gave reformers sufficient public support for the Laboratory Animal Welfare Act to be signed into law by President Johnson on 24 August of that year. This Act, renamed the Animal Welfare Act in 1970 and amended in 1976 and 1985 (following further pressure brought by Stevens and her colleagues) sets humane standards for laboratory animals, among them the requirement for the appropriate use of anaesthetic, analgesic and tranquillizing drugs.

From 1955 onwards Stevens also lobbied for the better protection of animals at slaughter, and in 1958 the first federal Humane Slaughter Act was passed requiring pre-stunning. Other legislation followed to protect horses, marine mammals and other wildlife.[9] Stevens could rightly claim that whereas only two federal laws existed to protect animals in 1955 (prior to the foundation of the Society for Animal Protective Legislation), fifteen had been passed by 1998.

In 1975 Peter Singer's *Animal Liberation* was published in New York and immediately had an impact on a younger generation, triggering a long public debate on the ethical issues raised by speciesism. Tom Regan became the leading American-born philosopher of animal rights and, in some quarters, the more conservative "animal welfare" attitudes of the older generation were subjected to fierce analysis and criticism. Some of the older campaigners such as Helen Jones and Cleveland Amory moved with the times, welcoming the more radical approach. Others held aloof. The quiet achievements of the 1950s and 1960s tended to be overlooked.

Inspired by Singer's message, Henry Spira in New York demonstrated how to campaign effectively, organizing pickets in front of the Museum of Natural History against the cat sex experiments being performed there. After eighteen months of protest the research was stopped. Spira then led the campaign to repeal the Metcalf–Hatch Act and succeeded in this aim in 1979. This good work was continued by Ingrid Newkirk and Alex Pacheco who founded People for the Ethical Treatment of Animals (PETA) in 1980. Paradoxically, however, as the subject gained a higher public profile in America, and as a large number of new animal-rights groups proliferated, old supporters such as Senators Clark, Neuberger and Young and Congressmen Reswick, Poage and Dole gradually disappeared from Congress and the issue languished politically during the later 1980s and 1990s. Campaigning became based more upon philosophical purity than political credibility and achievement. As Spira put it, "the war cry has been 'all or nothing' with the almost inevitable result being nothing."[10]

MODERN TIMES

The 1980s, in retrospect, was a period of consolidation rather than progress for British animal welfare. As we have seen, the radical breakthrough had been achieved in the previous decade by groups such as the Hunt Saboteurs Association, the RSPCA Reform Group, the General Election Coordinating Committee for Animal Protection (GECCAP) and the informal Oxford Group (see pp. 6–7). In the Britain of the 1980s there was a conservative reaction; the media adopted a new and menacing tone, attacking animal-rights organizations in terms more appropriate for terrorists or revolutionaries. For those not familiar with the sensationalistic tactics of the media, practised chiefly in order to create excitement and thus to boost sales, the new and idealistic crusade against speciesism was easily made to appear a sinister conspiracy of the political Left. In fact, Marxists were conspicuous by their absence from the animal-rights movement and, indeed, often openly despised it. Yet an ultra-conservative group regained control of the RSPCA and proceeded to purge the Society of some of its leading modernizers. Almost overnight in 1979 the new Conservative government under Margaret Thatcher had changed the climate of opinion, fuelling right-wing paranoia which condemned out of hand liberal reformers in almost every field. Yet despite all this an underlying change had occurred. Even the arch reactionaries of the RSPCA now accepted the necessity for many of the reforms which, only a few years previously, they had opposed. Most of the structural changes in the Society which, as a leader of the reformers I had instigated, had survived and, in the wider community, attitudes among younger scientists and veterinarians had swung the way of the animals. Above all, led by the British, the body politic of the European Community grew to perceive animal welfare as a credible political issue. While RSPCA Chairman I had initiated the establishment of the Eurogroup for Animal Welfare and, under the direction of Mike Seymour-Rouse, Ian Fergusson and David Wilkins, it had gradually expanded its influence with the Members of the European Parliament and with the officials of the European Commission in Brussels. Indeed, more progress was made on continental Europe than in Britain itself during the 1980s. Animal welfare in Britain had been squeezed off the political agenda again. Only the Liberal Party had built up animal-welfare policy following the GECCAP breakthrough of 1979 and the meetings of the Liberal Animal Welfare Group were among the best-attended fringe events of Liberal Party Conferences in the early 1980s.

In America things were different. The Vietnam War had preoccupied the younger generation of the 1960s and early 1970s and, initially, America had shown resistance to the new animal-rights awakening which was emanating from Oxford. The first serious philosophical book on the subject for eighty years, *Animals Men and Morals*, published in Britain in 1971, scarcely sold in America and my own *Victims of Science,* which was to trigger the laboratory welfare reforms in Britain (and the EU), was rejected by several leading American publishers when it was offered to them in 1973 and 1974; it was, they said, "subversive". Only the enlightened attitude of editors of the *New York Review of Books,* and the brilliance of Peter Singer's writing, caused the intellectual breakthrough in America with the publication of his *Animal Liberation* in 1975. This brought the Oxford message across the Atlantic and so started the ball rolling some five or ten years later than in Britain. But it rolled differently. While we in Britain had to contend with active opposition in the 1980s, the American movement boomed, at least on the philosophical level, with publications on animal rights peaking in the early years of that decade.[11]

In the 1990s, with the decline of Thatcherism, the British animal-welfare movement began to move forward again. The RSPCA was by now a far more effective organization than it had been. In particular, its staff were better qualified and more able than they were in earlier years. Then, in December 1990, Brian Davies set up the Political Animal Lobby (PAL) and made me its Director. Over the next six years PAL broke new ground politically. Instead of doing what most lobbyists did, that is to say, lobby "backbench" Members of Parliament (who have considerably less influence on legislation than do their American counterparts), I concentrated upon getting to know individual Ministers, their senior staff and advisers. I softened my old tactics of bombarding them with demands for new legislation (many other groups were doing this enthusiastically) and, instead, offered technical advice and trust. The declared intention of PAL was to raise funds to give to the political parties and the fund-raising was done with great success by Michael Espley and appropriate agencies. Over the years PAL made substantial donations to all three of the main British parties, culminating in a donation of £1 million to the Labour Party in 1996. I did not attach strings to these donations but, of course, it hardly escaped the attention of senior party figures that money was coming from a new and unexpected source. Gradually, I gained access to leading figures and, for example, arranged meetings for Brian Davies and myself with Neil Kinnock (Labour Party Leader), Chris Patten (Conservative Party Chairman), Paddy Ashdown (Liberal Democrat Leader) and, in 1992, with Prime Minister John Major. We had at least engaged the attention of some of the most powerful politicians in the country. Major wrote a year later: "animal welfare is no longer a fringe issue".[12] PAL subsidized party leaflets on animal welfare for all three parties, proposed and funded the establishment of party animal-welfare researchers and helped to set up and fund party grass-roots animal-welfare organizations. I also established good contacts with senior Whitehall officials and entertained Ministers and Shadow Ministers over meals. PAL persuaded the Liberal Democrat and Labour Parties to appoint Parliamentary animal-welfare spokespeople – Simon Hughes MP and Matthew Taylor MP for the former party and Ron Davies MP and Elliot Morley MP for the latter. I made sure that PAL supported ongoing campaigns on a wide range of issues – for example, against cosmetics testing on animals, the use of apes in research, farrowing crates and tethers for sows, for better conditions for poultry and for animals being transported, for amending the Dangerous Dogs Act and in support of new pet quarantine requirements, for the better protection of whales, seals and elephants and in support of the introduction of new legislation to protect wild mammals from cruelty. Some of these campaigns were targetted at Strasbourg and Brussels and PAL gave support to Eurogroup in these instances. The existing specialist organizations were all working well in the early 1990s – laboratory animals were dealt with by the National Anti-Vivisection Society (NAVS) under Jan Creamer and by the British Union for the Abolition of Vivisection (BUAV) under Mike Baker (who, in 1998 became UK Director of IFAW), farm animals by Compassion in World Farming (CIWF) exceptionally led by Joyce D'Silva and Peter Stevenson, farmed poultry by Clare Druce, dogs by Clarissa Baldwin at the Canine Defence League, and wild animals by Wildlife Link, IFAW, Mark Glover at Lynx and by John Bryant and Angela Smith at the League Against Cruel Sports (LACS). Mark Gold and Andrew Tyler at Animal Aid provided more-generalized support for the younger and more radical parts of the animal-protection community. PAL assisted where it could with the many issues campaigned upon expertly by the specialists, usually by raising them in face-to-face contacts with those in government. Just as PAL specialized in talking to government rather than lobbying Parliament, so also, I decided, PAL should specialise in the *structural* problems of animal politics rather than with its myriad manifestations – the problems behind the problems, so to speak. To this end PAL campaigned (ineffectually due to resistance from within Whitehall) to improve the machinery of government dealing with animal welfare. I had, as early as 1979, obtained a pledge from Prime Minister Jim Callaghan that a Labour government would set up an Animal Welfare Council as a coordinating body. In the 1990s PAL called for some similar structure to be established and suggested the Health and Safety Commission as a model. The Liberal Democrats had supported such a move when I was Chairman of the Liberal Democrats Animal Welfare Group in 1985.[13] But the Home Office in particular proved reluctant to give up its existing powers and responsibilities in this field.[14]

As PAL Director I addressed with success other structural issues such as "subsidiarity" (the proposed decentralization of animal welfare by the EU to its Member States) and initiated the campaign to introduce the animal-welfare protocol into the Treaty of Rome. PAL and CIWF brought IFAW, the RSPCA, WSPA and Eurogroup into this operation and I lobbied the Foreign Office. In 1997 the protocol was proposed by the UK government and was agreed in Amsterdam as follows:

DESIRING to ensure improved protection and respect for the welfare of animals as sentient beings [the parties] AGREED upon the following provision which shall be annexed to the Treaty establishing the European Community.

In formulating and implementing the Community's agriculture, transport, internal market and research policies, the Community and the Member States shall pay full regard to the welfare requirements of animals, while respecting the legislative or administrative provisions and customs of the Member States relating in particular to religious rites, cultural traditions and regional heritage [Amsterdam 1997].

This was, almost certainly, one of the most gratifying animal-welfare achievements of the 1990s.

The other major structural issue was the effect of global free trade. The General Agreement on Tarriffs and Trade (GATT) had become the World Trade Organisation (WTO) in January 1995 and been given the power to sanction countries that erected barriers to trade.[15] Measures to protect the environment or to promote animal welfare could come into this category. Attempts, for example, to restrict the import of cruelly trapped furs or to stop the import of seal products became vulnerable. Countries with higher welfare standards found themselves at a disadvantage, being forced to accept cheaper but cruelly produced goods from abroad. In an effort to prevent this position becoming established, I arranged meetings with the Director General of the WTO and the European Trade Commissioner Sir Leon Brittan in 1995 asking that animal welfare be included under the existing exemptions for "public morality" and "animal health" (see page 000).

The 1990s were characterized by three high-profile campaigns in Britain – that to outlaw cruelty to wild mammals (achieved with the passage of Alan Meale's Wild Mammals Protection Act of 1996), the live exports debate (1994–1996) and the anti-hunting campaign (which was reactivated from 1992). I will consider each in a little more detail. There was also a prolonged campaign by activists against the breeding of cats for laboratory use at Hill Grove Farm in Oxfordshire; its picketing allegedly costing the police more than £1 million in 1997. The farm closed in 1999.

Attempts to include wild animals in the standard legislation against cruelty (the Protection of Animals Act 1911) had always been opposed by the hunting lobby. When Labour MPs Kevin McNamara and John McFall had introduced Private Members Bills to protect wild mammals in 1991 and 1994 respectively, they, too, had encountered opposition from this quarter. It was therefore necessary to exclude hunting with dogs as a possible offence and, with this exemption, the hunters dropped their opposition to the Bill and Alan Meale finally succeeded when his Wild Mammals (Protection) Bill became law in 1996. Outside Parliament, the campaign had been led by Angela Smith and John Bryant of the LACS and Kate Parminter of the RSPCA, but many others had participated, including myself at PAL. IFAW had helped to ensure that a record half a million cards and letters had been received by MPs on this issue during the Bill's Second Reading.

The live exports debate had been prominent in the late 1970s when I had led the RSPCA in its first massed street protest. The issue was revived in

1994 by grass-roots protesters and not by any of the major animal-welfare bodies. Once the initial protests had been reported in the media, the movement spread and protesters gathered at the main ports where live animals were being exported, mostly by sea, across the English Channel – principally at Dover, Plymouth, Shoreham and Brightlingsea. One protester, Jill Phipps, was accidentally crushed to death by a truck carrying calves outside Coventry airport. Mark Glover of Respect for Animals (a key figure in the 1980s, along with the author Richard Adams, in driving fur coats off the streets of London) was involved from 1994, as was CIWF. But in general, it was the ordinary compassionate citizenry which participated. The journalist Penny Lewis played a key role in highlighting the issue as did Carla Lane and her allies Celia Hammond and the well-known actress Joanna Lumley. Attempts instigated by Stanley Johnson of IFAW and myself to use Article 36 of the Treaty of Rome to stop live exports were rejected by the European Court in 1998. But the BSE crisis, in effect, supervened to put an end to live cattle exports and by 1995 the campaign had persuaded the main cross-channel ferry companies to abandon the trade. At least temporarily this form of cruelty was suspended.[16] In Brussels, too, massed protests had taken place where German- and French-speaking demonstrators far outnumbered the British by 1995.

The anti-hunting debate flared up just before the General Election of 1992 when IFAW, under Brian Davies's direction, had placed prominent advertisements in the national press. Once the Wild Mammals Protection Act was on the statute book the issue became prominent again when the winner of the Private Members Ballot, Michael Foster, Labour MP for Worcester, agreed, under persuasion from animal-welfare organizations, to introduce his Wild Mammals (Hunting with Dogs) Bill in June 1997. The RSPCA, LACS and IFAW came together in an alliance called the Campaign for the Protection of Hunted Animals (CPHA) and, advised by leading agencies such as Shandwick and Lawson Lucas Mendlessohn, succeeded in achieving the greatest attendance of MPs for any Private Members Bill when, at its Second Reading on 28 November 1997, the Bill was supported by 411 votes to 151. An extraordinary 85 per cent of the House had attended this Friday afternoon debate and it was the first time that an overall majority of the House (62.4 per cent) had ever voted for a Private Members Bill. Despite this massive Parliamentary support, a handful of pro-hunting MPs, mostly Conservatives, managed to talk the Bill out in July 1998. On 1 March 1998 the pro-hunting lobby under the slightly deceptive title of the Countryside Alliance (in fact a coalition principally of the British Field Sports Society, the Countryside Movement and the Countryside Business Group) organized a well-attended march in London. Although they claimed a turnout of 300,000 in support of hunting, a scientific count that I commissioned for IFAW revealed that only approximately 142,000 protesters walked down Piccadilly and only 40% of these said that hunting with dogs was their single main reason for attending.[17] Shortly before the Election, in April 1997, Tony Blair had written to Tony Banks saying that if Parliament voted, on a free vote, to ban hunting, "parliamentary time will be made available for appropriate legislation to progress in the normal way". This pledge was repeated by Blair's office in letters to members of the public.[18] Nevertheless, the Countryside March unsettled the government, and Home Secretary Jack Straw was reported as saying that he "saw no role for government" in legislating to end hunting.[19] The campaign, however, continued and I commissioned research for IFAW which demonstrated that few jobs would be threatened by a ban on hunting (and that many jobs might be created by a switch to draghunting or blood hounds), that the fox was of actual benefit to most farmers, that hunting did not control fox populations, that the hare population was declining and that there are no valid grounds for using a civil-liberties argument against a legislated ban. The results of public-opinion surveys continued to move increasingly in support of a ban, even after the Countryside March had received massive support from the media. A Gallup survey for the *Daily Telegraph* in August 1997, for example, showed that 84 per cent of town people and 77 per cent of country people disapproved of hunting foxes with hounds and 83 per cent and 78 per cent respectively considered it to be cruel.[20] A year later, after the Countryside March, Gallup repeated the poll. Professor Anthony King commented: "the proportions backing a ban on foxhunting have increased since Gallup last asked the relevant questions."[21] The anti-hunting campaign languished after late 1998 but was revived when over 500 pro-hunting infiltrators attended the RSPCA's AGM at the end of June 1999 and massively defeated my motion calling upon the government to reform the Private Members Bill procedure. This helped to revive media interest in the subject for some days and may have been partly responsible for Prime Minister Blair's unexpected pledge to ban hunting made on television a week or so later on 8 July.[22]

INTERNATIONALISM

The first international conferences on animal welfare had been held in the nineteenth century but work on such a scale was not revived until after the Second World War when the RSPCA and the Massachusetts Animal Welfare Society established the International Society for the Protection of Animals (ISPA). ISPA specialized in much-publicized rescue operations of wild animals but always remained a small operation dependent for funding upon its parent bodies. Later, the World Federation for the Protection of Animals (WFPA) started in Zurich and played a more political role in making links with the Council of Europe. In 1969 the Council, a purely advisory body, published a comprehensive seven-point plan on animal welfare which stated the need to regulate intensive rearing, slaughter, animal experimentation, the protection of birds, the protection of wild animals, the protection of animals abused in sport and show business, and the need to find "a uniform legal status for animals". This important seven-point plan marked the beginning of a coordinated European approach to animal protection and led to the publication in 1976 of the Council of Europe's European Convention on the Protection of Animals Kept for Farming Purposes, and conventions on slaughter and laboratory animals. Karl Frucht, Tony Carding and Hans-Jurgen Weichert of WFPA had made an excellent beginning. In December 1976 the RSPCA began financial support of the WFPA, and in 1980 persuaded it to merge with the ISPA to form the World Society for the Protection of Animals (WSPA). At the same time, the major animal-welfare bodies from each of the member states of the European Community came together in the Eurogroup for Animal Welfare which the RSPCA had instigated in 1979. The northern states continued to be more sympathetic on animal-protection issues generally than were the southern countries of Europe, and the balance swung the animals' way in the 1990s when countries such as Austria, Finland and Sweden joined the Union. In 1983, the European Parliament set up its own all-party 'Intergroup' on animal welfare and asked Eurogroup to provide its secretariat. The whole subject of animal protection had caught the imagination of Members of the European Parliament during the massive lobbying on behalf of seals in 1982 by Eurogroup and the International Fund for Animal Welfare (IFAW), coordinated by Ian McPhail. Members had found themselves the unaccustomed centre of worldwide attention and their mailbags reflected this sudden awareness, among thousands of constituents, of the role and importance of the European Parliament. Indeed, the good progress made in Europe, in part, can be explained in this way: animal protection was the first issue on which the European Parliament captured the support of a mass public.

In 1969 Brian Davies had set up the IFAW. As its executive director, he began the long campaign that culminated in the ban of baby-seal imports into the EEC in 1983 and in the consequent collapse of the Canadian seal hunt which previously had accounted for the deaths of around a hundred-thousand seals annually off the east coast of Canada. Davies's tools were publicity, the mobilization of public opinion and political pressure. He proved adroit at using all three. He had learned to fly a helicopter in order to ferry the media people of the world to the treacherous ice floes of the Gulf of St Lawrence, and in 1977 this massive publicity exercise reached its zenith, with Davies transporting forty-five television and newspaper reporters on to the ice to witness the slaughter. They duly passed on what they saw to millions in America, Canada, Britain, France, Scandinavia, Holland, Germany and Australia, and, for the most part, they did so sympathetically, the main exception being elements in the Canadian media, virtually alone in the English-speaking world at that time in continuing a dogged opposition to the work and ideals of animal protection. Davies remained the inspirational leader of IFAW until his retirement in 1997 when he handed over to Fred O'Regan. By that time, IFAW had grown into a worldwide multi-million-dollar network of loosely coordinated offices, many headed by entrepreneurial and dedicated campaigners. IFAW had specialized in wildlife welfare and focused upon the plight of seals, whales and elephants. In 1985 I collated evidence from leading international experts for IFAW's report to the Canadian Royal Commission on Seals and the Sealing Industry.[23] For the next ten years, chiefly as a result of IFAW's campaigns, the Canadian seal industry remained in a state of collapse.

In the 1990s, as trade and finance became increasingly global, the animal-protection movement responded with increased cooperation between the major organizations on both sides of the Atlantic. In December 1995, for example, the meeting I arranged with the Director General of the World Trade Organisation (WTO) involved the leaders of the RSPCA, WSPA, Humane Society of the United States (HSUS), Humane Society International (HSI) and Eurogroup in order to challenge the new and powerful threat to animal-welfare legislation posed by the powers of the WTO to censure laws deemed to interfere with the freedom of international trade.

After the collapse of the Soviet Empire, there was also a revival of interest in animal protection manifested in the countries of Eastern Europe and both WSPA and the RSPCA conducted training programmes in these countries.

THE MAIN ISSUES

The field of animal welfare has grown in scope commensurate with the expanding exploitation of animals in the twentieth century. New technologies have led to an increase in the use of animals for research and in new forms of intensive agriculture. The population of pet animals has grown in the West while expanding human populations and the destruction of habitats have created massive problems for the welfare of wild animals. Increasing specialization within the animal welfare field has become characteristic of the movement. In each of the five major subdivisions of animal protection – those concerned with pets, laboratory animals, farm animals, wildlife and the use of animals in entertainment – specialized bodies have proliferated. Wildlife welfare has, to an extent, evolved out of the 1960s' concern for conservation. Ian Macphail, initially as a founder of the World Wildlife Fund and later as an IFAW campaigner, was a pioneer. In Europe, the two sides of the movement have worked fairly amicably together and the concern for individual animals and the focus on the protection of species have been found, for the most part, to coincide. In America, however, clashes have occurred occasionally between environmentalists and animal rightists deriving, perhaps, from their different ethical positions – the former essentially anthropocentric and the latter concerned for the animals themselves. The killing of seals, the ivory trade, the plight of whales and dolphins have all attracted massive publicity and the welfare emphasis has grown over the years to complement the conservation argument. On its own the wildlife-welfare movement has campaigned against the use of cruel trapping methods in the fur trade and the European Union banned the importation of furs from countries (such as the US, Canada and Russia) still using steel-toothed leghold traps. More local wildlife-welfare issues have included campaigns to prevent the cruel treatment of kangaroos in Australia, of vicuña in South America, of apes in Africa, of bears in China and of hunted animals in Britain.

Laboratory animals became the leading issue in Britain in the 1970s (especially following the story of the ICI Smoking Beagles and the publication of my book *Victims of Science*) and our campaign continued until new laws were introduced both in Britain and in the European Community in 1986. The latter was largely due to the initiative taken by Stanley Johnson in Brussels. Central to the British campaign was the Committee for the Reform of Animal Experimentation (CRAE) set up by Douglas Houghton, Clive Hollands and myself in 1975. In America, too, the laboratory-animal issue has preoccupied animal protectionists from the 1950s and, especially, since the revival of interest following the publication of Peter Singer's *Animal Liberation* in 1975. Campaigns against the use of animals for trivial research purposes, such as the testing of cosmetics, produced a ban in Britain in 1998, and the development of humane alternative techniques for research has been funded by the European Union under the influence of Michael Balls, Gill Langley and others.

The concern for pet animals has, to an extent, remained partly a matter for education, the rescuing of stray animals and the promotion of sterilization programmes. Specific gains have been made in Europe in the registration of pets and in the relaxation of strict and often cruel quarantine regulations. The control of dangerous pets has also proved a contentious issue.

The concern for the use of animals in entertainment (other than hunting for sport) has flared fitfully when films or television programmes have apparently exploited animals cruelly. A growing antipathy towards inadequate zoos and the use of animals in circuses has led to improved standards in Europe and to some circuses using no animals at all. Campaigners such as Bill Jordan, Virginia McKenna and Wil Travers have achieved some great successes. Even in Spain voices were raised against bullfighting in the 1990s.

A marked difference in emphasis between Europe and North America can be seen in attitudes towards farm-animal welfare. In America, despite every effort by skilled campaigners such as Henry Spira, Alex Herschaft, Peter Singer, Jim Mason, John Kullberg and David Pryor of the Farm Animal Reform Movement (FARM), among others, to push farm-animal welfare up the agenda, it has never yet attained the prominence achieved in Europe. In Britain, Joyce D'Silva and Peter Stephenson of CIWF (founded by Peter Roberts in 1967) have often led the way with battery-hen campaigner Clare Druce. The writers Rebecca Hall and Gordon Newman skilfully used publicity to highlight the predicament of caged poultry. With help from Richard Body MP and the RSPCA, the use of sow stalls and tethers was phased out by 1999. Britain also led the way in the development of the science of farm-animal welfare with centres at Edinburgh (Dr Natalie Waran and

Dr Mike Appleby), Oxford (Professor Marian Stamp Dawkins), Bristol (Professor John Webster) and Cambridge (Professor Don Broom). The huge level of publicity generated over the opposition to the long-distance live transportation of meat animals in the early 1990s exceeded even that concerned with animal experiments in the 1970s or the killing of seals in the early 1980s. The health scares surrounding meat-eating also contributed powerfully to the vegetarian movement at this time. With the worldwide *weekly* consumption of meat estimated in 1999 to be 35 million pigs, 5 million cattle, 5 million sheep and 500 million poultry, the treatment of farmed animals remains a huge challenge facing those concerned about cruelty.[24]

After twenty years or more of active campaigning against battery cages it was gratifying when the European Parliament (EP) voted in January 1999 for a ban on keeping hens in these conditions. But such humane decisions by the EP had usually been ignored by the all-powerful Council of Ministers. It therefore took the key lobbyists (CIWF, RSPCA and Eurogroup) rather by surprise when, on 14 June 1999, the Council voted to ban battery cages throughout the EU from the year 2012. The usual opposition from the southern states surprisingly had melted away led by a volte face by Italy, inspired by the hunger-striking lobbyist, Adolpho Sansolini. The reasons for such sudden breakthroughs are often unclear – was it due to a softening approach by the UK egg industry, was it the Belgian dioxin food scare which was then raging or was it some hidden "horse trading" that caused the southern states, apparently reluctantly, to change their position? Both Sansolini and the improved Belgian campaigning had received UK funding aimed at boosting the lobbying performance of weaker member states - a policy some of us had advocated for many years. It was certainly a great victory.

By the end of the millennium the battles over bloodsports in Britain, the use of animals in genetic engineering and the threat to animal welfare posed by world free trade joined the transportation of live food animals as the leading issues. Grass-roots activists, however, independently of the main campaigning bodies, in addition to their protests against bloodsports, continued their direct action against fur farms and vivisection laboratories. One of them, Barry Horne, sentenced to a draconian eighteen years jail for arson, gained much media attention when he went on hunger strike in 1998 in order to protest against animal experiments.

THE DEVELOPMENT OF ANIMAL WELFARE STUDIES

Until quite recently the idea that the welfare of animals, or even the relationship between human and nonhuman animals, should be subjects of serious study, seemed ridiculous to many scientists and academics. Veterinary science was all very well but the proposal that historians, academic lawyers, zoologists, ethologists, political scientists or psychologists should study such areas appeared absurd. This negative attitude is itself curious and seems to stem from the macho feeling that a sympathetic interest for animals is emotional rather than rational, characteristically infantile or effeminate and, furthermore, undermines the emotional detachment necessary in a speciesist society for the exploitation of animals for research, food and other products. In almost every aspect of life human beings interact with or utilize the other species, yet this relationship has only begun to be studied seriously since about 1970. The revival of serious interest in the subject in Oxford[25] at that time gradually gave the subject some academic credibility as did Jon Wynne-Tysons's reminder that many great intellectual and literary figures of the past had expressed their deep compassion for animals.[26]

During the 1970s the RSPCA made its first research grants. Among these were support to David Macdonald and Marian Stamp Dawkins in Oxford; the former to study the behaviour of foxes and the latter to test the preferences of poultry. Grants were also made to Professor D. G. Wood-Gush in Edinburgh to study the welfare of other farm animals. Since then, animal-welfare science has expanded rapidly in the Western World, particularly in Britain and Australia but also in other countries of Northern Europe and North America. The British emphasis, inspiringly led by Donald Broom and John Webster, has mainly been on the behaviour and welfare of farm animals, while in America the human – nonhuman interaction has been examined widely by philosophers and social scientists.[27] Other academic disciplines have also become involved. From the 1970s departments of philosophy have considered at length the treatment of nonhumans as an ethical issue[28] and, more recently, in Britain, academic lawyers such as Mike Radford of the University of East Anglia have promoted the study of the relevant legislation,[29] historians such as Hilda Kean have begun to write about the animal-protection movement,[30] anthrozoologists such as James Serpell have studied the human – nonhuman relationship, as have psychologists like Elizabeth Paul, and the subject has also gained recognition as a matter for research by political science, the leading exponent being Robert Garner of Leicester University.[31] In America, Temple Grandin, Ray Stricklin and Joy Mench have pioneered farm-animal-welfare research, historians such as Harriet Ritvo and Laurence and Susan Finsen have brilliantly examined the reform movements, and lawyers like Gary Francione, David Favre, Steven Wise, David Wolfson, philosophers such as Bernard Rollin, Tom Regan, Steve Sapontzis, Evelyn Pluhar and David De Grazia, biological scientists like Andrew Rowan and Barbara Orlans, social scientists like Kenneth Shapiro, Arnold Arluke, Randall Lockwood, Linda Pifer, Alan Felthous, John Broida, Clint Sanders, Hal Hertzog and many others have helped to establish the issue on the academic agenda. The increasingly well-established and important link between violence to humans and violence to animals, for example, has become a well-publicized product of such research.[32]

Most recently, new initiatives have stimulated widespread interest in animal welfare among academic libraries on both sides of the Atlantic, and the professional collection of animal-protection archives has begun. The oral historical study of animal protection has been promoted by Recording Animal

Advocacy, based in Philadelphia, while in London, Robert Perks, the Director of the National Life Story Collection, commissioned Melanie Oxley in 1998 to carry out a series of oral-history interviews of animal campaigners for the British Library. In the same decade, Kim Stallwood, the influential editor of the *Animals Agenda*, had pioneered the way forward in the collection and safeguarding of books and documents relating mainly to the US movement. Anne Summers and William Frame at the British Library have expanded their archival records covering the UK based movement.

PAINISM

Since the first publication of this book the character of the animal-protection movement has evolved. As we have seen, it has become more professional, more academic and, in Britain at least, more direct in its contact with government. My own philosophical position, too, has been more clearly expressed and I have published my long-held views based upon my concern for the suffering of individuals. I used to call this position sentientism[33] but, since the late 1980s, I have more often referred to it as painism.[34] Painism, like Utilitarianism (or, more precisely, Negative Utilitarianism), is concerned with pain in all its manifestations – painful emotions, thoughts and moods as well as "physical" pains. I include all these experiences under the term "pain". Unlike Utilitarians, however, I reject the notion that the pains of several individuals can be meaningfully aggregated. This is because unless one experiences a pain oneself it does not fully exist. The pains of others are entirely different things from the actual experience of my *own* pains. It makes sense, of course, to add up my own different pains. For example, while feeling anxious about my children and at the same time suffering from a headache I may have the misfortune of stubbing my toe! All these simultaneous experiences of pain *can* legitimately be aggregated because I actually experience them. However, it makes no real sense to add all *your* pains as well into my own aggregated pain score. Yours is a different world of experience. Knowing you are suffering may cause me some sympathetic pain of my own but I do not feel exactly the same pain that you feel. All I feel of others' pains is, as it were, their husks. Without directly experiencing pains they are not real. Around each individual is the boundary of consciousness. What goes on in the consciousness of others is a different universe. Trying to aggregate the pains of different individuals is like adding chalk to cheese. So it is a far more serious matter to inflict, say, ten units of pain on one other painient individual than to cause single units of pain to thousands of individuals – even though, in the latter case, the aggregated total of pains is far greater. *We should thus be concerned primarily with trying to reduce the pain of the individual (human or nonhuman) who is suffering most – the maximum sufferer.*

How, then, does *painism* differ from other ethical theories? Well, as we have seen, it differs from Utilitarianism in that it rejects the aggregation of pain scores across individuals. Is it then a form of Rights Theory? Yes, but it posits pain (in all its forms) as the only criterion of what is bad. Unlike Tom Regan, for example, who bases rights upon the "inherent value" of a human or nonhuman animal, I consider that rights should be attributed on the basis of painience alone. So all painient individuals have the prima facie right not to be caused pain by others. To put it another way, we, as moral beings, have responsibilities to relieve the pain of others and not to cause it. ("Rights language" and "responsibilities language" are, in my book, two sides of the same coin.)

TRADE-OFFS

Aggregating the pains of several individuals is not the same as trading off the pains of one against the benefits to another. One of the great difficulties facing all ethical theories is this problem of trade-offs. How far, if at all, is it right to permit or inflict pain on A in order to reduce the pain (or increase the pleasure) of B? Utilitarians, we know, say that such trade-offs are acceptable when the pain of A is outweighed by the aggregated advantages to all those affected by the action (i.e. not just B's advantage, but C's and D's as well). Extreme Rights Theorists, on the other hand, might argue that no pain at all, however trivial, should be caused to A no matter how much pain could thereby be reduced for B. Both theories, therefore, when carried to the extreme, produce absurd results. Utilitarianism can justify torture if torture produces a greater aggregation of benefits to others and extreme Rights Theory could forbid the reduction of another's agony if it caused mere inconvenience for a third party. The trade-off problem remains a thorn in the flesh for every ethical theory. Some set of approximate rules of action, outlining our duties and responsibilities, have to be invoked to reduce the absurdity of its implications. I have suggested the following:[35]

SOME MORAL RULES OF THUMB

1 **Speciesism is always wrong.** So try to act as though human and nonhuman suffering carry equal weight.
2 **The aggregation of pains or pleasures across individuals is meaningless.** So try to act as though the sufferings of the many count for no more than the sufferings of the one. (This challenges orthodox opinion and has considerable implications for human society.)
3 **Our primary moral concern, therefore, should always be for the individual who is the maximum sufferer.** So try not so much to reduce the *quantity* of individuals who are suffering, as to reduce the *severity of the pain* experienced by every one of them, giving priority to those who suffer most.
4 **It is always wrong to cause pain to A merely in order to increase the *pleasure* of B.** So inflicting even mild pain for fun or luxury is never justified.
5 **It is always wrong, whatever the benefits, to cause severe or prolonged pain.** So, regardless of benefits, torture is never justified.

We then arrive at the huge grey area of decision-taking where causing (or permitting) mild or momentary pain or distress causes (or may cause) marked pain reduction in others. This is the so-called "cost-benefit" calculation that we see, for example, in the administration of the British law controlling animal experimentation. Obviously it is extremely difficult to estimate the value of pains, particularly when two separate variables are involved – *intensity* and *duration*. For example, is a mild pain lasting a week worse than an intense pain lasting a minute? Furthermore, there is also the problem of *probability of outcome* or the *predictability* of the pains and benefits. In the case of animal experiments the outcome can never be entirely certain. Usually, the further ahead in time the predicted effects are, the less certain they become. We can, in other words, be fairly sure that a particular type of experiment will be painful but we will be less certain that it will produce the hoped-for long-term benefits. In my opinion this tilts the moral balance a little further against the experimenter. He is trying to trade off the *probable* pain of A (the experimental animal) against the *uncertain* pain-reduction of B (e.g. the patient whose illness is to be treated). In extreme cases it will be a trade-off of certain pain against hypothetical benefit. Is this allowable? There is also the problem that the experimenter will be deliberately (knowingly) causing pains that did not exist before he intervened and which otherwise would not have occurred. This, too, seems more ethically questionable than causing pain inadvertently or observing pain that is already "naturally" occurring. For all these reasons those who conduct painful animal experiments stand on particularly difficult ground, ethically speaking. The trade-off problem affects them almost uniquely. They are trying to alleviate suffering by causing suffering. NATO faced the same dilemma in Kosovo!

The case of animal experimentation vividly illustrates what are general problems for all ethical theories. These problems apply in human-to-human treatment no less than in human-to-nonhuman. The Western World is currently in a state of moral muddle. It could do worse, perhaps, than consider following the ethical rules I have tentatively proposed. Take the Christmas 1998 attack on Iraq by the US and Britain, for example. This illustrated all the aforementioned difficulties of *trade-offs*. Agony and death were inflicted upon innocent Iraqi civilians in order to reduce the probability that their leader, Saddam Hussein, would be possessed of weapons of mass destruction which could kill and cause agony to others. To say that *fewer* Iraqis (and others) were affected by the attack than *might* be affected by Saddam Hussein's possible future use of chemical, biological or nuclear weapons, is to fall into the all-too-common trap of *aggregation*, as well as the *prediction* problem, that we have been discussing. The parallel between pre-emptive war of this sort and vivisection is quite striking. There is, however, a difference: every effort was made by the attackers to avoid any deleterious effect upon innocent Iraqi civilians. Those planning the attack knew that some would, accidentally, be hurt, but it was not an intended result of their action.

It is almost impossible to frame an arbitrary rule that deals satisfactorily with such situations. We could, perhaps, argue that causing *mild* pain to A might conceivably be justified if it is the *only* way to reduce, *beyond all reasonable doubt*, an *unquestionably great and highly probable* pain for B. Causing even mild pain or discomfort is, of course, always quite wrong (regardless of benefit) if there are painless alternative ways of achieving the same results or ways to alleviate the pain. These should always be tried first. But to be consistent, and to avoid speciesism, would mean that this rule, too, should be applied in our treatment of all species, including humans. Would it be wiser to go the other way and to avoid all deliberate infliction of pain without consent, except in the most extreme and desperate of cases?

Perhaps there is the basis for a sixth rule of thumb here, namely, that *it is never right to cause a pain that has a probability of occurrence of* x, *on the grounds that a (greater) pain will thereby be reduced with a probability of reduction of less than* x.

Animal protection has been much discussed by philosophers since 1970 and this discussion has helped clarify ethical thinking generally. I believe that this debate has produced ethical theories and rules of thumb that are of relevance to the human no less than to the animal condition, and at a time when human society is showing a need for a new morality. Painism is a case in point. It is universally applicable.

WHY IS PAIN EVIL?

At the start of the third millennium the world seems to be floundering in ethical confusion. The media, exploiting our natural fascination with others' sexual behaviour, and anxious only to sell more copy, promote sex outside marriage as the main moral misdemeanour when in reality, when it causes only pleasure, it can be exactly the opposite. Meanwhile, those politicians who talk seriously about morality persist in claiming that the final moral objectives are equality or liberty or justice or democracy or the defeat of poverty or some other half-truth. They rarely explain *why* such things are to be considered good or their denial bad. It is time that the moral debate became unstuck from this endless recitation of unanalysed nostrums. Psychological research produces growing evidence that most of these moral objectives are, broadly speaking, conducive to happiness. Their absence causes pain. So do unrealistically high expectations. Wealth may not be necessary for happiness but the avoidance of poverty most certainly is. So we *want* equality, liberty, justice, democracy and affluence because we believe (often quite rightly) that their denial causes pain and suffering. But why, one might ask, is pain to be considered evil? Well, what property is it that all bad things share? The answer is that they all cause pain (in its broad sense). Most examples of killing, lying, cheating and stealing cause pain and are therefore bad. (Even the painless killing of the proverbial "hermit about whom nobody cares" is wrong, not least because somebody, at some time, may find out about the killing and be upset by it or feel insecure as a consequence). Injustice, inequality and lack of liberty are bad because they, too, cause pain. Neglecting and rejecting are bad for the same reason. Pain is the common feature of all bad things. A bad thing is that which causes pain. But pain is the great motivator. When I apply this to *myself* it is a fundamental of *psychology*. When I concern myself with my reaction to the pain of *others* I am also dealing with a fundamental of *ethics*. Morality and psychology point in the same direction if I accept that I should do to others what I would like others to do to me.

DOUBLE STANDARDS

A concern for the individual is often a basis for laws protecting humans but not for those protecting nonhumans. The latter are almost invariably based upon Utilitarian principles where the suffering of an individual can be justified in the name of a greater benefit. Hence the typical offence is to cause "unnecessary" suffering. In most laws protecting humans, however, each *individual* is protected absolutely. For example, it is considered wrong to experiment upon a human being without consent (except in certain very low risk and nonharmful cases), even if that experiment may bring some advantage to others. This is despite the fact that with human rather than nonhuman subjects the likelihood of achieving useful results would certainly be higher. Why is there this double standard? Clearly, because of human self-interest. Once again it is a question of speciesism.

The much-quoted ethicist John Rawls argues that if we did not know what our position would be in society, we would be forced to choose a form of "justice as fairness" that would guarantee basic liberties and maximize the condition of the least advantaged.[36] He requires us to act as if we were behind a "veil of ignorance" concerning our current sex, ethnicity, class and status. To this list I would like to propose that "species" be added. In other words, we should include all "painients" (that is, all beings capable of suffering any kind of pain) in our scheme of justice, as if we did not know of which species we might find ourselves to be members.

IS EXTREMISM JUSTIFIED?

The modern era has seen a questioning of basic attitudes. Are humans part of nature or not? Is there a moral and biological gulf between our species and all other animals? Is it good enough for kindly people to dispense charity towards dogs and cats or is a more fundamental reappraisal of the human–nonhuman relationship required? Ultimately, should animal and human rights be put on the same legal basis? Why not a UN Convention on Painients' Rights to mark the millennium? The dispute between animal welfarists and self-styled animal rightists, particularly evident in the United States, is about such issues.

A debate also rages about *tactics*. How far can direct or illegal or even violent tactics be justified even in a good cause? If governments ignore, decade after decade, constitutionally expressed pressures for reform that are *supported by the majority*, then is it surprising that a few impatient people adopt unconstitutional methods? The Animal Liberation Front was begun in 1982, and its alleged supporters have since caused considerable damage to property in animal laboratories, factory farms and abattoirs around the world. How far are such tactics justified? Similar behaviour by the opponents of slavery are, in retrospect, extolled. So are the far more violent tactics once supported by leaders of the ANC in South Africa. Nelson Mandela is universally admired. There seems to be a lack of ethical consistency in these matters. Peter Singer and most of the other philosophical contributors to the animal-liberation movement, including myself, have made a distinction between *direct* and *violent* tactics. If constitutional tactics fail in a democracy then *peaceful* civil disobedience may be the only course. Gandhi certainly thought so.

In Britain in the 1990s, the controversy over animal experimentation, begun in the 1970s, still continued. At the centre of the storm for decades has been Professor Colin Blakemore of Oxford University, cast in the role of the "wicked" vivisector. Castigated by the tabloid media in the 1970s for his experiments on the eyes of kittens, Blakemore has, however, also been a worker for reform. As an active member of the moderate Boyd Group (convened by Professor Kenneth Boyd of Edinburgh and by Les Ward of the Scottish Society for the Prevention of Vivisection), he has lobbied the Home Office for more humane measures. Yet he continues to be considered an emblem of speciesism and has been a target of death threats for many years.[37] To an extent this seems unfair and arbitrary. Many other animal researchers have merely kept their heads below the parapet and continued experimenting. There are some 14,000 of them in Britain alone. Blakemore, however, has always joined the public debate, arguing on one hand for the medical benefits of research and, on the other, for the better care of animals. Would he agree to experiment on humans in order to achieve his laudable ends? He sits painfully on the horns of the moral dilemma – how far is it justifiable to inflict suffering in order to reduce suffering? Ironically, the same moral predicament applies no less forcefully to his tormentors – are they right to cause him suffering in order to reduce suffering? Extremists can sometimes be hoisted by their own moral petards. It is idle, however, to pretend that either side is all wrong or all right. Rightness is on *both* sides! That is the essence of the problem.

ALTRUISM

Evolutionary psychologists argue that our feelings of compassion and resultant altruistic actions are born into us because they have proved to have survival value. We help others because one day they may be able to help us. But can this theory account for my feelings of compassion for kittens, crabs or, even, for caterpillars? How will caterpillars or crabs be able to help me? Surely, our altruism towards the weak and disabled is not so selfish. Not all of our innate feelings must necessarily have survival value for our genes. Some must be "spill-overs" of parental and other impulses. Furthermore, sometimes I can fail to act upon my compassion and, conversely, sometimes I can act altruistically out of rational principle alone *without* feeling compassion. I consider that ethics should be like this - dictated by reason but fuelled intermittently by compassion.

CONSCIOUSNESS AND CLEVERNESS

How consciousness is caused remains a mystery. Some people dislike the idea of explaining themselves and their consciousness in terms of physical laws. Yet these physical laws are very complex and mysterious. There is nothing dull nor demeaning about them. Subatomic particles, for example, behave as if they had free will; their behaviour is unpredictable. Individual particles will come into existence suddenly and unexpectedly. Furthermore, one particle may instantaneously affect the behaviour of another even over huge distances. On the subatomic scale, things do not happen as they do in the everyday world with which we are familiar.[38] The solid material world is really composed of continuously changing particles and forces. Yet "solidity" emerges from this maelstrom. Solidity is one of only many emergent qualities which have an entirely different character from their constituent parts. Music emerges from the plastic and metal of a radio, images of beauty from the cathode rays of a television. Consciousness itself emerges from the blood and tissue of the brain. It is partly a question of scale; the emergent entity inevitably seems larger. Scale matters for emergence. It does, too, when it comes to explaining the universe. Big events (by our standards of scale) can be explained by the laws of Relativity whereas tiny events are best explained by Quantum Mechanics. These two great theories appear, however, partly incompatible. Brains are at a scale where both theories may apply – is this somehow connected with their generation of consciousness? If one equates consciousness with "observation" it raises new possibilities because the role of the observer is crucial in Quantum Theory (and also, in a different way, in Relativity). The possibility is raised, therefore, that consciousness is no mere by-product of complex systems but an ingredient as basic, perhaps, as time or space, or energy or mass. On the other hand, to assume that because I am conscious I necessarily have freedom of will may be a mistake. Being conscious may make me *feel* as though I have complete control over my choices of action, and that I am neither a slave to my genes nor to my neurones. But this could be an illusion. Why should consciousness exempt me from conforming to the laws of nature? Those who dislike the implication that they are "mere" machines or "mere" animals probably are unaware of the subtleties of modern science. The strangeness of consciousness is no more strange than the behaviour of subatomic particles, the power of gravity nor the size and character of the universe.

If we look again at those who have argued that the human animal is different in *kind* rather than *degree* from the other animals we can see that they are usually basing this assertion on the hunch that nonhumans lack consciousness.

Many other words have been used – 'reason', 'understanding' or 'soul' for example. The word 'consciousness' did not come into use until the seventeenth century and, even then, with scarcely today's meaning. Yet, to many, if not most, intelligent people it has always seemed quite obvious that dogs and cats and many other nonhumans are conscious. Why should they not be? They behave as if they are conscious and many have similar, although not identical, nervous systems to our own. It is impossible to *prove* absolutely that another human being is conscious and, in the same strict sense, it is impossible to prove consciousness in another animal. But all the signs are there. An animal howls when injured just as we do, trembles when faced with danger, heroically defends her young just as good human parents will do. These are the sort of actions that we humans perform *most* consciously because they are charged with intense emotion yet they are also performed by nonhumans. Dogs may not be able to think about income tax or geology but they may be just as conscious as we are, or more so, of love, fear, jealousy and pain.

Some nonhumans, we suspect, are also conscious of *themselves*. In the 1970s Gordon Gallup in New York tried to find out if chimpanzees could recognise themselves in a mirror. He found that the chimpanzees began to use the mirror to groom parts of their body which they normally had difficulty in seeing. Gallup then placed spots of red dye on the chimpanzees' foreheads and found that, while looking in the mirror, they frequently touched these spots. Similar results in the 1990s have been found with gorillas, orang-utans and some monkeys.

Pigeons, too, have responded in ways suggesting possible self-recognition, as have dolphins.[39] It is, perhaps, particularly striking that animals can show self-awareness using *vision*. In a state of nature many animals will never *see* their clear reflection. They do, however, constantly *hear* themselves, *smell* themselves and *feel* stimuli that come into contact with their skin. There is also increasing evidence from experimental psychology that animals can imitate, deceive others deliberately, reveal phenomenal powers of memory, use tools, fashion them, show ingenuity in solving problems and even learn to use abstract concepts. Pigeons, for example, have learned to peck for food only at keys that carry images of spherical objects (pearls, buttons or balls etc) or watery objects (droplets, a lake, a glass of water and so on) or symmetrical (but not asymmetrical) subjects. In other words, they can apply abstract concepts such as sphericity, wetness and symmetry.[40] Better-known studies have demonstrated that apes and birds can use signs and vocalizations meaningfully and creatively. All these lines of research demonstrate that many animals are surprisingly clever, although they do not, of course, strictly speaking, prove that they are conscious. Many nonhumans show brain (and hand) lateralizations, as humans do, and the left hemisphere is characteristically linked with communication in mammals, birds and frogs, whereas the right side is linked with solving spatial problems and the processing of emotions. As Lesley Rogers concludes: "We know of no single structure in the brain that is unique to humans".[41] If this is so, then why should humans be the only conscious species? Provided we accept that the brain is the organ of consciousness, it seems most unlikely that we are.

Those who, like Descartes, are desperate to look for differences between humans and the other species, will not like these findings. The old battle against Darwinism continues to rage.[42] For many of those who wish to widen the perceived gap between human and nonhuman the underlying motive seems to be a sense of guilt about our speciesism and our cruel exploitation of the other animals. For others it is the fear that the acceptance of our animality implies the loss of our freedom of will. Such critics can accept that nonhumans are machines governed by the laws of nature, but cannot accept that humans are similarly determined. They dislike the notion that we, as humans, are, to an extent, subservient to our genes. However, science has progressed beyond the Newtonian age in which nature was perceived as performing like a rigidly determined machine. We now live in the quantum age when we perceive the universe as a vast and mysterious place based upon uncertainty. Things happen in unpredictable ways. The more we know the more we realize that we can neither fully predict nor comprehend. The universal reality is so different from the appearances of our everyday world. So there is no shame, surely, in recognizing that we, the human animal, are a part of this great mystery. Instead of trying to maintain an artificial gulf between ourselves and the other animals on the grounds that they are machines and we are not, we should recognize that we are all part of the same complex reality where there is no such thing as simple causation nor crude determinism nor "mere" machinery. Perhaps to the same extent that subatomic particles appear to have freedom of will, so do we. On the cosmic scale we are but particles. Taken *en masse* we conform to the same rules of order and disorder, acting probabilistically rather than mechanistically, linked by fields, maybe, of which we are unaware.[43] The whole universe is awesome! It is no insult to be part of it. We, as conscious individuals, should be humble in accepting that we are an element in this cosmic conundrum, and should not, out of insecurity or arrogance, try to separate ourselves from the other animals nor from the rest of nature. It is irrational and degrading to do so.

Ethically speaking, of course, none of this really matters. What is important is painience. Pain (in all its manifestations) is a matter of vital importance for the individual. Distress, fear, discomfort, grief, boredom and anxiety are all manifestations of pain. They are almost constant features in our daily lives. This is what unites us with the other animals. We are all part of the community of pain. This is the universal ethic that should govern our relationship with all other painient things – that we have a responsibility to try to reduce their pain. All our current ideals of freedom, equality, justice, democracy, prosperity and peace, indeed, all the constituents of the human- and animal-rights ethics, are subordinate to the eternal and universal psychological rule that we seek to enjoy happiness and, as far as possible, to avoid pain. Our moral duty is to endeavour to help others achieve these aims.

12 Speciesism

We have seen in the first part of this book how humankind's relationship with nonhumans, far from being a peripheral issue, has often been a matter of practical, religious and intellectual importance. Nonhumans have played principal, not supporting, roles in literature, religion, science, folklore and philosophy, as well as in everyday economics. Although the distinction between human and nonhuman was emphasized in Christian countries, especially during the cruel and anthropocentric centuries of the Renaissance period, the way in which nonhuman animals have been treated, for example in their culpability in the eyes of the law during medieval times, suggests that many men and women continued to regard them as being in many respects like themselves.

There has always been a strange ambivalence towards nonhumans; a tendency to exploit them mercilessly combined with a common respect for some, but not all, things natural. Throughout the middle ages some animals were regarded as models of virtue and, later, as examples of God's beneficence to humankind; it was believed that all creatures were made to serve man, either as objects of exploitation or as teachers of goodness.

NATURAL AND UNNATURAL

This ambivalence, encouraged as it probably was by the contradictory human instincts of compassion and dominance, led to some confusion about what was to be considered natural and what unnatural.

Doing what was 'unnatural' was always considered to be wrong, but fashions changed as to how 'unnatural' should be defined. Those, like the Puritans, who saw great differences between human and other animals believed it was unnatural for men to show beast-like behaviour. Those who felt that men *were* animals tended to take a more lenient view. Sexual and aggressive behaviours, in particular, were often regarded as 'animal', and doing what nonhumans did was thus regarded with contempt.[1] Some viewed the whole process of civilization as a concealment of humankind's animal impulses; an idea to be reiterated by Freud in the twentieth century in his assertion that the 'higher' aspects of human civilization are sublimations of thwarted 'animal' instincts. For many, doing sexually that which not even the nonhuman animals were believed to do was considered still more wicked than the mere venting of animal lusts; thus child sexual abuse, masturbation and homosexuality were especially tainted.

Concerns over what was natural and about the connection between natural behaviour and virtue have always been strong, yet the arguments have often been inconsistent.

Although some of the 'natural' impulses of animals have been considered abhorrent, yet it has also been thought natural and quite right for a parent to protect its child, and natural and right for a child to respect its parents; parallels from nature are often used to support the 'rightness' of this idea. Some have also argued that artifice and affectation are to be mistrusted, along with fine clothes and elaborate decoration, in part at least because they are 'unnatural'. Shakespeare glimpsed man as 'a poor bare forked animal' in *King Lear* − a play deeply preoccupied with the intellectual search for the true nature of human beings. The stripping away of the trimmings of royal pomp and luxury is precisely Lear's predicament as, unnaturally rejected by his children, he flounders his storm-racked way between what is right and what is natural.

During the Renaissance period, in particular, witchcraft was associated with breaches of the natural order epitomized by the 'unnatural' intimacy between witch and cat or some other animal 'familiar'; such animals, if apprehended, could be burned alive. Similarly, any cock 'unnaturally' laying an egg was at once killed and the egg destroyed, lest it produce a deadly cockatrice.

Thus, although the naturalness of nonhuman animals was sometimes despised, any unnaturalness on their part was regarded with even greater horror. The Inquisition, for example, was ruthless in its suppression of what it considered unnatural familiarity between man and beast. The sin was to mix the categories. But why was it a sin? Was this attitude provoked by the fear of repressed human sexuality which appeared to be mocked and perhaps stimulated by the animal's brazenness? Or was it motivated by a sort of snobbery: a 'parvenu' need to feel superior?

We have seen that the Judaeo-Christian tradition taught that man was different, and was halfway between the beasts and the angels and made in the image of God; the animals being despised not only for their unbridled lusts of gluttony, lechery and ferocity, but also for their nakedness, dirtiness and hairiness.[2] Even to portray an animal on stage was unacceptable to some seventeenth-century Puritans. Furthermore, there was a tendency for humans to project on to the other animals qualities within themselves of which they were afraid or ashamed. But which came first − the control and concealment of humankind's natural impulses through religious or 'civilizing' pressures which led to the perceived separation from the other animals, or a basic urge to feel superior to the (feared) other species, which led to the suppresion of 'the animal' in man, which in turn led to religious and moral rationalizations for this control? Or was the reason for emphasizing the gulf between human and nonhuman chiefly the need to provide an excuse for the continued exploitation of the nonhuman animals?

Probably all three factors have played a part. By the sixteenth century at least lust had become almost synonymous with animality,[3] and the Puritan period, with its emphasis upon sexual restraint, was a bad time for animals; too often they seemed to remind men and women of their own sexuality, of which they were ashamed. In consequence, perhaps, people punished nonhumans for their own sexual weaknesses. But nonhuman animals in England were treated with particular contempt during the Tudor period, which also happened to be a time of middle-class advancement, when many felt a need to look down upon nonhumans much as they did upon the poor and vulgar of their own species. And in all ages, probably, there was perennial guilt surrounding humankind's speciesism and a need to alleviate this by arguing that human and nonhuman were so different that morality did not transcend the species barriers.

Fear of sex, 'snobbery' and guilt have all contributed to the development of speciesism. A fourth factor, too, has sometimes appeared — the displacement on to animals of the feelings of resentment against other humans felt by oppressed individuals in human society; Mary Wollstonecraft noted as much in 1792 when she observed that the lower classes tyrannized the animals 'to revenge the insults they are obliged to bear from their superiors'.[4]

This tension between those people who wish to 'rise above' their own animality and those who want to accept and 'liberate' it is still a fundamental division in modern society, between conservatives and liberals, obsessionals and hysterics, right and left, classicists and romantics.

In the eighteenth century it had been Rousseau who argued for a return to a more simple and natural way of life. Later it would be Thoreau who advocated a closer intimacy with nature. This is a recurrent theme in Western cultures, extolled sometimes by those who need to come to terms with their own natures, through greater sexual honesty, for example, or the abandonment of social pretension.

In the twentieth century the scientific preoccupation with nature continues not least in the behavioural sciences. The challenge has been to establish not a moral code but an explanatory theory of behaviour as, with the coming of Freud, psychology elbowed religion off the centre of the intellectual stage. Yet, from Wundt, Pavlov and Lloyd Morgan onwards, the psychologists turned constantly to the nonhuman animals for their answers, much as the moralists had done before them. After Freud, educated humankind began to feel that it was right, or at least healthy, to be true to their own animal natures, and nonhumans were closely observed in order to ascertain what these were like. Socio-biology, too, the science of the biological basis for social behaviour, would become a mid-twentieth century manifestation of this traditional preoccupation.

CIVILIZATION, SADISM AND COMPASSION

Nonhumans probably constituted an important impetus for the growth of human civilization because it was imperative for human creatures to defend their interests against competing species, and it was helpful that many could be eaten, ridden or employed as beasts of burden. Hunting clearly was a case in point. In the 'civilized' world of today it is an unnecessary relic of what was once a vital enterprise. Before effective agriculture, those with a strong propensity to collaborate with others in expeditionary searches for sustenance may have survived lean years better than the stay-at-homes. They were more likely to find food, whether meat or fruits or leaves or grains. So this adventurous spirit was bred selectively into humankind, as into most other animals, and has not been totally lost beneath the far more sedentary agricultural cultures of the last ten thousand years. Searching is thus instinctive, and since the fulfilment of an instinct is itself pleasurable, many hunters today who dislike the killing of the quarry still enjoy the simple pleasures of the preliminary search. Such motives help to explain the popularity of those sports which involve, literally, 'hunting'. The same can be said of many children's games of the 'hide and seek' variety.

Less attractive is the equally innate human desire to dominate and to exercise power over inanimate and animate things, which can all too often be seen in young children, especially boys, from infancy. In its most unpleasant form it is frankly sadistic, and accounts for much of the pleasure obviously experienced by those who bait and torment captive creatures. In most civilizations this power-lust is usually constrained in human relationships except in times of war or intense personal crisis. Against other adult human beings its crude manifestations are partly or totally prohibited, and are permitted only in certain disguised forms in business, politics or games. But, for centuries, nonhumans were regarded as acceptable targets, becoming not only the butt for humankind's lust for power, but also aunt sallies for venting individual frustrations, and particularly those of the more deprived members of the human race.

This continues to be true. It not only affects those engaged in blood-sports but also those being cruel in other ways. I have known a male vivisector discover sadistic pleasure during the 'punishment' of laboratory animals in a psychological experiment, and, in her brilliant *Animals and Man*, Professor Miriam Rothschild recorded the common link between cruelty and sexual arousal:

I was once taken aback by an unusually able assistant of mine suddenly deciding to quit zoology. Apparently she had been given a live, instead of a dead mouse, to feed to a stoat, in which we were studying pelage change. Not having the courage to kill the mouse herself, she hurriedly pushed it into the cage. She watched fascinated while the animal crouched terrified in a corner, facing the tense, bright-eyed stoat preparing for the kill. To the girl's consternation she then experienced a violent orgasm.[5]

I am aware of the unfashionable nature of such words as 'instinct' and 'innate', but I use them deliberately. The human animal, no less than other creatures, is programmed before birth with certain behavioural potentials. These can be channelled and coloured by cultural and other environmental influences, and indeed suppressed entirely. Nevertheless I am saying that in *all* cultures the human animal tends to show two conflicting and instinctual ways of relating to other individuals – the compassionate and the dominating. These two basic impulses – call them what you will – are fundamental to the human predicament generally, and nowhere are they revealed more clearly than in the human-to-nonhuman relationship.

The spectators of baitings, in addition to enjoying vicariously the satisfaction of domination, derived an additional pleasure: the thrill of feeling fear while at the same time knowing that they were safe. This must have been the origin of much of the excitement felt by audiences in the Roman amphitheatre and medieval bear garden, as well as in the bull ring of today. Such people identify with the man who is fighting the allegedly ferocious beast. The fact that many bulls do not want to fight, or indeed that many lions did not seem particularly eager to eat Christians, is unlikely to spoil the viewer's fantasy; such people do not identify with the object of their fear. Men are invariably the 'good guys' while the nonhuman is cast in the role of villain.

As with most human activities, the motivation for cruel sports is multiple. Not all hunters today hunt for the same mixture of reasons; some, as I have said, do so mainly because they enjoy searching, some for the love of outdoor exercise, others for social reasons, and only a few, probably, for the pleasure of the kill. Instinctive drives and culturally acquired ones have become compounded. The macho motive is probably strong in some men but not in others.[6]

In the late medieval mind the indulgence in bloody and sadistic behaviour towards nonhumans was not only unashamed but taken to be a sign of virility. Despite the steady disappearance of really dangerous species in Europe (the lion had gone around AD 80 and the wolf disappeared in England during the sixteenth century), men continued to convince themselves that the pursuit and torture of animals which were often timid and sometimes inedible was nevertheless heroic. The pleasures of bloodsports were largely on the level of unreality. As humans gained ever-greater control over the other animals, so they used this control to enjoy their 'macho' fantasies, while reducing their risks: sports became safer and easier. Deer were kept in parks and rounded up to be presented to the 'sportsman' to be shot at from point-blank range. Bears and bulls were chained safely before being whipped and bullied. It really took very little courage to watch while a pack of large hounds caught a timid and heavily outnumbered quarry, or to squeeze a trigger from a safe distance, yet men did, and still do, regard such activities as evidence of manliness.

The requirements of the state sometimes encouraged such sports, as in Roman times, when they were considered to breed the martial spirit while distracting the people from their social grievances. Certainly the suppression of compassion and habituation to the sight of blood and injury may have been useful training for soldiers and, later, the tricks of horsemanship learned on the hunting field were rated highly as an apprenticeship for the cavalryman, as were the skills of hunting with bow and arrow for the bowman. Indeed, the similarity between some of the techniques of sport and those of war added to their macho appeal. Sport was war without the danger; like today's child with a plastic gun, the bloodsportsmen could enjoy their fantasies of derring-do in relative safety.

Sports were extolled as a means of maintaining physical and mental fitness in an otherwise idle class – a perennial attitude immortalized in the present century by A. P. Herbert in *Tantivy Towers*:

> Well a chap must do something, I always tell chaps.
> For if a chap doesn't a chap will collapse,
> And a chap keeps as fit as a chap could be wishin'
> As long as there's huntin' and shootin' and fishin'.

Yet, surely, all men and women have a spark of compassion within them; it, too, is natural and universal. Was there not always a tendency for some, particularly the children and the more sensitive adults, to extend their sympathies to the nonhuman animals? It was surely this which generated widespread guilt about our treatment of nonhumans – a guilt which had to be reduced through various rationalizations, including the assertions that animals had been created by God for precisely the uses that man found for them, or that animals lacked souls or could feel nothing (see Part I).

We have seen that differences between human and all other forms of creation have often been emphasized. Only men and women could laugh, suggested Aristotle, or could observe religion, said Edmund Burke. The drawing of a firm line between humankind and the other animals helped to satisfy many scruples, and may have been done unconsciously for this reason. But additional arguments were needed to reduce the guilt felt over unnecessary bloodsports and other more recent forms of exploitation. One popular line was to argue that the exploited animal was more of a threat than it really was, or that it displayed morally reprehensible qualities; foxes are an example.

Too often, since Freud, we tend to assume that kindness is a form of behaviour which has to be learned, and that our natural impulses are all aggressive or sexual. Yet in earlier days sympathy was considered to be part of human nature. Even the word 'kind' itself, according to the *Shorter Oxford Dictionary*, denotes in Middle English both 'natural' and 'sympathetic', and kindness meant 'kinship' as well as the 'natural affection arising from this'.

I use the words 'compassion', 'empathy' and 'sympathy' interchangeably, although I recognize that 'compassion' suggests not only fellow feeling but the helpful and protective actions which follow from it. Where, then, does compassion come from? Maybe it is not uniquely human, as anyone who has seen a dog licking a wounded human or canine friend will suspect. Clearly it is as strong an instinct, or collection of behaviours, as any other, and is at its most powerful in the parental role. More than this, it is surely one of those behaviours with high survival value, which helps us and other species to work together effectively in groups. Yet frequently it is suppressed, often by other primitive motivations such as those arising from anger or fear, as in battle. Or, as I shall argue, it may be stifled by cultural factors such as the macho ideal and the consequent fear of ridicule. (The macho motive has much to answer for.) Ambition and any sort of stoical training may inhibit the natural expression of sympathy, just as over-exposure to scenes of suffering may, in some individuals, lead to habituation or de-sensitization.

The psychologist Randall Lockwood described what he calls the 'empathy crisis' in America − 'the problem of insensitivity among doctors, nurses, veterinarians, teachers, psychologists and psychiatrists', and tellingly attributed this to the pressure to conform to the 'scientific model' and the identification of this model 'with the exorcism of emotionality, empathy and compassion'.[7] Science has indeed been given these values by those who see it as being in opposition to human feeling, which it does not have to be. Science is, however, much concerned with the control of nature, and so is, in this sense, the continuation of the age-old story of human conquest. Hence it can all too easily become a bastion of speciesism.

Lockwood traces five paths to feeling compassion towards non-humans: traumatic suffering; a sense of oneness with nature; close familiarity with animals; logical deduction; and a supportive and nurturant family background. Surely Lockwood is right: any or all of these can and do play an important part in the free flowing of compassion. Perhaps, however, a distinction should be made between the emotional and the cognitive aspects of compassion; between the *feeling* and the *objects* of that feeling. Traumatic suffering (or indeed prolonged suffer-ing) may accentuate natural compassion, and an affectionate family background will surely nurture it, and, although compassionate people almost always tend to spread their compassion to nonhuman and human objects alike, the special emphasis upon the nonhuman may be encour-aged by Lockwood's other factors — a sense of oneness with nature, close familiarity with animals and logical deduction (i.e. the force of the animal rights argument). One may go further and speculate that a disappointment in human relationships may be an experience which drives some into putting a far greater emphasis upon nonhuman than human objects of compassion. Early experiences are, as usual, probably of special importance here. Certainly, some recently reported survey findings in America confirm the view that a positive attitude towards the idea of animal rights is formed early in a child's life and remains relatively unchanged in adulthood.[8] Children do not seem to feel much difference between themselves and nonhumans; instead, they tend to assume a great deal of similarity. They are probably right. The psycholo-gical difference we perceive between ourselves and other animals is due chiefly to the accumulated human knowledge and sophistication which we acquire through learning. Such cultural factors, based largely on language and writing, which tend to obscure the similarities be-tween human and nonhuman, are not present in children to the same degree.

One can distinguish between several types of compassion. First, there is the intellectually held belief that helping others is the 'right' thing to do; second, the emotional urge to give comfort and (parental) protection; third, the 'gut' feeling of hurt at seeing another's hurt. Squeamishness is not the same as compassion, but is very much linked to the latter type of it. Perhaps those who are most compassionate are those who have themselves suffered badly, but whose sufferings have not dulled their sensitivity nor made them bitter.

It is intriguing to speculate whether or not civilization is marked by an underlying greater gentleness, as Lecky suggested, or whether it merely shows a widening of the moral 'in-group'. From the seventeenth century onwards there may have been an average decline in the use of state torture in Western Europe, and the twentieth century advent of the welfare state demonstrates, at least in theory, the increasing power of humanitarian feeling for other humans in times of peace. But beside this general increase in the average humanitarianism of the state there has also been an erosion of the feeling of 'us and them' which, in past centuries, so often led to double standards. Whereas in the seventeenth century an Englishman would feel considerable duties towards and compassion for members of his own family, he might not have extended such scruples to his treatment of, say, foreigners or those of another religious group. In the following century the differentials between family and others were challenged by the universal thinkers of the Enlightenment, who wrote for *all* human beings. The status of women gradually improved (after periods of active feminist campaigning) in the succeeding two centuries, and foreigners, blacks, the lower classes, orphans and the insane were all more fully admitted into the circle of moral concern in Europe during the nineteenth century.

Nonhumans, too, began to be admitted. Since Stuart times at least, people had found it repugnant to eat any pet, and, as Bernard de Mandeville remarked, some people found it difficult to consume any creature they had daily seen and become acquainted with. In nineteenth-century England it was common for families to exchange pigs at slaughtering time so as to avoid eating a pig who had, to some extent, been a family member.

Was it growing affluence or a further extension of the 'family circle' that caused English people gradually to cease eating small song-birds from the seventeenth century onwards? Certainly, by the early Victorian period it sounded more like the latter, if Mountstuart Elphinstone's reaction to an Italian dish was typical: 'What! Robins! Our household birds! I would as soon eat a child!'[9]

Indeed, it is possible to see the growth of animal liberation not so much in terms of increased overall compassion so much as an *expansion of the family circle*; the perception of other animals as our 'brothers and sisters', literally as our evolutionary kin to whom we feel 'kindness'. We see a similar expansion of the moral circle in twentieth-century internationalism, fostered by the increasing speed of travel and (televised) communication; increased knowledge of others apparently leading to increased sympathy.

As we have seen, the development of the humane movement has been erratic. The Renaissance was quite a setback and little progress has been made during periods of war and insecurity. After the First World War, for example, the movement in Britain lacked political drive, academic acceptability and intellectual flair. As the importance of the traditional upper classes declined, so did animal protection as a moral and political issue. Many of the new social reformers, mostly socialists, saw animal welfare at best as a mild absurdity and at worst as an aristocratic and bourgeois confusion of priorities which had encouraged the disgraceful neglect of the needs of the human working classes. The decline in the influence of the Liberal party probably made the situation worse.

In addition, the Victorian emphasis upon associating kindness to nonhuman animals with nursery education had helped to make the issue appear sentimental, childish, unworthy of mature intellectual consideration and, in the most prejudiced sense, 'womanly'; an imperial culture which valued the martial virtues found it difficult to assimilate a concern for animal welfare with its worship of 'manliness', especially after the searing experiences of war. It was not until the 1960s and 1970s that the

moral and biological differences between human and nonhuman began
to seem less absolute.

The real and awful prospect of interbreeding human and nonhuman in
the 1990s becomes daily more probable, as agriculturalists scramble to
produce cheaper meat and the American administration decides to permit
the patenting of new animal forms created by genetic engineering.[10]
Within years, the ancient conceptual gulf between man and beast will be
closed by the scientists. Will this lead to increased callousness to humans,
or to a sudden dawning that we owe duties towards *all* sentient life?

Two other developments have been important in the growth of the
humane movement – the gradual removal of animals as *visible* threats to
human safety and the decline in dependence upon them. As a larger
proportion of the European population became town-dwellers, they felt
their interests less threatened by the depredations of pests than did their
country cousins and they decreasingly thought of nonhumans as being a
source of real danger to them. It was not itself that they lived in the
town or in the country which made people more humane. It was simply
that fewer town-dwellers felt directly imperilled by nonhumans or had
interests visibly bound up with their exploitation. All these trends made
it far easier for men and women to begin to extend the circle of
compassion. Indeed, it is tempting to postulate that between any alienated
groups, *if fear and exploitation are absent*, then feelings of sympathy
seep into the vacuum, and that this process can be rapidly accelerated if
close personal contact is maintained. This seems gradually to have happened, in the case of nonhumans in Europe, in the four hundred years
since the sixteenth century.

Pet-keeping, too, played an important part in this; nonhumans treated
as members of the family naturally became eligible for compassionate
treatment. Dogs and cats were widely domesticated in early medieval
times, although the cat fell out of favour with the Church in the late
fourteenth and fifteenth centuries and became shamefully mistreated –
further evidence that cruelty to nonhumans increased during the Renaissance period. By the eighteenth century cats were back in favour at both
French and English courts and subsequently became special favourites
among artists and writers as well as the aristocracy – precisely those
groups which led the animal welfare movement in Europe.[11]

Animal rights pioneers such as Montaigne, Johnson, Bentham and
Lawrence were all cat-admirers, and it is interesting to speculate on the
role played by cats in the promotion of the cause generally. The relationship between cat and human is, at least in the cat's eyes, more or less
one of parity. The cat-lover therefore is more likely to be someone who
respects animal equality than the dog-lover, who may enjoy the dominant
role which the subservient dog encourages.

Today we can see that pets satisfy our psychological needs in a
number of ways, some not especially selfish but others extremely so:

they give us physical tactile comfort; they flatter us and make us feel important; they help us to drop our social façades and to be ourselves; they give us a feeling of companionship and security, especially at night; and they can boost our egos as extensions of ourselves or as compensations for our weaknesses. We can gain satisfaction from showing off our pets to others; they increase our self-confidence by submitting to our authority; and sometimes, alas, they relieve our hostilities by acting as our scapegoats — they pander to the tyrant in us by becoming our slaves. They also play with us and so allow expression of the eternal child inside most adults; in playing with children they allow the child to develop his or her fantasies and thoughts; and they can act as go-betweens in human relationships, often facilitating the flow of emotion between people. Above all, pets allow us to love and to be loved — the experience of feeling loved and needed being the greatest service which they give to us. To each member of a family they can become something different — another child to the mother, a sibling to the child, a grandchild to the elderly. As companions they are particularly supportive — especially for the old and lonely. It is hardly surprising that, provided they are happy, pets can make excellent psychotherapists.

SQUEAMISHNESS

It is strange that we have no other word for this phenomenon; so ashamed have we been to admit that the sight of our own or another's blood or injury may make us feel ill or cause us to become 'medically shocked'. Yet various writers over the centuries have described this reaction, and today it is taken for granted (and widely joked about) in medical circles. Patients, particularly intelligent males, so the folklore avers, are liable to faint or feel nauseated when undergoing blood tests or injections. Anecdotes are told about war heroes who feared inoculations more than the enemy or who collapsed when they saw the wounds of others.

This could be regarded as an abnormality, some sort of phobia. Yet even phobias (such as the fear of insects, snakes and the dark) are probably based upon sound instincts which have good survival value. When so many people seem to be afflicted, it suggests a significant aspect of human behaviour, and probably one that has itself promoted survival by encouraging the avoidance of injury and illness. The lesser squeamishnesses, too, associated with aversions to vomit and excrement, may have the same function. Indeed there seems to be a general mild squeamishness which causes an aversion towards other individuals' bodies generally, their odours for example, which may also help to avoid infectious illness by maintaining separation. Is this why the sexual drive has to be so powerful in humans — to overcome these varieties of squeamishness?

What is particularly strange is that these culturally widespread behaviours have not been seriously studied. They have, instead, been studiously ignored. Yet they are clearly powerful phenomena, and far more powerful than many aspects of behaviour which do receive considerable study. Squeamishness can, after all, make grown men faint, or cause doctors to abandon careers in surgery; it may even have caused Darwin to give up his career in medicine. His biographer reports that Darwin was disgusted by the study of anatomy, and 'found that he was squeamish in the operating theatre: he attended two operations, one on a child, and ran away in the middle. The memory of them haunted him for many years.'[12]

Surgeons and nurses must develop a resistance to squeamishness, but even those most accustomed can continue to flinch. One distinguished pathologist has claimed that even his selectively hardy profession 'universally suffers from bad dreams' as a result of their work.[13]

In 1977 I surveyed a group of schoolgirls in Oxford who had recently started studying biology. One of the items in my questionnaire was about the dissection of dead animals. Although these fifteen-year-olds had chosen to do biology no less than 55 per cent indicated that they 'disliked' dissecting and 33 per cent said such procedures made them feel 'sick or ill'.[14] It appears that before habituation to dissection occurs a large proportion of schoolchildren are deeply moved by it. This is true even, it seems, of those who have self-selected for dissection and even when the nonhumans being dissected are dead.

Boys, it is true, quickly cotton on to the idea that it is 'macho' not to flinch at dissections. To an extent some may overcome, or at least conceal, their squeamishness by employing bombast. But I suspect the tendency is still there.

What does all this mean? It means, surely, that there is something inherently disturbing in seeing another creature injured, impaled, dismantled or killed — particularly if this is done cold-bloodedly; that is to say when the observer is not already aroused by fear, anger or other extreme emotion. Leo Tolstoy saw humankind's aversion to all killing as both strong and natural,[15] and so do I.

The excitement generated by a dissection class is often very noticeable, and seems to touch upon sadism on one hand and pity on the other. Some children are shocked to discover sadism within themselves and others by their teacher's apparent callousness. Teachers, so it seems, can become 'bloodied' by the process, which leads them sometimes to defend it almost irrationally, as if it were an initiation ceremony with valued religious undertones. Yet after many years working with disturbed children, I strongly suspect that persuading a reluctant child to dissect, and thus 'brainwashing' or corrupting him or her into this form of speciesism, can be as damaging to that child as sexual abuse or physical attack. Furthermore, I have noticed that children who profess indifference to dissection tend to score high on the 'P' scale of the Eysenck Personality Inventory — itself often a feature of teenage delinquency.

Putting young adults through ordeals of blood and injury is culturally widespread. Once through the gate of initiation there is no coming back, the intense sense of pride in the conquering of fear and squeamishness is a powerful part of the process of maturity, especially, perhaps, in warlike groups. Yet because of our shame at our squeamishness, because it does not conform with our macho culture's view of what is mature and manly, we try to pretend that it does not exist. But it *does exist*, and surely the lesson we should learn is that instinctively we are not programmed to destroy other living things cold-bloodedly; and that possibly we cause emotional damage when we force ourselves to do so. Above all it suggests we can care *innately*.

D. O. Hebb years ago discovered that nonhuman apes were deeply disturbed by the sight of an isolated ape's head, so perhaps we are not alone in being squeamish.

Why have I been concerned to argue that squeamishness and compassion are innate (although they can also be learned)? I am not saying that this is what therefore makes them a good thing. My reason for rejoicing at this is that it suggests that it is quite easy for human beings to be compassionate and it therefore gives us some hope for a kinder and more gentle future.

MACHISMO

Squeamishness is certainly not encouraged in militaristic cultures. This not only explains why the phenomenon has remained intellectually taboo in the West, but why cruelty towards nonhumans has sometimes been seen as a sign of virility. Bloodsports in particular have tended to fall into this category. Writing in 1853, Harry Hieover saw such sports 'as producing a manliness of mind and hardihood of frame that have (as yet) characterised my countrymen.'[16] Demonstrations of manhood are often culturally defined as including the ability to steel oneself to do things which one's natural sympathies shy away from. The teaching of such macho motivation is, surely, still one of the main causes of speciesism.

Roberta Kalechofsky has argued that male fear of female sexuality produced a new sadistic element in the pornography of the nineteenth century. Vivisection was associated by both men and women, so she argues, with this male hostility towards women. Certainly this very much ties in with my belief in the importance of a compensating 'machismo' motive for the oppression of both women and nonhumans.[17] The whole cult of machismo in nineteenth-century Britain is indeed very pronounced. Dr Arnold at Rugby started the 'muscular Christian' fashion for 'godliness and manliness' which led to the cultivation of dangerous team sports intended to mould the character of the English public-school man.[18] What was produced at the end of this educational procedure? Men who could endure and inflict physical and mental suffering in obedience to authority or out of loyalty to the team – ideal specimens so it happened, for the extension and maintenance of the British empire.

The middle-class trend towards respectability, together with the fear of uncontrolled working-class disorder, helped to motivate the suppression of violent working-class recreations, including bloodsports. Any occasion – such as a prize fight or a cock-fight – which attracted an unruly crowd was an object of middle-class apprehension. One response was to suppress; another, defensively, was to toughen up the middle- or upper-class male and to instil in him an intense class loyalty.

In the twentieth century this learned machismo dynamic is still very strong in the Western world of James Bond and Rambo; boys are still encouraged to be tough and brave and to eschew emotion. Historically, this was helpful for survival and was accentuated, perhaps, by fear of revolution, invasion or attack generally. But whatever the reason in the past, machismo is surely responsible nowadays for much unnecessary violence and loutishness of various sorts, including many instances of human oppression of the other species.

Significantly, many who have been involved in real wars and had to prove their bravery or strength in battle no longer feel the need to maintain a macho image: some outstanding war heroes have not been ashamed to express a tenderness towards nonhuman animals. The Duke of Wellington was kind to a toad, Lord Nelson felt open revulsion at a bull-fight, and Lord Dowding and Douglas Bader attacked vivisection. Winston Churchill, too, angrily declined to attend a bull-fight arranged in his honour when visiting Seville in 1958.[19]

It remains true that one of the surest ways of promoting speciesism is to imply that cruelty is akin to manliness. Geoffrey Gorer pointed out that this link between cruelty and manliness is culturally widespread. In the public torturing of prisoners by the Japanese, 'the torturer is demonstrating his manliness to his companions by showing his ability to inflict pain without flinching', and the situation is similar to the almost universal admiration accorded to those who *endure* pain stoically in initiation ceremonies or in other contexts.[20]

Women, in most cultures, have not been enslaved by this macho imperative. If, with emancipation, they can continue to escape its coils, then the growing female influence in the future may make the world a better place for all sentient beings. Yet, when enslaved by machismo, the individual female victim – as one has seen in the cases of certain vivisectors – can become particularly deadly.

Nonhumans, like children, are often our scapegoats. Humans will avenge themselves upon them for their own misfortunes, and this mechanism may well be behind the apparent increase in cruelty in Britain at a time of poverty and unemployment in the 1980s. Research by the World Society for the Protection of Animals carried out in America has found that aggressive criminals report being cruel to animals far more frequently than do less aggressive criminals. Significantly, three-quarters of the aggressive criminals studied were abused and beaten as children, compared with only 10 per cent of non-criminals. One criminal said; 'I beat on animals to get back for the beatings I got.'[21]

In 1986 there were nearly 19,000 more cases of cruelty reported to the RSPCA than in the previous year, an increase of 75 per cent on 1984. The highest increase in complaints by region was the 42.14 per cent increase over one year reported from the severely depressed north-east of England. In the three-month period May to July 1987, of 277 people in England and Wales disqualified from keeping animals because they were convicted of cruelty, 54 were housewives, 104 were otherwise employed and 119 (including 8 retired people) were unemployed.[22] Was idleness encouraging cruelty?

Andrew Tyler found in 1988 that 'blood sports are now all the rage with the inner-city set. Badgers, domestic cats, rats, pet-shop apes and horses are all fair game'.[23] In a revealing report he quoted one young unemployed animal-baiter as saying that from the early 1980s this trend had been associated with unemployment: 'a street lad with nothing to do would take to ratting.' Furthermore he would treat his own terriers with speciesist contempt, consigning them to travel in the car boot. All the familiar motives are described – the alienated young using non-humans as scapegoats for their anger, the emulation of the rich hunting set, the macho cult – 'all so that these fellas could stand around in boozers all night boasting how hard they were'. Even genuine erotic sadism was admitted by one young yob, describing his reaction to watching ferrets kill forty captive rabbits – 'I couldn't believe it, but I was getting off on it.' Tyler concluded:

It would perhaps be comfortable to think of them as an aberrant strain, a kind of runt city litter. In reality they express, in a heightened way, both a traditional smash-and-grab attitude to the natural world and a peculiarly late Eighties malaise whose symptoms are spite, selfishness and violent nihilism.

The man who keeps a dog, unfortunately, may gain satisfaction from the scapegoat relationship; the need for a 'whipping boy', a creature to dominate, and its constant admiration and undying loyalty – these things flatter the sagging ego, they may make him feel 'a man' partly because here he is in control to a degree that is not true in other areas of his life.

NONHUMAN *VERSUS* NONHUMAN?

The relationhip between species is a neglected field of study. Yet such relationships are not merely those of fight, flight or indifference. Prey species do not always show fear of a predator, they sometimes pester it as smaller birds do a buzzard. Cows, and particularly heifers and bullocks, are fascinated by dogs or cats who enter their field; young chimpanzees make friends with young baboons; even cats and dogs can play together. Such interspecies relationships can be strong and amicable. Similarly, people can sometimes relate more openly to their pets than to their human associates. Does this mean that we should interfere in the behaviour of nonhumans when this causes suffering to other nonhumans? Of course we should unless we are speciesists, or unless such behaviour has immediate survival value (as in, for example, a natural carnivore–prey interaction). I rescue mice who are being tortured by cats because the torture (almost certainly accentuated by human selective breeding over centuries) is unnecessary for the survival of the aggressor, just as I restrain a large dog from attacking a small one.

PAIN, PLEASURE AND CONSCIOUSNESS

At least since Epicurus in the fourth century BC, philosophers have suggested that all creatures seek pleasure and avoid pain. When questioned as to why they consider something to be good or bad most people produce an explanation which ultimately can be boiled down to whether or not it causes pain or pleasure, happiness or unhappiness. Intermediary goals such as liberty or equality or justice are ultimately valued for this reason. The two best-known utilitarian philosophers who identified this truth, Jeremy Bentham and John Stuart Mill, both included nonhuman animals in their calculations of pain and pleasure. For them, as we have seen this widening of the circle of compassion, to which both Einstein and Schweitzer have referred, was already explicit.

It is debatable how far this has ever been the case with the world's major religions. Some sense of it is present in Hinduism and Buddhism, as we have seen (chapter 2), but less so in the others. Yet in almost all is the general proposition that it is right to treat others as you would wish to be treated yourself. This is clear in Christianity,[24] Taoism, Confucianism, Sikhism, Zoroastrianism, Judaism and Islam. The problem comes with the definition of 'others'. Aristotle did not include slaves in his definition. Yet gradually over the centuries the definition has been widened to include those of other tribes, other nations and other faiths. The next great step forward, surely, is to include those of other species. That is what the animal revolution is about.

Gradually, more evidence accrues to suggest that nonhumans are conscious and feel pain. Nonhuman primates show electrical activity in their brains which is characteristic of consciousness in humans[25] and all vertebrate classes contain chemicals in their nervous system which are known to mediate the human experience of pain. Consciousness emerges from the material of the brain as mysteriously as electricity emerges from the copper wires of a dynamo, and the brains of many species are materially similar to those of humans. Although there is no conclusive evidence that any animal or insect lacks consciousness, it may be that consciousness increases with the complexity of the nervous system of the species, and when sufficiently complex machines are made they too may become conscious and need protection from cruelty.

Whatever are the *causes* of consciousness, its moral importance is clearly paramount. It matters not if an animal, whether human or nonhuman, is intelligent or communicative, or has an immortal soul. All that matters is that it is conscious: in particular that it can be conscious of pain and pleasure. This should be the bedrock of our morality. Pain is pain regardless of the species suffering it.

SINGER AND REGAN: INHERENT VALUE OR SUFFERING?

An interesting difference of opinion has appeared between Peter Singer and Tom Regan, the two leading philosophers of the movement. Singer argues, as I do, that sentience, or the capacity for suffering, is at the heart of the matter. It is because nonhumans can suffer that they have interests which must be considered. Regan, on the other hand, argues that nonhumans as well as humans have a certain 'inherent value' which may be independent of the pleasures and pain which they experience. This inherent value is possessed by all 'subjects of a life', that is to say beings with beliefs, desires, perception, memory, a sense of the future, an emotional life, preferences, the ability to initiate action in pursuit of goals, psycho-physical identity over time and an individual welfare in the sense that things can go well or badly for them.[27] Regan concludes that an 'equal right' to respectful treatment is possessed by all things with inherent value.

So Regan is using the term 'rights', whereas Singer is not. Singer prefers to use my word 'speciesism'. Singer is basing his position on 'suffering' (or sentience) and Regan is basing it on 'inherent value'. One of the advantages of Regan's use of the term 'rights' is that he can avoid getting into the argument about whether or not the suffering of one can be justified by the greater advantage or pleasure of another. He is, as I am, against such trade-offs. For Regan, to experiment upon an animal is to violate its rights and therefore it is wrong, regardless of any advantage to others. Singer, on the other hand, believes in aggregative trade-offs, and argues, for example, that it is possible to imagine a situation in which a painful experiment upon an unwilling subject (whether non-human or human) *is* justified by its beneficial consequences. Whereas I agree with Singer on the importance of *suffering* as the bedrock of morality, I tend to agree with Regan that it is *wrong to aggregate across individual sentients.* This is because I believe that in such matters the individual consciousness is everything. It is therefore wrong for me to inflict suffering *unless* it brings greater advantages to the *same* individual, or unless that individual gives consent. Surely, to take the aggregative line is to accept that performing agonizing experiments upon a few infants, for example,would be justified if we could be sure that it would lead to a cure for many others. The ends are said to justify the means. This must be wrong.

Besides, there are so many uncertainties in such a cost–benefit analysis. How many infants can be sacrificed for the benefit of how many others? How much agony is justified by what quantity of benefit? How certain must I be of the success of the experiment in advance? One could lay down certain rules. For example, pains and pleasures which are *certain* to occur could be said to count for more than *uncertain* ones, *deliberately* caused pain more than that accompanying *natural* events such as disease, and so on. But none of this is really satisfactory. Whatever our disagreements, however, most of us are agreed that pain and distress are bad and that the suffering of nonhumans should count equally with the same quantity of suffering in humans.

But how can 'quantities of suffering' be measured and compared? They might, for example, be measured by psychological indices of stress (such as heart rate, blood pressure, cortisol levels, galvanic skin response and so on) or by the individual's choice between two or more situations, one less painful than another.[28] Clearly in practice, however, it is extremely difficult to make valid measurements of this sort. It is psychological *experience* which matters, after all, not the physical magnitude of the painful stimulus itself, and stress can accompany pleasure as well as pain. Although pain can be said to vary along two basic dimensions – intensity and duration – its experience varies greatly between individuals and is dependent upon other circumstances, particularly psychological ones. In the heat of battle, for instance, a soldier may scarcely notice a wound which in 'cold blood' might be agonizing.

But how about painless killing? Why is that bad? The utilitarian answer is that it deprives a sentient creature of future happiness, as well as upsetting friends and family of the victim. Strangely, Singer has hinted that because nonhumans are at a lower 'mental level' than most humans, it may matter less to kill them. He concluded that:

In general, though, the question of when it is wrong to kill (painlessly) an animal is one to which we need give no precise answer. As long as we remember that we should give the same respect to the lives of animals as we give to the lives of those human beings at a similar mental level we shall not go far wrong.[29]

Is Singer here assuming that a higher mental level (and that, for Singer, appears to mean 'self-awareness, intelligence, the capacity for meaningful relations with others and so on') is linked with greater happiness? Surely the connection, and there may well be one, is by no means inevitable. In killing a normal human being one may be depriving him or her, not of future happiness, but of future sorrow. One can rarely be certain of such things; it is difficult to predict the future.

But Singer may be edging towards the view that certain qualities, in addition to the experience of happiness, have value in themselves: I find this hard to accept. Surely all such qualities have moral value only in the pain or pleasure they bring. Where Singer is surely right, however, is in the case of inflicting suffering rather than death. Here he maintains that the greater 'mental capacities' of the average human being can sometimes increase and sometimes reduce suffering compared with the suffering experienced by nonhumans in the same circumstances. For example, knowing that one is about to be tortured could very much *increase* the quantity of suffering in the total experience. But, conversely, knowing that the pain one experiences is in a very good cause could *reduce* the total suffering. Such cognitive factors, absent in most nonhuman cases and in some human cases (such as the severely mentally handicapped and infants), can work either way.

One thing remains certain. As Singer puts it:

Pain and suffering are bad and should be prevented or minimised, irrespective of the race, sex, or species of the being that suffers. How bad a pain is depends on how intense it is and how long it lasts, but pains of the same magnitude are equally bad regardless of species.[30]

Despite the difficulties in the measurement and comparison of pain, it is surely true that in very many areas humankind is inflicting severe suffering upon nonhumans – in slaughter houses, factory-farms and laboratories, for example. The most fundamental rights of nonhumans are being overthrown often merely for the convenience or luxury of our own species. Such discrimination, based as it is only upon the difference of species, is sheer speciesism.

For me Singer is right in his emphasis upon pain and pleasure but Regan is right in isolating the importance of the individual; ends, however glorious, can never justify means if the latter themselves entail suffering. Indeed, a common mistake made by those defending speciesism (e.g. animal experimentation) on the grounds of the benefits it brings (e.g. medical advances) is to then complain about those militant groups who damage laboratories and factory-farms and to attack them on the same grounds – namely that compassionate ends cannot justify violent means. If this is the case, then how can human benefits from research or other exploitation justify the infliction of violence and suffering upon nonhumans?

DUTIES OR RIGHTS? SPECIESISM AND SENTIENTISM

Whereas Singer avoids the use of the word 'rights' for the very best of reasons, I do so principally because it seems to me to be synthetic and unconvincing — whether applied in the human case or otherwise. This is one reason why I coined the word 'speciesism' in 1970. There are interesting differences in the psychological aspects of the terms. The word 'rights' has gained in popularity very considerably during this century taking over from the nineteenth century's favourite term, which was 'duty'.[31] One obvious difference between the two words is that rights are said to reside in the victim, whereas duties are in the perpetrator. Moral instruction used to place the emphasis upon the doer now it emphasizes the done-to. Why is this? Is it not partly because the doers, usually of the ruling classes, used to have real power over others, whereas today morality is a concern for *all* classes including many who feel powerless? Significantly, it is only in the late twentieth century that the welfare of nonhumans has very publicly become the concern of the working class. The Victorians, of course, sometimes appeared more worried about the righteousness of the doer than the suffering of the victim.

Speciesism is, I suppose, a compromise word.[32] It is applied mainly to the doer, but it is not as high-minded as words such as 'duty' or 'responsibility'. It describes the doer's negative attitude and actions, rather than his or her positive qualities. It denotes not merely discrimination but prejudice, and, far more importantly, the exploitation, oppression and cruel injustice which flow from this prejudice.

Perhaps there is some correlation with personality. Maybe the authoritarian or right-winger (who may feel confident in the efficacy of his or her action) talks in terms of responsibilities and duties, whereas the less authoritarian (who feels rather more of a victim) uses concepts like justice, liberty and rights. The basic difference here is with whom the speaker naturally tends to identify — the doer or the victim.

Whereas 'speciesism' is semantically equivalent to 'sexism' (or male chauvinism) and Animal Liberation has an equivalent meaning to Women's Lib, what then is the equivalent of 'feminism', one wonders? Will it be necessary to revive zoophilism, or would 'sentientism' be possible? This is, after all, what we are asserting — the overwhelming importance in moral (and political) terms of the capacity to feel. We are saying that whatever feels pain, whether an animal or some machine of the future, should have moral rights.

Such word-play is not, I think, entirely frivolous. Words condition how we feel and act. So much of the problem in our mistreatment of the other sentients is due to outmoded habits of thought which new words can play a part in breaking. They can expand our awareness and alter attitudes. If we proclaim sentientism, then the puzzlement this initially causes may help some people to stop and think. Furthermore it is a term which is positive rather than negative in tone.

THE NEW HEDONISM

We have seen that pain has been the overriding concern of most of the authors and artists who have contributed to the development of the modern animal liberation ethic, although sometimes there are *additional* reasons why they advocate compassion; the sense of oneness with nature, for instance, expresssed by Rebecca Hall as a regard for: 'the natural order of things; an order, a communion, we have forgotten, which we ignore to the detriment of ourselves and all that lives.'[33] Yet even here, presumably, the 'detriment' mentioned can ultimately be reduced to nonhuman and human suffering.

Is it possible that animal liberation, with its foundation partly in utilitarian philosophy, may have an effect upon wider morality and politics generally? The gradual decline in the overt importance attached to Christian values has left a moral vacuum. What more natural, in a hedonistic society, than to fill this void with an explicit morality that all can understand and accept: that to cause pain is wrong and to give pleasure is good; that virtue lies in giving pleasure to others and evil is the deliberate causing of pain or distress?

We have seen in Britain's Animal (Scientific Procedures) Act of 1986 the introduction of an overt utilitarian principle of a speciesist sort: namely that the pain of nonhumans should be weighed against the benefits to humans, and this same spirit could permeate government decisions entirely affecting people. Perhaps nowhere more clearly is this equation tested than in the decisions that governments have to make on whether or not to make concessions to terrorists in order to effect the release of hostages. The conventional wisdom dictates that governments should not do so because the relief of the hostages' sufferings would be outweighed in the future by the greater sufferings of further hostages being taken. The White House, it seems, sided more with Tom Regan's approach than with Peter Singer's in deciding that the relief of the current sufferings of hostages should not be aggregated against future cases, when it traded arms with Iran in 1986. The rights of the individual in the here and now were considered to be of paramount importance. Present and certain effects were thus deemed to count for more than the uncertain pains and pleasures of the future.

Health and welfare policies, too, are based, however vaguely, on utilitarianism. With the increasing cost of heart transplant surgery and other advanced medical techniques, administrators are being faced with awkward decisions. Should money be channelled into the comfort of the many or saving the lives of a few? One or many? The young or the old? Pain or life? Prevention or cure?

It is also interesting that viewing pain and pleasure (or suffering and happiness) as the bases of morality is a bringing together of what ought to be and what is, for pain and pleasure are the bases also for both Freudian and modern Behaviourist theories of behaviour. Just as Rousseau and Locke had believed that humankind had rights and liberties rooted in nature, so in the twentieth century nature again can be claimed as the foundation of morality. Certainly, natural impulses (especially aggressive ones) will clash with mores, and 'id' will conflict with 'superego', but at least there is widespread agreement that conscious contentment is the common natural goal.

The less discrepancy, perhaps, between a moral code and natural impulses the less psychological tension there will be, and this growing together of a *code* for behaviour with the *theory* of behaviour is epitomized in the case of animal liberation; both the criteria for morality and those for behaviour lie in the consciousness of the individual sentient. Consciousness is central. Certainly our clothing, our language and our technology emphasize the differences between species. But science itself has demystified the human–nonhuman difference and some psychologists now assert that nonhumans can indeed be credited with 'thought'[34] and even with the ability to deceive deliberately.[35] Certainly some clever apes are more intelligent than many mentally handicapped human primates. But what (to paraphrase Bentham) if it was otherwise? Intelligence does not matter in this context. The important thing to remember is that we can all *suffer*.

MODERN DARWINISM

I am aware that my emphasis upon Darwinism as grounds for asserting the *moral* kinship of all animals raises the question – 'But didn't Darwin claim that only the fittest survive, and isn't this an argument in support of human dominion?' Such an attitude, by no means incompatible with the political ethos of Reaganism and Thatcherism, would also seem to encourage the exploitation of weaker sexes, races and individuals. The strongest objection to this argument, however, is that 'fittest' does not necessarily mean strongest or most selfish or ruthless. The Darwinian definition of what is fittest to survive is made by the environment itself, and environments change. In a nuclear age and a polluted one, and one where the human conquest of the other vertebrates is all but complete, 'fittest' takes on a more subtle meaning. It may mean the opposite to aggressive, macho, selfish or destructive of the balance of nature. Darwinists today are by no means unwilling to support the idea of animal liberation. Indeed, one of this century's leading Darwinists shows a major concern for the ethics of the human-to-nonhuman relationship, and has confirmed that speciesism ' has no proper basis in evolutionary biology'.[36] Writing in his *The Blind Watchmaker*, Dr Richard Dawkins stated:

Such is the breathtaking speciesism of our Christian-inspired attitudes, the abortion of a single human zygote (most of them are destined to be spontaneously aborted anyway) can arouse more moral solicitude and righteous indignation than the vivisection of any number of intelligent adult chimpanzees! I have heard decent, liberal scientists, who had no intention of actually cutting up live chimpanzees, nevertheless passionately defending their right to do so if they chose, without interference from the law. Such people are often the first to bristle at the smallest infringement of human rights.[37]

Dawkins points out that speciesism is made easier by the convenient fact that the intermediates between humans and other apes are now extinct but reminds us that we share more than 99 per cent of our genes with chimpanzees.

Arguments about humankind's closeness to the other apes have waxed and waned over the years since Darwin. Today it is known that the composition of human blood and DNA put us closer to the chimpanzee than horses are to donkeys.[38] Yet still scientists and politicians behave as if no moral implications ensue. The scientific evidence accumulates to support the view that nonhumans suffer pain and distress very much like ourselves, yet the same men and women who produce the evidence continue to ignore its message.

Biologists more than any other group are guilty of this inconsistency. They cruelly experiment upon nonhumans very often in order to find information they hope will be relevant to the human condition. They scientifically justify these experiments on the grounds that the research tool is physically and psychologically like the human, but they fail to condemn their own cruelty on the same grounds. Either nonhumans are unlike humans, in which case they can have little value as models for research, or they are like us, in which case they should be shown similar respect.

We have seen that Darwinism, despite establishing the almost universally held belief in the *physical* kinship of men and animals, did not cause most people to take the logical next step of admitting *moral* kinship. The nineteenth century witnessed progress in the humane movement for quite other reasons, principally affluence and peace. Yet now, belatedly, the implications of the Darwinian message are beginning to be realized.

THE FUTURE

The worldwide campaign must continue, in all its aspects, undaunted by the apparent slowness of change. It may take thirty or forty years for a movement such as ours to turn the great ships of commerce and custom. But the up-and-coming generations of legislators and managers will be those who have heard about animal liberation and had time to think about it. They may not accept the whole ethic, but mindful of its *logic*, of public opinion and the twinges of their own consciences, they will turn the rudder by degrees until we have a full revolution.

The campaign must continue to strive to alter attitudes and reform the law. The five main areas of speciesist abuse remain the same: those affecting domestic sentients, and those in laboratories, farms, places of entertainment and in the wild. By mobilizing public compassion, we can persuade governments around the world that the treatment of non-humans is a legitimate political concern and that it is up to them, and not the individual politician, to effect change. Some changes will have revolutionary effects upon our life-styles, but in almost every case we are no longer as dependent upon the other animals as once we were; alternatives exist or can be found.

In the past our economic dependence upon the other animals surely helped to fashion our speciesism. As the highly anthropocentric Karl Marx noted, it was not religion but the coming of a money economy which led Christians to exploit nature in a way in which earlier Jewish society had not done.[39] In an age in which our technology can take us to the moon, is it not now possible to develop humane alternatives to laboratory animals? Why is so little spent on researching delicious and nutritious foods as alternatives to eating the dead bodies of our evolutionary kin? Surely there is commercial potential here. Cannot we create far more exotic textiles than the raped skins of creatures who have died in agony? As for sports – there are already draghunts, bloodhounds and clay-pigeon; and if more ingenious quarry are required then surely it is not beyond our computerized creativity to invent them.

The next step is to face up to the logic of anti-speciesism by bringing the law into line with philosophy. The gulf between human and non-human in the eyes of the law is almost everywhere still as great or greater than that between master and slave. The law must be made to recognize, and progressively, that nonhumans have claims to life, freedom and the pursuit of happiness just as we do; and among the liberties that individual nonhumans should be able to enjoy is the freedom from exploitation by humankind. Animal liberation is an idea that is easy to ridicule but hard to refute. So hard to refute indeed that one of the very few philosophers to have argued against the idea, Dr Michael Allen Fox of Ontario, has had the courage publicly to recant.[40]

Perhaps the advances in the law should initially cover those species assumed to possess a high level of sentience, such as vertebrates, octopuses and squid. On the premise, albeit an unproven one, that sentience fades with descent of the phylogenetic scale, then a graduated scale of legal rights may be the politically expedient way to proceed. Legal protection primarily should be against the infliction of suffering, then the causing of death, and then such considerations as the encroachment on and pollution of habitats.

People should not be required to *like* nonhumans before they show them respect. Observing duties of justice and kindness towards other humans should be regardless of any personal feelings of affection for individuals. Likewise with nonhuman sentients; I should not be required to *like* a boa-constrictor before wishing to safeguard her or his quality of life.

Nature's two fundamental aspects, ferocious and tranquil, have inspired fear and romantic fascination in human beings. Sometimes the response has been to dominate or to sentimentalize; to fear Nature 'red in tooth and claw' or to love her; or, more profoundly, to separate humankind from nature on one hand or to identify romantically or mystically with nature on the other. Gradually, our view of our own species as being above nature and central in the scheme of things has been eroded. The theories of Copernicus, Marx, Darwin and Freud have been four major blows to human pride. We must now continue this process by discarding speciesism along with all our other delusions of grandeur, and accept our natural place in the universe.

The feeling of oneness with the natural cycle is in all of us; the dim awareness of the dialectical process within our minds and the great spirals of history which bear us all along together, whether human or nonhuman. Yet we try to stand against this tide; we still strive to be masters of our own fate and tyrants over the other animals. A child may show this ambivalence by loving nonhuman animals and by bullying them at the same time: this microcosm of good and evil remains within all of us.

The future demands a reappraisal of the relationship between humankind and nature; both ruthlessness and sentimentality must make way for rationality and compassion, based upon our awareness of the common capacity for consciousness among all us animals.

CONCLUSIONS

In summary, what does our survey of the centuries suggest? The motives for speciesist exploitation are multiple. Many have an instinctive quality and all are culturally shaped. Material benefits are obvious and today they are very often commercial — in the production of food, fur, ivory or scientific products, for example. Sometimes they are connected with personal ambition and prestige — as is often the case in nonhuman experimentation. In sport, too, the motives are complex. Our bullying of nonhumans is a hangover from past millennia when we feared them.

The institutionalized subjugation of nonhumans is widely accepted, usually out of habit. People do it because it has been conventional in

Western cultures for centuries. We all tend to accept orthodoxies; just as ordinary and decent men and women once accepted the need for slavery and torture, so today the greatest moral blindspots are in our exploitation of the other animals.

Idiosyncratic cruelty, on the other hand, is differently motivated. It is usually the effect of individual deprivation or frustration, or a displacement of anger and revenge from human targets on to nonhuman — the scapegoat principle. In extreme cases it can be a sign of mental illness. Child and animal abuse have much in common psychologically and often their causes are the same.

The inherent urge to dominate is as widespread as are the natural surges of compassion; sadism and sympathy can co-exist and neither is uncommon. Sadism is usually concealed because it is recognized as being unacceptable in a civilized society. But sympathy, too, is often denied because men have been taught to regard some forms of cruelty as manifestations of manliness, and sympathy as a sign of weakness.

What, on the other hand, are the reasons for anti-speciesism and for the growing campaigns to help the 'Fourth World' of the nonhuman sentients? Those whose minds have shown an independence from their own culture, and who have not accepted the conventions of their age without question, have frequently expressed their sympathy for nonhumans; we have seen this in the case of numerous writers and thinkers, and in the lives of the saints. They would, on the whole, be described as intelligent and sensitive individuals, who have not been afraid to speak out against orthodoxy.

That compassion, like squeamishness, is a natural impulse, is an unfashionable idea. Yet it is accepted that parental feelings of protectiveness are largely inherent, and by caring for nonhuman sentients we may only be extending our sense of family, thus maintaining the traditional link between kindness and kinship. It is this widening of the family circle, caused partly by our increasing contact with other sentients through easier travel and the medium of television, which underlies our revolution in outlook.

As in all human behaviour (and in more nonhuman behaviour, too, than is usually recognized), cultural factors play a part. The liberation of our natural compassion and the inhibition of our sadistic, exploitative and domineering tendencies towards nonhumans can be assisted by a change in attitudes, values and, ultimately, sanctions. This is the revolution in which we are now immersed.

In the Introduction I raised a number of questions. Even if our perusal of the history of humankind's attitudes towards nonhumans has not always provided firm answers, it has, I feel, helped us to provide some provisional ones.

In Europe, overt human sympathy for nonhumans (the widening of the moral circle) has probably increased over the centuries, but has been far from universal or continuous, suffering a setback during the Renaissance. When the great religions were formed all of them treated the human—nonhuman relationship as a matter of importance. With the exception of Christianity, all placed some emphasis upon the rightness of treating nonhuman life with respect, for its own sake. Yet, in almost every case, practitioners of these religions today fail to show an organized concern for nonhumans. Paradoxically, it is those living in countries affected mainly by the Christian tradition who do so.

Affluence, and, to a lesser extent urbanization, seem to have fostered greater sympathy for nonhumans. Feelings of personal security and the increasing awareness of the scientific evidence for our kinship with other animals, and for our shared capacity for suffering, have also been instrumental. The animal welfare movement has been a particular feature of Northern Europe and of the English-speaking nations and appears to have made progress in periods of peace in the seventeenth, eighteenth and nineteenth centuries. Often its pioneers, such as Wilberforce and Shaftesbury, have also been noted for their concern for human welfare.

Typically, the leaders of the movement have been intellectuals, secular just as often as religious, and their followers in the nineteenth century were from the upper rather than the middle or lower classes. Only in the late twentieth century have we seen anti-speciesism receive active support from *all* classes.

Although sympathy for nonhumans can, of course, be encouraged through education and example, the way in which individuals have emerged as champions of reform suggest that the potentials for compassion and aggression are innate. These two instincts can produce conflicting behaviours of care and cruelty, and are probably one of the reasons why humankind's relationship with nonhumans has been so remarkably inconsistent and ambivalent. Sadism, too, a particularly virulent and eroticized form of aggression, although widely suppressed, is far from being uncommon.

Humankind, for thousands of years, has striven to conquer nature, and the domination of nonhumans has been regarded as a mark of manhood. In consequence, the culturally based macho ideal is a major additional source of cruelty; primarily in sport, but also in other areas of speciesist exploitation.

The absurdity and exaggeration of the traditional excuses for speciesism – that nonhumans feel no pain, that God created them for human use, that they have no souls or that the benefits of their exploitation are overwhelmingly necessary – suggest very strongly that humankind often, perhaps always, feels guilt over its speciesism. None of the excuses for speciesism are rationally convincing. Ultimately, the reasons are selfish, and the modern animal liberation movement, which has entered a new phase since the late 1960s, has exposed their weakness with its own, far stronger, rationale; its militancy, much condemned, suggesting a failure of the democratic process. Yet, gradually, politicians have taken on board the public's environmental concerns and animal protection is being seen, increasingly, as a major part of that 'green' movement.

In the late twentieth century we are in an era of extraordinary change and ambivalence — some people baiting badgers while others build tunnels for them under railway lines, and children stabbing whales to death in one advanced country while in another they strive to keep them alive.

People who are cruel to nonhumans are not all wicked; most are just unthinking. Those of us who seek change must not resort to hatred or violence, but press on with our campaigns to educate and legislate. We want people to open their eyes and to see the other animals as they really are — our kindred and our potential friends with whom we share a brief period of consciousness upon this planet.

Notes

CHAPTER 1 INTRODUCTION

1 See, for example, Ruth Harrison, *Animal Machines* (Stuart, 1964); Richard D. Ryder, *Victims of Science: The Use of Animals in Research* (Davis-Poynter, 1975); Peter Singer, *Animal Liberation: A New Ethic for our Treatment of Animals* (New York Review, 1975).

2 W. E. H. Lecky, *The History of European Morals from Augustus to Charlemagne* (Longman, Green, 1869), vol. 2, p. 174.

3 See Harlan B. Miller, 'Introduction', in Miller and William H. Williams (eds), *Ethics and Animals*, (Humana Press, 1983), p. 7.

4 *Sunday Times*, 10 October 1965. See also Brophy's 'In Pursuit of Fantasy' in Stanley and Roslind Godlovitch and John Harris (eds), *Animals, Men and Morals: An Enquiry into the Maltreatment of Non-humans* (Gollancz, 1971); id., 'Amnesty and Animal Rights', *Free Thinker*, June 1978; id., 'The Darwinist's Dilemma' in David Paterson and Richard D. Ryder (eds), *Animals' Rights: A Symposium* (Centaur, 1979).

5 Roslind Godlovitch, 'Animals and Morals', *Philosophy*, October 1978.

6 Richard D. Ryder, 'Rights of Non Human Animals', *Daily Telegraph*, 3 May 1969. My other letters to this newspaper at this time were on 7 April and 20 May.

7 Peter Singer, 'Animal Liberation', *New York Review of Books*, 5 April 1973.

8 Others include: Andrew Linzey, *Animal Rights* (SCM Press, 1976); Tom Regan and Peter Singer (eds), *Animal Rights and Human Obligations* (Prentice-Hall, 1976); Stephen Clark, *The Moral Status of Animals* (Clarendon, 1977); David Paterson and Richard D. Ryder (eds), *Animals' Rights: A Symposium* (Centaur, 1979). For reviews of the latter see: Richard Dawkins, 'Brute Beasts', *New Statesman*, 10 September 1979; Alan Whittaker, 'Revolutionary Ideas', *Nursing Times*, 30 August 1979; J. H. Benson, 'Books', *New Scientist*, 26 July 1979, p. 303; Ruth Lumley-Smith: 'Man and Beast', *Ecologist*, July-Aug. 1979. Robin Page's

'Sportsman's Bookshelf' in *Shooting Times*, 26 July 1979, ridicules the whole movement.

9 For example, see Richard D. Ryder, *Speciesism* (privately printed leaflet, Oxford, 1970); id., *Speciesism: The Ethics of Vivisection* (leaflet, Scottish Society for the Prevention of Vivisection, Edinburgh, 1974); id., *Speciesism: The Ethics of Animal Abuse* (RSPCA, 1979).

10 *The Times*, 13 April 1988.

11 'Report of the Panel of Enquiry into Shooting and Angling (1976–1979)', Chairman: Lord Medway (RSPCA, 1980).

12 Marion Stamp Dawkins, *Animal Suffering* (Chapman and Hall, 1980). See also this author's 'How Should Humans Treat Non-Humans?', *New Scientist*, 25 August 1983.

13 Hansard, 1 March 1799.

14 Hansard, 12 May 1799.

15 Hansard, 22 February 1818.

16 Robin Hanbury-Tenison, personal communication, September 1988.

17 James Serpell, 'Attitudes to Animals', paper read to 'The Status of Animals' Conference, Nottingham, 20 September 1988.

18 'The Role of the Veterinarian', papers presented to 'The Status of Animals' Conference, Nottingham, 20 September 1988.

19 C. S. Lewis, *Vivisection* (leaflet, National Anti-Vivisection Society, c. 1950).

CHAPTER 2   THE ANCIENT WORLD

1 Angela P. Thomas, *Egyptian Gods and Myths* (Shire Publications, 1986).

2 Quoted by Kenneth Clark, *Animals and Men: Their Relationship as Reflected in Western Art from Prehistory to the Present Day* (Thames and Hudson, 1977), p. 76.

3 Aristotle, *Politics* (Everyman's Library edition), p. 16.

4 Pliny, *Naturalis Historia*, Books 8, 9.

5 W. E. H. Lecky, *The History of European Morals from Augustus to Charlemagne* (Longman, Green and Co., 1869), pp. 175–6.

6 Cicero, *Ad Familiares*, 7.1.3.

7 Aulus Gellius, *Noctes Atticae*, 5.14.

8 Bukkyo Dendo Kyokai, *The Teaching of Buddha* (Kosaido, Tokyo, 1966).

9 James Serpell, *In the Company of Animals: A Study of Human–Animal Relationships* (Basil Blackwell, 1986), p. 168.

10 Al-Hafiz Basheer Ahmad Masri, *Islamic Concern for Animals* (Athene Trust, 1987).

11 Ibid., p. 18.

12 Ibid., p. 21.

13 Ibid., p. 31.

14 Ibid., p. 29.
15 Authorised Version, *Genesis* 1:26–8.
16 I am indebted to Rabbi Julia Neuberger and the Revd Andrew Linzey for their comments in this subject.
17 Isaiah 1:11.
18 Hosea 2:18.
19 Isaiah 66:3.
20 Genesis 1:29.
21 Genesis 9:3.
22 Exodus 20:10; 23:12.
23 Deuteronomy 14:21.
24 Deuteronomy 22:6–7.
25 Deuteronomy 22:10.
26 Proverbs 12:10.
27 Ecclesiastes 3:19.
28 Leviticus 20:15.
29 Lisa Silcock, 'My Life as a Giant', *Sunday Times Magazine*, 1 November 1987.
30 Serpell, *In the Company of Animals*, p. 142.
31 Ibid., p. 7; and Maureen Duffy, *Men and Beasts: An Animal Rights Handbook* (Paladin, 1984), p. 7.
32 Serpell, *'In the Company of Animals'*, p. 66.

CHAPTER 3   THE CHRISTIAN LEGACY: MEDIEVAL ATTITUDES

1 Luke 12:6.
2 I am indebted to the Revd Peter Sanders for this explanation (personal communication, 1987).
3 W. E. H. Lecky, *The History of European Morals from Augustus to Charlemagne* (Longman, Green and Co., 1869), vol. 1, p. 244.
4 Keith Thomas, *Man and the Natural World: Changing Attitudes in England 1500–1800* (Allen Lane, 1983), p. 24.
5 Aquinas, like Augustine, was of the opinion that only humans had 'rational' souls. Animals had 'sensitive' souls which were not 'rational'.
6 Thomas Aquinas, *Summa Contra Gentiles*, iii. 113.
7 Id., *Summa Theologica* II, i, Q. 102, art. 6.
8 Peter Singer, *Animal Liberation: A New Ethic for our Treatment of Animals* (New York Review, 1975), pp. 214–16.
9 *Dives and Pauper*, ed. Priscilla Heath Barnum (EETS, 1976), 1 (2), pp. 35–6. See also Thomas, *Man and the Natural World*, p. 152.
10 H. R. Hays, *Birds, Beasts and Men* (J. M. Dent, 1973), p. 40.
11 'Homily 39, on the Epistle to the Romans', quoted in C. W. Hume, *The Status of Animals in the Christian Religion* (Universities Federation for Animal Welfare, 1957).

12   Quoted by C. W. Hume, in *Universities Federation for Animal Welfare Theological Bulletin*, 2 (1962), p. 3.
13   Thomas, *Man and the Natural World*, p. 152.
14   Florence H. Suckling, *The Brotherhood of Love* (George Bell and Sons, 1910).
15   Peter Singer, *The Animal Liberation Movement* (Old Hammond Press, 1987), p. 4.
16   Thomas, *Man and the Natural World*, pp. 94–7.
17   John Caius, *Of English Dogges* (1576).
18   John Swain, *Brutes and Beasts* (Noel Douglas, 1933).
19   Nicholas Humphrey, Preface to E. P. Evans, *The Criminal Prosecution and Capital Punishment of Animals* (republished by Faber, 1987).
20   Quoted in E. S. Turner, *All Heaven in a Rage* (Michael Joseph, 1964), p. 24.
21   Wynkyn De Worde, *The Demaundes Joyous* (1511). This collection of medieval riddles was the first to be published in England and was republished in 1971, edited by John Wardroper, by the Gordon Fraser Gallery.
22   Quoted in Turner, *All Heaven in a Rage*, p. 28.
23   Thomas, *Man and the Natural World*, p. 164.
24   Lecky, *History of European Morals*, p. 185.

CHAPTER 4   THE RENAISSANCE AND ITS AFTERMATH

1   C. W. Hume has argued, in *The Status of Animals in the Christian Religion* (Universities Federation for Animal Welfare, 1957), that the Renaissance was a revival of paganism which gave new life to astrology and witchcraft. It was during this period, according to Hume, that neighbourliness towards animals dwindled to a new low.
2   Keith Thomas, *Man and the Natural World: Changing Attitudes in England 1500–1800* (Allen Lane, 1983), p. 164.
3   Ibid., p. 152.
4   Ibid., p. 147. Queen Elizabeth's interest in bloodsports was, for a woman, outstanding even for her time. Was there a sadistic streak in her make-up, or was it merely politically expedient for her to emphasize her 'masculinity' in this way?
5   Paul Hentzner, *Travels in England* (1598).
6   E. S. Turner, *All Heaven in a Rage* (Michael Joseph, 1964), p. 37.
7   Thomas, *Man and the Natural World*, p. 147.
8   Ibid., p. 18.
9   Ibid., pp. 19–20.
10   E. McCurdy, *The Mind of Leonardo da Vinci* (Jonathan Cape, 1928).

11 John Vyvyan, *In Pity and in Anger* (Michael Joseph, 1969), p. 16.

12 *The Utopia of Sir Thomas More*, tr. Ralph Robinson (George Sampson, 1910), book 2, pp. 128–9, 181.

13 William Shakespeare, *Measure for Measure*, III. i; *As You Like It*, II. i. 33–40; *Henry VI Part 2*, III. i. 210–18; *Cymbeline*, I. v. 21–30.

14 Michel de Montaigne, 'Of Crueltie', *Montaigne's Essayes*, tr. Florio (republished 1890), book 2, ch. 11.

15 Id., 'An apologie of Raymond Sebond', *Montaigne's Essayes*, book 2, ch. 12.

16 Philip Stubbes, *Anatomie of Abuses* (1583), pp. 177–9 of Colliers Reprints edition.

17 John Calvin, *Sermons*, tr. Arthur Golding (1583) (republished, edited by John Wardroper, Gordon Fraser Gallery).

18 *The Poems of Sir Philip Sidney*, ed. W. Ringler (Oxford University Press, 1962), p. 103.

19 *Magnum Bullarium Romanum*, vol. 2, p. 260: Bull de Salute Gregis, 1 November 1567.

20 Francis Quarles, *Enchiridion* (1641), Century 2, no. 100.

21 Ibid., Century 3, no. 23.

22 Matthew Hale, *The Counsels of a Father* (reprinted London, 1817).

23 Thomas Tryon, *The Countryman's Companion* (*c.* 1683) p. 140.

24 Thomas Tryon, *Wisdom's Dictates* (1691), p. 94.

25 Thomas Babington Macaulay, *History of England* (1849), vol. 1.

26 Henry More, *An Antidote Against Atheism* (1655).

27 John Locke, *Thoughts on Education* (1693), republished in *The Works of John Locke: A New Edition* (London, 1823), vol. ix, pp. 112–14.

28 *The Statutes at Large* (Dublin, 1786), ch. 15, pp. 168–9.

29 W. E. H. Lecky, *The History of European Morals from Augustus to Charlemagne* (Longman, Green and Co., 1869), p. 173.

30 See Emily Stewart Leavitt, *Animals and their Legal Rights* (Animal Welfare Institute, Washington 1968); Richard D. Ryder, 'The Struggle Against Speciesism', in *Animal Rights: A Symposium*, edited by David Paterson and Richard D. Ryder (Centaur, 1978), p. 5.

31 Thomas, *Man and the Natural World*, p. 122.

32 W. Howell, *The Spirit of Prophecy* (1679).

33 Turner, *All Heaven in a Rage*, p. 45.

34 Sir James Thornton, *The Principal Claims on Behalf of Vivisection: A Refutation* (National Anti-Vivisection Society, 1901).

35 Vyvyan, *In Pity and in Anger*, pp. 22–4.

36 Peter Singer, *Animal Liberation: A New Ethic for our Treatment of Animals* (New York Review, 1975), p. 204.

37 Ibid., p. 204.

38 Robert Hooke, letter to Robert Boyle, 10 November 1664, in Gunther, *Early Science in Oxford*, vol. 6, pp. 216–18.

39 Quoted in Singer, *Animal Liberation*, p. 205.

40 John Hildrop, *Free Thoughts Upon the Brute Creation* (1742), pp. 8–9.

41 Quoted by Andreas-Holger Maehle and Ulrich Tröhler in 'Animal Experimentation from Antiquity to the End of the Eighteenth Century: Attitudes and Arguments', in Nicolaas A. Rupke (ed.), *Vivisection in Historical Perspective* (Croom Helm, 1987), p. 22.

CHAPTER 5   THE AGE OF ENLIGHTENMENT: THE EIGHTEENTH CENTURY

1 Richard Steele, *Tatler*, no. 134, 14–16 February 1709.

2 Joseph Addison, *Spectator*, no. 120, 18 July 1711.

3 Joseph Addison, *Maxims, Observations and Reflections*.

4 Alexander Pope, *Guardian*, 21 May 1713.

5 This argument between Pope and a vivisector, Dr Stephen Hales, is recorded in *Spence's Anecdotes* (1820).

6 Alexander Pope, *Windsor Forest* (1713).

7 Maurice Dommanget, *Le Curé Meslier* (Paris, 1965), pp. 62–3, 249.

8 Voltaire, *Dictionnaire philosophique* (Paris, 1775), under 'Bêtes'.

9 Voltaire, *Eléments de la Philosophie de Newton* (1733).

10 Jean-Jacques Rousseau, *Discourses on the Origin of Inequality* (1755), Preface.

11 Id., *Émile* (Montmorency, 1762).

12 See Andreas-Holger Maehle and Ulrich Tröhler, 'Animal Experimentation from Antiquity to the End of the Eighteenth Century: Attitudes and Arguments', in Nicolaas A. Rupke (ed.), *Vivisection in Historical Perspective* (Croom Helm, 1987), p. 35.

13 Immanuel Kant, *Lectures on Ethics*, trans. J. Infield (Methuen, 1930), p. 240.

14 Arthur Schopenhauer, *On the Basis of Morality* (1841).

15 Keith Thomas, *Man and the Natural World: Changing Attitudes in England 1500–1800* (Allen Lane, 1983), pp. 288–300.

16 David Hartley, *Observations on Man* (London, 1741), p. 222.

17 William Paley, *Moral Philosophy* (London, 1785), vol. 2, BR 6, p. 599.

18 John Oswald, *The Cry of Nature, or An Appeal to Mercy and Justice on Behalf of the Persecuted Animals* (London, 1791).

19 Oliver Goldsmith, *The Citizen of the World* (Everyman's Library, 1934), p. 38.

20 George Nicholson, *On the Conduct of Man to the Inferior Animals* (Manchester, 1797).

21 Ibid., p. 88.

22 Ibid., p. 89.

23 *Tatler*, no. 134, 14–16 February 1709.

24 *Guardian*, 21 May 1713, p. 7.

25   Lord Kames, *Essay on Morals* (1751).

26   Rousseau, *Émile* (1762).

27   Thomas Young, *An Essay on Humanity to Animals* (2nd edn, 1809), p. 20.

28   Susanna Watts, *The Animals' Friend: A Collection of Observations and Facts Tending to Restrain Cruelty and to Inculcate Kindness towards Animals* (William Darton, n.d.), p. 1.

29   H. V. Morton, *Stranger in Spain* (Methuen, 1955).

30   'A Surprisingly Rational Speech of a Hen', *Gentleman's Magazine*, April 1749, pp. 147–8.

31   *Gentleman's Magazine*, May 1754, p. 255.

32   James Ferguson, *Lectures on Select Subjects in Mechanics, Pneumatics, Hydrostatics and Optics* (1764).

33   David Hume, *Enquiry Concerning the Principles of Morals* (1751), ch. MI.

34   *Idler*, 5 August 1758.

35   Richard Dean, *An Essay on the Future Life of Brutes* (1767).

36   James Granger, *An Apology for the Brute Creation or Abuse of Animals Censured* (T. Davies, London, 1772).

37   Religious Society of Friends, *Christian Faith and Practice in the Experience of the Society of Friends* (1960), paras. 47 and 51.

38   Humphry Primatt, *The Duty of Mercy and the Sin of Cruelty to Brute Animals* (London, 1776; Edinburgh 1834), pp. 14–15.

39   Ibid., pp. 17–18.

40   Ibid., p. 18.

41   G. H. Toulmin, *The Antiquity and Duration of the World* (1780).

42   Primatt, *The Duty of Mercy*, p. 73.

43   James Yorke, *Country Life*, 23 June 1988.

44   Quoted in Lawrence Gowing, *Hogarth* (Tate Gallery, 1971), p. 69.

45   Ibid., p. 69.

46   Young, *Essay on Humanity to Animals* (2nd edn), p. 59.

47   James Thomson, *The Seasons* (1730).

48   William Cowper, *The Task* (1785).

49   Robert Burns, 'On Seeing A Wounded Hare' (1785).

50   Id., 'On Scaring Some Waterfowl in Loch Turit'.

51   Robert Burns, quoted in E. S. Turner, *All Heaven in a Rage* (Michael Joseph, 1964) p. 71 ('To a Mouse on Turning Her up in Her Nest with the Plough').

52   William Wordsworth, *Hart-Leap Well* (1800).

53   Robert Southey, *The Dancing Bear: Recommended to the Advocates for the Slave Trade*, lines 21–30. Quoted in Bertram Lloyd (ed.), *The Great Kinship* (Allen and Unwin, 1921), p. 51.

54   Alfred de Vigny (1797–1863) and D. M. Moir (1798–1851) are examples.

55   'In Memoriam', lines 15–16. Quoted in Frances E. Clarke (ed.),

Poetry's Pleas for Animals (Lothrop, Lee and Shepherd, Boston, 1927).
56 Percy Bysshe Shelley, *On the Vegetable System of Diet*, quoted in Jon Wynne-Tyson (ed.), *The Extended Circle* (Centaur, 1985), p. 333.
57 Shelley, *Queen Mab* (1813).
58 Frances E. Clarke, *Poetry's Plea for Animals* (Boston, 1927), p. 280.
59 Ibid., p. 132.
60 Thomas, *Man and the Natural World* (Allen Lane, 1983), p. 132; Edward Tyson, *Orang-Utang, sive Homo Sylvestris* (1699); Sir Thomas Browne, *Religio Medici* (1643).
61 William Smellie, *Philosophy of Natural History* (Edinburgh, 1790).
62 Lord Monboddo, *Ancient Metaphysics* (Edinburgh, 1779), vol. 2.
63 Edward Long, *History of Jamaica* (1774).
64 Joseph Ritson, *An Essay on Abstinence from Animal Food, As a Moral Duty* (1802), pp. 13–14.
65 Jeremy Bentham, *Introduction to the Principles of Morals and Legislation* (1780), ch. 17.
66 An alternative version of this story gives the cat's name as Sir John Langborn.
67 *The Works of Jeremy Bentham*, ed. John Bowring (1843), vol. 10, p. 17.
68 Ibid., vol. 11, p. 81.
69 Ibid., vol. 10, pp. 549–50.
70 Oswald, *The Cry of Nature*.
71 Soame Jenyns, *Disquisitions on Several Subjects* (1782).
72 Nicholson, *On the Conduct of Man to the Inferior Animals*, pp. 255–6; John Lawrence, *A Philosophical Treatise on Horses, and on the Moral Duties of Man towards the Brute Creation* (2 vols, 1796, 1798), vol. 1, p. 132, tells a similar story.
73 *Gentleman's Magazine*, January 1789, pp. 15–17.
74 Lawrence, *Philosophical Treatise*, vol. 1, p. 131.
75 Ibid., vol. 1, p. 154.
76 Adam Fitz Adam, *World*, no. 190, 19 August 1756, p. 1139.

CHAPTER 6   TIME FOR ACTION

1 Henry Alken, *British Sports* (1821).
2 John Scott (pseudonym), *The Sportsman's Repository* (London 1820), p. 18.
3 *Sporting Magazine*, December 1801.
4 Edward G. Fairholme and Wellesley Pain, *A Century of Work for Animals: The History of the RSPCA 1824–1924* (John Murray, 1924), pp. 32–3.
5 Ibid., pp. 27–8.
6 E. S. Turner, *All Heaven in a Rage* (Michael Joseph, 1964), p. 129.
7 Three histories of the RSPCA have been written. They are: Fairholme and Pain, *A Century of Work for Animals*; Arthur W. Moss, *Valiant*

Crusade: The History of the RSPCA (Cassell, 1961); Antony Brown, *Who Cares for Animals?* (Heinemann, 1974).

8 Margaret Blount, *Animal Land: The Creatures of Children's Fiction* (Hutchinson, 1974).

9 Sarah Trimmer's *The History of the Robins* was first published in 1786 under the title *Fabulous Histories: Designed for Children, Respecting their Treatment of Animals.*

10 Mrs Trimmer, *The History of the Robins* (1786; 9th edn, 1811), p. 165.

11 *Pity's Gift: A Collection of Interesting Tales to Excite the Compassion of Youth for the Animal Creation, Ornamented with Vignettes from the Writings of Mr. Pratt, Selected by a Lady* (5th edn, London, 1810), Preface.

12 For example in *Stories from Natural History* (anon., 1832).

13 Keith Thomas, *Man and the Natural World: Changing Attitudes in England 1500–1800* (Allen Lane, 1983), p. 167.

14 *Insects and Their Habitations: A Book for Children* (Society for Promoting Christian Knowledge, London, 1833), p. 48.

15 Mary R. Capes, *The Life of Richard of Wyche* (Sands & Co., 1913), p. 43.

16 William Smellie, *The Philosophy of Natural History* (1824; 7th edn, William Milner, Halifax, 1845), p. 271.

17 Jon Wynne-Tyson, *Food for a Future* (Thorsons, 1988), Appendix.

CHAPTER 7 VICTORIAN CONSOLIDATION

1 For example: E. S. Turner, *All Heaven in a Rage* (Michael Joseph, 1964); Edward G. Fairholme and Wellesley Pain, *A Century of Work for the Animals: The History of the RSPCA 1824–1924* (John Murray, 1924).

2 Arthur W. Moss, *Valiant Crusade: The History of the RSPCA* (Cassell, 1961). The other members attending this meeting were T. G. Meymott in the chair, Captain Charles Bernard and Thomas Butt.

3 RSPCA minute book, no. 1.

4 I am indebted to Derek Sayce and Olive Martyn of the RSPCA for their assistance.

5 Quoted in Ronald Fletcher (ed.), *John Stuart Mill: A Logical Critique of Sociology* (Michael Joseph, 1971), p. 416.

6 RSPCA Tract, London, *c.* 1860.

7 Ibid.

8 Quoted in M. R. L. Freshel (ed.), *Selections from Three Essays by Richard Wagner* (Millennium Guild, Rochester, NH, 1933).

9 Christina Rossetti, *To What Purpose this Waste?* (1872).

10 Quoted by John Vyvyan, *In Pity and in Anger* (Michael Joseph, 1969), p. 38.

11 *British Medical Journal*, 22 August 1863, p. 215.

12   Keith Thomas, *Man and the Natural World: Changing Attitudes in England 1500–1800* (Allen Lane, 1983), p. 174.

13   Quoted by Vyvyan, *In Pity and in Anger*, p. 22.

14   *Report of the Royal Commission on the Practice of Subjecting Live Animals to Experiments for Scientific Purposes* (HMSO, 1876), C-1397 p. 23, Q. 444.

15   Claude Bernard, *Introduction to the Study of Experimental Medicine* (Paris, 1865).

16   Ibid., 1926 edition, vol. 1, p. 35.

17   Richard D. French, *Antivivisection and Medical Science in Victorian Society* (Princeton University Press, Princeton, NJ, 1975), p. 260.

18   *British Medical Journal*, 11 May 1861.

19   Quoted by Vyvyan, *In Pity and in Anger*, p. 68.

20   Ibid., p. 69.

21   Frances Power Cobbe, *Life of Frances Power Cobbe* (London, 1894), vol. 2, p. 16.

22   Gladstone Papers, British Museum, quoted by John Vyvyan, *In Pity and in Anger*, p. 162.

23   French, *Antivivisection*, p. 66.

24   Quoted by Vyvyan, *In Pity and in Anger*, p. 86.

25   Royal Commission 1876, p. 183, Q. 3538–41.

26   Ibid., p. 183, Q. 3549–54.

27   Richard Hutton, *Spectator* (1875), 48.

28   Cobbe, *Life of Frances Power Cobbe*, vol. 1, p. 652.

29   Moss, *Valiant Crusade*, p. 163.

30   *Animal World*, 7 (1876), p. 132.

31   Mary Shelley, *Frankenstein or the Modern Prometheus* (1818); R. L. Stevenson, *The Strange Case of Dr. Jekyll and Mr. Hyde* (1886).

32   French, *Antivivisection*, p. 408.

33   Ibid., p. 412.

34   Ibid., p. 409.

35   S. D. Collingwood, *The Life and Letters of Lewis Carroll* (Fisher Unwin, 1898), pp. 165–71.

36   Ibid., p. 299.

37   Lewis Carroll, 'Some Popular Fallacies About Vivisection', *Fortnightly Review*, 23 (1875), p. 854.

38   *The Diaries of John Ruskin* ed. Joan Evans (Oxford University Press, 1959), p. 1102.

39   L. I. Lumsden, *Ruskin as a Moral Teacher* (Scottish Society for the Prevention of Vivisection, Edinburgh c. 1916, undated), pp. 5–7.

40   Ruskin, too, had once had tea with the 'delightful' young Misses Liddell together with the Archbishop of Canterbury (on 24 October 1873) and, indeed, had a perplexing dream the following night that he had 'starved a hermit-crab whom I had packed away in his shell'. Was this vivisectional nightmare a premonition of the battle he was to fight

with old Liddell, or was the dream a sign that Dodgson was not alone in being titillated by little Alice and that Ruskin was having to 'pack away' his feelings for her? Freudians could interpret it as a masterpiece of symbolic repression: 'The metaphysics of this', Ruskin notes, ' — which came to looking at the starved creature and wondering if I could revive it — are highly curious.'

41 French, *Antivivisection*, pp. 184–9.

42 Ibid., pp. 204–14.

43 Quoted by Turner, *In Pity and in Anger*, p. 176.

44 It was, however, not until murderous millinery and dove slaughter had passed out of fashion in the twentieth century that either would be entirely prohibited by law; the latter by an Act piloted through Parliament in 1921 by Lord Lambourne and Sir Burton Chadwick, the former by Lord Buckmaster and Lord Tweedsmuir's Act of 1933. Under the influence of the Swede, Axel Munthe, even Mussolini would become involved in bird protection, in 1933 declaring the island of Capri a bird sanctuary, thereby earning a congratulatory telegram from the League Against Cruel Sports and no less than the Queen Victoria Silver Medal from the RSPCA — the society's highest award.

45 Richard Thomas, *The Politics of Hunting* (Gower, 1983), p. 182.

46 Reprinted as *The Morality of Field Sports* by the Animals' Friend Society, (London, *c.* 1910, undated).

47 James Walvin, *Leisure and Society* (Longman, 1978), p. 26.

CHAPTER 8   EDWARDIAN VIGOUR AND POST-WAR APATHY, 1900–1960

1 Henry Salt, *Animal's Rights Considered in Relation to Social Progress, with a Bibliographical Appendix* (Macmillan, 1894).

2 Stephen Winsten, *Salt and His Circle* (Hutchinson, 1951), Preface.

3 Ibid., p. 122.

4 Salt's other animal rights works include *The Humanities of Diet: Some Reasonings and Rhymings* (Vegetarian Society, 1914); *The Story of My Cousins: Brief Animal Biographies* (Watts, 1923); *The Creed of Kinship* (Constable, 1935).

5 Ernest Seton-Thompson, *Wild Animals I Have Known* (Charles Scribner's Sons, New York, 1900), pp. 12–13.

6 D. H. Lawrence, *Snake*, quoted by Jon Wynne-Tyson, 'The Extended Circle: A Dictionary of Humane Thought' (Centaur, 1985), p. 167; Albert Schweitzer, *The Philosophy of Civilization* (1923); George Orwell, quoted by Richard D. Ryder, 'Victims of Science' (Centaur, 1983), p. 143.

7 Coleridge was described by William Watson as 'The Swordsman of Mercy' — an epithet equally appropriate for many other animal rights activists.

8   The *Animal World* of July 1911 contains some lengthy correspondence between Stephen Coleridge and the RSPCA's secretary, Edward Fairholme. The former had chided the RSPCA in the pages of the *Zoophilist* for being lukewarm in the battle against vivisection and for allowing on to its council a veterinary surgeon who was also a vivisector, a Mr Stockman; a familiar tale.

9   Arthur W. Moss, *Valiant Crusade* (Cassell, 1961), p. 50.

10   Henry Salt (ed.), *Killing for Sport: Essays by Various Writers* (George Bell, 1917).

11   R. Gordon Cummings, *Five Years of a Hunter's Life in the Far Interior of South Africa* (London, 1850).

12   Maureen Duffy, *Men and Beasts* (Paladin, 1984), p. 103.

13   Henry Seton-Karr, *My Sporting Holidays* (London, 1904).

14   William Shakespeare, *Much Ado About Nothing*, III.i.

15   A. E. Freeman, 'The Morality of Field Sports', in *Fortnightly Review*, 1869-70, reprinted by the Animals' Friend Society, London, *c.* 1910.

16   Edward G. Fairholme and Wellesley Pain, *A Century of Work for Animals: The History of the RSPCA 1824-1924* (John Murray, 1924), p. 100.

17   Patrick Moore (ed.), *Against Hunting: A Symposium* (Gollancz, 1965).

18   Moss, *Valiant Crusade*, p. 174.

19   The story is given in the *Report of the Animal Defence and Anti-Vivisection Society* (1911).

20   Ibid., pp. 11, 12.

21   *Report of the Animal Defence and Anti-Vivisection Society* (1923), p. 5.

22   Richard D. French, *Antivivisection and Medical Science in Victorian Society* (Princeton University Press, Princeton, NJ, 1975), p. 260.

23   Wilfred Risdon, *Lawson Tait* (National Anti-Vivisection Society, 1967).

24   Lawson Tait, paper presented to the Birmingham Philosophical Society, 20 April 1882.

25   Bernard Shaw, 'Looking Backward', in G. H. Bowker (ed.), *Shaw on Vivisection* (Allen and Unwin, 1949), pp. 63-4.

26   Dr A. de Watteville, letter to the *Standard*, 24 November 1882.

27   Edward Carpenter, 'Vivisection and the Labour Movement', *Humanity* (November 1895), p. 68.

28   C. W. Hume, *Man and Beast* (UFAW, 1962), p. 202.

CHAPTER 9   WHY BRITAIN? PAIN, EVOLUTION AND
SECURITY

1   James Turner, *Reckoning with the Beast* (Johns Hopkins University Press, 1980), p. 27.

2   *Commons Journals*, 23 and 28 April, 1802.

3   Turner, *Reckoning with the Beast*, p. 27.

4   Nicolaas A. Rupke (ed.), *Vivisection in Historical Perspective* (Croom Helm, 1987), p. 11.

5   Keith Thomas, *Man and the Natural World: Changing Attitudes in England 1500–1800* (Allen Lane, 1983), p. 150.

6   John Pollack, *Wilberforce* (Constable, 1977), p. 80.

7   Georgina Battiscombe, *Shaftesbury* (Constable, 1975), p. 332.

8   Lord Coleridge, *The Nineteenth Century Defenders of Vivisection* (leaflet, Animals' Friend Society, London, 1882).

9   Miriam Rothschild, *Animals and Man* (Clarendon Press, 1986), p. 50.

10   Spinoza, *Ethics* (1675), part iv, prop. 37, n. 1.

11   *British Medical Journal*, no. 2, 28 May 1904.

12   Francis Darwin, 'Charles Darwin', *Dictionary of National Biography*. See also John Chancellor, *Charles Darwin* (Weidenfeld and Nicolson, 1973), pp 55–6.

13   Charles Darwin, *The Descent of Man* (1871), i, pp. 35, 48–9, 78.

14   *Report of the Royal Commission on the Practice of Subjecting Live Animals to Experiments for Scientific Purposes* (HMSO, London, 1876), C-1397, pp. 233–4, Q. 4662–6 and Q. 4672.

15   John R. Durrant, 'Darwin Unbuttoned', *New York Review of Books*, 28 April 1988.

16   M. R. L. Freshel (ed.), *Selections from Three Essays By Richard Wagner* (Millenium Guild, New York, 1933).

17   T. H. Huxley, *Evidence as to Man's Place in Nature* (1863; Macmillan edition of 1901), pp. 151–2.

18   Lauder Lindsay, *Mind in the Lower Animals* (Kegan Paul, 1879). vol. 1, pp. 118–25.

19   Charles Darwin, *The Descent of Man* (1871).

20   A. Armitt, *Man and His Relatives: A Question of Morality* (London, 1885), pp. 6–7. See also Richard D. French, *Antivivisection and Medical Science in Victorian Society* (Princeton University Press, Princeton, NJ, 1975), p. 384.

21   John Lubbock, *The Beauties of Nature* (Macmillan, London, 1892), p. 41.

22   Wilhelm Wundt, *Lectures on Human and Animal Psychology* (1892; trans. J. E. Creighton and E. B. Titchener, Swan Sonnenschein, New York, 1894), pp. 358–66.

23   C. Lloyd Morgan, *An Introduction to Comparative Psychology*, (Edward Arnold, 1894), p. 51.

24   Ivan Pavlov, *Conditioned Reflexes* (1927).

25   C. Lloyd Morgan, *Animal Sketches* (Edward Arnold, 1891). p. 5.

CHAPTER 10   THE REVIVAL OF THE MOVEMENT AFTER 1960

1   Personal communication, April 1973.

2   The three principal histories, as previously mentioned, of the RSPCA are: Edward G. Fairholme and Wellesley Pain, *A Century of Work for Animals: The History of the RSPCA 1824–1924* (John Murray, 1924); Arthur W. Moss, *Valiant Crusade: The History of the RSPCA* (Cassell, 1961); Antony Brown, *Who Cares for Animals?* (Heinemann, 1974).

3   Brigid Brophy, 'The Rights of Animals', *Sunday Times*, 10 October 1965.

4   Personal communication, 1985.

5   Monica Hutchings and Mavis Caver, *Man's Dominion* (Hart-Davis, 1970).

6   It was after the failure of one such Bill introduced by Seymour Cocks MP in 1949 that the matter was referred to a special committee chaired by Scott Henderson KC. Its report condemned the gin (leghold) trap and the snaring of deer, but condoned bloodsports.

7   Richard H. Thomas, *The Politics of Hunting* (Gower, 1983), p. 228.

8   The influence of the British Field Sports Society within the Conservative party still remains considerable, as was clearly demonstrated in April 1983 when the Conservative prospective parliamentary candidate for South-West Cambridge was forced to withdraw his candidacy after it was revealed that his wife had once supported the League Against Cruel Sports.

9   Thomas, *The Politics of Hunting*, p. 159.

10   Hunt Saboteurs Association Constitution, as agreed at its AGMs in 1977 and 1984.

11   Personal communication, August 1988.

12   Otters became protected in Scotland in 1981.

13   Lord Houghton of Sowerby, letter to the *Halifax Evening Courier*, 16 March 1978.

14   *Sunday Times*, 21 August 1977.

15   *Howl*, the magazine of the Hunt Saboteurs Association, Autumn 1981, Obituary, p. 6.

16   *Western Morning News*, 24 December 1986.

17   Robert Churchward, *A Master of Hounds Speaks* (National Society for the Abolition of Cruel Sports, 1960), p. 38. Churchward's real name was Paul Rycaut de Shordiche-Churchward. An explorer, soldier and big-game hunter, he denounced his 'sporting' past and became vice-president of the National Society for the Abolition of Cruel Sports in 1959 and a life patron of the League Against Cruel Sports. He contributed a chapter on fox-hunting to Patrick Moore's *Against Hunting* in 1965.

18   Vera Sheppard, *My Head Against the Wall: A Decade in the Fight Against Bloodsports* (Moonraker Press, 1979).

19   For example, Lord Halifax, then chairman of the Masters of Foxhounds' Association had written to *Horse and Hound* on 2 July 1960 stating that it was: 'absolutely essential that we should try to get foxhunting people to join

NOTES TO PAGES 173–179

the RSPCA so that they are in a position to vote'. Sheppard also referred to a letter in the *West Sussex Gazette* of 26 January 1961 from Sir Ralph Clarke, which stated that 'It was the desire of the Masters of Foxhounds' Association and the British Field Sports Society to increase the RSPCA membership in this way with the object of capturing control of the policy of the RSPCA. We are anxious to get as many members as possible.' She went on to quote more recent letters in *Horse and Hound* from John Hobhouse, the new RSPCA chairman (27 November 1970 and 1 January 1971) to the effect that he hoped that readers would join the RSPCA. (A council member defended this by asserting that by joining the society bloodsports people would in time become educated against bloodsports.) A rather similar case arose in 1988 when it was reported that members of the BFSS were urged to join the National Trust to prevent a ban on hunting on Trust land (see *Independent*, 5 September 1988). So much for 'entryism'.

20   The Reform Group, however, went from strength to strength under its indefatigable leaders. Under John Bryant's name the group issued the following statement in 1971: 'We of the RSPCA Reform Group, representing more than one hundred RSPCA officials and other members are very concerned for the future wellbeing of the society. We believe the facts given below show that people with a vested interest in a particular form of cruelty have infiltrated the RSPCA in an effort to subdue the society's criticism of their activities. That the subject is bloodsports is not important — it could have been infiltration by the factory farming community or any large body of people who gain pleasure or profit from cruelty to animals.'

21   The group of younger and more radical members of the RSPCA council remained in a minority except from June 1979 to June 1980. The passage of their reforms throughout the period 1972—9 depended, therefore, upon the support of moderates such as Michael Kay, Lady Dunn, Marjorie Sutcliffe and Roy Crisp. The radicals included, besides those already mentioned, Jan Rennison and Robin Howard.

22   Celia Hammond, one of Britain's top models in the 'swinging sixties' and a pioneer campaigner in the modern anti-fur campaign, went on to rescue hundreds of cats in and around London, forming her own charity CHAT (the Celia Hammond Animal Trust) in 1986. Her fund-raising events were supported by many well-known people such as Joanna Lumley, Marie Helvin, Jonathan Ross, Uri Geller, Linda McCartney and Dudley Moore.

23   JACOPIS was largely the idea of Peter Mann, president of the British Small Animals Veterinary Association and, later, the Chief Veterinary Surgeon of the People's Dispensary for Sick Animals.

24   For a description of the formation of FAWCE and CRAE see Clive Hollands, *Compassion is the Bugler: The Struggle for Animal Rights* (Macdonald, 1980), pp. 73—7.

25   Speakers at the conference included Brigid Brophy, John Bryant, Stephen Clark, Maureen Duffy, Lord Houghton, Clive Hollands, the Revd Andrew Linzey, David Paterson, Tom Regan, Timothy Sprigge, John Aspinall, Michael

Fox, Ruth Harrison, Peter Roberts, Jon WynneTyson, Bill Jordan, David Macdonald, John Harris and myself.

26   Signatories included all the speakers and, among others, Richard Adams, Peter Singer, John Alexander-Sinclair, Raymond Frey, Ruth Plant, Angela Walder, David Wetton, Clare Druce, Violet Spalding, Ronnie Lee, Cliff Goodman, Ian Macphail, Jan Rennison and Robin Howard.

27   See, for example, *Observer*, 26 June 1977.

28   Charles Bellairs, 'Animal Welfare', *Politics Today*, no. 13, 17 September 1979.

29   One of the most effective supporters of GECCAP was Richard Course, director of the League Against Cruel Sports, which gave £20,000 to the campaign. Course's tough approach and his flair for publicity often achieved results, but sometimes controversially. Some societies, worried about GECCAP's direct lobbying of the parties at their annual conferences, objected, and the Universities Federation for Animal Welfare withdrew its support from GECCAP.

30   The parties' election promises were as follows:

Liberal party: 'Support the demand of the General Election CoOrdinating Committee for Animal Protection for a Royal Commission on Animal Welfare. Ban the importation and manufacture of any product derived from any species whose survival is threatened, and work for a total ban on commercial whaling. We also need a co-ordinated approach to the needs of food production and conservation of natural wildlife which recognises their interdependence. Increase the number of abattoirs to EEC standard to discourage the export of live animals.'

Conservative party: 'The welfare of animals is an issue that concerns us all. There are problems in certain areas and we will act immediately where it is necessary. More specifically, we still give full support to the EEC proposals on the transportation of animals. We shall update the Brambell Report, the codes of welfare for farm animals, and the legislation on experiments on live animals. We shall also re-examine the rules and enforcement applying to the export of live animals and shall halt the export of cows and ewes recently calved and lambed.'

Labour party: 'Under Labour's new Council for Animal Welfare we will have stronger control on the export of live animals for export, on conditions of factory farms and on experiments on living animals. Legislation to end cruelty to animals will include the banning of hare-coursing and stag and deer hunting. Angling and shooting will in no way be affected by our proposals.'

31   Richard Sayer, *RSPCA Parliamentary Report* (October 1985).

32   Katya Lester and Richard D. Ryder, *Animal Protection Commission* (Liberal/SDP Alliance, August 1986).

33   Editorial, *British Farmer and Stockbreeder*, 18 August 1979.

34   Richard D. Ryder, letter to the *Daily Telegraph*, 17 December 1979.

35   The defence case rested largely on my shoulders. During the debate I was physically attacked by Frederick Burden MP. A few months later he was

knighted. (See photo and report in the *Guardian*, 25 February 1980.)

36   A. L. Smith-Maxwell, letter in *Horse and Hound*, 15 February 1980.

37   'Militants Pull RSPCA Off Welfare Council', *Poultry World*, 15 November 1979.

38   For example, Mike Nelson, 'What is the RSPCA Council Really Up To?' *Veterinary Practice*, 4 February 1980.

39   In 1979 RSPCA membership had increased to more than 65,000. By 1988 it was less than 20,000. See, for example, Richard D. Ryder, 'Animal Revolution', *Outrage*, November/December 1981.

40   'Politics and the RSPCA', *Daily Telegraph*, 1 March 1980. See also Brian Seager and Vera Sheppard's letters in reply, *Daily Telegraph*, 5 March 1980.

41   *Daily Telegraph*, 22 March 1980.

42   Personal communication, 17 March 1980.

43   BBC *Panorama*, 6 December 1982.

44   See Sir David Napley's letter, *Sunday Telegraph*, 11 November 1980, and Janet Fookes's view of the situation on 26 October. See also *Daily Telegraph*, 12 April 1980. The unsuccessful attempt to expel me from the society was on 26 November 1980. Miss Fookes's views are also reported in the *Evening Standard* of 12 December 1980. Those of the president of the society, Richard Adams, and the vice-presidents, Lord Houghton, Lady Dowding and Clive Hollands, who all supported my calls for an investigation of the society's finances, are reported in the *Daily Mail* of 12 January and 13 January 1981. See also further relevant reports in the *Daily Mail*, 1 October 1981 and 2 October 1981.

45   *Guardian*, 30 September 1982.

46   The reaction to the disputes and obvious mismanagement of the period 1980–3 was reflected in a temporary dip in legacy income in 1984; but soon legacies resumed their steady climb and by 1986 they were at a record £12 million.

47   For example, Stefan Ormrod at Wildlife, Cindy Milburn and John Callaghan, Mike Smithson, Caroline Vodden, and Gavin Grant.

48   'Blood-letting at the RSPCA', Daily Telegraph, 29 November 1988; BBC Radio 4 News, 30 November 1988; George Hill, 'Should You Kill a Healthy Cat?', *The Times*, 3 January 1989, p. 7.

49   Personnal communication, March 1979.

50   Personnal communication, October 1980.

51   Royal College of Veterinary Surgeons, *Guide to Professional Conduct* (1978), p. 4.

52   *Veterinary Record*, 8 April 1972, pp. 416–18.

53   *Sunday Mirror*, 26 June 1988.

54   Clive Hollands, 'What the Animal Welfare Movement Expects of the Veterinarian', Biological Council Lecture, British Veterinary Association Congress, 10 September 1987.

55   *Mail on Sunday*, 12 December 1982.

56   For example, Professor N. Anderson's comment that 'Animal welfare

issues generate a puzzling lack of interest among the academic members of the veterinary profession' (*Veterinary Record*, 4 July 1987).

57   John Webster, *Veterinary Record*, 4 October 1986. Most encouraging of all was P. G. Dunn's letter to the *Veterinary Record* of 9 February 1980: 'Animal Welfare is a subject to which too little attention is paid; many have grown immune to the insidious development of unsatisfactory husbandry conditions for our farm animals. By tolerating such practices we support a system of animal agriculture which is immoral. How many veterinarians feel totally unconcerned at the sight of dry sows in confinement stalls on a cold winter's day? How many of us have a completely clear conscience when we see four layers in a small battery cage?'

58   *Sunday Times*, 12 June 1988.

59   Angela Walder at the Annual General Meeting of the RSPCA, 25 June 1988.

60   Jolyon Jenkins, *New Statesman*, 21 February 1986.

61   From the world of entertainment Doris Day, Brigitte Bardot, Joanna Lumley, Julie Christie, Judi Dench, Geraldine James, Julia McKenzie, Hayley Mills, Linda McCartney, Carol Royle, Spike Milligan, Johnny Morris, Sir John Gielgud, Dudley Moore, James Mason, Uri Geller, Virginia McKenna and Bill Travers are examples, and the writers Iris Murdoch, Fay Weldon, Jan Morris, Brigid Brophy, Gordon Newman, Rebecca Hall, Maureen Duffy, Richard Adams and Desmond Morris also stand out. Clare Francis, novelist and round-the-world yachtswoman, motivated to 'try to make the world a tiny bit better', became a leading anti-fur campaigner in the 1980s. Amongst royalty, Princess Diana has made it clear that she does not wear fur and Princess Anne and Prince Charles have made sympathetic public statements about farm animals (e.g. *Daily Telegraph,* 13 September 1986, RSPCA Statement of 24 January 1986 and *The Observer,* 8 January 1989, p. 3); and the latter has lamented that 'we see ourselves as somehow separate from and superior to nature' (*Daily Telegraph,* 23 March 1988). Prince Sadruddin Aga Khan has attacked animal experimentation (e.g. Prince Sadruddin Aga Khan, 'Penalising Animals for our Indulgence', *Observer,* 16 August 1981).

62   Hugh Hudson added to the fiction of *Greystoke* – Edgar Rice Burrough's story of the human baby Tarzan nurtured into adulthood by apes – a final chapter in which Tarzan, by this time the Earl of Greystoke, discovers his own ape foster-father in a laboratory cage in London; he at once liberates him and together they flee across Hyde Park. Hudson was here questioning human dominion and was conscious of the parallel with the Nazi ideal of the super-race (personal communication, December 1986). Spielberg, too, inserts an animal liberation theme in *E. T.,* and the late James Mason's final film performance in *The Shooting Party* subtly expresses the actor's own profound interest in animal rights.

Tarzan is one of the century's most popular fantasies and has a relevance to our story. For decades Hollywood depicted most of the nonhumans in Tarzan movies as the 'good guys' who assisted Tarzan in his battles against the (usually human) villains; in the Tarzan epic human dominion has become a friendly partnership. Also for decades Walt Disney, reportedly concerned about the mistreatment of nonhuman animals, portrayed nonhumans as the allies of humans in, for example, his *Snow White and the Seven Dwarfs* of 1938. According to Marc Davis, a Disney animator, Disney sought to combine life-like animal movement with anthropomorphic character *(The Art of Walt Disney,* ITV South Bank Show, 25 September 1988).

63   Anna Sewell's *Black Beauty,* published in 1877, had had a similar effect. Not too strenuously preaching humanity, this very popular 'autobiography of a horse' had reminded thousands that animals can suffer, and persuaded many to change their ways accordingly. In recent times, Richard Adams's novels *Watership Down* and *The Plague Dogs* (1977), both turned into films, have had similar impacts, affecting the outlook of millions. Indeed, the twentieth century has seen a growing number of novels touching the cause of animal protection. Examples are *Crowleigh Hall* by Emily Robinson (1906); *The Difficulties of Dr. Deguerre* by Walter Hadwen (1926); *Morwyn or the Vengeance of God* by John Cowper Powys (1937); Roald Dahl's *The Magic Finger* (1966); *Doctor Rat* by William Kotzwinkle (1976); *Hackenfeller's Ape* by Brigid Brophy and *I Want to Go to Moscow* by Maureen Duffy (1973); Innis Hamilton's *The Beagle Brigade* (1980), and *Bobbie* (1986); and *Set a Thief* by G. F. Newman (1986).

64   First was Richard French's meticulous *Antivivisection and Medical Science in Victorian Society* (Princeton University Press, Princeton, NJ, 1975), which coincided with the new wave of philosophical books on animal liberation. Inspired by Bill Jordan and the new radicals within the RSPCA, there followed *Animal Marking,* edited by Bernard Stonehouse (Macmillan, 1978); *Animals in Research,* edited by David Sperlinger (John Wiley, 1981); and *The RSPCA Book of British Mammals,* edited by C. L. Boyle (Collins, 1981). Later came Mary Midgeley's *Animals and Why They Matter* (Penguin, 1983); James Serpell's stimulating *In the Company of Animals* (Blackwell, 1986), and the excellent *Vivisection in Historical Perspective,* edited by Nicolaas A. Rupke (Croom Helm, 1987).

65   *The Beast* in 1979 and *Black Beast* in 1985 (renamed *Turning Point* in 1986). *The Beast,* subtitled *The Magazine that Bites Back,* was published by Clanose Publishers Ltd in London between June 1979 and June 1981. Its founding editor was John May.

66   For example: BBC Radio 4's *Animals for Man,* 27 May 1975, *Woman's Hour,* 6 September 1976, *A Word in Edgeways,* 16 January 1983; LWT *Credo,* 26 February 1980; BBC 2 *Rabbits Can't Cry,* 20 October 1982; LWT *Credo,* 21 October 1982; Channel Four *The Animals Film,* 4 November 1982, and *Heart of the Matter,* 4 October 1984.

67   The 1970s had been another golden era for the animal welfare movement in Britain and, by the end of the decade, its influence could be seen in revived movements throughout Europe and the English-speaking world. Many outstanding campaigners had emerged in Britain, among them Richard

Adams, John Alexander-Sinclair, Mary-Rose Barrington, Eileen Bezet, May Bocking, Joanne Bower, John Bryant, Nick Carter, Vivien Clifford, Richard Course, Muriel Lady Dowding, Clare Druce, Lady Dunn, Roy Forster, Fay Funnell, Penny Goater, Basil Goldstone, Brian Gunn, Rebecca Hall, Celia Hammond, Dr Harold Hewitt, Cathy Hodgson, Clive Hollands, Lord Houghton, Margery Jones, Bill Jordan, Bruce Kent, Joan Latto, Dr Alan Long, Ruth Murray, Melanie Oxley, Jean Pink, Ruth Plant, Peter Roberts, Eileen Ryan, Violet Spalding, Kim Stallwood, Marjorie Sutcliffe, Betty Svendsen, Allan Thornton, Angela Walder, David Wetton, Jon Wynne-Tyson and Vera Yorke. In America there were Dr Michael Fox, Murdaugh Madden, Dr Charles Magel, Dr Dallas Pratt, Dr Tom Regan, Dr Andrew Rowan, Dr Ken Shapiro and Henry Spira. In Australia, Elizabeth Ahlston, Rosemary Bor, 'Mick' Fearnside, Richard Jones, Patty Mark, Graeme McEwan, Glenys Oogjes, Peter Singer, and Christine Townend. External constraints do not allow me the space to describe in detail all the superb work of these and other leaders of the contemporary movement.

68   A few probably already disturbed and sensitive individuals have taken their protests tragically too far. In March 1986, for example, Robert Blackman poured petrol over himself from a lemonade bottle and burned himself to death in Colchester: 'He gave his life', said his mother, 'because he thought the cruelty would never stop' *(Today,* 31 March 1986).

69   The Thatcher governments, despite constant lobbying, failed to implement the far-reaching reforms to protect farm animals recommended by their official Farm Animal Welfare Council, failed to introduce warning labels on furs that came from trapped species, failed to help charities to get to grips with the chronic problems of stray dogs and cats, and introduced new legislation affecting laboratory animals which was highly controversial. On the positive side, however, they rather reluctantly supported the European import ban on baby seal products, and supported amendments in 1988 to the Protection of Animals Act 1911 (steered through the House of Lords by the nonagenarian Lord Houghton) which made it illegal to tether equines so as to cause unnecessary suffering or to advertise or attend dog-fights, and gave powers to the courts to disqualify from ownership in first cases of cruelty to any species.

70   Speech at the Royal Society, 27 September 1988.

71   See, for example, *Daily Telegraph,* 20 October 1988; *Sunday Times,* 30 October 1988, p. A13.

CHAPTER 11   A WIDER PERSPECTIVE

1   See Chapter 9.

2   Arthur Schopenhauer, *On the Basis of Morality,* 1841.

3   Quoted by John Vivyan, *In Pity and In Anger* (Michael Joseph, 1969), p. 21. (Pro animal sentiments also appear in Wagner's Opera *Parsifal*).

4   Susan E. Lederer, 'Controversy in America, 1880–1914 in *Vivisection*

8 Harold Takooshian, *PsyFTA Bulletin,* Spring 1988, pp. 8–9.

9 Thomas, *Man and the Natural World,* p. 117.

10 *Daily Telegraph,* 18 April 1987.

11 French writers, as well as British, have extolled feline charm, among them Chateaubriand, Victor Hugo, Baudelaire and Alexandre Dumas; later still, Colette and Cocteau (Fernand Mery, *The Life, History and Magic of the Cat* (Hamlyn, 1967), pp. 223–5). In England, there have been Dickens, H. G. Wells and Hardy, and in America Mark Twain and Edgar Allan Poe; actresses, too, just as often as writers, have been outstanding cat-lovers, from Ellen Terry and Sarah Bernhardt to Sophia Loren.

12 John Chancellor, *Charles Darwin* (Weidenfeld and Nicolson, 1973) p. 76.

13 Professor Bernard Knight, BBC World Service, 25 August 1988.

14 This paper was read to the AGM of the British Psychological Society, Exeter, 1977. The sample of students was small – only 31.

15 Leo Tolstoy, 'Introduction', *The Ethics of Diet* (Russian translation). Quoted by Jon Wynne-Tyson, *Food for a Future* (Thorsons, 1988), pp. 165–6.

16 Harry Hieover, *Bipeds and Quadrupeds* (T. C. Newby, 1853), p. xi.

17 Roberta Kalechovfsky, 'Metaphors of Nature', *Behavioural and Political Animal Studies,* 1 (1) (1988).

18 James Walvin, *Leisure and Society 1830–1950* (Longman, 1978), pp. 84–5.

19 Anthony Montague Browne, letter in the *Financial Times,* 8 August 1987.

20 Geoffrey Gorer, *The Life and Ideas of the Marquis de Sade* (Peter Owen, 1934).

21 Carol McKenna, *Ag Scene,* September 1987, p. 5.

22 *RSPCA Conviction Returns,* September 1987.

23 Andrew Tyler, 'City Hunters', *Independent* 'Weekend', 10 September 1988.

24 See for example Matthew 7:12; Galatians 5:14; Leviticus 19:17–18.

25 The electro-encephalograph (EEG) record will show (a) blocking of alpha rhythm, (b) enhancement of N100 event-related potential, (c) 'Readiness Potential' and (d) P300 event-related potential. All these electrophysiological signs, which have been associated with human consciousness, have been found in nonhuman primates (Richard Latto, 'Making Decisions about the Conscious Experiences of Animals', *Behavioural and Political Animal Studies,* 1 (1) (1988), pp. 7–16).

26 Lord Medway, *RSPCA Panel Report* (1980), pp. 8–11.

27 Peter Singer, 'Ten Years of Animal Liberation', *New York Review of Books,* 17 January 1985, p. 6.

28 See Marian Stamp Dawkins, *Animal Suffering* (Chapman and Hall, 1980).

29 Peter Singer, *The Animal Liberation Movement* (Old Hammond Press, 1987), p. 8.

30   Ibid., p. 10.

31   For example, see the emphasis on 'duty' in William Smith, *Uses and Abuses of Domestic Animals* (Jarrold, 1884).

32   I coined the word speciesism in 1970. It entered the *Oxford English Dictionary* in 1986.

33   Rebecca Hall, *Voiceless Victims* (Wildwood House, 1984), p. xii.

34   Steven Walker, *Animal Thought* (Routledge and Kegan Paul, 1983).

35   Roger Fouts, *The Natural History Programme,* BBC Radio 4, 10 August 1988.

36   Richard Dawkins, *The Selfish Gene* (Oxford University Press, 1976), p. 11.

37   Richard Dawkins, *The Blind Watchmaker* (Longman 1986), p. 263.

38   Richard Leakey, 'Science Now', BBC Radio 4, 23 November 1985.

39   Karl Marx, *Early Writings,* trans. Rodney Livingstone and Gregor Benton (Penguin, 1975), p. 239. Marx was certainly a speciesist.

40   Marly Cornell, 'The Philosopher Who Came in from the Cold', *Animals Alert,* Summer 1988 (Magazine of the Australian and New Zealand Federation of Animal Societies, Collingwood, Victoria, Australia).

Index

Massachusetts Society for the
  Prevention of Cruelty to
  Animals, 198–9, 207
Mavor, William, 69
McFall, John, 205
McGinn, Colin, ix
McKenna, Virginia, 210
McNamara, Kevin, 205
Meale, Alan, 205
Medway, Lord, 7
Mench, Joy, 212
Meredith, George, 122
Merrett, Penny, ix
Meslier, Jean, 56
Mesopotamia, 17
Metcalfe, William, 92–3
Meymott, T.G., 86
Midgeley, Mary, ix
Milburn, Cindy, ix
Milgram, Stanley, 11
Mill, John Stuart, 97, 100, 238
Miller, Dr. Harlan, 3
Milne, Miss, 86
Milner, Frank, ix
Milton, John, 48, 57
Mithraism, 15
Monacella, St., 30
Montagu, Basil, 85,
Montaigne, Michel de, 45, 51, 55,
  71, 232
Moore, Patrick, 132
Moore, Thomas, 134
More, Henry, 49, 53
More, Thomas, 43
Morgan, Lloyd, 225
Morley, Elliot, 204
Morris, Desmond, 51
Morris, William, 122
Moses, 124,
Muckle, Richard, 197
Mudford, William, 85
Muhammad, 22, 23
Murdoch, Iris, 132
Myers, Fred, 200
Mylius, Christlob, 57

National Anti Vivisection Society,
  110, 112, 134, 204
National Society for the Abolition
  of Cruel Sports, 132
National Society for Medical
  Research, 200
National Society for the Prevention
  of Cruelty to Children, 200
Nelson (Horatio) Lord, 60, 236
Neot, St., 30
Neuberger, Julia, ix
New York Society for the
  Prevention of Cruelty to
  Animals, 200
Newall, J.T., 129
Newkirk, Ingrid, 201
Newman, Gordon, 210
Newton, Isaac, 43, 56–7
Nicholson, E.W.B., 75, 114
Nicholson, George, 58, 72, 75
Nordvall, Adolf, 196
Neuer, the, 25

O'Brien, Robert, 125
O'Meara, Edmund, 54
O'Regan, Fred, 209
Orlans, Barbara, 212
Orwell, George, 125
Oswald, John, 58, 72
Overton, Richard, 48
Ovid, 19, 55
Oxford Group, 6, 7, 202–3, 212
Oxley, Melanie, 213

Pacheco, Alex, 201
Paget, James, 113, 116
Pain, x, 6, 71–72, 238–243
Paine, Thomas, 72
Painient, Painience, Painism, x,
  213–221
Paley, William, 58
Pankhurst, Christabel, 131
Paracelsus, 52
Parminter, Kate, 205
Pasteur, Louis, 101, 103